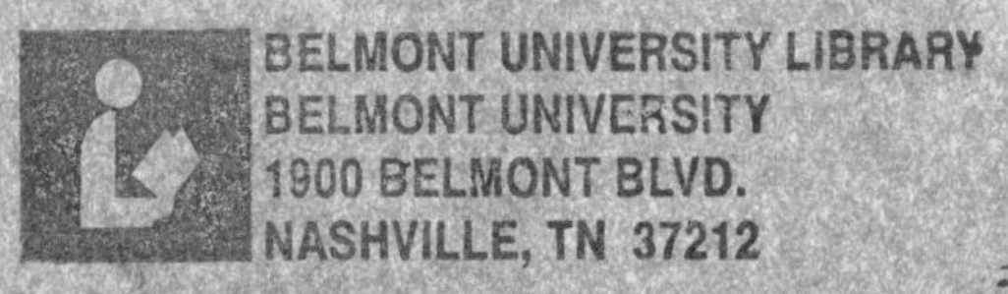

The Return of the Visible in British Romanticism

The Return of the Visible in British Romanticism

William H. Galperin

The Johns Hopkins University Press
Baltimore and London

Printed in the United States of America on acid-free paper

The Johns Hopkins University Press
2715 North Charles Street
Baltimore, Maryland 21218-4319
The Johns Hopkins Press Ltd., London

Illustration on pages ii–iii: Caspar David Friedrich, *Monk by the Sea,* 1808–1810. Nationalgalerie, Berlin.

Library of Congress Cataloging-in-Publication Data

Galperin, William H.
The return of the visible in British romanticism / William H. Galperin.
p. cm.
Includes bibliographical references and index.
ISBN 0-8018-4505-X (alk. paper)
1. English literature—19th century—History and criticism. 2. Art and literature—Great Britian—History—19th century. 3. Visual perception in literature. 4. Ut pictura poesis (Aesthetics) 5. Romanticism—Great Britain. 6. Description (Rhetoric) I. Title.
PR457.G35 1993
820.9'145—dc20 92-32622

A catalog record for this book is available from the British Library.

For Tina

The Poet, singing a song in which all human beings join with him, rejoices in the presence of truth as our visible friend and hourly companion.

—William Wordsworth

The world is *what we see* and . . . nonetheless, we must learn to see it.

—Maurice Merleau-Ponty

Contents

Illustrations

Acknowledgments

A portion of chapter 2 appeared originally in the *Centennial Review,* whose editors I thank for allowing me to reprint it. I also want to thank the following museums for allowing me to reproduce materials in their collections: British Museum, London; Kunsthalle, Hamburg; Museum Folkwang, Essen; Nationalgalerie, Berlin; National Gallery, London; National Gallery of Art, Washington, D.C.; Staatliche Kunstammlungen, Dresden; Tate Gallery, London; Victoria and Albert Museum, London; Walters Art Gallery, Baltimore; Yale Center for British Art, New Haven. I want to thank, too, the staffs of the following libraries: the British Library, the Guildhall Library, the John Johnson Collection of Printed Ephemera at the Bodleian Library, Oxford, the Library of the Victoria and Albert Museum, and the Van Pelt Library of the University of Pennsylvania. Special thanks go to Scott Wilcox at the Yale Center for British Art for advice on matters regarding the Panorama and the Diorama and for expediting the reproduction of several illustrations.

I want especially to acknowledge the very generous support I received from the George A. and Eliza Gardner Howard Foundation, which, in conjunction with Rutgers University's equally generous competitive leave program, provided me with a year's leave during which this study was brought to completion. I am grateful, too, to the Rutgers University Research Council for a travel grant, which enabled me to go to England.

Susan Wolfson and Jerry Flieger read the entire study with care and generosity, lending their considerable expertise in romanticism and contemporary theory respectively. Richard Macksey and Kate

Nicholson have followed this study from its inception and have continually encouraged me. Peter Manning and Anne Mellor presided over my earliest efforts at working on the problem of visibility in Wordsworth and were, as usual, both supporters and mentors. Garrett Stewart and Jay Clayton, who read the manuscript for the Johns Hopkins University Press, produced reports of such extraordinary insight and sympathy that they can (if they so wish) be credited as collaborators. And Timothy Corrigan, who would have collaborated on the study with me had other commitments not arisen, continues to rank as the prime mover and presiding spirit of the project. The book is dedicated to the person whose influence on me, emotionally and intellectually, has always mattered most.

The Return of the Visible in British Romanticism

INTRODUCTION

The Visible Subject and the Agency of the Text

The present study is an outgrowth of my interests in both romantic writing and cinema, although in ways that are restricted to romantic studies and to a series of disciplinary concerns within that field. Even so, the disciplinary concerns with which I am directly engaged—involving, among other issues, the politics of romanticism and romantic subjectivity at various points of conflict or contradiction—are related to disciplinary issues in film studies in the last twenty years. And it is this connection, which centers on the hegemonic formation of romantic culture, that my argument for the agency of the merely seen or seeable in romantic texts at once addresses and challenges.

My interest in the problem of the visible in romanticism, as well as my attempt here to see it in a different light, comes by a fairly circuitous route. Drawn to the cinema and to critical issues regarding it while at work on a study of Wordsworth, I was surprised to discover that film studies, unlike romantic and especially Wordsworth studies at the time, had discovered intentionality, or authority in film, to be no more viable theoretically than the possibility of either an indeterminate cinema or, in one critic's phrase, a "cinema without walls."[1] By the late 1970s studies in romanticism had leapfrogged from a fundamentally humanistic preoccupation with intention and individual authority to a more deconstructive position in which an increasingly overdetermined sense of intentionality had given way finally to indeterminacy. In contrast, film studies were firmly anchored in a structuralism or semiotics which held that such "intentional structures" as autonomy or imagination were the constituents, by and large, of bourgeois individualism. (I am, to be sure, simplifying matters greatly here, but I want to stress that it was through film studies, and my attempts to engage their compelling conjunction of psychoanalysis and Marxism through a "romantic" conjunction, alternately pre- *and* poststructural, that the present study first developed.)

It is not necessary at this point to detail all the specifics of these engagements but rather to observe that my efforts to reconceive or indeed to recuperate something on the order of "romanticism" in film were founded on a link between directorial will or knowledge, on the one hand, and an uncontainable or indeterminate image, on the other. Thus, I argued that Stanley Kubrick's 1962 adaptation of Vladimir Nabokov's *Lolita* stressed the antihumanistic dimension of the cinematic medium.[2] That Kubrick regarded the cinema in this light was clear not only in the transformation of the novel's hero and sovereign subject (Humbert Humbert) into something of a villain, but in the concomitant transformation of the novel's villain (Claire Quilty) who, as played by Peter Sellers, is characteristically many subjects in the film rather than a single or unitary self. Moreover, both the subversion of the novel's hero and the promotion of its protean villain were inextricably linked in the film to *seeing,* which is a matter, additionally, of *seeing through* an otherwise mystified subject-position. It is one thing, after all, to see a motel room through Humbert's eyes in the novel and quite another to see Humbert in a motel room, less a master of an environment than a victim—of wallpaper, TV, the detritus, quite literally, of Western culture.

Such detritus is not in itself indeterminate. In fact, such images may be said to underscore the control and containment that the novel with its remarkably imaginative hero, means to transcend. At the same time, however, the peculiar (and indeed visible) claustrophobia of this—and other—Kubrick films is not only a concession to a dominant order, whose power is mirrored by the cinematic framework within which details are both visible and comprehensible. The sheer abundance of cultural signs distracts and educates even as it contains in Kubrick's film, creating a tension ultimately between the various identificatory mechanisms (including voyeurism), which clearly link the viewer to Humbert, and a more reflexive or unstable subjectivity, whereby the visible is somehow marshaled (in identification with both

Quilty and, as it turns out, the expatriate Kubrick himself) against the very culture from which there is otherwise no escape. The "way out" in Kubrick's *Lolita* is not to some single, sovereign position of exteriority, as in the novel. Rather, it is to a position of *inclusion,* where the visible—whether as distraction, or knowledge, or both—necessarily prevents or at least impedes assimilation to an order whose inexorability (as the protean Quilty makes clear) is no longer overwhelming.

Such arguments on behalf of the cinema, needless to say, were more eccentric than definitive. But what must be emphasized about them is that the particular subjectivity and the particular *motivation* to which they referred—one responsive rather than resistant to a kind of real or visible—remains a subjectivity divided, in a decidedly romantic way, between the visible and the visionary. It remains a subjectivity divided, then, by its responsiveness to a visible or material world, on the one hand, and to a world *no sooner seen* than imaginatively appropriated, on the other. Such a subjectivity would seem to resemble closely the subjectivity that Wordsworth describes when he speaks in "Tintern Abbey" of a mind that half perceives and half creates. Nevertheless, the subjectivity—and, I would further urge, the romantic subjectivity—to which the cinema refers us in this instance, remains, with its necessary deference to the material, bodily condition of sight, which is unassimilable to control or conceptualization, a different and more mobile construction than Wordsworth's ultimately asymmetrical ideal. And this is because the visible, though seemingly non-existent in the romantic schema, is by its constitution as the "familiar thing that has undergone repression" (to borrow from Freud),[3] something that is no more forgotten than it is necessarily anterior.

If anything, the visible is the central and unrivaled repressed of romanticism precisely because it *has* been repressed and, like Freud's "uncanny," may "return" now on account of having never left. I am not suggesting, by any means—certainly not in the current climate of new historicism—that there are not other candidates for the role of the repressed in British romanticism, many of them quite legitimate. What I am proposing is that unlike "the nothing that is not there" in romantic writing, including the absence that new historical criticism has recently (and perhaps too virtuously) called "history," the romantic visible is a nothing whose return is often demonized by both the Romantics and their admirers because it is, more properly, the "nothing that is": because it is capable, on the sheer strength of its facticity, of wrenching the so-called "romantic ideology" from a potentially hegemonic or repressive formation to an orientation that is potentially a composite of positions rather than a single, unitary ideal.

Almost all accounts of romanticism, from Wordsworth to de Man, are far less sanguine about the presence or, for that matter, the return of the visible. In these accounts the visible is usually so repressed and defamiliarized that it virtually ceases as a repressed, remaining no more than a precondition to a world of sovereignty and imaginative autonomy, where the mind's mastery of the real routinely holds sway over what both Wordsworth and Coleridge disingenuously call the "tyranny of the eye."[4] Thus it is almost never remarked, not even by deconstructive critics, that the visible is less an absence in romanticism than the familiar thing, again, whose essential nothingness is both provisional and, paradoxical as it sounds, foundational.

To deconstruction, for example, the mastery of the familiar in romanticism is contested less by a material world that has been repressed than by an imagined world, whose materialization in language resists the very structures and hierarchies that mandate the removal of the familiar to a metaphysical or celestial plane.[5] Thus, instead of following romanticism's own gyrations, deconstruction merely moves romanticism to a position that can only approximate the positionality of which the visible is, in a very real sense, a mark: to a site whose peculiar "decomposition" (to borrow a deconstructive trope) allows romanticism—or what is left of romanticism—a freedom from the very containment, indeed from the very structures, hierarchies, and authority with which it can be said to consist.

It is this romantic residue, then—this peculiarly resistant reduction to which, either by agency or in form of the visible, romanticism sometimes returns—that is the subject of my study. For while it is tempting still to regard this materialization as a consequence of deconstruction (or as a figure, more pointedly, of critical wish fulfillment), the romantic visible or real is more properly a prolepsis to which deconstruction has, in a certain way, simply been responsive. The many recent attempts, then, to forge a link between romanticism and deconstruction, chiefly by showing the various ways romanticism yields up "its own temporal limits to register critical claims of a much more overwhelming kind"[6] are only partially relevant to the problem as I see it. For beyond the fact that these attempts—including those of de Man, Hillis Miller, and Lacoue-Labarthe and Nancy—no longer carry the political credit they once did or could have, there is the very real problem involving the visible itself, which is sufficiently local and particular to oppose the almost transhistorical will that deconstruction, like humanistic criticism, seeks to cull from romantic texts.[7]

Tilottama Rajan's brilliant and influential study *Dark Interpreter* (1980), which begins by tracing the lineage of deconstruction to romantic theory, is a particularly good example of a deconstructive study in which the visible must, by the logic of a certain kind of deconstruction, submit to a larger intentionality.[8] Beginning with Schiller's well-known distinction between naive and sentimental poetry, Rajan shows how Schiller's "dialectical separation of a classical past" (with its unconscious affinity for the actual and concrete) "from a Romantic" or more self-conscious "present" (32) is a pseudodialectic by which the subjective or modern orientation ultimately demystifies all notions of the real or objective. The ostensible "dichotomy" of "mind and matter," she shows, comes to "a union of fiction and actuality" (32) in that the idealization of the naive as a modern telos, as a reality to be "reapproximated" by imagination, reveals that the "naive" is "already sentimental" (33). A similar—and similarly deconstructive agency—is detectable in the theories of both Schopenhauer and Nietzsche, whose respective dichotomies of will/representation and Dionysian/Apollonian work to position the artist *against* a referential order at once real and ideal. Thus, in Nietzsche, the tragic "artist's simultaneous kinship with a chorus . . . bound to the pathos of existence, and with a hero elevated above the choric collectivity, forces the act of aesthetic representation to be at once a submission to existence and a liberating act" (42–43). To the extent, then, that deconstruction is in partnership with romantic theory, it is on account, Rajan shows, of a referentiality that is no sooner real than ideal, or according to a referentiality that is both a product of, and thus a figure for, the very idealizations that by their nature are self-reflexive.

It scarcely requires saying that, in contrast to a deconstructive view, in which the only materiality in a work of art is the material of the work itself—be it paint or language—the possibility of a material *referent,* of something at once visible, real or concrete, is not simply a mystification but a possibility that the very materiality of the sign would appear both to interrupt and forestall. Nevertheless, it is also clear that insofar as this interruption takes place—or is allowed to take place—it remains, in Rajan's or even de Man's way of reading, a consciousness that resembles a more conventionally romantic authority in its tendency to annihilate or displace the particular. Thus, in talking about the visible in romanticism, it is useful to think about it in accordance less with a kind of will than with a responsiveness or openness of which the visible may well be cause or effect or both. For in this way the visible is the issue no more of a single or unitary selfhood than of an equally authoritative self-reflexivity. A matter more, I think, of a shifting subjectivity or, following Quilty again, of a subjectivity in default, the peculiar responsiveness of the bodily eye (and of the mind in its influence), of which the visible is a mark, reveals a responsiveness provoked as much by details as by a potential willingness or consent to *being visible:* to being *a body,* or detail, within a visible field.

I will elaborate shortly on the political and theoretical yield of such a mutable position. But first I want to turn once more to the example of film to illustrate better what I mean by the visible as well as by the subjectivity-in-default with which the phenomenon of the visible—and the romantic visible in particular—is finally indissoluble.

Like Kubrick's *Lolita,* whose displaced vision is most fathomable in the way the visible—specifically visible "America"—is able to serve the dual functions of containment and subversion, Roman Polanski's *Chinatown* (1974) marshals the visible actuality of what I call "Chinatown" to similar effect.[9] Here, as in *Lolita,* the visible—a "suspension in the symbolic details themselves" as Garrett Stewart describes it[10]—figures a link between a displaced or expatriate vision on the one hand, in which *Chinatown* may be held distinct from the representational conventions to which it frequently refers, and a particular kind of subjectivity on the other, which is equally displaced from a central and totalizing narrative committed to the disclosure of "how things really are."[11] But there is also a difference between the two films. Where Kubrick has Sellers-Quilty as a kind of counterintelligence in his film—as a pastiche or quilt who embodies the numerous details and distractions among which he and the viewer circulate—it devolves upon the viewer of Polanski's film to see through, or apart from, a representation, which is alternately a representation *by and of* a more conventional or authoritative subjectivity.

That *Chinatown* does the work of both absorption and deconstruction, or is deconstructive by virtue of being cooptative, is clear from a number of things. The most immediate is the imbrication of two narratives and subject-positions in place of what—in most contemporary film theory—is usually just one.[12] The first of these narratives, whose position coincides with that of the central character, remains a narrative of discovery and comprehension, the authority of which is registered in an eventual assignment of blame. In this narrative, as viewers familiar with the film know, the conspiracy of evil that is darkly at work from the very outset of the film is eventually exposed by the hero and detective Jake Gittes (Jack Nicholson), whose discoveries—and judgments—are no sooner his than ours.

But there is, as viewers familiar with the film also know, a problem with this narrative. And it is the fact that knowledge or revelation turns out to be the only triumph associated with the heuristic position; the good, including Gittes, are variously punished in the end, and the blameworthy escape with only blame as their retribution. As a result, *Chinatown* becomes—in subsequent viewings—a rather different text, in which authority is characterized far less by moral revelation than by a remote, almost paralyzing omniscience. It is the viewer's prior (rather than anticipated) knowledge of the past and future fates of the various principals that, in subsequent viewings, remains the source of textual engagement, allowing virtually every gesture, every line, to become rife with dramatic irony. Details that were previously meaningless, or in which meaning was simply suspended, are suddenly immensely moving. Viewers will recall, for example, the foreshadowing of the catastrophic close when, wilting under the interrogation of Gittes, Evelyn Mulwray (Faye Dunaway) lets her head fall to the steering wheel, setting off a horn blast. And then, of course, there are the repeated allusions to "Chinatown"—the scene, we are always reminded, of an earlier catastrophe in which Gittes apparently hurt someone while trying to help her.

Certainly, the power of these details owes much to what, in subsequent viewings, amounts also to an advanced knowledge of Robert Towne's intricately wrought screenplay. But I would argue that the power of these details—as well as of other images or disruptions in the film—is indebted equally to an anterior *ignorance* that has presumably been erased in the initial viewing. While it would appear, that is, that one source of textual engagement (and its concomitant subject-position) has simply been replaced on second viewing by another source (and position), the situation is actually more complicated. What really affects the viewer on second or third viewing is not simply his or her intelligence—or the kind of knowledge "of how things really are" on which a drama such as *Oedipus Rex* depends for its effect. What is even more compelling in subsequent viewings is the kind of ignorance or consent onto which authority continually opens, making the omniscient position to which the viewer is privy a matter, to quote one of the film's characters, of having "ma[de] the same mistake twice."

Thus, instead of simply leading us from one dominant station to another, *Chinatown* juxtaposes the heuristic and omniscient positions not only to expose their respective limitations, but to expose something else as well. That is, no matter how much we are constructed by one or the other of the film's narratives, there is in the instability wrought by these constructions a necessary relaxation in which a merely visible world or a "suspension in the symbolic details themselves" becomes both an objective correlative for some other version of subjectivity and the product simultaneously of an intermediate or even failed subjectivity that is more responsive than authoritative.

It will appear from all I've said, then, that the visible to which *Chinatown* gives access requires that the film be seen more than once. However, it is more the case that the multiple viewing of *Chinatown* simply reenacts the conditions under which the visible is visible, thereby marking a subjectivity-in-default of which the subject's own materiality or visibility is a necessary end. What is accessible to the viewer in the aftermath of several viewings is also visible in an initial viewing of *Chinatown*—provided that one can *resist* the particular authority to which he or she is ordinarily attracted by such a text. Garrett Stewart construes this in terms of what he calls "atmospheric foreboding." "Ordinary narrative suspense," he writes,

> the train of multiplying clues and partial discoveries, is to a large extent replaced by a sense of atmospheric foreboding divorced from plot, and more importantly by a suspension in the symbolic details themselves, a consistently withheld relevance that defines the true plotline of the film. . . . What does it mean that Noah Cross [the film's villain] eats whole fish? Or that he is named Noah for that matter? That Mrs. Mulwray has a black flaw in her green eye? What have her Chinese servants to do with the film's title? What, in fact, has the title to do with the film? (28)

Many of these distractions, to be sure, are far less distracting and more absorbing in subsequent viewings. However, it must be stressed that in the very way that the initial viewing opens onto a world of distraction, which frequently threatens the absorptive or cooptative dimension of the initial text, so subsequent texts of *Chinatown,* in which many of the initial distractions are symbolically contained, are even more fraught—by virtue of these containments—by a world that is inchoate and uncontainable. Here, once again, the proliferation of subject-positions, and, I would further venture, positions of authority in *Chinatown,* is key. For just as authority is deferred in this film and the distractions of the initial text are allowed to become the components, so to speak, of subsequent texts, it is the case as well that the more authority is deferred or variously reconstituted in *Chinatown,* the more it will defer to a visible world shorn of meaning or containment.

Central to this deferral is the notion of "Chinatown," whose materialization in the film continually contests (along with other manifestations of the visible, such as the world viewed or refracted through Venetian blinds) the ostensible function of Chinatown as the telos of represented action. Here, the emphasis is not simply on China or the Chinese per se, which are subjected to the usual stereotypes and reductions. The emphasis is on China "town," on the alien order that infiltrates our own, challenging and resisting our idealized conceptions. "Chinatown" is, in the word of the Mulwrays' Chinese gardener concerned about the effect of saltwater on their lawn, "bad for the glass," bad for representation.

Space and occasion do not permit a more detailed analysis of "Chinatown's" function as the "real" in *Chinatown.* (Those interested in such a demonstration are strongly advised to review the scene of the gardener's observation. In this scene the confluence of East and West, beginning with the Chinese servant who meets Gittes at the door, becomes a signpost to the visible, which is not only irrepressible but implicitly linked to a shattering or complication of the mimetic plane: specifically, the reflective yet potentially troubled surface of the saltwater pond.) What I do want to address at present, though, is the peculiar *agency* of the visible: that the visible remains a vehicle for distraction as well as evidence that distraction has taken place, and that some other subject-position is therefore possible. And here, the discussion of both agency and the possibility of subjective resistance recently undertaken by Paul Smith in *Discerning the Subject* proves especially helpful.[13]

Smith's argument rests, somewhat oddly, on an Althusserian commonplace: namely, that there is no ultimate position of exteriority or "space of the nonideological" (25) in culture, as the human subject is in one way or another compelled (or "interpellated" in Althusser's term) to a "subjected state." Nevertheless, Smith also argues that neither the sheer prevalence of interpellation nor the fact that we are all in language, according to Lacan and others, necessarily "foreclose[s] upon the possibility of resistance" (xxxi). Instead, he maintains,

> resistance does take place, but . . . only within a social context which has already construed subject-positions for the human agent. The place of resistance has, then, to be glimpsed somewhere in the interstices of the subject-positions which are offered in any social formation. More precisely, resistance must be regarded as the by-product of contradictions in and among subject-positions. The subject/individual can be discerned but not by the supposition of some quasi-mystical will-to-resistance. [Rather] . . . resistance is best understood as a specific twist in the dialectic between individuation and ideological interpellation. (25)

And what of the visible in this regard? The answer, based on the way the visible functions in a film like *Chinatown,* is fairly obvious. The visible and, as I will show shortly, the romantic visible in both literature and spectacle, remains both a "by-product" and a sign of the very resistance that is a by-product of the subject's "negotiations among and between particular subject-positions" (40). The crucial difference, then, is that where Smith regards these negotiations as leading to what he calls "conscious resistance" or "choice," the visible and the kind of resistance it both signifies and attracts may be better thought of in terms of *consent* or, with respect again to the subject-position on which the visible may be said to verge, physical or material displacement.

The remarkable, and rather pragmatic, feature of agency, in Smith's characterization, is not the capacity to resist certain cultural constraints but, in fact, the very opposite: that is, agency's dependency on the very constraints by which it is "enabled" as well as bounded. As a result, Smith's version of agency would appear to differ from the visible in the way it is virtually surrounded by interpellated states, whose incessant subjectivity, no matter how changeable, necessarily limits both the objectification and the default of which the visible is mark and measure. Thus, Smith's agency also differs from the agency of the visible in its reliance on language as a kind of "edge or mediating border where," as Smith asserts, "relationships between self and other" or between one subject-position and another are invariably negotiated. I am not suggesting, of course, that the visible, particularly in romantic literature, is not also "in language." I am suggesting only that the central feature of the visible, and of the subjectivity on which it both relies and is simultaneously a sign, is its enunciation (to mix a metaphor) of the subject's failure or distraction. For this failure is the failure of both a symbolic order, as well as *any* position to which one might be interpellated by such an order, to contain or represent subjectivity.

Whether this failure or any failure is "outside of language" is really not the point, then. The point is that such enunciations mark a responsiveness to a material world that is simultaneously, and by the conditions under which such responsiveness is possible, an acknowledgment, however tacit, of the subject's *own* materiality or visibility. This materiality, furthermore, which is scarcely a position at all, is the only subject-position by which the visible is in any sense limited or contained. In *Chinatown,* then, the acknowledgment of the subject's materiality comes in the way repeated viewings of the film manage—in the very face of an interpellated omniscience—to return the viewer to an anterior (and, one might argue, parasubjective) state of distraction and dislocation, which in turn cancels or at least *can cancel* the interpellative work accomplished in all viewings of the film. In romanticism this acknowledgment comes more overtly in the kind of "levelling" (to use Charles Lamb's description) whereby the self in language—what the discourse of romanticism names the sovereign subject—is transposed under aegis of the visible to a materiality so overwhelming that its construction, by language or any other means, is literally and figuratively immaterial.

The fact, then, that the material, bodily condition of sight does return at certain junctures during the romantic period is important for two reasons. It is important to our understanding of the period itself, which is routinely viewed as an interval in which the visible or something like it was successfully contained, for better or for worse. And it is also important, in conjunction with this renewed understanding of the period, to recognize what in a more general sense we can, with some modification of Smith, call artistic agency or resistance. For romanticism, lest we forget, is that juncture where being in language is not only proven but virtually recapitulated by the language with which the romantic self routinely appropriates the world. Thus, I am proposing not only the potential for resistance—or agency—in *some* literary texts; I am proposing a potential that withstands an "ideology," whose mystified claim to a radical or humanistic function would, in the minds of many romanticists today, put it at cross-purposes with the very thing I am suggesting. Literary criticism, and romantic criticism in particular, need not come to a choice between what Jerome McGann calls "an uncritical absorption in Romanticism's own self-representations" and a "socio-historical method," which, as he and others propose, can expose the bad faith of such representations.[14] Criticism—and, I would further urge, an oppositional criticism—can also take a more sympathetic view of the texts it addresses. For the texts we write on, despite their apparent lack of circumspection, are rarely as uncritical as literary critics (and literary theorists especially) are inclined to permit. Rather, much like people—or human agents—including the many who do make a difference, literary texts are doing more than the best they can in spite of themselves; they are often, as we shall see, doing the best that can be done.[15]

That this "doing" is bound up with "being," or with a state of being of which the romantic visible is both sign and function, does not, therefore, minimize its social work. If anything, the always wrenching aspects of the visible, whether as something resisted or something wished for, perform a strangely communitarian function in romantic texts, jarring the subject just enough to make his individuality or separateness a condition no sooner bolstered than undone by his material integrity as a body seeing and hence a body seeable. Thus, in Constable's famous painting *The Hay-Wain* the comprehensive view of the landscape for which the painter is often praised is both a privileged vision of harmony and integration as well as a vision made possible by the merely *physical* elevation from which Constable has elected to view and to represent the world in this instance.

But painting, finally, is neither the most important nor the most productive site of the visible in romanticism. Indeed, precisely because it is responsive as a medium to a world seen, painting is incapable of allowing the visible to return as the "hidden, familiar thing," to quote Freud again, "that has undergone repression and then emerged from it." It devolves upon other kinds of texts, including poetry, theater criticism, as well as popular spectacle, to grant the visible its paradoxical and—given its peculiar agency—politically necessary role as the "thing" whose familiarity is marked by a capacity to distract and variously to remove the subject from what, at one level, may seem an even more familiar continuum.

The popularity of such precinematic spectacles as the Panorama and Diorama, for example, which is often attributed to their novelty and, in the case of the Panorama, to the public interest in larger painted images, turns out to be a more complicated affair. In both instances, the visible—with its capacity to distract—has the effect of destabilizing the viewer in ultimately militating against the absorptive potential of the image, which is always shifting, or, in the case of the Diorama, reduced to mere illusionism. Moreover, in so removing the viewer from an absorptive or privatized vantage, the "oramic" spectacles manage to return viewers to a visible field by effectively leveling them to a materialized condition. In the Panorama this leveling is managed through a virtual correspondence between the world viewed, notably the images of cities both in England and abroad, and the world viewing: the ever mobile urban audience circulating through the Panorama building. In the Diorama, whose viewers were seated (sometimes against their will) in a darkened amphitheater, the collective mandate is achieved less by submission to an incredibly illusionistic image than by an alliance of sorts, which positions an increasingly disbelieving audience against both the image itself and, more important, its power to captivate.

Both the Panorama and the Diorama are also, of course, relatively conventional in their appeal to audiences. The disorienting and destabilizing effects of the Panorama are often mitigated by elements ranging from the subject matter, which included "events" from the Napoleonic Wars with their patriotic interest, to the various keys and explanatory guides, which see to it, in effect, that details can also be comprehensible facts. Thus the peculiar work, and indeed the social work of the oramic displays, is accomplished less through simple opposition than by a *continued* shifting or sliding away, in which agency—the resistance to absorption and to the viewer's role as a gazing, meditative subject—is essentially underwritten, although not bounded, by another apparatus of repression.

There are, of course, instances in romanticism in which both the visible and, more important, the subjectivity responsive to it take on what look to be a more boldly oppositional character. Both Wordsworth's later poetry, beginning with *The Excursion,*, and the first two cantos of Byron's *Childe Harold's Pilgrimage* are quite explicit, as we shall see, in their efforts to remove a world viewed or described from one narrated and possessed. Yet, as even these examples make clear, the return of the visible in British romanticism is invariably shadowed by the memory and thus by the always intrusive possibility of an order, where both the seen and the equally visible material character of the beholder are inclined simultaneously to invisibility and omniscience. In Byron, this tension is registered by contrasting the figure of Harold, who stares at the world uncomprehendingly, to a series of authoritative narrative voices, the last of which nearly subsumes Harold's perspective in reducing it to mere memory. In Wordsworth, the specter of a more appropriative orientation is raised by the sheer insufficiency of many of the later poems, whose rather unremarkable contribution to the sonnet tradition recalls a more aggressively figurative apparatus that is no longer apparent or apparently necessary.

Thus, it is not at all surprising that the majority of this study is given over to materializations of the visible in romanticism, which irrupt or return under pressure of resistance. For it is by resistance to the visible rather than by the resistance that, as Smith describes it, is alternately a circuit of subversion and containment that the uncontainable and potentially communitarian aspects of the visible are most in evidence. The sections of *The Prelude* detailing Wordsworth's experiences in London allow the spectacular nature of London, which both anticipates and (in retrospect) refigures the spectacular nature of France during the Revolution, a primacy that—in spite of the poet's aversion—overrides and even trivializes the detached, meditative solitude that Wordsworth remembers experiencing during this time. So, too, the theater criticism of both Charles Lamb and William Hazlitt admits, by way of resistance, the "levelling" that takes place when "genius" is represented on stage in bodily form. For Lamb, this leveling involves two things. It entails the reduction that transpires when the Shakespearean hero—Hamlet, Othello, or Lear—is represented by a human actor suddenly visible to the "bodily eye." And it involves as well the effect of this reduction on the closeted, romantic reader, whose previously exclusive relationship to the hero in the act of reading is disrupted and demystified in actual performance. Beyond the outrage, then, of simply seeing the word made flesh, which is especially "revolting" in *Othello* with its necessary endorsement of miscegenation, Lamb must suffer the ultimate indignity of his own visibility or materiality, which, given his capacity to see (a capacity miraculously suspended in the act of "reading"), now renders him a body like everyone else.

For Hazlitt, by contrast, the embodiment of genius on stage is a more complicated matter, largely because the very leveling of genius to bodily form that Lamb reviles is another description of the democratization that Hazlitt, for his part, supports. Yet precisely because the democratic ideal is based also on a hierarchized notion of individuality and enfranchisement, Hazlitt's recuperation of the theatrical representation of Shakespeare entails a modification, but not a refutation, of Lamb's conception. While Hazlitt does not deny the importance of genius, be it Shakespeare's or his characters', he manages to deflect attention from the authority represented (or "articulated" as he calls it) by concentrating instead on the articulator—notably the actor Edmund Kean—who is effectively poised between man and god. Hazlitt's defense of theatricality is tantamount, then, to a deconstruction of the democratic ideal, since Kean turns out, like the idea of universal enfranchisement, to be an impossible conflation. Drawing its power less from the actor's corporeality, or from the fact that Kean is really one of us, the idea (and ideal) to which Hazlitt's "Kean" refers derives its strength finally from the actor's privileged and increasingly discrete relationship to an invisible, omniscient power to which Kean alone—and an increasingly disembodied Kean—has special access.

With this in mind, it is perhaps fitting, though not necessarily surprising, that the hero of this study (or at least one of its heroes) is Samuel Taylor Coleridge, whose contradictory, even apostate, position (as Hazlitt reviled it) may be also linked to the peculiar agency, and to the communitarian possibilities, of which the visible is, again, a sign. Coleridge's Shakespeare criticism, for example, is not only taken up with a characteristically romantic (and indeed borrowed) defense of genius as essentially godlike; it is also capable of undoing its own mystification in regarding genius from the opposite angle of vision—or from the outside in. The representation of Hamlet as someone whose "retire[ment] from all reality" is the "result of having [the greatness of genius] we express by the terms a world within himself," certainly echoes Coleridge's description of Hamlet's creator as an artist who necessarily stands apart from "the iron compulsion of space & time." Yet it also, in the very midst of hagiography, opens onto the spectacle of a man "living in meditation." All of which returns "genius" to a materialized form and, in the process, cancels the difference or superiority to which genius, like romantic subjectivity, is routinely interpellated.

A similar reversal takes place in the *Biographia Literaria,* whose defense of genius—chiefly Wordsworth's—is sharply qualified in the sections Coleridge elected to append to the second volume, which are variously concerned with issues of theatricality and with the return of genius to bodily form. Thus, the eventual consignment of Wordsworth to anonymity—indeed, to a vomiting body accompanying Coleridge on his trip to Germany—is ultimately recapitulated in the peculiar solidarity that Coleridge demonstrates in literally dramatizing, thereby demystifying, his antitheatrical stance. His critique of Maturin's play *Bertram,* which at one level is a diatribe against the trivialization of genius in theater, also enlists the apparatus of theatricality so as to grant Coleridge his place among the community and, more specifically, among the very audience from which he has held himself distinct.

The image of Coleridge with which the *Biographia* leaves us—a Coleridge alternately mindful of the materializations before his view and of his own materiality as someone sighted and thus, like Hamlet, also sightable as part of a community or audience—is scarcely without relevance to the cinematic culture of which the theater in the nineteenth century is a precursor. However, the relevance of Coleridge's position to film culture comes less, in my view, to a tale of two hegemonies than to a counterhegemony that he and Wordsworth were partly right to call the "tyranny of eye." The problem with accepting their demonization of the eye—which is the same problem, I would argue, as accepting the male gaze as the sine qua non of narrative cinema—involves more than a misreading of the materialized hegemony or solidarity that is the visible's only orientation or limit; the real problem with such characterizations is that they invariably describe the visible and its work solely in terms of the very order—or orders—that the visible otherwise threatens. Paul Smith is certainly right, then, when he charges contemporary film theory, and the *Screen* group in particular, with seeking to rescue the subject variously interpellated by narrative cinema by removing him or her to "another" —presumably better—"level of determination" (37–38). For very much like the antitheatrical posture that Coleridge breaks with in the penultimate chapter of the *Biographia,* the anticinema orientation of much recent film theory patently ignores the possibilities that a more microscopic, less virtuous, approach to the cinema can yield. Recent work, particularly regarding early cinema, has already begun, in the spirit of Walter Benjamin, to reassess and revalue the hegemony with which cinema, in its classic formation, has been routinely associated.[16] It is the argument here, then, that a counterhegemony of the sort that these investigations are turning up—with its intimations of solidarity —is also an important legacy of romanticism.

Part I

The Romantic Visible and the Visibly Romantic

CHAPTER ONE

The Return of the Visible

I

The thesis of this study is somewhat simple but also problematic: that a visible world—accessible to the material, bodily condition of sight and thus prior to idealization—is manifest in certain texts, including verbal texts, of the British romantic period. This thesis is problematic less for its implications regarding romantic painting, which is always seeking in a way to assimilate the material world to conceptualization (and vice versa), than for its reversal of the imaginative iconoclasm—that is, the fear of both visual images and the material world such images admit—endemic to romantic poetics.[1] Unlike the "pictorialist" poets of the eighteenth century, who "accepted as axiomatic the doctine of *ut pictura poesis* [as a painting, so a poem],"[2] the romantic poets were generally determined to distinguish their representations from the other arts in defense of what they believed was poetry's greater accessibility to "truth" (Mitchell, "Visible Language," 52)—the "knowledge" that, as Wordsworth described it, "cleaves to us as a necessary part of our existence, our natural and unalienable inheritance."

Whether it is Wordsworth's and Coleridge's complaint, then, about the "tyranny of the eye," or Coleridge's criticism of certain poetic techniques as akin to the "touches" of a "[painter's] brush," or even Lamb's attack on the artificial theatricality of what he disparagingly termed the "last century," the Romantics seem virtually united in their suspicions regarding the world viewed as against a world of imagination, whose scope for them, as W. J. T. Mitchell describes it, "transcends mere visualization" (49).

It is Shelley, not surprisingly, who is the most eloquent and decisive on this issue. In discussing the genesis of language in imagination—"that imperial faculty, whose throne is curtained within the invisible nature of man"—Shelley credits language as a "more direct" and, by implication, more powerful "representation of the actions and passions of our internal being,"

> and is susceptible of more various and delicate combinations, than colour, form, or motion. . . . For language is arbitrarily produced by the Imagination and has relation to thoughts alone; but all other materials, instruments and conditions of art, have relations among each other, which limit and interpose between conception and expression. The former [language] is as a mirror which reflects, the latter [the other materials] as a cloud which enfeebles, the light of which both are mediums of communication. Hence the fame of sculptors, painters and musicians, although the intrinsic powers of the great masters of these arts, may yield in no degree to that of those who have employed language as the hieroglyphic of their thoughts, has never equalled that of poets in the restricted sense of the term; as two performers of equal skill will produce unequal effects from a guitar and a harp.[3]

Behind Shelley's "defence of poetry," particularly poetry's privileged "relation to thoughts alone," is not only an empirical legacy that allows the world and its perception to be collapsed into "conception" but an idealist negotiation, in the course of which conception and its linguistic representation become synonymous. To reflect or to represent the "light" all one need do, according to Shelley, is write it; for unlike painting, a highly mediated form of representation, writing is effectively that juncture where conception and expression are indistinguishable and immune to adulteration.[4]

Still, for all its range and authority, there is also something narrow to poetry's purview here. This narrowness owes mostly to the way perception, with its particular grounding in an objective, sensible world, is virtually forgotten in deference to "conception," whose "expression" in turn—and the "hieroglyphic" produced thereby—subsume and, by recourse to a now "visible language," supersede all other modes of representation. Yet the question remains: Is the typology of visual perception—"hieroglyphic," "mirror," "reflection"—sufficient in actually *describing* poetry's function, not to mention its predominance among competing modes of representation? The answer, particularly if one accepts what Shelley claims for poetry, is decidedly no. If anything, Shelley's recourse to a typology of seeing in his defense of poetry puts substantial limits on poetry by recalling—and by actually recuperating poetry in terms of—what it lacks and can be said even to eschew: specifically, access to a visible, perceivable world.

Reflected "light," Rudolf Arnheim reminds us, is the "first caus[e] of visual perception."[5] Consequently, by extrapolating or distilling "light" *from* the world in accordance with the function of imagination, poetry not only forsakes perception as a necessary prelude to conception; it remains, in its correspondent deference to "our internal being," left with almost nothing—that is, nothing visible—to illumine or to reflect. To the extent that poetry reflects anything, it reflects not "light" (as the *Defence* contends) but darkness, since it is the function of poetry merely to represent "our internal being"—the "light," as it were, emanating from no visible object—which Shelley previously (and perspicaciously) calls the "invisible nature of man."

In alluding to man's "invisible nature" Shelley was undoubtedly referring to one's enormous power as an autonomous subject possessed of imagination. Nevertheless, it is symptomatic of the contradictions of this humanistic argument, which renders everyman a boundless, omniscient god and makes the visible invisible, that it is immediately vulnerable to a return of the visible. For what the visible constitutes in its resistant or insufficiently repressed status now is not what imagination and its representation (i.e., poetry) necessarily subsume in their various operations; rather what the visible suddenly adumbrates is the "visible nature," the "light" *of the world*, which imagination and its linguistic manifestations must avoid to function as they do. Although the gap between conception and expression is, as Shelley would have it, sufficient to distinguish poetry's operation from the operations of, say, painting and sculpture, the fact remains that poetry's economy and remarkable luminosity owe entirely to the narcissistic completeness that obtains when darkness supersedes light as the first cause of perception—or when there is no longer, in effect, a perceptible, visible world for the subject to contend with.

The repeated recourse to the typology of seeing as a way of describing imagination's function becomes a way, then, of magnifying an ostensible narrowness that is as much a virtue in poetry as it remains, with the identity of conception and expression, something of a liability. Thus, a related and possibly more important effect of Shelley's "allegory of seeing" is that it actually glimpses what poetry is *not* by allowing us to see, or to *imagine* seeing, in ways that poets are apparently not capable of. In reading the act of seeing in the way that Shelley's allegory permits, we are able, even in the sway of his polemic, to distinguish and to recall the "light," which is the "first cause of visual perception," from the light of the mind that emanates from nowhere.

This capacity of romantic writing, even a humanistic manifesto such as *A Defence of Poetry*, to open up onto the very vistas to which it remains opposed—and which, for their part, strenuously oppose what one ordinarily considers the romantic project of interiorization[6]—can hardly be deemed a capacity of all romantic writing. Indeed, for the "first generation" British Romantics in particular, whose preoccupation with imagination and the individual mind in the aftermath of the French Revolution has been described by E. P. Thompson as "Jacobinism-in-recoil," the visible or the "earthly" is no sooner broached than subsumed in a symbolic, intentional structure.[7] The example of William Blake, who illuminated and engraved his own poems as well as the works of other poets, including Dante, Milton and Thomas Gray, may be taken, curiously, as representative of the antipathy to the visible in romanticism's primary, oppositional phase.

Blake, of course, can hardly be considered an "iconoclast" in the sense that Wordsworth or Coleridge would have proclaimed themselves (though he is surely an iconoclast in other ways), and he is undoubtedly unique among the romantic poets in his continued and simultaneous reliance upon the visual medium. However, Blake's "composite art," as W. J. T. Mitchell has brilliantly shown, is sufficiently "synthetic" or dialectical in function—preserving the "rivalry of text and design" so as to undo it—to have ultimately raised romantic iconoclasm, or "iconology" (as Mitchell would have it), to a new, seemingly unassailable plateau.[8] What aspects of language Blake relinquishes to the realm of the visible, whether in the illustrations to his poems or in the printed lines themselves, are more than compensated for by the way the visible as such is displaced—either by the mythmaker himself or by our act of reading him—to those "invisible reaches" of which language, according to Shelley, remains the "more direct representation."[9]

Identifying Blake as a dialectician is scarcely to impugn his achievement or to charge him with having somehow used that achievement to mask a unitary, totalizing project. I am suggesting only that Blake's continued interest in and reliance upon visual signs had the effect of protecting him and his poetry from certain accidental, underdetermined images to which more overtly iconoclastic writers like Wordsworth were staunchly opposed and ultimately more vulnerable. To "return" in the way that I conceive it, and in the way that Wordsworth, for his part, would eventually experience and even embrace it, the visible must be banished or resisted at a prior juncture. Or, to paraphrase Freud, from whom I take my title, again: the visible, like the "uncanny," is a "familiar thing that has undergone repression and then emerged from it." This "repression," which characterizes romanticism in a primary phase of postrevolutionary interiorization, was for Blake, then, a process of immunization as well: a repression that he effected simply by *resisting* in turn. But for other Romantics, or for romanticism at other sites—be it the "second generation" writings of a Byron, or the writings of critics such as Hazlitt or Lamb, or even the works of Wordsworth and Coleridge in their middle and later stages—the visible comes to have a different and less congenial function. Not only does the visible return, however consciously or intentionally, as an adversary once banished and subsequently reassimilated in the struggle with and against authority; the visible returns now as a contradiction—as "something" whose "familiarity" is a function of its repression and continued strangeness—which is also a response to the contradiction that *is romanticism*.

The contradiction "that is romanticism" may be as specific as the narcissism masquerading as comprehension in Shelley's conception of imagination, or it may be as general as the authoritative dispensation—manifest in the ideal of the individual and his enfranchisement—under which progressive social change will, according to many versions of romanticism, come to fruition. But whatever the nature of this contradiction, it was, as the repression and return of the visible shows, assimilated by romanticism in more than one way. Not only was it assimilated as part of a humanistic or romantic ideology and its characteristic fear of visible images. It was reassimilated both prior to and in conjunction with a self-reflexive initiative that criticism has, for the most part, chosen to ignore. Nor is it hard to see why this has been the case, why romanticism-in-recoil is invariably domesticated and—in the case of writers such as Coleridge and Wordsworth—dismissed by critics of all persuasions as political conservatism.[10] For the possibility of a romanticism beside itself, capable at any juncture of redressing and even reinscribing its central inconsistencies—a romanticism capable, like Shelley's *Defence*, of *seeing* through itself—is not simply anathema to a humanistic approach to romanticism, with its particular faith in a liberal imagination; a romanticism beside itself is equally inimical to the varieties of poststructuralism, which have undertaken to expose romanticism's affinity with the very tradition and authoritarianism of which it is a particularly seductive manifestation.

The return of the visible in British romanticism is consistent, then, with romanticism's program of alleged progress and liberation, but to the extent that it is able to expose the inconsistencies of a program whose inability always to repress the visible, or to accept the leveling that a reduction of the world by sight will accomplish, figures a deficiency of romanticism's own to which it now attests. Thus the visible, like "return of the repressed," is a contradiction whose radical productivity in this instance goes a long way in relieving "contradiction" of its pejorative implications. Visibly an intervention *against* romanticism, resisting through its irrepressible and unrecuperable manifestations the symbolic, appropriative tendencies of a putatively democratic, nonauthoritarian, antinomian orientation, the visible is no less, if less perceptibly, an intervention *within* romanticism, whose fidelity to the "light" of the world—with its necessary deauthorization of the perceiving subject—goes a long way in saving the individual from tradition and in saving the world viewed from both of them.[11]

Moreover, the visible also suggests something about the capacity of texts—and, I would further venture, literary texts—to intervene in ways that to most fashions of theory and criticism appear static or beside the point. This is because the particular subjectivity that the visible brings to romantic writing—a subjectivity-in-default or in distraction—opposes by its attachment to the particular, and by the reciprocally leveled status of a subject so distracted, a millenarian or redemptive teleology. That is, the visible is opposed not only to the narrative of universal suffrage characteristic of British romanticism in its revolutionary phase, or to the narrative of personal or representative redemption characteristic of romanticism in its postrevolutionary phase; the return of the visible also challenges the narrative of *contemporary* criticism as it seeks to remove romanticism from the very notions and goals that only critical theory may be expected to serve properly. Thus, if what I am ultmately talking about, again, is some kind of agency of the visible in romantic literature, it is an agency both tantamount to and actually distinguishable *by* what Coleridge would have termed its "accidentality." It is an agency, in other words, sufficient to mobilize literature, indeed to recuperate it as agency, so long as the text remains accessible to the unrecuperable and to the quotidian: to the "light" that, in variously distracting and arresting the subject, necessarily opposes any intentional narrative of symbolic transformation and control.[12]

II

It is on this very issue of intentionality, in fact—the way a resistance to the visible endemic to romanticism provides for a continued, if less manageable, return of the visible—that literature of the romantic period may be distinguished from the art of the period seemingly most concerned with representing the visible world: namely, painting. For just as the visible intervenes in literature in the ways I have suggested, so narrative in a very real sense—or what, after E. H. Gombrich, we may call a "conceptual schema"—invariably consumes and interrupts the world represented in romantic painting.[13] In the case of a painter like Turner such narrative interventions are, Ruskin notwithstanding, hardly news to students of the period. However, if the current Constable boom in art studies is any sign, such interventions represent an important discovery regarding the more naturalistic painter, whose declared fidelity to the visible, or to what Constable consistently called the "truth," had the ironic effect of introducing a range of narrative cathexes, none ultimately involving those "slimy posts" and other detritus that Constable claimed were his true subjects. In fact, just as the return of the visible in romantic literature signals a peculiarly literary resistance that finds similar provocations and manifestations in other kinds of texts, including spectacle and film, so Constable's painting, as Gombrich was perhaps the first to demonstrate, represents painting's ultimate and somewhat astonishing failure to accommodate the merely visible—or what, in some sense, is its principal means of production.

Now, it was scarcely Gombrich's intention to excoriate Constable for having somewhow failed to reduplicate the world or with not achieving what Norman Bryson calls an "essential copy."[14] It was Gombrich's altogether more subtle argument that the represented world in Constable—for all its similarities to our world—is no more and no less an illusion than the worlds represented by Giotto and, before him, by the ancient Greeks. Although art, as Gombrich contends, is committed to an illusionistic program of "matching" the world seen, it is simultaneously committed to "making" or "representing" the world in accordance with the conceptual conventions of the medium. "Without a medium," writes Gombrich, "and without a schema which can be molded and modified, no artist could imitate reality" (*Art and Illusion,* 146). Thus Constable, as Gombrich shows, can have claimed to have forgotten ever having seen a picture of nature whenever he made a sketch despite the fact that he had previously and demonstrably learned to draw nature by imitating the examples of other painters.

My point in stressing Constable's necessary cooptation as an illusionistic painter is not to dwell on the inevitable fallacy of realistic representation so much as to suggest how—in a manner similar to Blake's—the romantic antipathy to the visible is usually better served in the versions of art that make no ostensible or concerted effort to resist and suppress the eye's mediation. This paradox becomes especially clear when we turn to romantic literature. For in literature, be it poetry or criticism, the stated and demonstrated resistance to the "most despotic of our senses" not only thematizes what Derrida wryly calls "the truth in painting"; it also manages—given its peculiarly authoritative opposition to the eye's "tyranny"—to charge this tyranny to the "invisible nature of man" and not to his capacity of sight.

There are many ways, of course, to discuss this tyranny of conception. We can describe it, as Paul de Man does, as the tendency to negotiate a course from the "earthly and material" to the "mental and celestial" in representing nature ("Intentional Structure," 75); or we can describe it as a tendency to renegotiate the passage from the semiotic to the symbolic, resubstantiating the evolution of individuality under the aegis of patriarchy, as Julia Kristeva warrants;[15] or we may follow Norman Bryson in regarding this tyranny as the colonization of the "glance," which (like Kristeva's semiotic) is chiefly a bodily function, by the culturally determined and, as such, more gratifying "logic" of the "gaze." But however we describe it, the tyranny of which we speak is not only diametrically opposed to what Wordsworth and Coleridge called the "tyranny of the eye"; indeed, as the example of Wordsworth (among others) shows, it remains a tyranny against which *only the eye* can effect anything resembling an intervention.[16]

We can return now to the problem with which I began: that as the familiar thing that has undergone repression the visible is usually better served in verbal rather than in visual texts of the romantic period. This is so because the antipathy to the visible in romantic literature creates a possibility for the visible as something *other* or opposed, which painting, in its necessary recourse to the visible as a primary or originating percept, subsequently militates against. Indeed, as criticism after Gombrich has shown, it is the function of Western illusionistic painting to domesticate the "glance"—that bodily activity by which we may perceive the visible—by systematically transposing the visible to the plane of "vision" and to a more symbolic, more encoded realm. For Gombrich, this transposition happens at the very inception of the image, at which point the real is sufficiently conceptualized or determined by both prior knowledge and expectation to ensure that any representation of the real in painting is likely to be an "interaction between narrative intent and pictorial realism" (131).

For Norman Bryson, on the other hand, the suppression of the visible is a more complicated and disturbing affair. In its approximation toward and away from the real, Bryson shows, painting contains what is excessive or immaterial to its denotative, narrative dimension by making all incidental and seemingly extraneous "information" a matter of "recognition." For as something "*found*" (rather than "made"), excess not only legitimizes denotation (lending credence, for example, to the coded figures of Christ and Judas in Giotto's *Betrayal* by positioning them against a "semantically neutral" background); it allows the more transparent social agency of denotation to be naturalized merely by the coexistence of an excessive connotative dimension and the "interpretive effort" provoked thereby. This hermeneutic effort, then, which both provokes and grounds a belief that "meaning" can "inhere in an objective world," necessarily represents a "consciousness" that is "socially constructed" and "socially located" (*Vision,* 53–64).

A particularly revealing function of such a consciousness, according to Bryson, is the transformation of the viewer into a disembodied gazer, whose lack of a body—as demonstrated, for example, in the inability to absorb the various details of Vermeer's *Art of Painting* from a single vantage—is the effective (if somehow deserved) consequence of a socially constructed omniscience. But the more immediate, if necessary, operation of this hermeneutic consciousness, and the tradition of which it is obviously a part, involves continual opposition to the merely visible—the world as unmediated excess or produce of the "glance"—by continually suppressing it. If the glance is, by anatomical necessity, intermingled with the gaze in illusionistic painting, then it remains, with its relationship to the visible and its particularly visceral attachment to the viewer, what is actually "separated out, repressed, and as it is repressed . . . also constructed as the hidden term on whose disavowal the whole system depends" (121). "Against the Gaze," Bryson argues, "the Glance proposes desire, proposes the body, in the *durée* of its practical activity," all of "which the tradition seeks to repress" (122).

Bryson's, it should be emphasized, is a revisionist thesis, marked by its efforts to emend Gombrich's too genial approach to illusionism and by its contestation as well of the linguistic imperialism to which semioticians such as Roland Barthes have been quite eager to subscribe. The verdict from Bryson may in the end be no more encouraging than that from Barthes, both of whom lament the prevalence of the "system." But Bryson's *dolour* clearly bears the stamp of Gombrich and a belief in art's allegiance, however attenuated, to the "truth," in the refusal to dispense with the possibility (if it is only a theoretical one) of the "glance." I certainly join with Bryson in an unwillingness to relinquish the glance and the visible, even if they must still be exceptions that prove the rule. Yet where Bryson is largely content to regard the visible as a theoretical other in painting, whose necessary hiddenness simply confirms to what degree it has been separated and written over, I am somewhat more sanguine about the possibility of the glance and about the return of the visible. These last are potentially a condition of those texts and media—be they poems or popular spectacles or even photographs—that, by definition and operation, can (following the Freudian logic) enjoy no real success in repressing the repressed.

Chief among such texts, as I have been suggesting, are the literary artifacts bearing a revolutionary or postrevolutionary cast, whose demonstrable fear of the glance ironically thematizes the usurpation of the glance in painting, where the visible is initially admitted and even relied upon. Painting, of course, gradually immunizes itself against the visible by admitting it to, and otherwise placing itself at the disposal of, a cultural or semiotic field. But romantic literature—which staunchly resists the visible (and consequently eschews any immunization against it)—routinely dictates its vulnerability as host. It is not important whether this imperative on the part of literature is conscious or intentional. What is important is that it is necessarily "willed" in the sense that Schopenhauer, and later Freud, would describe. The particular hostility of romantic literature to what Walter Benjamin later termed "distraction" simply makes it more vulnerable to distraction—to the technically visible which is presently (or no sooner seen than) invisible—than its visualized counterparts are. In language more than in other media one is able paradoxically to *see* how the visible has been reconceived in all versions of art and consequently to imagine, along with Shelley, the steps necessary to reexperience the *durée* of the body in the *durée* of representation.

This peculiarly "romantic imagination" is not simply about technique, or even about technologies of beholding the world in the relatively random or distracting fashion of such (then) contemporary media as the Panorama, the Diorama, the kaleidoscope, or even photography. This imagination also involves the cultural politics of wanting, or of being forced, to see differently, which is alternately a way of seeing and displacing a culture of signs. Thus, Byron's juxtaposition of two beholders in *Childe Harold's Pilgrimage* works to differentiate and to extract the world viewed from a world read or described in virtually the same way that Charles Lamb, with rather different motivations, distinguishes between the world according to the "bodily eye," which is an object of loathing, and the world as "object of meditation." Returned by sight to a borderline condition in which the "incredible" is suddenly too real to be anything but "hateful," Lamb signals the denial by which the critic *and* his culture are able—albeit tenuously—to maintain sovereignty over visible things. And in still other criticism of the period, notably the theater criticism of Hazlitt and Coleridge, the very sight of genius in bodily form admits a leveling of distinction regarding *all* "creatures" against which the putatively radical notions of democracy and freedom appear both hopelessly inadequate and utterly conventional.

III

These instances of the visible—and others—are explored in ensuing chapters. But first, it will help to distinguish my approach from its critical or aesthetic genealogy, which, not surprisingly, turns out to be still another way of talking about romanticism's unappreciated rejection of itself. I alluded earlier to romanticism's rejection of the neoclassic doctrine *ut pictura poesis*: a resistance that provided, in the end, for a return of the visible, though not necessarily the picture, of which the visible might have been a grounding. As a result, my identification of the verbal medium as a crucial site of the visible in British romanticism is no more an endorsement of the doctrine of the sister arts (which romanticism rather explicitly and properly rejects) than of the equally conventional if more romantic opposition of the verbal and the visual as expressive and mimetic media respectively. Indeed, these latter distinctions tend even more than neoclassic aesthetics to obfuscate and resist those larger cultural imperatives (or, as the case may be, imperatives against culture) that are demonstrably cross-generic and sufficiently prolific that a literary artifact may in the end have more in common with a Diorama or a photograph than with a painting.[17]

That it would devolve upon photography and later film, in addition to such precinematic institutions as the Panorama or the Diorama—and not necessarily upon painting—to register these imperatives attests more to the restraints and controls exerted on painting by the academy and the marketplace, which saw to it that innovation proceeded only by increments and in accordance with an essentially benevolent tradition. Such stewardship might also explain why, from the perspective of the visible as I conceive it, and its related manifestations of particularity and detailism, the Pre-Raphaelitism of the mid-nineteenth century represents something of a failure or, at the least, an anomoly, whose totalizing, symbolic dimension jibes uncomfortably with an impulse to realism.[18] And, more to the point, such "ownership of the image" (to borrow Bernard Edelman's term)[19] explains the tendency of romantic painting—the painting to which Pre-Raphaelitism is clearly a reaction—to vitiate and subordinate the visible in deference to the visionary.

Indeed, despite the tendency of preromantic aesthetics, chiefly those of Burke and Lessing, to distinguish poetry and painting as expressive and mimetic media whose respective commitments were to the sublime and the beautiful or (in Lessing) to the temporal and the spatial, these distinctions—as the genesis of the picturesque as an intermediate category in painting later demonstrated—eventually proved unnecessary.[20] For as romanticism became increasingly phenomenological in focus, granting "truth" status to individual perception and imaginative experience, the mirror, as M. H. Abrams famously reminds us, became the lamp, suppressing even more the visible or putatively objective truths, which to a critic such as Burke were apparently still the domain of the visual arts.

Just as the lamp or light of the mind became a more truthful reflection of the real than the merely reflected light of visual perception, so romantic painting and aesthetics saw to it, in effect, that sensory perception and the representation of it were ideally indistinguishable. To represent and to reconstitute the world seen, according to romantic dogma, is no different from, and in no way a departure from, the experience of actually seeing the world. This is so much the case, in fact, that travelers would, as Jane Austen brilliantly satirizes in *Northanger Abbey*, be known to seek out and quite literally see only those pictureseque vistas that resembled their representations. The comparatively recent efforts, then, of Rudolph Arnheim and others to attach the representations of the visible in painting to physiological and psychological processes of visual organization common to all of us are sharply tried in romantic painting, whose representations are likely to be as discrete and arbitrary as the representation of the landscape a few miles above Tintern Abbey in Wordsworth's poem.

And yet, in the very way that the "I" demonstrably supplants the *eye* as the prime agent of perception in romantic aesthetics, so the bracketing of the eye simultaneously underscores the arbitrariness and the remarkable conventionality of romantic aesthetics. Thus, the visible is critical for understanding romanticism (and vice versa) not only in the way it is obviously the "hidden," on whose suppression the "system" depends; it is critical in the way this virtually institutionalized bracketing both measures and, with the return of the visible, figures the resistance of a seemingly revolutionary or democratic movement to its own radical imperatives. The very marginality of the visible in romantic writing is what ensures its centrality, then, since the visible represents both the disruptive imperative that was always present in romanticism—the "unmediated vision" of which apocalyptic or subjective vision was arguably an issue—as well as the disruption that was always resistable, according to a humanistic ideology and its particular claim for individual authority.

In this way, too, the return of the visible suggests something about romanticism that criticism, it is no exaggeration to say, has adamantly refused to concede. And this last, quite simply, is the variousness and remarkable mobility of romanticism, both as movement against itself, or what we ordinarily consider the "romantic movement," as well as a counterculture that opposes both its typical mystification as revolution and its typical demystification as bourgeois humanism. In fact, as the prevalence of the visible before and after the fact—as a disruption that becomes absorbed and resisted by romanticism—suggests, there is much more to romanticism, and much more going on during (and after) the interval nominated as "the romantic period," than the somewhat bellicose individualism on which proponents and deconstructers are remarkably agreed. As my choice of "representative" writers of the visible shows—a selection ranging from the margins of the period (the late Wordsworth), to critics once removed (Lamb and Hazlitt), to the more familiar instances of Coleridge, Byron, and the earlier Wordsworth—not only was there remarkable mobility, or resistance to a "set" sensibility, on the part of writers of the time; there was, in conjunction with the popular culture, a greater flexibility and range to the movement of which all of these figures were still a part.

Thus criticism can, I submit, talk responsibly and credibly not only about a romanticism whose informing feature is its productive decenteredness but about a romanticism whose manifestations and interventions extend well beyond the literary instances whose importance, in comparison to painting for example, is chiefly their ability to theorize what has in our time been frequently written in the name of theory. These instances, which embrace contemporary technological innovations and other transformations in the culture of seeing (for example, the new public art galleries) that in turn comprise what Benjamin and others see as an "archaeology of cinema," extend inevitably—through such institutions as the Panorama and the Diorama—to the example of cinema itself.

I am scarcely the first, of course, to contend that cinema represents a culmination, or more modestly perhaps an extension, of a romantic way of seeing. Beginning indeed with Eisenstein's claim for cinema as an instrument of intentionality, it has been the "tradition" of cinema studies, in a peculiar sense, to locate cinema's genealogy in the very humanism whose care and feeding were unquestionably one of romanticism's projects. Nor will it surprise students of romanticism to discover that this genealogy is generally distinguished only by the degree of praise or blame attached to its interpretation. From the phenomenological claims of Stanley Cavell and Frank McConnell, who otherwise promote film as an imagined or "spoken seen," to the neo-Marxist readings of Laura Mulvey and others, who take a dimmer viewer of film's cooperation with the viewer, film studies are remarkably agreed on the primacy of the sovereign subject.[21]

Thus if romanticism and cinema have been rendered uniform by the controversy surrounding each, they remain, in the contemporary critical imagination at least, copies of one another. The "agnostic humanism," for example, on which the generally honorific reassessment of romanticism in the 1960s was based has not been significantly challenged or revised by the revisionist tendencies in romantic studies (in which "humanism" is now a stigma) any more than film studies have succeeded in avoiding the subject. Instead, what has been initiated under the banner of revisionism in both areas has attempted merely to expose and more recently to historicize the humanistic ideology by which the Romantics—and their cinematic successors—have apparently upheld the very authoritarianism that romanticism (and film, according to both Eisenstein and Benjamin) presumably opposed.

I do not mean, of course, to discredit the revisionist tendencies in romantic studies (on which I obviously depend) any more than I mean to discredit film studies for their similar fixation on the bourgeois subject. Subjectivism of a certain order, whether an invention of romanticism or not, is very much a romantic legacy that demands both attention and critique. I am troubled simply by the remarkable consensus regarding this problem. Such consensus, as I see it, does more than limit the possibilities of romanticism and film respectively; it ultimately renders the continuity of romanticism and film (or the issue of the romantic visible *in* film) a hegemony, for better or worse. I agree with the criticism that theorizes an indisputable link between romanticism and film. I disagree with the extent to which such criticism makes no provision for the agency—much of it clustering around the prospect of the visible and the contingent—that is as much a matter of romanticism's intervention against the very tradition it was destined in some measure to become as of a variety of other institutions of seeing that are fundamental and fundamentally opposed to the romantic "movement" as such.

CHAPTER TWO

The Panorama and the Diorama: Aids to Distraction

I

Of the various "oramic" displays that captivated London viewers in the late eighteenth and early nineteenth centuries, "fixing the attention to objects which the eye might possibly pass unheeded, and . . . exercising various mental faculties, which wanting some impulsion, would never be manifested" (*Examiner,* 22 April 1832), the most popular and significant by far were the Panorama and the Diorama. Panoramic painting and its near cousin, the prospect, had been features of British art and culture throughout the eighteenth century, numbering among their practioners such artists and draughtsman as Paul Sandby, Matthew Read, Thomas Bowles, John Bowen, and Robert Whitworth, as well as internationally renowned painters such as Canaletto, who was invited to London in the 1740s and subsequently painted panoramas of the city from both Somerset House and Lambeth.[1] However, it was not until the turn of the century, or during the romantic period to be precise, that the Panorama achieved a form and magnitude that not only must be reckoned a response to a public need to view things differently—or beyond prevailing standards of taste—but must also be measured in accordance with the various *reactions* to these shows, which underscored the particular resistance that panoramic "responsiveness," with its notably unique version of the visible, represented.

A similar tension characterized the Diorama, which was brought to England in 1823 by the great French theatrical designer and inventor Louis-Jacques-Mandé Daguerre. Even more than viewers of the

Panorama, who moved through the two-tiered exhibitions, which effected a continuum between the world viewed and the world viewing it, the seated audience for the Diorama was noticeably unfamiliar to *and with* the orders of art and exhibition. Such an audience, then, was not only a more "public" public than the one that both shaped and was simultaneously constructed by the Panorama. The Diorama's audience was a public drawn inevitably, or so it seemed, to a peculiarly stubborn, if ultimately disorienting, experience: an experience that, according to numerous accounts in both periodicals and newspapers, amounted less in the end to a suspension of disbelief than to a resistance toward the illusions ordinarily fostered by art.

A hybrid of theater and the fine arts that has been largely overlooked in the histories of both, the huge circular panoramas developed by Robert Barker and his son Henry Aston Barker at the turn of the eighteenth century (and continued in the nineteenth century by Robert Burford and his son John) are increasingly recognized as a crucial development in the visual and artistic culture of modern England. Thanks in large measure to the studies of Richard Altick and Hubert Pragnell, and to the perceptive inclusion of the Barkers' work in such revisionist exhibitions as Peter Galassi's Before Photography (Museum of Modern Art [New York], 1981) and Ralph Hyde's Gilded Scenes and Shining Prospects (Yale Center for British Art, 1985) and Panoramania! (Barbican Art Gallery [London], 1988), Barker's Panorama stands prominently among a series of developments—notably the rise of photography and, following it, the cinema—that can no longer be understood independent of the Panorama, its impetus, and its often startling effects.[2]

Nevertheless, while these studies and exhibitions are materially correct in the importance they grant the Panorama, both as a new form and as the progenitor of later representational modes, they are noticeably silent on the broader significance of these developments, both at the time and later on. Concerned largely with material culture and altogether less with the ideological underpinnings of certain cultural productions, these studies leave mostly unexamined the various ways such oramic displays—as registers of social and political change—bear upon or were influenced in turn by the "age of revolution" in which they were spawned. Thus, such studies not only sidestep the influence of a discrete but arguably valid version of "romanticism" on later generations and their productions; they leave unexamined as well the competing romanticisms, or, more properly, the competing ide-

Figure 1. Frederick Birnie after Robert Barker, *Panorama of London from the Albion Mills,* 1792–93. Yale Center for British Art, New Haven, Connecticut.

ologies within the romantic period, that a popular culture in this case, rather than a "higher" culture dialectically positioned by and against tradition, was successful in staging.

Both Pragnell and Altick describe at length the various experiments by which the Barkers came upon the decision to paint panoramic views on a large circular surface and their entrepreneurial decision to display such a painting in a gallery of their own built in 1793 "expressly for the exhibition of panoramas." This building, which "contained three circular rooms, the largest ninety feet in diameter and forty feet in height, for the display of full-circle works to be viewed from a distance of thirty feet," became, as Pragnell observes, "the talk of the town" and was subsequently visited by a host of notables, including Sir Joshua Reynolds and King George III (*The London Panoramas,* 12).

Barker's Panorama, both the building in Leicester Square and the numerous representations displayed therein, have long since vanished. The seminal 1792 Panorama of London taken from the rooftop of the Albion sugar mills survives, for example, only in a small aquatint made by Frederick Birnie (fig. 1), which was published while the painting—a prototype for the 360-degree view of the city subsequently displayed in the upper rotunda of the new building (Fig. 2)—was initially on exhibit.

The irretrievability of Barker's Panorama as a viewable object is undoubtedly an impediment to understanding it. But even more critical perhaps is the relative unavailability of public response to the Panorama, especially during its early and critical stage of development. The periodicals at the turn of the century, including newspapers such as the *Morning Chronicle* and the *Times,* not only were restricted in what

space they could allow for reportage of the fine arts; they were altogether unprepared to comment on something that clearly extended both the audience for the fine arts and the boundaries of pictorial representation. Attention was given, to be sure, to Thomas Girtin's less innovative panorama of London, his so-called Eidometropolis, which was exhibited a decade later in 1802. But attention in this instance owed as much to the work itself, which at 1,944 square feet was a little larger than Barker's London Panorama (but much smaller than many of Barker's other Panoramas, including, for example, the 10,000-square-foot painting of the fleet moored at Spithead pictured beneath the painting of London [fig. 2]), as to Girtin's untimely death shortly after the exhibition opened. Commenting on the "recent death of that extraordinary and celebrated artist, Mr. Thomas Girtin," the *Morning Herald* remarked rather hyperbolically that the "Eidometropolis exhibited at Spring Gardens, both in magnitude and effect, stands unrivalled" (Pragnell, 21). The *Monthly Magazine* echoed these sentiments in an uncharacteristically lengthy review of Girtin's "new and extraordinary appropriation of perspective to painting," spelling out the differences between a "connoisseur's panorama" such as Girtin's, with its "most picturesque display," and other "pictures of this description" that, according to the *Monthly,* "take the common way of measuring and reducing . . . objects" (14 [1802]: 254–55).

Nor could the *Monthly Magazine* resist lampooning the Panorama and its originator, who had sole rights to the Panorama by royal patent. Earlier that same year, the *Monthly* made public a letter to Barker from Lord Nelson attesting to the the accuracy of the Panorama of the battle of Copenhagen then on display (13 [1802]: 597). While we can only speculate on the circumstances that led eventually to the publi-

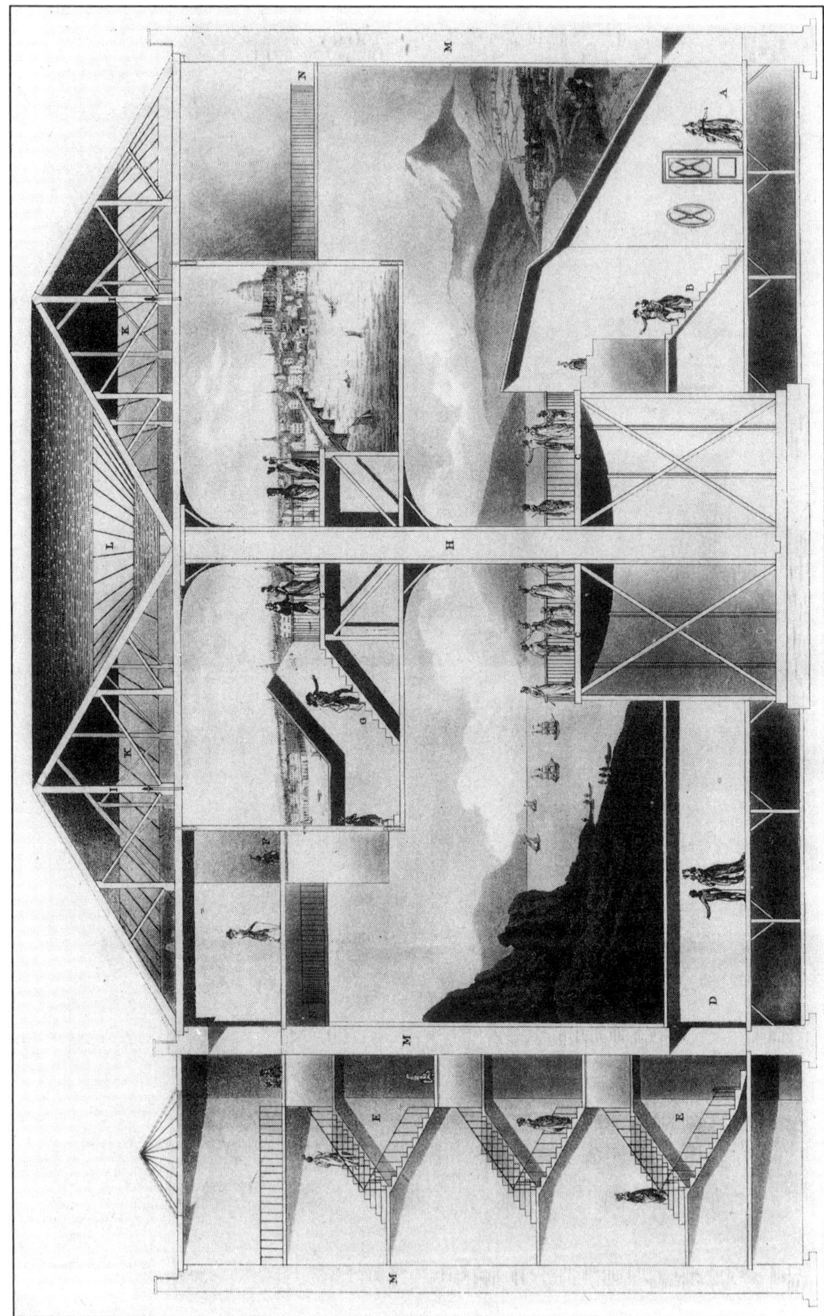

cation of this correspondence, the *Monthly*'s disdain for both Barker's work and his tendency to self-promotion was clear enough. Lord Nelson, whatever his virtues, was no particular connoisseur of the arts. Thus, to have made available a letter from him pronouncing the Panorama "the most correct picture of any event I have ever seen"—a judgment in which the admiral's two subordinates, "who have examined the picture with [him]," are reported to have concurred—not only reflects a certain obtuseness on Barker's part (if only to the vagaries of consensus); it manages in its present incarnation to draw a parallel between the meanness of Barker's motives in soliciting such testimony in the first place, whatever its purpose, and the "particular merit," as the *Monthly* dryly put it, of his more formal "exhibition."

It is easy to imagine the conditions that might have forced the *Monthly* into this hostile posture. In addition to eschewing the various conventions, notably the picturesque style, by which Girtin's work had gained legitimacy as a fine art, Barker's Panorama was, for the duration of the Napoleonic Wars, a frequently topical affair whose rapid (and occasionally haphazard) production was paradoxically, or so it appeared, a guarantor of success. Moreover, the Panorama's other major function, the representation of cities both in England and abroad, remained a function about as far removed from the meditative disposition of Claudean and other (then) conventionally fashionable versions of locodescriptive painting as was possible.

And yet, for all their hostility, the periodicals are vital to our understanding of what was *at stake* in the Panorama and in the resistance to it. Not only did their resistance to the Panorama refer (however obliquely) to the particular threat to convention that the Panorama posed. The notices and advertisements for the Panorama and related entertainments that ran on the front pages of newspapers like the *Times* and the *Morning Chronicle* adumbrated an audience and, by extension, a public imperative that the remaining pages of the *Times* either seemed unaware of or pretended was of little consequence in the course of human events.

The notices for the Panorama were, like Barker's circulation of Nelson's letter to him, entrepreneurial gestures intended to gain as

---

Figure 2 (opposite). Robert Mitchell, "Section of the Rotunda, Leicester Square, in Which Is Exhibited the Panorama," *Plans and Views in Perspective of Buildings in England and Scotland,* 1801. Yale Center for British Art, New Haven, Connecticut.

large an audience as possible for the building in Leicester Square (and later, the Panorama in the Strand). Yet they manage to tell us a good deal about the Panorama: they give a sense of who was attending it, the impetus behind their attendance, and a way, finally, to assess the bearing of this public upon a new and very different version of art (and vice versa). By no means, then, are the notices always at odds with the prevailing standards of taste, by which the Panorama was kept a virtual secret for more than twenty years—at least to those who relied on newspapers and magazines for reportage of the fine arts. In fact, what is clearly dramatized in the notices—and in almost equal degree in the panoramic exhibits themselves—is a conflict between a conventional aesthetic and a newer, more public desideratum, which the Panorama can be said to have both cultivated and satisfied.

Thus, while the Panorama was introduced (and, at one shilling, priced) as an entertainment for the public at large—early announcements for Barker's painting of London were addressed, for example, to the "public" rather than, like other notices, to the "nobility, gentry, and the public"—the exhibitors were mindful of the division of the public into classes and of the aesthetics pursuant to that division. A 1794 Panorama of Bath, for instance, of which the public was, as usual, "respectfully informed" (*Times,* 7 October 1794), was directed (like Barker's earlier three-shilling exhibit in Edinburgh) at an audience arguably smaller and more exclusive than the public whose "sphere" ultimately *was* the Panorama. The "subject" of this painting—a fashionable resort—was clearly not without its interest. But whether this interest was in any way identical with the interest provided and provoked by the quotidian details of urban life in the earlier painting of London is doubtful. If anything, the representation of Bath effectively followed its presumed audience in the control it claimed to maintain over the world viewed. Unlike the majority of Panoramas, which were consumed by details and sufficiently distracting to remove the viewer from an otherwise stable and controlling subject-position, the "view of the City of Bath, and the surrounding country, commanding a distant prospect of Bristol and part of South Wales," was promoted less as an eidometropolis than as a vantage in which the viewer would be privileged to "command."

Nor was Barker, for his part, at all hesitant in either his quest for respectability or his conviction that his art, however popular or well suited to a larger viewing public, was art of an ultimately conventional and respectable sort. An article on the Panorama "with memoirs of its inventor, Robert Barker, and his son, the late Henry Aston Barker," which appeared in the *Art Journal* in 1857 shortly after the younger Barker's death (Barker himself had died in 1806), reported that the elder Barker first took his invention to Joshua Reynolds, who was then president of the Royal Academy. Although initially unimpressed, Reynolds reversed his opinion after viewing the picture of London. According to the younger Barker, Reynolds admitted his "error in supposing [the] invention could never succeed" and further credited its capability in "producing effects, and representing nature in a manner far superior to the limited scale of pictures in general" ("The Panorama," 46).

The Barkers' recollections are not the only evidence of Sir Joshua's interest in the Panorama. James Northcote later recalled that Reynolds was not only a "prodigious admirer of the invention and striking effect of the Panorama," but that he had personally urged Northcote "to go also, saying it would surprise me more than anything of the kind I had ever seen in my life" (*Panoramania!*, 25). The point to stress, then, is not that the Barkers necessarily misrepresented Reynolds's response, construing his "surprise" as a sign of legitimation. What must be emphasized is that the Panorama was from the beginning, and in particular accordance with its destabilizing effect on viewers such as Reynolds, beyond the grasp of virtually everyone, including its patentees.

Nor can the confusion surrounding the Panorama be separated from the Panorama's ability to achieve an *already desired* effect. While it was surely unconventional as an art form, the version of painting that the Barkers may be credited with having developed and perfected was also strangely congenial to viewers: an art whose "surprises" were more "striking" than they were disappointing. It was an art of uncanny simultaneity, in which surprises were sufficiently anticipated to be striking, yet sufficiently striking to be surprising. In fact, like photography, which it anticipates in important ways, the Panorama was less an accident of technology than a technology of "accidentality," a phenomenon so surprising and beyond the grasp of its inventors and viewers alike that its particular interest either superseded or at the very least adumbrated a desire it had *already* requited. Effectively fulfilling a wish to view things differently, the Panorama achieved success not because this wish was somehow comprehensible to the Barkers and their audience; it was successful on account of the incomprehensibility (to borrow Schlegel's concept) by which satisfaction and surprise were somehow identical. Its success owed to a confusion in which the act of viewing was less a matter of being wrenched or startled than of being enticed *in being startled* from a stable or commanding vantage.

II

The incomprehensibility regarding both the Panorama and its contestation of a subject-position, wherein the privilege to behold was simultaneously the privilege to command or to control, is evident in a number of ways. Chief among these are the panoramic subjects themselves, which in the early years especially were either "events" from the Napoleonic Wars or views of particular cities. The latter subjects, needless to say, were suited to the Panorama and its "public" audience. But it is the former subject, with its distinctly patriotic interest, that reveals the confusion surrounding the Panorama and, worse, the resistance of the institution itself to the impetus behind its appeal in the first place.

Although the panoramic views of cities exhibited by Barker derive clearly from the prospects and panoramas of the eighteenth century, their uniqueness consisted in their lack of a frame or controlling perspective. The giant panoramas with their mobile, circulating audiences worked, however directly, to establish an equivalency between the "familiar"—the perceiving subject's recognition of himself as part of a public and as coextensive with the peculiar aggregate now viewing the world—and the unfamiliar, or the world currently on view. Constantinople (1801), for instance, was no longer a place about which the viewer was suddenly empowered to know more. It was a place, rather, whose uncanny familiarity *as a place apart,* as the boundless site of many selves and objects, worked to eliminate a distinction between a commanding viewer, on the one hand, and an object in apparent want of control, on the other. Unable, in effect, to separate the world viewed and the world viewing it, the panoramic views of cities both played to and at the same time underwrote a uniformitarianism *in excess* of human equality, or beyond the individual enfranchisement we customarily associate with romanticism and the revolutionary imperatives of the Enlightenment. Indeed, the uniformity of the Panorama was arguably one in which the capacity of sight was more a prelude to the viewer's sudden and even simultaneous visibility: a dislocation in which, in light of what one saw or was distracted by, one was inexorably relocated.[3]

We need only turn to book 7 of Wordsworth's *Prelude* (1805), where London's "thickening hubbub" (227) joins with the Panorama (among other spectacles) in threatening to cancel the speaker's sovereignty as a self and as an artist, to see this dislocation at work. And yet an even better measure of the changes produced by the Panorama was its own continued resistance to its productions. This internal resistance took a number of different forms, none of them particularly conscious, or any more knowing, say, than the resistance that Wordsworth himself waged when he accused the Panorama of the very appropriation and control—of greedily "taking in / A whole horizon on all sides—with power / Like that of angels" (258–60)—for which his poetry was at least as blameworthy. Such resistance was, if anything, inevitable and altogether typical of the confusion to which the exhibitors, as much as their "public," were continually prone. It was especially evident in the Panorama's attention to the Napoleonic Wars, whose various engagements accounted for about half of the Panorama's subjects, even as late as the 1820s.

Although the representation of battles may be counted as a shrewd business decision in response to the public's desire to be informed of the progress of these events, the exhibitions also had the effect of resisting the uniformitarian imperative and its challenge to an otherwise stable subject-position. Now, according to the adversarial imperatives of king and country, the Panorama was no longer one thing to an increasingly homogeneous public—an experience whose "surprising" *effect* had arguably been the elimination of difference. In a virtual mockery of that initiative, the Panorama was suddenly all things to all people: a theater of consensus whose adversarial base proved the base in turn of a variety of superstructures (including class and, by extension, self) whose mitigation was impossible in light of a common enemy, or other. Resisting the very instability it was able elsewhere to support, the patriotic Panorama saw to it that its audience would be equally opposed to distraction—that both the visible and its peculiar work would remain secondary to a process of reading and, by implication, a process of framing, which both reinforced and were in turn reinforced by a more conventional cultural framework.[4]

Nor was it simply through its subject matter alone that the Panorama waged a resistance to its disruptive tendencies. The strictly visual and, as such, disorienting aspects of the Panorama were further mitigated by the printed guides, which were initially distributed free of charge, allowing patrons to read and thereby to control what they could otherwise only see. The guides were comprised of two parts.

There was the "explanation" or key to the Panorama, which was composed of both a small (often barely recognizable) facsimile of the actual painting with its details numbered and an accompanying legend with explanatory cross-references (fig. 3). The second part of the guide was the so-called "description," which, true to its designation, provided basic information regarding the history, disposition, and current affairs of a specific city or place. In the case of a battle such as Waterloo or Trafalgar, the description would recount both the development and progress of the engagement as well as isolated exploits and moments of heroism, which though separated by hours and (sometimes) days were often represented in the actual painting as occurring all at the same time.

These accompanying narratives were undoubtedly a boon to those who came to the Panorama to learn more about a place or an event—a motivation that many commentators, including Ruskin, assume to have been the public's reason for being there, and hence, to have been the Panorama's most important function.[5] Yet the notices for the Panorama, which are a more accurate measure by far of what the public wanted or otherwise demanded of the Panorama, give a different account. In these notices, which appeared routinely in the *Times* and in the *Morning Chronicle,* frequently in the company of other notices appealing to the same or to a similar audience, the overwhelming interest and appeal of the Panorama was more visual and sensational. This was so even in the advertisements featuring patriotic Panoramas, where a more stubborn structure, or deferential behavior, clearly militated against mere sensory engagement.

Thus, even though the accompanying guides to the Panorama may have joined with the subject matter in effectively marginalizing and writing over what was visibly before the viewer, the Panorama *as a panorama* never stopped either responding to public pressure or, for that matter, exerting pressure on the public. It may, at times, have resisted those pressures as did many viewers and later the many reviewers who were finally disposed, under pressure of its popularity, to report on the Panorama phenomenon. However, to the extent that the Panorama remained advertisable and a source of revenue to exhibitors and newspapers alike, it was committed above all else to a return of the visible (if only as a condition of economic return) and, its various confusions notwithstanding, to working toward a uniformitarian goal. The public notices therefore did more than provide a foretaste of the Panorama—promising in the case of Lord Howe's de-

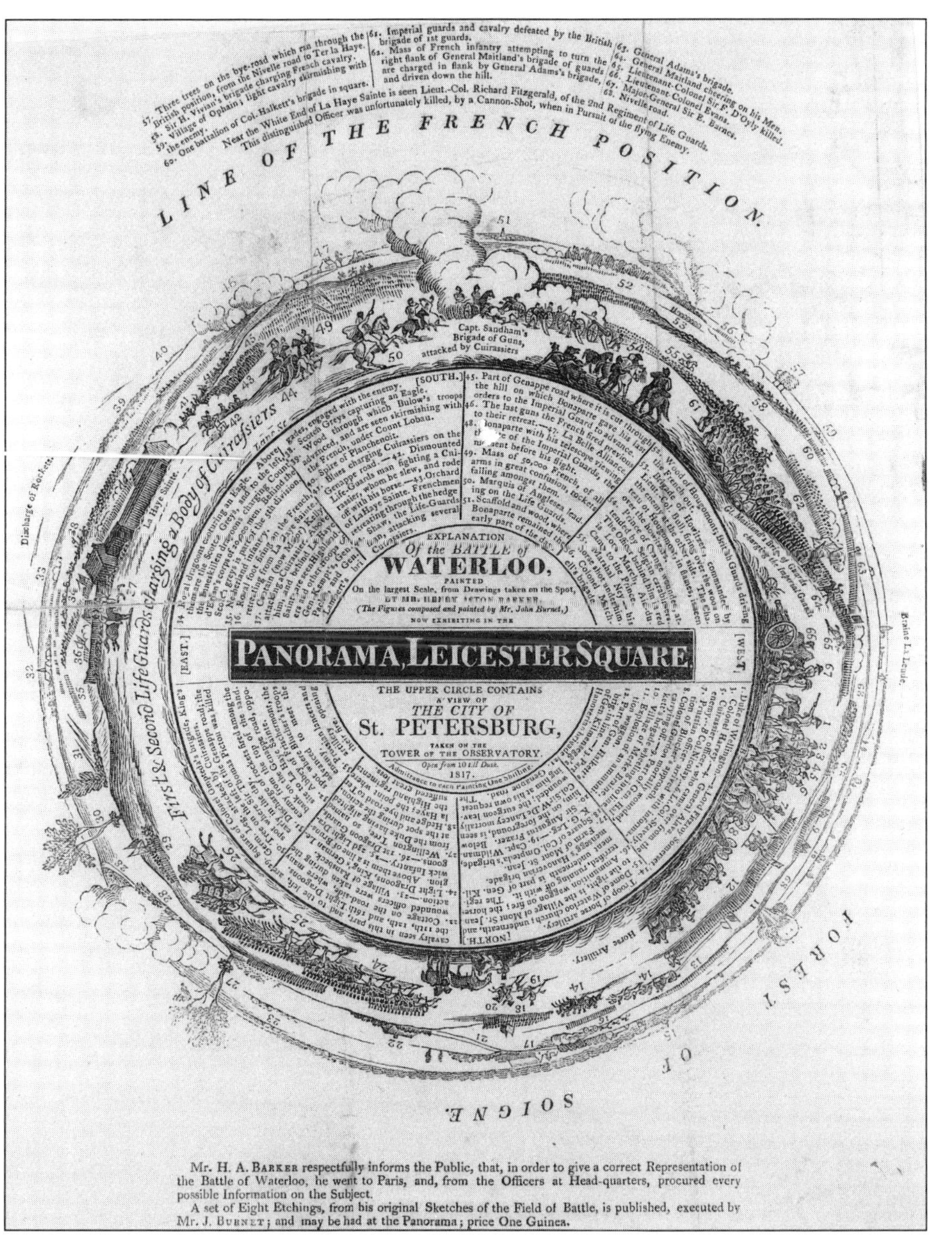

Figure 3. Henry Aston Barker and John Burnet (after Barker), *Explanation of the Battle of Waterloo,* 1817. Yale Center for British Art, New Haven, Connecticut.

feat of the French to locate the viewer "on the open sea, in the centre of both fleets" (*Times,* 1 June 1795). They made promises that were always to some extent recollections; as *advert*isements, they recalled a desire for distraction that could be satisfied either by the Panorama itself, or by the public experience—past, passing, and to come—with which panoramic views were coextensive.

While notices for the Panorama sought initially to distinguish it from such popular and spectacular entertainments as the Mechanic Theatre, which featured automatons of various kinds (usually by proclaiming the accuracy of the panoramic "views" at issue), it was not long before the experience, and the invariably wrenching effect, of the Panorama was publicized as its principal feature. A notice for the relatively early Panorama of Windsor (*Times,* 9 June 1798) is an excellent case in point. Promising to locate the "observer" on "the highest turret on the Castle" from where "at one view a part of 14 Counties" could be seen, the advertisement went on to list the many details therein and finally to note how the "whole" would be "interspersed with Towns and Noblemen and Gentlemen's Seats." To the extent, in other words, that a command of the landscape in "one view" was initially promised, it was also disappointed by the world viewed: a vista which, as the ad suggested (and as the actual painting undoubtedly demonstrated), was an aggregate of details rather than a picturesque totality. What viewers of the Panorama could count on—and what the advertisement sought (however consciously) to promote—was less a painting in the customary sense than a collection of fragmentary sights, ranging from St. Paul's at one glance to Shooter's Hill and part of Wilshire in others.

Such sights, inasmuch as they would have disrupted the observer's association with Windsor, bear very strongly on the painting's other significant aspect: namely, its situation of the viewer *in* the landscape—or among the public metonymically pictured there. Rather than providing control over the landscape by allowing a whole, in this instance, to be a product of "one view" or gaze (and vice versa), the Panorama with its continually shifting interest reconstituted and, in effect, redistributed subjectivity by transforming the beholder—a previously sovereign subject associated with the castle—into a detail among details.

It is easy undoubtedly to overread these notices or to attribute a consciousness to them that is contingent at best. However, it is this contingency ultimately that is the issue. By adverting and attracting

Figure 4. Frederick Birnie after Robert Barker, *Panorama of London from the Albion Mills,* 1792–93, detail of Blackfriars Bridge. Trustees of the British Museum, London.

as large an audience as possible, such notices not only anticipate or, as the case may be, recapitulate, the panoramic experience; they manage actually to defer to potential viewers by allowing how the event to which they have been adverted is—if only on the evidence of that advertence—about *them.* In the view of London taken from Albion Mills this particular responsiveness is figured, for example, in the veritable spectrum of society crossing Blackfriars Bridge (figs. 4 and 5).

Similarly, in the notice of the view of Windsor, viewers are invited not only to picture themselves in the landscape, but to picture themselves among an audience whose particular division into noblemen, townsmen, and gentry serves less to uphold these classifications than as pretext for their conflation or reformation as a visible "public." Cut off or displaced from the structural base of Windsor and the divisions, oppositions, and deferences the "castle" fosters, the houses in

Figure 5. Frederick Birnie after Robert Barker, *Panorama of London from the Albion Mills,* 1792–93, detail of Blackfriars Bridge. Trustees of the British Museum, London.

the landscape, like the viewer in their adverting sway, are (like the people pictured in the London Panorama) very much in a state of transition or crossing. No less than viewers, whose sovereignty and individuality are contested both in the capacity to see as well as by the company they keep as viewers of this particular painting, the residences currently on view shuttle between significance and loss of significance: between a value or status that is describable and readable and a visibility or uncitability that, like the "scene" advertised, may be properly reckoned "rich beyond description."

It is difficult, of course, to view such democratic vistas as anything but excessive to the business—and indeed it was a business—of getting people through the doors of Barker's Panorama. And it was not many decades, in fact, before the public that Barker was both creating and satisfying would begin to bear the marks of a less mobile, less tractable, hegemony. However, during its inception and early development, the Panorama remained, along with other versions of art at the time, a site in flux—an art that both created and *in creating* submitted to the taste by which it was to be enjoyed. Thus, the Panorama also differed from other contemporary art forms—including such transitional art as Wordsworth's early poetry—in extending the "uniformitarianism" that Wordsworth, by alignment with tradition and with the literary culture that empowered him as a writer, managed also to restrict.[6]

Like the more popular entertainments of the time such as the Mechanic Theatre and "Invisible Girl," the Panorama was not only more responsive to change than, say, *Lyrical Ballads*; it was, on the evidence of both "high" romanticism and the necessary resistance of that romanticism to such entertainments, more responsive to the needs of an increasingly fathomable and mobile public. A manifestation, then, of the transformation of the bourgeois public sphere of which Jürgen Habermas has written, the Panorama was scarcely content with a transformation that, as Habermas observes, made the public its sole patron. Indeed, the Panorama can be said to have transformed or resisted Habermas's transformation in the way it effectively separated the public from the privacy on which membership in the public, and access to a public forum, had been based. Thus, the Panorama can be said to have collaborated with the public in producing the very "masses" that Marx would shortly theorize: in attracting a public, that is, whose "autonomy" was no longer based on privatization but, as Habermas states, was based "in the public sphere itself."[7]

The notices for the Panorama as well as those for related entertainments continually attest to this particular responsiveness and to the Panorama's particular role as a public sphere for a public in flux. The notice for the "View of Windsor," for example, anticipates the actual image through a proliferation of details, which is in turn linked to their leveling effect. This is equally true of other notices, whose advertisement of the Panorama and its effect frequently involve contrasting the panoramic image to something more conventional. A View of Ramsgate exhibited in 1800, which promised "a faithful representation of an Embarkation of both Horse and Foot," not to mention "Deal, Dover Castle and a Fleet at the Downs," concluded by assuring viewers that the "whole" would "appea[r] the same as reality" (*Times*, 22 May 1800). Caught between two conceptions of "reality"—between the overwhelming experience of seeing many things and the experience of a recoverable, representable reality, in which "whole"-ness suggests a totality contained—the notice effectively contrasted art so called, and its particular work of illusion, to the more public, more visceral reality of simply seeing.[8]

This notice, like many others, is concerned with satisfying many different people and with gaining as large an audience as possible. But this is a concern that runs up against the uniformitarian (or, if you prefer, counterhegemonic) imperative of the Panorama itself. For just as Joshua Reynolds was ultimately forced by its various "surprises" to frequent the Panorama "repeatedly" and compelled in doing so to forget both his aversion and the various criteria legitimating it, so it can be argued that the differences and divisions previously pertinent to art and its audiences—specifically, the categories of high and low or fine and popular—submitted under pressure of the Panorama to an uncategorical imperative (so to speak) by which the "ocular," the body in the sway of its capacity to see, was now and properly the last word.

The increasingly discrete and public disposition of the panoramic experience becomes clear when we compare the Panorama to Robert Ker Porter's "historical picture" of the *Storming of Seringpatam by the British Troops and Their Allies, May 4th 1799*. Although sometimes likened to the Panorama on account of its enormous size (2,550 square feet) and semicircular shape, Porter's painting adhered very clearly to the categorical imperative resisted by the Panorama. This is evident in the painting's subject matter, which, like many patriotic Panoramas, resisted a "public" or even "internationalist" imperative through a more conservative promotion of deferential behavior. And it is evident in the apparent appeal of the painting to complete accuracy over (and against) the details rendered. The "painting," readers of the *Times* (26 April 1800) were informed,

> is designed from the most authentic and correct information, relative to the Scenery of the Place, the Costume of the Soldiery, and the various circumstances of the Attack. It is executed upon a Scale comprehending 2550 square feet of Canvas, and contains several Hundred figures, with Portraits of the British Officers who distinguished themselves on that occasion. Explanatory Descriptions will be given at the Exhibition Room.

"Explanatory Descriptions," to be sure, were available at all Panoramic exhibits. But that the exhibitors of this painting felt obliged to stress their availability—and to do so, it appears, in order to placate viewers likely to be distressed by the overwhelming prospect of hundreds of potentially anonymous figures spread over two thousand square feet of canvas—cannot be overlooked. It underscores, if nothing else, the very different and, as the Panorama's exhibitors realized, comparatively nondifferentiating experience of the Panorama.

Where the Panorama can be said to appeal to the body seeing, to a body that is anybody's and therefore *any body,* Porter's picture appeals to the body reading and ultimately to a body readable and identifiable. It appeals to a public—in this case, Habermas's "public"—which, far from being homogenized into one viewer, necessarily remains divided and individuated. This public is, in fact, so privatized that the painting may be said to follow the established order of things in providing more to those who are apparently entitled to it: affording some viewers the delight of recognizing certain friends, kinsmen, or acquaintances portrayed therein. Just as difference per se, then—the division separating England and France—served to bring observers to Porter's painting in the first place, so it was difference and individuation that the *Storming* worked also to preserve, ensuring that the public imitated by the painting would depart in exactly the same disposition as they came.

Porter's painting was hardly the only such version of art that, as Habermas has shown, had this effect. It can be argued, in fact, that much of the art produced during the romantic period, including the particularly innovative works we deem romantic, was as exclusive as it was inclusive. From Wordsworth's paradoxical designation of the Poet as different in degree but not in kind from "other men," to Shelley's efforts to divide the Poet and his privileged constituency from "those unforeseeing multitudes" (preface to *Alastor*), to even Coleridge's brilliantly bombastic definition of imagination as the repetition in the finite mind of "the infinite I AM," high romanticism, as many of its students have long maintained, was more than half in love and more than half aligned with the very autocracy it purported to deplore.

In the case of patriotic paintings, specifically those of the Napoleonic Wars, which were abundant at this time, this characteristic exclusivity was underscored in their availability to the "public" in the form of engravings that, compared to the Panorama, were partly a means of containment: an expansion of the "fashionable" gallery to *include* the reading or sitting room. The Panorama defied ownership in both its lack of a frame and, more important perhaps, its necessarily limited tenure as an image. By contrast, the accessibility and malleability of other kinds of images through reproduction and ownership identified the owner, like the viewer located on Windsor's highest turret, as a subject owned or constructed by the ability to do likewise.

This accessibility of the image was not always complicit with the more conventional and exclusive tendencies of exhibition. Indeed, it was a development that, particularly in the eighteenth century, can be said to have also anticipated the Panorama. Such public issues as Boydell's *Shakespeare Gallery,* for example, reflected more than the growing demand for illustrated books; they represented, along with the Panorama, both a transformation and the inevitable expansion of the conditions for the exhibition of art in response to a burgeoning audience (Altick, 106). Undoubtedly, the marketing of engravings in print shops throughout London worked also to *protect* the image from the "mob"—from the very crowds who routinely gathered in front of the shops' window displays (Altick, 109–10)—by returning it to those who could rightfully afford it. And yet, the engravings also constitute a mechanical reproduction of images such as Walter Benjamin would later describe: a proliferation or excess that ultimately intrudes, even as it depends, upon their exclusivity as purchasable objects. Notices for such "national galleries" as the European Museum might well have continued to appeal to their tradition as "the favourite rendezvous for the fashionable world and distinguished cognoscenti," as one memorable notice indicated (*Times,* 5 April 1817). But there is little doubt that by the first quarter of the nineteenth century the picture gallery was—in the image of multiple "galleries" in homes throughout London at this time—an increasingly permeable space.[9]

Barker, for his part, saw matters differently and, despite calling it an improvement on painting, regarded the Panorama as a version of painting similar to the most conventional art. Nevertheless, his efforts to imagine the Panorama in conventional terms ultimately met the resistance of the Panorama itself. An "Advantageous Proposal" of 1797 (*Times,* 12 December), announcing the disposal of paintings "which have been exhibited, and which are now exhibiting in the Panorama," not only garnered little response; its particular rejection by the public pointed ultimately to the Panorama's equally particular success in attracting the public. Appealing simultaneously to entrepreneurs and speculators, who might wish to set up Panoramas in other cities such as "Dublin, Edinburgh, &c.," and to "any Nobleman or Gentleman," who might "chuse to purchase [Panoramas] for amusement," Barker's proposal did more than simply reenact the Panorama and its peculiarly "social work" by collecting and combining in this one advertisement—or under the Panorama's influence—a public hitherto separated or unrecognizable as a public; it emphasized, in failing to identify a specific owner for these paintings, the resistance of the works to ownership.[10]

Far from admitting the public to a previously exclusive order, or expanding that order so as to include a previously excluded public, the Panorama, both in form and in effect, tended to resist any attempt merely to preserve the public sphere. Circulating among an increasingly mobile constituency to which it responded even as it worked simultaneously to reform, the Panorama, like the examples in our time of Smithson's *Spiral Getty* or even Christo's *Running Fence,* was a version of art whose peculiar uncontainability, and unmarketability in this instance, was perfectly consistent with its refusal to contain.

III

The reviews of the Panorama that began to appear regularly in newspapers and journals beginning in the 1820s may be taken as a sign of its growing respectability. Yet even as this attention points directly to the social transformations, or to the changes in audience of which the Panorama remained an early manifestation (and against which the early silence regarding the Panorama remained a bulwark), the reviews are by no means inured to their subject. If anything, the reviews, which appeared in a variety of places including the *Examiner, Blackwood's,* the *Times,* the *Athenaeum,* and the (wonderfully and appropriately titled) *Mirror of Literature, Amusement, and Instruction,* are remarkably uniform both in their response to the Panorama and in their fear of or resistance to that response.

In its review of Burford and Barker's Panorama of Pompeii in April 1824, for example, *Blackwood's Edinburgh Magazine*—hardly the most conservative of publications—was at pains to discuss everything except what was visibly before the beholder. Beginning, as did many accounts, by remarking on the money saved by visiting the Panorama in lieu of the place represented ("what cost a couple of hundred pounds and half a year a century ago, now costs a shilling and a quarter of an hour" [472]), the review proceeded to a rather lengthy and jingoistic account of the history of Pompeii before offering a number of brief observations on its present representation.

Unlike the droll, altogether controlled history that precedes them, these concluding observations are striking in the way their belated, seemingly obligatory appearance clearly bears the mark of denial or of something suppressed. "The Panorama," wrote the reviewer,

> gives a striking coup-d'oeil of one of the two great excavations of Pompeii. The Forum, the narrow streets, the little Greek houses, with their remnants of ornamental painting, their corridores and their tesselated floors, are seen, as they might have been seen the day before the eruption. The surrounding landscape has the grandeur that the eye looks for in a volcanic country. Wild hills, fragments of old lavas, richly broken shores, and in the centre the most picturesque and sublime of all volcanoes, Vesuvius, throwing up its eternal volumes of smoke to the heavens. (475)

Although this is only one viewer's description of what it was like to have viewed the Panorama of Pompeii, it is both noteworthy and representative in the way it directs attention away from the perceiving subject toward a visible object (or objects) whose interest is overwhelming.

The timescape, under pressure from what is suddenly visible, is wrenched from a historical, geopolitical framework to a more contingent, uncontainable present: to an orientation marked by distraction, by an irresistible attention to details, over and against either the narrative irony of impending doom or the descriptive imperative that makes "this most picturesque and sublime of all volcanoes, Vesuvius." Vesuvius, to be sure, is mentioned here, as indeed it must be, but its designation is strangely parenthetical and bracketed in virtually the same way that the contingent, the sheer wonder of distraction, is held back until *its* irruption.

Nor is *Blackwood's* at all unique in recording this experience. Time and again, reviewers of the Panorama are compelled by the details before them, and by the impossibility of attending to the entire composition at once, to a completely visceral wonder. Almost without exception, in fact, accounts of the Panorama, particularly of Barker and Burford's at Leicester Square, reach that moment where, like the viewer of Pompeii, they are simply reciting details.

Such accounts, then, invariably recall the view of London in Wordsworth's 1802 sonnet composed from Westminster Bridge, the details of which—"Ships, towers, domes, theaters, and temples lie / Open unto the fields, and to the sky"—bear a remarkable similarity, as Alan Liu suggested, to Barker's 1793 exhibition with its paintings of London and the grand fleet.[11] Yet withal, it is important to distinguish what is visible in Wordsworth from what is visible in the Panorama. In the poem, London is apparently accessible only to persons of sensibility and imagination such as the speaker ("Dull would he be of soul who could pass by / A sight so touching in its majesty"), whose ability to see is an imposition not unlike amalgamating two separate paintings into a single, continuous vision. By contrast, the actual and less retrospective accounts of the Panorama, both in magazines and newspapers, sharply distinguish between the narrated or imaginable and the merely visible. Many of these discriminations owe their existence to the accompanying "keys," which reviewers often quoted at length. Thus, unlike Wordsworth, whose poem may have conflated randomness and intentionality, the reviews, in their inevitable recourse to an apparatus of control, manage to set the Panoramic experience *against* what was gained or lost for failure to submit to that experience.

What was gained first and foremost through strategies of containment—and what the keys undoubtedly accommodated—was a commanding vantage. While the Panorama clearly fascinated viewers, it generally did so at the cost of the beholder's authority. Remarking, again, on "those mimic sights that ape / The absolute presence of reality," Wordsworth typically construed this loss of authority in terms of someone else's gain: "the painter," in this case, who "with his greedy pencil [had taken] in / A whole horizon on all sides—with power / Like that of angels or commissioned spirits" (*Prelude* 7. 247–60). The "lofty pinnacle" (261), in other words, that Wordsworth suddenly found deplorable was so not simply because it was a height from which the painter, and by extension the viewer, could suddenly regard "Nature's circumambient scenery" (257); it was deplorable to him because it was no longer, in effect, *his* vantage, but rather a "pinnacle" that, by agency of the painting (and under pressure of seeing), he was obliged suddenly to descend.

Similarly, in its review of Burford's 1828 Panorama of Sidney, the *Examiner* (21 December 1828) moved quickly from recounting what it was like to view the Panorama—that is, from a host of details ranging from "the irregular and singular buildings stretching to the very edge of the extensive bay" to "an infinite variety of hill and dale, backed by immense and towering forests"—to a more authoritative position. This position, initially revealed in a mapping impulse, where things are given names—Botany Bay, the Blue Mountains, New

South Wales, George Street, St. James's Church—modulated in the end to a more socially constructed subjectivity by reference to the social distance separating the residents of Sidney, specifically the many prisoners there, from the viewers of its representation. "Such," concluded the *Examiner,*

> is Sidney and its vicinity, the abode, unfortunately, of gentlemen, whose enjoyments, for the main part, do not arise from the contemplation of subjects especially calculated for the *fine* Arts. But this, by the way, is perhaps quite as well; for were a certain numerous body of individuals, whose notions respecting the rights of property not over strict, in the habit of visiting Panoramas, this of Sidney would cause such a yearning after a residence in that attractive spot, that a transportable offence would become as common as lying, and Hick's Hall and the Old Bailey be looked upon merely as rude passages leading to an earthly paradise. (821)

This concluding excursus on the criminal body, whose dangerous proximity to individuals such as the *Examiner*'s reviewer had been responsible for its removal elsewhere, may seem nothing more than a bit of waggishness. However, the vision here of a public under assault in the very bastions where it might have previously been considered safe, represents a very real fear that no amount of wit can occlude. With the Panorama's admission fee of a single shilling, the imagined union of spectator and spectacle may well have been less a fiction than a fact, reflecting the changes wrought both by the Panorama itself and by the "numerous body of individuals" that had pressured the Panorama into existence.[12]

Thus, despite the *Examiner*'s wish to remove the public (or the people that it feared would soon constitute the public) to Australia, this removal was no more likely than the possibility of a public made up exclusively of the *Examiner*'s implied readers. Indeed, just as the Panorama can be said to have altered subjectivity, reducing its beholder to a detail among details, so the *Examiner,* despite clinging to a more authoritative subject-position (and to a smaller, more discrete public), confirmed a transformation already afoot. It marked a public not only coextensive with the numerous body it saw but one whose visibility was sufficiently a feature of the Panorama that the view of Sidney became, as the *Examiner* fantasized, a view of Sidney seeing itself.

Not all accounts of the Panorama are as revealing in their strategies of denial and fear. Yet many of them try, in one degree or another, to dominate the Panorama for fear of being subsumed by it. Sometimes this will to dominance comes to nothing more than misunderstanding or misreading, to an aesthetic lexicon (e.g., the picturesque) that is plainly inadequate to the occasion. At other times, it involves recourse to a more immediate and, I would venture to argue, more desperately sought stay against confusion. The accounts of the Panoramas of Stirling, Hobart Town, and the Thames from Westminster Bridge to Richmond that appeared in the *Mirror* between 1830 (15: 232) and 1832 (20:410–12) read as if they were about the locations themselves rather than their representations, so dependent are they on the accompanying guides, which the *Mirror* either paraphrases or quotes at length. This is similarly the case with the Panorama of Milan, which the *Times* (30 May 1832), though crediting for its representation of Il Duomo, criticizes—in apparent sway of that "masterpiece"—for lacking the "sentiment of painting."

As we have seen, the Panoramas were not always innocent of provoking their own resistance, or of neutralizing their effect through some uncertainty or confusion. Much of the appeal of Thomas Hornor's bird's-eye view of London, which was developed from sketches that Hornor heroically produced a decade earlier from an elaborate scaffold atop St. Paul's (fig. 6), lay in its faithful representation of a city already familiar to most of its viewers. It was only later, when the cityscape had changed, when the viewers could no longer experience the gratification of recognizing what they knew (a gratification Hornor had initially exploited in publishing a prospectus in which the painting he hoped eventually to display was made available to potential subscribers in a folio of individual sketches), that the panorama in the Colosseum was turned to a more spectacular purpose and became "London by Night."[13] Such resistance of spectacle was also evident in some of the historical Panoramas—for example, Burford's Siege of Antwerp (1833), whose "vast and varied scene" provoked more than a measure of sententiousness, inspiring the *Mirror* (21:182–83) to moralize over "the exhaustless ingenuities and the wholesale cruelties of man to entrap and annihilate his fellow man." This was also the case with the Panorama of the Battle of Navarino (1828), in which a contemporary and, as the guide termed it, "untoward event" was subsumed in a landscape of memory (specifically the Peloponnesian War and its various annals), telescoping past and present.[14]

Figure 6. Thomas Hornor, "View of the Observatory Erected over the Cross of St. Paul's," *Prospectus View of London, and the Surrounding Country,* 1822. Yale Center for British Art, New Haven, Connecticut.

And yet, for all the resistance to it, there can be little doubt—as the resistance attests—of the Panorama's destabilizing effect on a privatized subject-position. Evidence of this effect—quite literally an invasion of privacy—can be found in the diary of an unnamed Panorama painter who worked with Robert Burford in the 1830s and who, like Robert Barker before him, appears to have had remarkably little sense of what he was involved in. The diary chronicles a period of eighteen months when, as a single male with no apparent prospects for marriage, the painter followed a fairly routine schedule of painting for Burford during the day, playing the cello in the evening, and dining with a range of friends.[15] Although he appears to have taken his vocation seriously, painting is clearly less important to the painter—certainly less important as an art—than his music making, which he pursues with great diligence. "Panorama painting," he says at one point, "causes a very slovenly and loose style" (3 November 1833), and several weeks later he complains that the "panorama consumes my best days" (1 December 1833).

Furthermore, when not complaining either about the deleterious effects of the Panorama on his artistry or about Burford's failure to pay him promptly for his work, the painter is convinced that his sole function as a painter of Panoramas—and by extension the function of the Panorama itself—is simply to render a scene as accurately as possible. "It is a great pity," he writes while at work on a Panorama of an expedition to the North Pole, "that men that go out upon these expeditions do not attend more to drawing or at least endeavour to get some one that can" (23 November 1833)—a condition he has even greater cause to lament when the expedition leader arrives on the scene and ultimately does him and Burford "the favour of obliterating half our sketch" (26 November 1833).

Still, for all his apparent disaffection with the Panorama, which he generally likens to a chore more than to an art (much less to an art experienced), the painter is sometimes curiously under its influence. Shortly after having labored over certain details in the polar sky and having discovered "a novel and beautiful way of managing the stars" (6 December 1833), he describes an experience that indicates how his habits of seeing and of regarding the world have been influenced by the canvas constantly before him:

> As I was going home, I saw a . . . phenomenon in the heavens which I imagined to be the Aurora Borealis. It appeared like a

> white cloud brilliant but so transparent that the stars appeared through it. It spread rapidly from north to south and at intervals there proceeded (from this cloud as it appeared) small pencils of light parting upwards and slowly disappearing. The whole lasted about one half of an hour. (29 December 1833)

Such epiphanies, to be sure, are scarcely uncommon, especially in certain romantic lyrics—Wordsworth's "A Night-Piece" comes immediately to mind—that by the 1830s had become modern classics. However, what is striking in this experience is not its triteness or its seemingly conventional romanticism; what is striking is its startling uniqueness. The visible order at which the painter had been laboring for weeks, and over which he had been able to exert control, suddenly "returns" in the guise of experience, liberating him from his private existence and, just as important, from its equally private (if routine) documentation. The impact of the Panorama is apparently such that even a painter cognizant of its artifice remains, like any other viewer, susceptible to its influence and capable, according to that influence, of admitting a world doubly screened by habit and, in the painter's case, by its habitual representation.

Nor is this the only occasion on which the Panorama succeeds in penetrating and interrupting the subject's order of things. Six weeks later, on 13 February 1834, the painter confesses to having "never experienced a greater treat in viewing Nature than I did today in looking on the Thames striped as it was with small craft. The sails and rigging reflected in the clear, calm, water and backed up by two or three large Indianmen towering above and seeming to form a nucleus for the lesser boats to congegrate around." The establishment of a nucleus in a scene that clearly lacks an order recalls the resistance frequently waged against (and sometimes by) the Panorama itself. Still, where resistance to the Panorama invariably involves the reassertion of a private or commanding vantage, it is interesting that command is never assumed by the painter and is in fact the province of the larger ships, whose centrality is illusory. The view of "Nature," in other words, that exceeds all previous views in delighting the subject, exceeds them because it is emphatically a view *of nature,* and not a naturalization: because the "nucleus" in the scene, as the Panorama painter's "panoramic" observations confirm, is constantly shifting.

One Panorama, then, that is especially noteworthy in its staging and, further, in its particular thematization of the fundamental disparity between private and public, or between a readable order and an ultimately incomprehensible one, turns out not to have been a painting of an actual metropolis—Calcutta, or Madras, or Rome (all of which were the subjects of Panoramas)—but of an imagined city: Milton's Pandemonium. In this 1829 display, the resistance to the visionary came to more than simply retrieving the viewer through the introjection of some narrative or moral argument; it was a matter in the end of representing what was in fact a representation. "Here is a sight for one shilling" reported the *Examiner,* (26 April 1829), though this "sight" and its value were soon blemished (according to the review) by its unreadability, specifically the difficulty in distinguishing Satan from his "compeers."

One can understand, of course, the impulse to reread and to repossess, as did those Londoners who flocked to see London in the Colosseum, what was undoubtedly familiar to the reviewer in another context. Yet it is clear, too, that the "defects" in representing Pandemonium were not merely defects. They were also *effects,* in which the erosion or obscuring of narrative was necessarily consistent with the obscuring of identity of both the "Archangel ruined" and the viewer seeking to behold him. Where the identity of Satan (a prototypical Romantic) was evidently challenged by the Panorama of Pandemonium, or by a vision made visible, the identity of the romantic spectator, for whom seeing was too often an act of reading, was reciprocally "ruined" by the pandemonium of a Panorama: a "sight" accessible to anyone and anybody with a "shilling" to spend.

IV

If it was the effect of the Panorama, then, to marshal the visible against its containment, the Diorama, which was introduced in 1823, worked by opposite means, transfixing viewers with its "great illusion," as Constable described it, only to lead them to a threshold where both representation and the subject-position controlling it (and controlled by it) were apparently rejected. One of several related innovations developed in France by Daguerre, the Diorama was brought to England through a business arrangement involving Daguerre and his British brother-in-law Charles Arrowsmith. According to this agreement, dioramic exhibitions, which premiered in Paris, would be brought to London, where, as newspaper accounts attest, news of them had already traveled and they were eagerly awaited.[16]

Unlike the Panorama, which constituted a 360-degree view of a particular city or event, the Diorama in Regents Park was composed of two rectangular pictures, each measuring about eighty by forty-five feet. These "two distinct pictures, delineating different objects"—one, "the interior of a large edifice," the other, a "picturesque view of some delightful valley" (as the *Mirror* described it [6 September 1823: 245])—were displayed in two picture rooms and were viewable from a darkened amphitheater accommodating approximately three hundred people, which "pivot[ed] on a 73 degree arc" (fig. 7). "Built on eighteen-foot piles, and so delicately balanced that, even when loaded with a capacity audience, it could," as Altick remarks, "be moved by a boy and a ram engine" (165), the amphitheater was separated from the actual image by a corridor "thirty or forty feet long." The "charmingly painted transparenc[ies] through which light [was] admitted" (*Mirror*) were viewable individually for intervals of approximately fifteen minutes. During this time the admission of light—controlled through "a combination of lines and chords, pulleys and counterweights," which in turn activated "an elaborate system of screens, shutters, and curtains" (Altick, 165)—was responsible for the Diorama's celebrated "dynamic effects," including, for example, the passage of light from dawn to dusk and the arrival and dissipation of both fog and mist.

Although the Diorama at Regents Park always featured both interior and exterior views, there was, for the most part, a clear division of labor in the production of these representations. The majority of the interiors were by Daguerre himself, and most of the exterior views were by his collaborator, Charles-Marie Bouton. Occasionally the artists would exchange responsibilities, with Bouton painting such transparencies as the Cloister of St. Wandrille in Normandy, as well as the first interior to be exhibited in England, which was of Trinity Chapel in Canterbury. Nevertheless it is no coincidence that the innovator of the Diorama, Daguerre, was responsible in the main for what must be counted as the Diorama's most substantial achievement—namely, the interior views, which, as the *Mirror* (6 September 1823: 246) commented of the inaugural representation of Trinity Chapel, "[created] an astonishment . . . difficult to express: a person may almost imagine that he sees the edifice itself standing before him, so true to nature are the effects of light which gleams amongst its massive arches."

Time and again, as almost every review attested, it was this *unwilling* suspension of disbelief—a wonderment countered by an in-

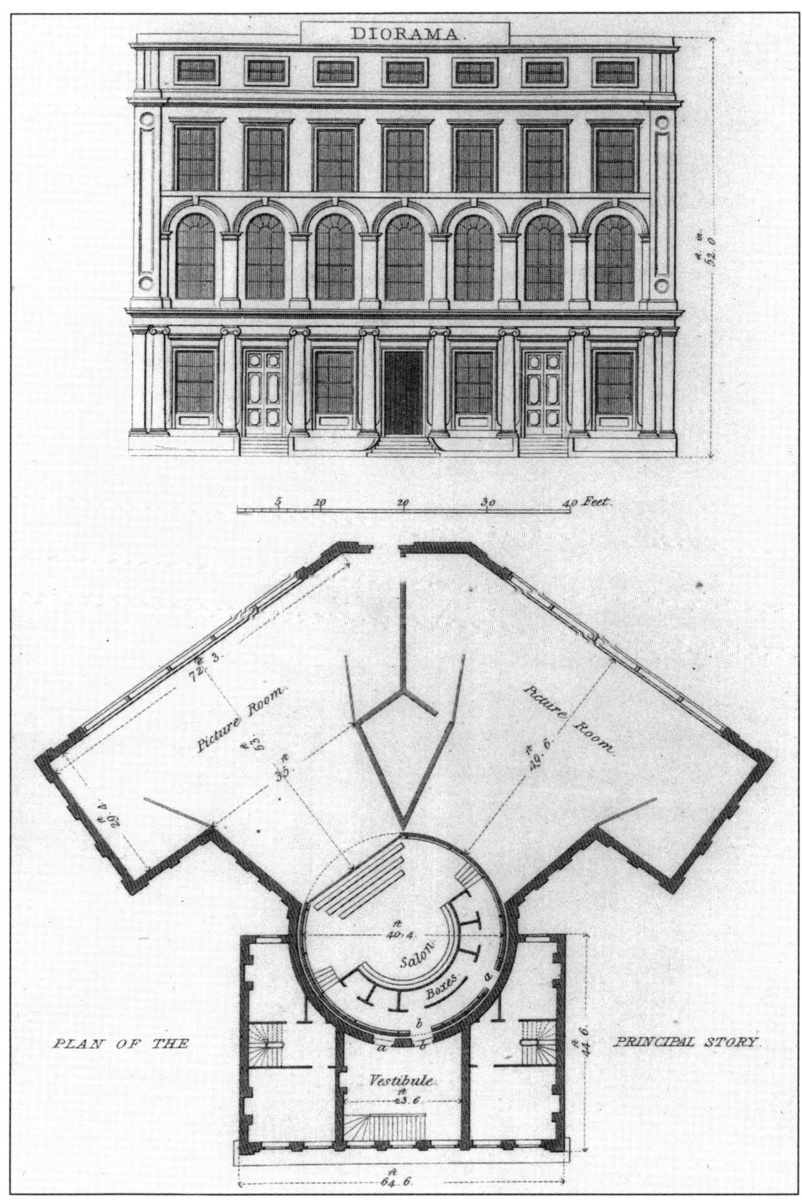

Figure 7. John Britton and A. Pugin, "Diorama, Park Square, Regents Park," *Illustrations of the Public Buildings of London,* 1825. Yale Center for British Art, New Haven, Connecticut.

creasing skepticism toward the "illusion" at hand—that characterized the "dioramic" experience, particularly the transparencies of Gothic churches. Any interruption of this circuit, in fact—by which skepticism would be either allayed or, more often than not, immediately unleashed—was clearly to the Diorama's detriment. This was often the case when a larger edifice or cathedral was represented—for example, St. Peter's in Rome, which, as the *Times* noted, failed "to impress the beholder with an adequate notion of immense size" (28 May 1829).

Indeed, the impression of "immensity" was never ultimately an achievement or an attraction of the Diorama. As the reviews continually document, the exhibit's interest was forever leagued with a peculiar indeterminacy—and not with the totality, as it were—to which the dioramic experience ideally led: with an instability of subject-position wherein "it bec[ame] difficult to imagine that [it was] not reality" one was seeing (*Athenaeum,* 25 March 1828:284), or where the "apparent reality" was such that "[we] suspec[ted] that we [were] under some magical illusion" (*Mirror,* 26 March 1825:195).

This instability, moreover, was no accident or simply testimony, however reluctant, to the "reality" of a particular illusion. It was an instability, strongly and deliberately abetted by *what* Daguerre, in particular, chose invariably to represent—namely, Gothic *churches*. By choosing these smaller edifices over the more sublime and more famous cathedrals, Daguerre served the dioramic experience in two related ways: first, he chose edifices whose more probable declension to ruin allowed for the remarkable effects of light, the admission of which was no longer restricted only to windows; and second, he chose a subject *theoretically* in ruins—a subject that, as Erwin Panofsky describes it, "enclose[d] an often wildly and always apparently boundless interior, and thus create[d] a space determinate and impenetrable from without but indeterminate and penetrable within."[17]

Part of the "penetrab[ility] within" involved the penetration of light and weather among other dioramic effects. But more crucial by far was the war on totality that such vulnerability—whether by design or by the vicissitudes of weather and time—could wage. Unlike the Gothic cathedral, whose immensity renders it (in Panofsky's formulation) the architectural equivalent of the high scholastic summa, the particular indeterminacy of the Gothic church both echoed and, in a peculiar way, portended the phenomenological instability to which its dioramic representation gave rise. While it is certainly possible to construe the fascination with ruin merely in terms of a "romantic" nostalgia for a prior and therefore recoverable wholeness,[18] most striking about the representation of ruin in the Diorama is the way it militated against that totalizing act of imagination. More often than not, viewers were left suspended between an admiration of the illusion before them and a reluctance to accept as real or as authoritative what was, after all, only a representation.

This last is perhaps better understood in light of the exterior views that were exhibited alongside the interior views. The majority of the former, it is safe to say, suffered by comparison with a more "legitimate landscape style," as the *Times* termed it, or with views that were in one way or another versions of the picturesque. In its review of the Diorama of Paris, for example, which accompanied the much praised "Ruins in a Fog," the *Times* (5 June 1827) summarized the dioramic experience to date by reiterating that the "great curiosity of the Dioramic pictures," chiefly "their powerful management of the engines of light and shade," is generally less effective "in wide and extended scenes, in which the circumstances of strong relief (and the illusion consequent upon it) are necessarily less attended to."

While it is possible to regard this as a fairly local observation pertaining to the way light works better in relief, it is clear that the "curiosity of the Dioramic pictures"—the illusion attendant upon their "management of . . . light and shade"—was, like the "surprise" of the Panorama, a matter of astonishment and disbelief. By contrast, the exterior views yielded both a lack of curiosity and, in accordance with their relative deficiency, an abiding conviction in the legitimacy of more conventional landscape styles. Where the dioramic interiors drove a wedge between "art" and "illusion," effectively distinguishing "illusions of enchantment" from what the *Times* suggestively termed the "mere creations of art" (22 April 1830), the dioramic exteriors worked to heal that breach, recalling the legitimacy of creativity and those products of imagination whose success involved the suppression of what was fathomable or visible in the *space between* art and illusion.

What was fathomable in this space, therefore (and in the darkened amphitheater especially), was not always visible to the viewer. As with other "oramic" effects, in fact, it was the case that the visible remained on a continuum with the invisible, insofar as the ability to see was often a prelude to a more profound sense of dislocation. In the Panorama, as I have discussed, this dislocation was tantamount to the relocation of beholders in the painting, transforming them through distraction into details among details. In the Diorama, by contrast, such dislocation—following the very arrangement of the exhibit—involved the removal of viewers to a space whose darkness or indeterminacy was quite literally a reflection of what they saw. That is, in the very way that the Diorama worked to denaturalize the image by making representation invisible *except* as an illusion, it had the reciprocal effect of disrupting the social order simply in resisting the position to which beholders might be interpellated by the sign, and by their absorption.

The Diorama also represented, then—in contrast to theaters that were still illuminated—the first commercially successful emplacement of audiences as passively invisible before an actively visible world. (Later, of course, the cinema would exploit this confining darkness as the cornerstone, according to many, of classical cinematic perception—specifically voyeurism.) More than just enhancing the illusion of reality, however, this confining and darkening of an audience position—in clear contrast to the elaboration of that position in the Panorama—had major repercussions in the definition of the visible. In effect, it worked to remove viewers from the scene, and (until such time as the image could be psychologically naturalized in cinematic narrative) left them excluded from the very space they simultaneously inhabited.

Fully more bound to the technological activity of placing sharply contrasting images before the secreted and physically constricted vision of its audience, the dioramic scenes were, like those of the Panorama, equally faithful to the central flux and the essential contingency of an always visible world. Through the alternation or "doubling" of images and the use of light and transparencies, the Diorama tended to fracture and loosen narrative coherencies, distracting, instead of locating, the look of the viewer. Accordingly, the *Times* observed of the dioramic exhibition of the Cathedral of Rheims,

> We have only a small portion of this cathedral exposed to our gaze, and then that portion is "sawed into quantities," and frittered away in parts, in a manner which can hardly be conceived by those who have not seen it. Next, we have a partial insight into other portions of the cathedral,—a circumstance which distracts our attention, but does not gratify our curiosity,—and lastly, we have that portion which we are permitted to see distinctly, fitted up more like a lady's cabinet than a Christian temple. The central

> object of the picture—a table with half a dozen candlesticks upon it—has nothing either grand or picturesque about it; on the contrary, there is a meanness and littleness about it which impairs the effect of the whole view. (22 April 1830)

The indeterminancy of contingent relationships that characterizes the dioramic experience in this account suggests an instability of subject-position that is a resistance of *and by* what the subject saw. That is, the resistance of "imagination" to a visible "reality," as the *Athenaeum* earlier described the phenomenon, is no less, in the experience of this spectacle, a resistance of visible reality *to* imagination: a suspicion fostered by what the *Mirror,* with characteristic indeciveness, later termed an "apparent reality."

Thus, it comes as little surprise that the viewers *least* disturbed or dislocated by the Diorama were the viewers most inclined to regard the paintings as art, or as the "beginning," as the *Examiner* put it, "which may lead to the enjoyment of the luxury physical and mental, which the higher branches of art offer" (22 April 1832). In fact, the only thing that disturbed *these viewers* was the company they were obliged to keep in viewing the transparencies—since the "untutored," "child"-like viewers who also frequented the Diorama seemed not at all impressed with or capable of heeding the "instruction" immediately before them. Constable, who was alternately impressed and disturbed by the Diorama's "great illusion," reserved his greatest animus for the particular audience attending the "private view" with him. "The place was filled with foreigners," he wrote, "[and] I seemed to be in a cage of magpies."[19] And Lady Morgan, whose reviews of the Diorama appeared regularly in the *Athenaeum,* found herself compelled to comment not only on the Diorama's "miracle of optic illusion" and its historical importance but simultaneously, or so it seemed, on the audience's failure to fathom this.

Lady Morgan's essay (*Athenaeum,* 13 August 1836:570–72), which was published more than a decade after the Diorama first appeared, is—for all its efforts to the contrary—the best evidence we have of what dioramic illusionism worked ultimately to resist or, short of that, to foreground. Thus, it ultimately devolves upon "the visitors of the Diorama" to whom it "is merely a show-box" to dismantle the essay's claims for illusionism and for the Diorama's historical importance. Beginning with a survey of illusionism from Cimabue to seventeenth-century Dutch painting, the essay goes on to grant the Diorama a historical position in Western art, whose development, as Morgan construes it, is essentially a progress toward achieving ever more convincing or lifelike illusions. "Produc[ing] an illusion so perfect, that the mind, when left to itself, is never for a moment awakened to the belief that this wondrous exhibition is not the thing it represents," the Diorama is, if nothing else, on a continuum with "an art, which the mighty geniuses of the middle ages have consecrated with an almost religious character."

To readers familiar with the writings of E. H. Gombrich, not to mention the art produced in the interval since the Diorama, there is something ill informed (and even shocking) in the implication that Cimabue or Giotto would have produced dioramic transparencies had they only had the means at their disposal. Nevertheless, it is Morgan herself who gives us the most cause to question her claims. She does this by basing her argument for illusionism less on a sense of what illusionism *is* than on a demonstration of what it is *not* or of what it masks *as illusionism*—especially to viewers who are inclined, like Lady Morgan, to "believe" what they see.

As a result, the better part of Lady Morgan's essay is taken up less with the history of Western art or with the Diorama's position in it, than with a history of Lady Morgan, specifically with her visits to the actual sites—the Alpine village of Alagna and the Church of Santa Croce in Florence—whose representations are "now exhibiting at the Diorama." These paintings are powerful illusions not because of their verisimilitude but on account of what they recall: because they are illusions "to which the imagination [is] an accomplice, and against which the mind and senses ma[k]e no resistance." Before the picture of the eye can convince, in other words, the picture in the mind must first revive. For without this revival, it would be impossible for the "Alpine scenery [to rise] at once upon the eye in all the vraisemblance of the region it represented."

In showing how an idea in this instance remains—more than what is actually pictured—essential to the "vraisemblance" of the image before her, Lady Morgan has furnished what Gombrich among others would undoubtedly deem an anatomy of illusionism.[20] This is further illustrated in the way the very image in which the "imagination [is] an accomplice," according to Morgan, is simultaneously an image "before which the imagination lies captive." In order for illusionism to work, that is, for a painting to be able to present itself as something more than an illusion, the beholder must be convinced that what she, in fact, sees is what she, in fact, saw: it must allow a conceptual scheme or memory to heal rather than to expose the difference between Lady Morgan's imaginary relations to the world and the "real relations" that, according to Althusser, the imaginary relations mask. In the example of Lady Morgan, the real relations come to more than the relations between a human subject and an illuminated object constructed of canvas and papier-mâché; for they are the relations of the subject to itself, or relations by which absorption is leagued with the *private* privilege of visiting the sites depicted. These real relations, then, pertain less to Morgan's memory of Switzerland, or to her knowledge of Cimabue, than to an individuation measured by absorption or by her interpellation as one absorbed. Lady Morgan is a subject now whose particular privilege is at once figured and masked by the veracity of what is only a memory.

Still, if the Diorama can lend itself to the business of interpellating viewers such as Lady Morgan, its more important and commoner function is to demystify this work by exposing and disrupting the ideological circuit (as Althusser would deem it) in which the imagination is alternately accomplice and captive. It does this typically with the assistance of an audience, whose instability before the image—both as a public disposed to attend a public exhibition and as the audience in attendance—spells misfortune, as even Lady Morgan admits, "for the imagination and its pleasures." For Lady Morgan this misfortune comes in the distraction that an audience, with little sense of how to behave—and with no pictures of the mind to be revived by the image at hand—necessarily poses. However, insofar as this misfortune becomes one that she is compelled to recount and to recount by way of conclusion, it also reveals how the Diorama and its audience ultimately conspire and work to thwart a particular order of private subjectivity.

The "obtrusion" that "such visitors" present remains an obtrusion that, for all her absorption and her aversion to these people and their "prosaic vulgarity," Lady Morgan is necessarily and strangely prone to. Detailing the entry of a family into the darkened amphitheater, she is at pains to note how the wife "is sure to be in advance of the husband, who holds cautiously by her dress," and how "the mother pioneers for her son, who clings to her side." Nor can she restrain from blurting the blurtings out of her co-viewers, which range in her account from "Jesus where am I going to" to "I'll trouble you, Miss, to remove your humbrella off my toe please."

Last but not least, there is the testimony of a woman who

> during the whole first beautiful exhibition of the Alpine scenery . . . narrated, in an audible voice, her trip to Italy in 1830, beginning with the loss of her dressing-box at Tower Stairs, and ending with her *coup de soleil* at Naples,—disputing the fidelity of every feature of the Piedmontese Alps, and every trait of the Santa Croce, (which she mistook for the Duomo of Florence,) describing a night spent at St. Mary's Major, at Rome,—strenuously advising her not alas! *sole* auditor, to read Mrs. Starke's book on Italy, in preference to every other: it would prevent him being cheated on the road, and enable him to detect the impositions of those universal impostors everywhere, the washerwomen, or, as you must call them in Italy, "the *Blanchishoes*." (571)

Whether it is the challenge that this woman poses as someone capable of "disputing the fidelity" of the two paintings, or simply the threat that she poses as a version of her chronicler—after all, the "lady" can no more stop complaining about Italy than *Lady* Morgan can resist detailing and thereby complaining of the lady's obtrusion—is difficult to say. But the distraction that this woman represents is important because it attests in no small measure both to her resistance to the illusion before her and to the resistance, by implication, of the Diorama to illusionism. The distraction serves not merely to displace the image but also to displace the subject, forcing Lady Morgan into a position where the failure to be absorbed—to stand in imaginary, stable relation to the image—is accompanied by an absorption in that failure: by attention to a "lady" who, were she not so distracted and therefore not so much a distraction, might very well have been Lady Morgan herself.

All of this, of course, is not what Lady Morgan means to say; she means to describe a vulgar imposition that we are expected to join her in deploring and in condescending to. Yet what she achieves is more on the order of a deconstruction of absorption in that the object of her most sustained attention is alternately a disruption and *a figure* of the positionality disrupted. Thus, the disruption of the Diorama, specifically of Morgan's absorption, is of a piece really with the peculiar and subversive effect of the Diorama (and of "oramic" displays in general), whose particular effect can be understood only in light of the constituency attracted: in conjunction with a public that, despite its occasional similarities to an earlier, more exclusive public, is more willing, or at the very least more able for a time, *not* to have imagined what it saw.

The historical impact of the Diorama and of the visible order it made available is another matter altogether, and it would be foolhardy to contend that whatever effect the Diorama and the Panorama achieved at the time of their development continued unabated throughout the nineteenth century. But it is equally foolhardy to use the fate of these displays in order to show that the particular hegemony of romanticism—and of the selfhood contained thereby—necessarily persisted or could have ever persisted without some disruption. As the oramic displays show, the romantic subject-position was not only challenged by competing orders of culture at the time and by competing versions of art; its persistence, on the evidence of viewers such as Wordsworth, Constable, and Lady Morgan, was always a function of competition—of both the resistance and the counterresistance, which romanticism can be said to have fostered.

Thus, although the fate of the oramic displays—which proliferated along with a growing and ultimately more stable public—may well be a less interesting story than their development and capacity for resistance, we can better appreciate their particular bearing on subsequent versions of art such as film, where, as recent criticism has shown, spectatorship is more often than not an experience of containment. For in the very way that romanticism and the subject-position associated with it remain, with few exceptions, prototypical of the similarly dominant, yet contained, position of the cinematic spectator, it is no less true that the Diorama and the Panorama as prototypes—or, better still, as the components of an "archaeology of cinema"—*remember* the agency that a visible image, in cooperation with a romantic spectator, is capable of producing. Whether this agency is evident in the popular cinema of our time or in the classic cinema that precedes it is, as Wordsworth put it, matter for another song. My point here is that the visible, and the subject-position of which it is both cause and effect, are there to be seen.

CHAPTER THREE

Constable's Deception

I

Writing to his good friend and patron John Fisher in 1823, Constable concluded a letter—divided by the antithetical themes of gratitude to Fisher and the painter's own sense of entitlement—with an equally ambivalent description of "the private view of the '*Diorama*'" he had just attended:

> It is a transparency, the spectator in a dark chamber—it is very pleasing & has great illusion—it is without the pale of Art because its object is deception—Claude's never was—or any other great landscape painter's. The style of the pictures is French, which is decidedly against them. Some real stones, as bits of brown paper & a bit of silver lace turned on a wheel glides through the stone—to help. The place was filled with foreigners—& I seemed to be in a cage of magpies. (*Correspondence,* 6:134)

Most remarkable about Constable's account (though by no means unique to it, as we have seen) is its failure, even in retrospect, to exert more than a modicum of control over what was (and obviously still is) an unsettling experience. Fascination proceeds to pleasure, which in turn modulates to disapproval before culminating in a sense of dislocation. Further, while there is no reason to doubt that the painter's fellow spectators were in fact foreigners, the more important point to stress is that the experience of seeing the Diorama served to estrange

Constable from a public that, however foreign, represented *at that moment* an exclusive group to which the painter was privileged to belong.

The question, then, is not simply: Why was Constable so dislocated by this "private view?" As we have just seen, dislocation or some circuit of disbelief was both a common response to the Diorama and a source of the Diorama's appeal. The question that must be asked, rather, is why the experience of viewing an art that (by comparison to the paintings of Claude Lorrain) remained mechanically reproduced was sufficient to throw Constable back upon a sole self whose distinguishing feature was less his artistry or connoisseurship than his intense individualism? The answer to this is not easy. Yet in light of my previous discussion of the innovations in the culture of seeing and of the challenges to sovereign subjectivity they variously posed, the movement toward individuation here is bound up, even more directly than Lady Morgan's, in a necessary resistance to the Diorama, whose "pleasing" work is effectively tarred by the imprecation of "deception."

The charge of deception, had it come from Turner or any other expressionistic, even picturesque, painter, would have made sense, since it was Turner's project—as it was the project of romantic painting generally—to militate against an illusionistic or "Zeuxian" view of art. (I am referring, of course, to Pliny's anecdote about the painter Zeuxis, whose painted grapes were so "lifelike" that "birds began to fly down to eat from the painted vine" [cited in Bryson, *Vision,* 1]). But for Constable, who had professed a fidelity to "truth," and whose version of "truth" was almost always characterized in terms of visible particularity and by its appeal to "common sense," the accusation of deception has a defensive and, one might even argue, apostate ring. What Constable is ultimately conceding by the charge of deception and, in a related way, by the relegation of his fellow spectators to the aviary (were these "magpies" also the birds in Pliny?) is that *his* art was no more deceptive or a copy of the real than it was a matter of common sense or, as the case may have been, of common experience. Rather, the truth to which Constable had (in a famous earlier letter to Fisher) pledged fidelity and had vowed "never [to] cease to paint"—the "Old rotten Banks, slimy posts, & brickwork"—was not "truth" as he had brashly (and not a little sanctimoniously) claimed; it was, as his criticism of the Diorama now shows, a decidedly private vision of things (6:76–78).

Constable was not unaware of the egoistic dimension of his art.

In the same letter, he was quick to add that the things he vowed to paint were, in effect, his "own places." "Painting," he observed,

> is but another word for feeling. I associate my 'careless boyhood' to all that lies on the banks of the *Stour*. They made me a painter (& I am gratefull) that is I had often thought of pictures of them before I had ever touched a pencil, and your picture [Fisher's description of his "fishing excursion"] is one of the strongest instances I can recollect of it. But I will say no more—for I am fond of being an Egotist, in whatever relates to painting. (78)

Constable might well have reversed this last line by expressing his fondness for painting whatever related to his ego. But it is symptomatic of Constable's dilemma as a painter—and therefore central to his ambivalence regarding the Diorama, which was anything but a "private" experience—that he was motivated to justify his personal imprimatur in terms of the subjects of his paintings and not the other way around. Unlike a writer such as Wordsworth, whose fidelity to nature was continually characterized, all statements to the contrary, by his bearing on *it*, Constable could never bring himself to admit that his art was not, in some fundamental way, a representation of recoverable, perceptible truth. As late as 1833, when his painting had, by all accounts, become more personal and impressionistic, Constable was still speaking, albeit cryptically, of the "CHIAR'OSCURO OF NATURE," which neatly transferred to the object a process of both perceiving and representing that was unquestionably the artist's own.

Thus if, as he maintained in 1833, it remained Constable's purpose as a painter to "mark the influence of light and shadow upon Landscape," it is equally clear that marking had come to more than the capacity "to note 'the day, the hour, the sunshine and the shade'" so as "to give 'to one brief moment caught from fleeting time', a lasting and sober existence, and to render permanent many of those splendid but evanescent Exhibitions, which are ever occurring in the changes of external Nature."[1] Indeed, much like Shelley's notion of language, which collapses perception, conception, and expression into a single hieroglyphic, "marking" for Constable was precisely and indeterminately that: a gesture that was a matter of both perception *and* reinscription or, as the painter himself observed, a way for painting "to show its use and power as a medium of expression." Marking, then, not only corresponds to the dynamic of matching and making that

Gombrich makes a special point of locating in Constable.[2] "Marking" is the ambiguous activity that underlies Constable's equally ambivalent stance toward the Diorama as an instrument of deception. While it is surely tempting to join with Constable's biographer and interlocutor Charles Leslie in attributing the charge of deception to the conviction that art pleases by reminding, not by deceiving (*Correspondence,* 6:134), it is more the case that the Diorama, with its obvious appeal to the contingent, the unexpected, and the "evanescent," so exceeded the capability of painting to do the same that the painter's only recourse was to regard the truth—the truth of painting—as somehow distinct from that of "external Nature."

Thus, while the "private view of the Diorama" undoubtedly fascinated Constable, recapitulating in its fortuitous conjunction of the private and public the antithetical if not always contradictory claims of Constable's "ART," the view of the Diorama ultimately attenuated this synthetic conception in returning Constable to a private, personalized vantage in contrast to the public and increasingly *foreign* experience of re-viewing the external world. The Diorama deceived or was a deception not simply by approximating the truth of external nature which, as Constable had theorized, was properly the function of painting; rather, as we saw in the previous chapter, the Diorama deceived also by exposing the deception that *painting* had perpetuated.

Constable's response to the Diorama, then, was defensive in a variety of ways, none of them complementary. The subject-position to which the painter is returned by his own account distinguishes him as much for his dedication to the truth as it distinguishes his art—or what he is certain his paintings represent—on the basis of his uniqueness. And so the charge of deception comes to more than a simple instance of the pot calling the kettle black. If anything, it represents both a revaluation of "truth" as mere illusionism and at the same time (and paradoxically) a reinvention of truth in terms of what the artist saw. Where the Diorama deceives by avoiding or otherwise canceling the individual perceiving subject through its illusionistic procedures, "art" correspondingly functions by recourse to, and by representing as true, an experience no longer accessible or (on the evidence of the Diorama) necessarily relevant to "common sense."

That Constable would show little awareness of these contradictions, that he allowed his animus and fear to do the work of deconstruction, should not surprise us. After all, what Constable ultimately achieved as a painter, particularly in his famous Stour Valley scenes, could not have been accomplished had he been committed fundamentally to recovering a recoverable reality. It is the case, in fact, as Ronald Paulson has argued, that the recourse to the visible or to the world of common sense as an aesthetic desideratum—a recourse that Constable made much of—simply allowed for the introduction of narratives, which Constable might actually have foregrounded as narratives had he also understood to what extent marking or observing was also marking or narrating.

Thus, it is symptomatic of Constable's art and of the painter's continued belief in the veracity of his representations that what he narrated in his various paintings was not only necessarily unclear to him but is also a matter on which critics and art historians are necessarily in disagreement. For Michael Rosenthal, perhaps the most scrupulous and informed of the "new wave" of Constable students, the narrative is constantly shifting. Beginning with the early ideal of a "natural painture," which committed Constable, invariably against his own assertions, to a version of the true that, as Gombrich observes, was always/already a version of art,[3] Constable's putatively "pure and unaffected representation[s]" of the Stour Valley were consistently informed by a variety of schemas, allowing fiction the paradoxical if inevitable prerogative of underwriting fact.

The most notable of these fictions, as Rosenthal shows, was the georgic ideal of a "rural society in which all worked for the common good, and which divided workers into those who laboured, and those who dictated, their 'common' industry directed to the shared end of national advancement and glory decided on by the latter."[4] This ideal, which Constable inherited from the eighteenth century and which bears the stamp of the social authoritarianism that the Romantics, for their part, generally opposed, simultaneously enabled Constable to imitate the Romantics and actually to adhere to their democratic vistas in "shifting from the safe ground of convention" (Rosenthal, 57) by depicting the daily life of the Stour Valley. Hence, the very same Constable who radically wrenched landscape painting from the compositional ideal (and from the ideal world depicted therein) of Claude and his followers ultimately resembled Claude in his advocacy of, and nostalgia for, the prospect of a "golden age."

There were, to be sure, other narratives and other truths that would occupy Constable and would inform his representations. Yet none, in a way, was more seductive than the subjective narrative that was nicely accommodated by the impressionistic style that came to dominate his later canal scenes. This style, as anyone familiar with the painter knows, was already a dominant feature of the preliminary oil sketches, which Constable had composed in *plein air* and on which his studio paintings, the so-called six-footers, were based. What is significant, then, about the later canal scenes is their deconstruction of the assumptions behind Constable's unique compositional method—all of them clustered, again, around the ideal of a pure and unaffected representation of nature. In spite of its resistance to formal composition, what the oil sketch ultimately represented was not nature or the external world but the beholder himself, whose impressions, rapidly transcribed, were the basis of all subsequent compositions. The decidedly unfinished aura of a painting like *The Leaping Horse* (1825), with its uncomfortably, chaotically low viewpoint, underscores the ultimate primacy of painter over place, transmitting "pictorially the sensations, the flux of shifting lights, the feel of the wind, the shifts in perception caused by actual bodily movement, of *being* outdoors" (Rosenthal, 166, my emphasis). And this is even truer of the preliminary sketch (fig. 8) to which the final painting strenuously adheres.

Rosenthal is not at all troubled by these contradictions. It scarcely matters to him, for example, that the impressionism whose primary allegiance was to truth or to a natural painture was no more than a cover for an expressionism whose truth was more a matter of vision or intention. It is his purpose as a student of Constable simply to make sense of and to understand the logic behind a statement such as the "Chiar'oscuro of Nature" and not necessarily to unmask it. But other commentators are not so charitable or so uncritically disposed toward Constable's narrative introjections. Instead they tend with various degrees of praise and blame to treat Constable almost exclusively in terms of his narratives, allowing the painter's own statements and ideals to stand as no more than disingenuous guides to his work.[5]

These "readings" share more than the disposition simply to debunk or variously to amend Constable's own pronouncements on the veracity of his representations; they are determined, all of them, to amend Constable's art so that it remains, for better or for worse, a *romantic* art. Ronald Paulson, for his part, is generally appreciative of this dimension or, at the very least, able to regard it without disapproval: understanding Constable, for him, simply involves understanding the "literariness" of the painter's landscapes. But Ann Bermingham and John Barrell are far less sanguine. The literariness of the painter's landscapes is, as Bermingham describes it, complicit with a

tendency to appropriate, to dominate, to enclose—whose naturalization, in turn, cannot possibly cover the stigma to which the natural, as a result, remains testimony in Constable. And Barrell, while he does not underscore the subjective dimension of Constable as do the others, nevertheless identifies—in the distance separating the painter from both his landscape and its inhabitants—a nostalgia for harmony, both among men and between man and nature, which reciprocally constructs the painterly self as a mythmaking and, as such, alienated authority.

In other words, the revision of Constable currently underway corresponds almost identically to the revision of British romanticism in general: students of Constable readily concede the humanistic dimension of the paintings, on which they are characteristically divided, while bracketing out any bearing on Constable's art of the authentically visible or of the world "as it is." It scarcely requires saying that from my perspective such readings are in the main correct, rightly demystifying the particular access to the visible or to external nature that Constable—and his method as sketcher first and painter afterwards—effectively claimed.

My quarrel with such readings simply involves their virtual recapitulation of the contemporary stance toward romantic *literature,* which, along with such institutions as the Diorama, is more complicated and less predictably autocratic. Nor is it surprising that these complications are ones to which Constable gives testimony as well—to the extent at least of having been put in the untenable position of calling the Diorama an instrument of deception. While the accusation of deception is defensive to the extreme of implicitly condemning the painter's own work as untruthful, it implies, and even seems to draw justification from, a much greater illusionism inherent in the representation of places and things that were for Constable highly cathected. There was no way, in short, that Constable could have ultimately distinguished what was true from what was true *to him* and consequently quite arbitrary.

Constable's "truth," then, is precisely what the visible resists in turn. Yet even allowing this, there is enough that is sufficiently *proximate* to the visible in Constable not only to warrant its demystification

---

Figure 8 (opposite). John Constable, sketch for *The Leaping Horse,* 1824–25. Trustees of the Victoria and Albert Museum, London.

in Paulson, Barrell, Bermingham, Rosenthal and others, but to account in some way for the visible per se. Like the Diorama as a vehicle of deception, in fact, Constable's own paintings do more than demonstrate what Constable could not possibly have represented in the long run; they admit or represent the visible just enough to justify both the painter's blindnesses and his insights. Thus, I will conclude my discussion of Constable's "deception" with an examination of his well-known *Hay-Wain* (1821), which not only approximates the visible in its unmotivated resistance of narrative, but approximates it sufficiently, I think, to have transformed the famous letter to Fisher on old brickwork and mossy banks—written in reply to (among other matters) a query regarding this very painting—into something of a critical accompaniment.

Originally titled *Landscape-Noon, The Hay-Wain* (fig. 9) would appear to justify its initial designation (and thus to correspond to the aesthetic extrapolable from such a title) in its depiction of "one brief moment caught from fleeting time." In addition to "mark[ing] the influence of light and shadow upon Landscape" at a particular hour, *The Hay-Wain* is further distinguished by the way each of its inhabitants is captured *in medias res*. This is so much the case that all activity here and the continuum or narrative of which any action is necessarily an element are rendered secondary. The dog in the foreground, for example, who in a preliminary study was painted scampering away from the cottage on the far left (fig. 10), is arrested here and distracted by the sight of the hay wagon midstream, whose presence usurps purpose. For in the very way that the dog has been momentarily distracted from going to some place or thing, the hay-wain, as its position midstream and emptiness together thematize, is represented less in accordance with a particular narrative or goal (as the painting's final title would appear to assert) and more in accordance with the initial title. This is equally true of the various other figures in the painting, the woman with a pitcher (left), the man fishing (right), and the mowers in the distance (upper right), whose virtual invisibility is as much a function of Constable's impressionistic method (and of the rapidly executed sketch that, as Rosenthal observes, deviates hardly at all from the final version [132]) as it figures a resistance in the painting to representation: to circumscription by a larger temporality and causality. These figures may well be participants in a larger, fundamentally meaningful activity—as viewers are permitted certainly to discover; but this cannot be taken to countermand the fact that they are also merely (that is, barely) visible and, like the figures to the left of the mowers toward the center of the painting, privy to a less decidable, less comprehensible function.

It is always something of a surprise, then, to discover what various commentators have been able to read into *The Hay-Wain.* To Karl Kroeber, for example, whose comparative study of Wordsworth and Constable exceeds even Paulson's in its appreciation of the painter's literariness, *The Hay-Wain* may be likened to Wordsworth's "spots of time"—the privileged moments in which, as Wordsworth writes, the "mind / Is lord and master, and . . . the outward sense . . . but the obedient servant of her will"—in its "unity of mood."[6] This view is shared by James A. W. Heffernan, who, while observing that Constable effectively displaces history with rural incident, nevertheless concludes that the painting's projection of "the structure of a bower" (that "contains even as it expands") "symbolize[s] the mind's capacity to contain the outer world."[7]

In fact, there are virtually no modern instances that I know of in which commentary is not obliged, in some way, to come to terms with *The Hay-Wain*'s intentional structure. From Rosenthal's analysis of the georgic element of absorptive labor and the "social harmony it signifies" (129); to Bermingham's more personally inflected discussion, wherein the techniques of naturalism—the depiction here of the unity of man and nature—simultaneously construct Constable as a subject who can only project himself and his ideas *onto* nature (138–45); to Barrell's sharply critical analysis of the invisibility of the rural poor, notably the mowers here, whose very unobtrusiveness and lack of actuality help ensure "the stability of an ideally structured economic and social order" (146–49), there is a need apparently to ferret out what *The Hay-Wain* in a peculiar sense yields only by withholding. In other words, it is the extraordinary *readability* of *The Hay-Wain*—its unending capacity to yield up narratives—that accounts paradoxically for its *un*readability and its challenge to criticism, which commentators have lately met and, at the same time, have continued to abet.

It is in the intersection of readability and undecidability, or in the necessary excess of interpretability, that *The Hay-Wain* verges on the visible. For if the visible may be defined as the produce of the glance, whose images are excessive and inchoate rather than denotative, so *The Hay-Wain,* with its multiplicity of meanings, is plainly too suggestive, too cathected, too overdetermined, to say any one thing, much less anything. It is more the case, in fact, that the various freight

Figure 10. John Constable, *Willy Lott's House,* ca. 1811. Trustees of the Victoria and Albert Museum, London.

Figure 9 (opposite). John Constable, *The Hay-Wain,* 1820–21. Trustees of the National Gallery, London.

that the gazing Constable continued to bring to the painted scene, particularly as he moved from plein-air sketch to full-scale painting, simply exceeded, thereby subjecting to continuous revision, what may have motivated the painting in the first place. The effect of this, then, is to bring *The Hay-Wain* to a virtual standstill, to a peculiar momentariness that, however faithful to the initial title (*Landscape-Noon*), is on the far side still of "accidentality."

The only aspect of *The Hay-Wain,* indeed, that can be deemed contingent and genuinely excessive remains the failure of narrative always to repress the visible, which is always/never liberated and always/never apparent as one meaning competes with another for primacy. In turn, this allows what is clearly overdetermined to verge on (without obviously becoming) what I would again call the *under*determined. Hence, despite its uncanny abetting of a visible order, *The Hay-Wain* is opposed to the visible as I conceive it. What is ultimately visible in *The Hay-Wain* is neither a repressed returned nor what Constable himself arguably experienced when confronted by the Diorama: namely, the ungovernable produce of the glance in the space between illusion and reality, which cancels the gaze and, by implication, the gazing subject. Instead, what is visible in *The Hay-Wain* is as removed from the merely visible as the painter is from something or someone *not* Constable. And this last, not surprisingly, is actually figured by the painter himself, who was plainly too motivated not to have been obsessed with the very critical difference between his subject-position, on the one hand, and what was lost, on the other, for failure to see as he did. This is indicated in *The Hay-Wain* by recourse to the dog in the lower foreground (fig. 11), whose literally decentered position contrasts with the comparatively elevated, appropriative position of the painter, and whose sighting of the hay wagon, which is the object of the painter's attention as well, is distinguished from the painter's vision as a glance differs from a gaze.

That the dog and its positioning were of more than incidental concern to Constable, particularly in the final version, is clear from other evidence. In an oil sketch of Willy Lott's farm composed sometime before the study for *The Hay-Wain* (fig. 10), this same dog (or one nearly like it) is painted walking away from the cottage (represented at the same angle and from the same elevation as it is later painted) toward what subsequently became *The Hay-Wain*'s foreground. And in the actual study for the painting, which Constable painted (as Rosenthal reminds us) at great "speed" (132), the dog is

Figure 11. John Constable, *The Hay-Wain,* 1820–21, detail of dog. Trustees of the National Gallery, London.

rendered stationary next to both a horse and, significantly, a human rider (believed to be the painter's father) staring *with them* at the wagon in midstream (fig. 12).[8]

In other words, whatever parity exists in the preliminary studies between the canine and the human, whether in terms of purposefulness and motivation or simply in the degree of interest in something sighted,[9] is significantly amended in the final version of *The Hay-Wain,* where the human companion to the dog was initially included and then removed. (The outline of an elided figure can be seen very clearly in the actual painting.) Here, the dog is both the sole observer in the painting (the other figures in the foreground apparently too preoccupied even to notice the wagon), in addition to being an observer whose observations, unlike the painter's, are tantamount to distraction. Neither stationary like the dog in the study, nor in purposeful transit like the initial dog, the dog in his final incarnation is barely stopped and, one suspects, as incapable of being stopped here as he is

prevented, his attention momentarily captured, from proceeding forward. Instead, the dog is demonstrably (and, in contrast to his prototypes, *demonstrably painted*) in a kind of limbo.

All of which may be likened to what Constable was exposed to in the Diorama and what he resisted—then as now—by asserting both his individuality and, in the peculiarly and *impossibly* elevated vantage of the painting, his humanity.[10] For as his rather defensive homocentrism (recall the magpies) suggests, at issue in the romantic visible is more than simply an aesthetic possibility—the representation of a world uncontrolled by human or authorial intervention. At issue finally is a social possibility, what Baudrillard eloquently dubs "the haunting memory of a lost reality," whose necessary demystification of the individual (and the oppositional framework of subject and object) is resisted—but not disproven or eliminated in Constable—by imagining what the painter was clearly too afraid and thus too "human" to become.

II

In refusing, then, to envision what—by inclusion of the "little dog"—it imagines nonetheless, *The Hay-Wain* begs comparison with an aesthetic that, as Michael Fried details in his study of eighteenth-century French painting, is committed to an annihilation or "absorption" of the painting's beholder.[11] *The Hay-Wain* begs comparison on this score because the beholder of Constable's painting, who may be taken as a stand-in for the artist himself, is (as we will see) at the crossways of absorption, on the one hand, and the peculiar self-awareness or reflexity, on the other, that Fried calls "theatricality." The ideal of which Fried writes in *Absorption and Theatricality* is, with particular bearing on the question of the visible, a conventionally romantic, homocentric aesthetic. Fried's preferred term for this orientation is "modernism," largely because the virtues he perceives in paintings by artists like Chardin are ones he sees also in Courbet and more recently in canvases by, among others, Morris Louis. Although committed to recovering something that happened in eighteenth-century art in reaction to the rococo, Fried's real purpose is to construct a genealogy of modernism (or to recover what he calls an "ontological basis of modern art" [61]) for the purpose of legitimizing and, in cer-

---

Figure 12 (opposite). John Constable, sketch for *The Hay-Wain,* ca. 1820. Trustees of the Victoria and Albert Museum, London.

tain cases, discrediting more recent versions of art. Thus, Fried is especially averse to terms such as *neoclassicism,* not only because of their restrictive or taxonomic nature, but because the virtues of "neoclassic" art, as he perceives them, are virtues more apposite to the means and ends of romanticism—which is, if nothing else, a more modern movement. Fried would doubtless find romanticism a restrictive term as well. Nevertheless, it is a useful term (and a useful perspective on Fried) in light of the authority with which Fried's art is ideally invested. For this authority—ultimately figured by an omniscience of which the absorbed or invisible beholder is a lesser if still similar manifestation—is precisely what *The Hay-Wain* both manifests and yet militates against.

Drawing chiefly on Diderot's response to the Salons of the 1750s and 60s, particularly to those paintings singled out for admiration, Fried postulates a desideratum, which rests chiefly on the depiction of an absorptive state, whose success, in turn, depends on the neutralization, or absorption, of the painting's beholder. Beyond simply a "correlative" for the artist's "own engrossment in the act of painting" (51), the particular absorption to which Diderot was attentive (in, for example, a painting like Chardin's *Soap Bubble* [fig. 13]) virtually demands that the represented subject, or figure *in* the painting, be oblivious "to everything but the objec[t] of [his or her] absorption" (66). Fried continually terms this obliviousness a "fiction" because there is no way, after all, that a figure fashioned out of canvas and oil can be oblivious to whomever stands before it. At the same time, this obliviousness, however much a fiction, was an undeniable effect of certain paintings of the period and—in conjunction with this strange metamorphosis of fiction into fact—evidence of a special kind of authority.

The question of authority is in many ways a moot one in Fried's analysis and seemingly secondary to the effects of art, all of which take precedence over intentionality. The continued recourse to Diderot—over and against the stated intentions of the artists themselves—is emblematic of this subordination. Still, in examining the effects as Fried describes them—and in examining them, moreover, in conjunction with *The Hay-Wain*—we not only see what is at stake in the aesthetic of absorption; we see also why it is virtually mandatory that authority be *inferred* from this aesthetic, rather than the substance of it. For it is precisely the insubstantiality of the artist, and the mystified agency of which his insubstantiality is effectively a figure, that Fried's argument fosters and exploits. Instead of imagining the artist as some-

Figure 13. Jean-Baptiste-Simeon Chardin, *The Soap Bubble,* ca. 1733. National Gallery of Art, Washington, D.C. Gift of Mrs. John W. Simpson.

one who arbitrarily lays claim to power, Fried allows the power or the particular suasion of the image itself to legitimize the artist's claims.

Of the various means by which art in the eighteenth century was able to accomplish the work of absorption, essentially two stand out in Fried's account—both of them relevant to our understanding and appreciation of Constable's painting. The first of these, as I've already mentioned, involves obliviousness to the painting's beholder. Such obliviousness, as Fried elaborates it, is achieved not merely by depicting a given figure in a state of intense preoccupation but—most "efficacious[ly]" he observes—by taking "as subject matter the deeds and sufferings of conscious agents who were, to say the least, fully capable of evincing awareness of the beholder" only to "forestall or extinguish all traces of such awareness in and through the dramatic representation of those deeds and sufferings" (103).

The second means of absorption occurred in genres that in the main were less suited to the absorptive strategy, chiefly landscape and still life, whose illusory procedures, with their necessary emphasis on the "madeness" of their respective worlds, led inevitably (according to Diderot and others) to "dislocation and estrangement rather than [to] absorption, sympathy, self-transcendence" (104). Nevertheless, in the landscapes of a painter like Claude-Joseph Vernet (fig. 14), absorption was achieved by inducing beholders to the fiction of actually being in the painting, or before "a real scene" that they could proceed "to explore" (131). This fiction, which like other versions of absorption succeeded in removing the beholder "from in front of the painting," was managed by what Fried calls "a fracturing of perspectival unity." According to this procedure there are depicted "within the painting . . . numerous points of view, each of which competes with all the others for the beholder's attention and in a sense for his imagined presence at the spot." In this way, it is "virtually impossible for the beholder to grasp the scene as a single instantaneously apprehensible whole" and to remain fixed as a figure "in front of the canvas" (134).

Such dissolution, of course, is precisely the kind of disembodiment that Norman Bryson affiliates with the gaze and with the tendency of illusionistic art, in particular, to deploy the gaze against the materiality of both world viewed and the subject viewing it. Unlike the glance, with its more immediate relationship to the body, it is the function of the gaze, as it is the function of absorption, to remove the viewer from a fixed or materialized state. Correspondingly, as the

Figure 14. Claude-Joseph Vernet, *Landscape with Waterfall and Figures*, 1768. Walters Art Gallery, Baltimore.

mode of perception on whose suppression absorption necessarily depends, it is the effect of the glance to intervene against absorption: to provide an impedance in which the materiality of the viewer, and of the world viewed, may be marshaled *against* a subject-position (or social formation, if you prefer) whereby visual fascination, with its promise of omniscience and comprehension, remains abundant recompense.

The interposition of the glancing dog in *The Hay-Wain*'s foreground can be said, consequently, to accomplish a number of things. Not only does the dog militate against the aesthetic of absorption in replacing human contemplation with animal distraction; it effectively speculates, or allows us to speculate, on what *The Hay-Wain* can no more than threaten to become now—namely, a representation wherein both viewer *and* painter are consigned, at different levels of authority, to invisibility. The dog in the painting's foreground, distracted and unaccompanied, clearly differs from the absorptive figures Fried describes in obviously lacking the kind of awareness or capacity for involvement that a human figure might necessarily display. Far from neutralizing the viewer's presence by recalling him or her to a position of relative insignificance, the dog sees to it, if anything, that the beholder's sovereignty, signaled and bolstered by the elevated vantage from which the entire scene is visible, is sustained rather than unfixed. Thus, the dog also bears a peculiar relation to the actual humans in the painting, whose relative imperceptibility has prompted John Barrell to charge Constable with having ignored or otherwise dehumanized them.[12] That is, in the very way that the dog shores up a subject-position of exteriority in *The Hay-Wain,* so the position that the dog fixes, so to speak, is also proven through its apparent effects, which include (as Barrell shows) the consignment of other subjects to barely human status.

The various human agents in *The Hay-Wain*—the woman at the left, the fisherman at the right, and the two men in the hay wagon itself—are, to follow Fried more specifically, pictured at the crossways of absorption. Absorbed by their respective activities and thus oblivious to a beholder or viewer, these same figures are sufficiently assimilated to the represented scene to prohibit the viewer's absorption in kind. Like the dog, in fact, who can be said to have gotten into the painting first, preventing the beholder's absorption or involvement in the scene (and his removal correspondingly *from in front* of the picture), the figures in the painting contrast with at least two figures exterior to the painting now—the painter and the beholder—who stand in relative opposition to the world seen. Nor is it a coincidence, therefore, that unlike a Vernet landscape, whose many striking details are a means (according to Fried) to remove the viewer from a stable, fixed, or exterior position, *The Hay-Wain* additionally fixes the viewer to an exterior position in the way such *potential* sights or details (for example, the mowers in the distance) are scarcely visible and thus unable (as are the assimilated figures in the foreground) to disrupt the "perspectival unity" for which Constable's paintings are routinely praised.

These aspects, to be sure, are evident in other Constable paintings as well. Nevertheless, *The Hay-Wain* may be distinguished from these other works in the way its obstructions to absorption are somehow pressed in an intentionality, which recoils not only upon the aesthetic of truth that Constable was allegedly committed to, but upon the "truth" of the particular image at hand. And here, again, the deployment of the unaccompanied dog, whose obstruction coincidentally figures another way of seeing, is central. Although the dog is clearly leagued with a materialized world, and a materialized way of seeing, which contrasts to the painting as decomposition to composition, the very possibility of what one critic jocularly terms a "dog's-eye-view" succeeds in underscoring the equally materialized (if still mystified) vantage that *The Hay-Wain,* unlike the art of absorption, barely masks.[13] Where the art of absorption is curiously impervious to a visible field, or to a world whose palpability is forever tied to the work of a *bodily* eye, the orientation (and, I would further venture, the romanticism) to which Constable's art provides peculiar access in this instance, lies precisely in the accessibility of its world to a vantage characterized less by absence, omniscience, or invisibility (as Shelley might avow) than by a remarkably stable, if increasingly demystified, exteriority to things.

Such accessibility, needless to say, is not tied to Constable, much less to this one painting. Barker's Panorama in London, for example, easily exceeded *The Hay-Wain* in collapsing virtually all distinction between inside and outside, or between the world viewed and the world viewing it. Where Constable's painter/beholder maintains a position of material exteriority in this instance, which resists in some degree the omniscience to which such materiality is routinely elevated in romantic discourse, the Panorama extends that reflexive initiative in making the beholder (or beholders as was usually the case) coextensive with the image. Thus, where it is the goal of absorption—and of much romantic art—to remove the beholder to a state of virtual disembodiment and authority, it was the effect of the Panorama to recall the beholder to corporeality by creation of a "public" that the image did not encompass or contain so much as reflect. Fried, for his part, describes this "visuality"—which "address[es] or exploit[s] the visuality of the . . . audience" in refusing "to wall it off from the action taking place" (96)—as "theatricality," and it is a tendency that, like Diderot, he deplores. Furthermore, it is clear that at stake in theatricality for Fried is less the audience on whose visuality it depends than the lack or dispersal of *individual* authority in what he elsewhere calls a "negation of art."[14]

Such dispersal of authority was, as we shall see, both an ideal as well as a problem for the Romantics: a humanistic initiative that was also challenged and attenuated by the many selves to whom it could theoretically apply. As a result, the conception of the beholder as a physical entity, as a body incapable of "self-transcendence," was undoubtedly more subversive in the end than either skeptical or conservative. As the Panorama makes clear, in fact, it remained the function of such visuality—as it remains the function of the physically elevated beholder in *The Hay-Wain*—to resist that omniscience or difference which, in typically lesser form, issues in a dematerialization of the body seeing. The absorption, in other words, by which the beholder can become a disembodied gazer—in contrast, say, to Constable's dog—typically assimilates one to a hierarchy where individuality and privacy are the components, by and large, of a lesser though scarcely equitable godhead.

That it was one of the achievements of romanticism to have made peace with this lesser godhead—as *The Hay-Wain* manages simply by sustaining an exteriorized subject position—should scarcely be news to anyone. And yet, as the painter's reaction to the Diorama also suggests, this compromise could be managed only through a mystification in which one's visceral presence, or separate integrity as a body, was literally naturalized as existential difference or superiority. Nor is it at all surprising, therefore, that the detachment effected by the Diorama—which had summoned viewers to a nonabsorptive state—prompted both Constable and Lady Morgan to resist the summons in regarding their fellow viewers as lesser creatures. This is equally the case in Constable's painting, where a merely physical displacement from the represented scene is also a position from which the scene submits to organization and control. But this, fortunately, is not all that transpires in *The Hay-Wain*. The failure of absorption to do its work in removing the beholder from before the canvas effectively registers, in conjunction with other manifestations of the visible in romanticism (*including* the Diorama), the refusal of both a physical world and the physical subject to accede either to their negation here or, in the phrase of both Kracauer and Fried, to their "redemption."

A similar refusal, or resistance, is evident in reactions to theater of the period, the visuality of which led to a host of complaints in support of a privatized theatricality, whose constitution in the act of reading recapitulates the asymmetrical compact between an omniscient artist and unequally invisible—or, in this case, closeted—respondent. Nevertheless, in the very way that *The Hay-Wain* works to disrupt such a compact by replacement of the human with the canine, so the romantic reaction to the theater frequently admits the very visuality it seeks otherwise to contain. Sometimes this admission is simply a complaint against the leveling that a representation of genius on stage, or in bodily form, effects. However, in other instances, as we shall see, including the theater criticism appended to Coleridge's *Biographia*, this visuality is marked by an inability to wall the audience off. The effect of this default, or theatricalization of the audience, represents more than a leveling of distinction; it involves a visuality so comprehensive, so universal, that the critic—the subject disposed to praise or blame—is literally wrenched from his position of difference and authority to a place beside himself.

All of this will be explored in detail in subsequent chapters. What must be emphasized, in concluding this section, is that despite the efforts to annihilate the visible by removing the subject from a visuality in kind, the various imperatives to absorption and authority remain, as romanticism's reflexive efforts make clear, a "romantic crux" (to use Thomas McFarland's term) in which autonomy and individual enfranchisement are necessarily purchased at the cost of a more authentic freedom.

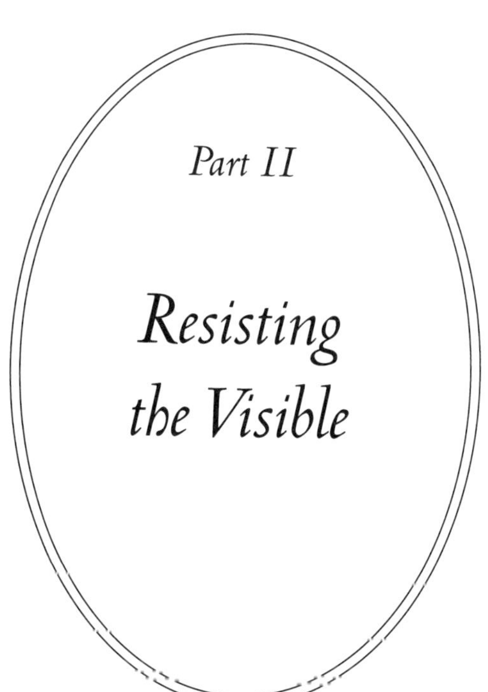

Part II

Resisting the Visible

CHAPTER FOUR

The Mind in the "Land of Technology": Resistance to Spectacle in Wordsworth's Prelude

I

Despite the many recent efforts to explore the "kinship" of "science and literature," particularly the way "they draw mutually on one culture," the separatist attitudes of romantic writers such as Wordsworth, who seemingly regarded science, education, and technology as the enemies of poetic sensibility, have gone unchallenged by critics of virtually every persuasion.[1] One reason for this reticence—especially among critics otherwise attuned to the poststructural mandate that locates science and literature equally in the realm of cultural discourse—is that the romantic hostility to science is, as we now read it, a shocking prejudice: a humanistic misconception against which more sophisticated and informed objections may at last be lodged.[2] Nevertheless, in undertaking these correctives, whose overall effect has been to demystify the privileged status of a subjective or poetic stance to reality, advocates of the "one culture" of science and literature (to borrow George Levine's term) find themselves in the paradoxical position of enlisting poststructuralism *against* poststructuralism—especially regarding literature's capacity as a discourse beside itself.[3]

To say, then, that Wordsworth's poetry is capable of self-intervention, even when it is most determined to resist intervention by preserving certain oppositions and hierarchies, is not to reify the romantic prejudice against science any more than it is to reverse that prejudice by disclosure of an "intentional structure" in scientific (as in symbolic) method sufficient to render observation and imagination versions of the same thing.[4] Rather, it is to take very seriously Wordsworth's animus to science not because such animus is necessarily justified or justifiable (as almost every commentator is convinced Wordsworth believed it was), but because this aversion is ultimately a desperate and transparent ruse: a fiction whose perpetuation succeeds only in exposing the need for its assertion in the first place.

That Wordsworth's attacks on science and modern education have a tendency to turn on themselves, sometimes in the guise of circumspection or amelioration, should be clear to anyone to whom Wordsworth's position on this issue has been of interest. Even the famous invective against the scientific "intellect" in "The Tables Turned" (1798)—"we murder to dissect"—is blunted by the subsequent equation of "science and . . . art" as "meddl[ers]" in kind, as well as by the fact that this very poem is merely a "reply" to an educator's expostulation against idleness, which began in a preceding and companion work, "Expostulation and Reply."[5] Not only does the poet's sustained reply over two poems lend a peculiarly defensive air to his appeals on behalf of "wise passiveness"; his antithesis, so to speak, has the effect of minimizing the defense of poetry in effectively requiring three times as much verse to contest the argument on behalf of education.

These problems are similarly evident in the Preface of 1802, where Wordsworth makes much of the privileged and unique status of the Poet, and has recourse to a comparison of the "Poet" and the "Man of Science."[6] Conceding that "the knowledge both of the Poet and the Man of Science is pleasure," Wordsworth immediately qualifies this comparison. Where the scientist's knowledge is a "personal and individual acquisition, slow to come to us, and by no habitual and direct sympathy connecting us with our fellow-beings," the "knowledge of [the Poet] cleaves to us as a necessary part of our existence, our natural and unalienable inheritance" (52). Still, Wordsworth means to be conciliatory: "If the time should ever come when what is now called Science, thus familiarized to men, shall be ready to put on, as it were, a form of flesh and blood, the Poet will lend his divine spirit to aid the transfiguration, and will welcome the Being thus produced, as a dear and genuine inmate of the household of man" (53).

Then, in a somewhat surprising conclusion, Wordsworth offers a final admonition:

> It is not, then, to be supposed that any one, who holds that sublime notion of Poetry which I have attempted to convey, will break in upon the sanctity and truth of his pictures *by transitory and accidental* ornaments, and endeavour to excite admiration of himself by arts, the necessity of which must manifestly depend upon the assumed meanness of his subject. (53, emphasis added)

This concluding observation would, on the face of it, appear to have little bearing on the comparison of poetry and science—except as this comparison is meant to bear chiefly on the function of poetry rather than on its analytic counterpart. Nevertheless, Wordsworth's warning to would-be poets and poetasters seems clearly to depend on the preceding comparison: the potential deficiencies of poetry as he imagines them, or as he implies his own critics may possibly construe them, are part of a dimension—specifically a proclivity to the accidental, the transitory, the mundane and, as Wordsworth later shows, to the spectacular—that is *potentially* the province of a *nonscientific* discourse. The millenarian marriage of science and poetry is, ironically enough, consummated less in the projected ability of science to imitate the more humanized example of poetry than in the more probable and deplorable tendency of poetry to resist its otherwise "sublime" or humanistic conception.

There are ways, of course, to account for and to justify Wordsworth's inability to oppose poetry to science successfully in his earlier works, or to make plain and unequivocal poetry's superiority to science. In the case of "The Tables Turned," for example, the seeming defensiveness on the part of the poet is (as the title implies) a repetition in form of Matthew's initial expostulation in defense of reading, which would have been unnecessary were it not vulnerable to the threat already posed by a "heart / That watches and receives" ("The Tables Turned"). And in the case of the Preface, the conciliatory nod to science may be nothing more than a way to defend *Lyrical Ballads* on the grounds of their uniqueness—particularly in terms of their rather ordinary subject matter.

None of this negates the fact, however, that in both instances a peculiar pressure is brought to bear on poetry through the very mention of a representational alternative. This pressure may be as slight as the bibliophobia, which implicitly links the "barren leaves" of books of science with those of books of "art" ("The Tables Turned"). Or it may be as serious as the privatization—the charge that scientific observation remains a largely "personal and individual acquisition"—that is potentially applicable (one might even argue more plausibly applicable) to poetic perception. But whatever its particular weight, this pressure registers two related uncertainties: it reflects an ambivalence regarding poetry that is additionally *and necessarily* an ambivalence regarding science and the "poet's" tendency to characterize science as an undesirable or debased mode of seeing.

It is not long before Wordsworth becomes more decisive in his opposition to science, as well as in his aversion to modern education and to the modes of seeing that may be similarly affiliated with scientific or technological media. However, in the same way that Matthew's expostulation against poetic knowledge bears the brunt of its own defensiveness in the two early poems, Wordsworth's subsequent attacks on science in his autobiographical epic, *The Prelude* (1805), on behalf of an unflinchingly "romantic" or "subjective" orientation, have the effect of disclosing what was repressed or unclear in the previous attacks. *The Prelude* reveals that a nominally scientific way of seeing—an experience that, following certain innovations in the culture of seeing in Wordsworth's own time, we may call spectacular—is demonstrably more revolutionary or communitarian in the end than the putatively "human" or specular orientation to which it is opposed.

Thus, it is the paradoxical, if seemingly unintended, effect of the treatment of science in *The Prelude* that it reverses and subverts the poet's invectives, past *and* present. Contrary to its announced and ostensible purpose of celebrating the growth of a poet's mind, *The Prelude* also postulates a "time" when what is now called *Poetry* will be able "to put on, as it were, [the] . . . flesh and blood [of Science]," whose proclivity to the transitory, the contingent, and the mundane, may be said to rescue perception from the very hegemony or containment that renders the "sanctity and truth" of any representation—artistic *or* scientific—a contradiction. This development—which is an intervention in *The Prelude*—would later find a powerful advocate in Walter Benjamin, whose well-known essay "The Work of Art in the Age of Mechanical Reproduction" (1936) imagines an art, in this case film, revolutionized by mechanical or technological agency. For Wordsworth, by contrast, this development is imagined through what may only be termed an "archaeology" or "genealogy" of the cinema. Thus Wordsworth anticipates Benjamin in two ways: first, by inadvertently theorizing a radical, antibourgeois "art," which is humanized and "true" on the condition of remaining antihumanistic, unsanctified and without "aura"; and second, in the way his own art, *The Prelude,* effectively rescues science, and a visible world made available by scientific means, from the very hegemony—from the "one culture," if you will—that is opposed now by the marriage of "art" and technology.

II

Nearly three hundred lines into *The Prelude*'s fifth book (titled "Books"), whose indirection to this point has prompted even the narrator to express "fear" that his "drift hath scarcely . . . been obvious" (290–91), Wordsworth moves to clarify matters by turning directly to his ostensible theme of "books" or, more broadly, education.[7] Noting the "monster birth / Engendered by these too industrious times" (293), the Poet[8] adopts a manner similar to a hawker's at Bartholomew Fair—a scene to which he returns later in the poem—before lapsing into a more sublime style:

> 'tis a child, no child,
> But a dwarf man; in knowledge, virtue, skill,
> In what he is not, and in what he is,
> The noontide shadow of a man complete.
> . . . .
> He is a prodigy. His discourse moves slow,
> Massy and ponderous as a prison door,
> Tremendously embossed with terms of art.
> Rank growth of propositions overruns
> The stripling's brain; the path in which he treads
> Is choked with grammars.
> . . . .
> The ensigns of the empire which he holds—
> The globe and sceptre of his royalties—
> Are telescopes, and crucibles, and maps.
> Ships he can guide across the pathless sea,
> And tell you all their cunning; he can read
> The inside of the earth, and spell the stars;
> He knows the policies of foreign lands,
> Can string you names of districts, cities, towns,
> The whole world over, tight as beads of dew
> Upon a gossamer thread. He sifts, he weighs,
> Takes nothing upon trust. His teachers stare,

The country people pray for God's good grace,
And tremble at his deep experiments.
(294–340)

Although the persona that Wordsworth temporarily adopts feigns a certain fascination with this freakish product of modernity, the speaker's antipathy to modern education and what it ideally produces is obvious enough. Such products "of our later age" (370) are far better suited to a sideshow, where they may amaze the bumpkins and appall the free, than to the putatively progressive aims of education—whose "broad highway . . . overbridg[ing] / The froward chaos of futurity" has, in this instance, "confine[d] us down / Like engines" (371–72, 382–83).

In the rhetorical structure of book 5, Wordsworth moves immediately—in the well-known boy of Winander passage—to offer an alternative to the infant prodigy and to promote an alternative model of education. But it is indicative of the pressure that the prodigy has exerted on the poem—which, like the prodigy's narrative, also involves the progress of an individual mind—that the Winander boy is not always distinguishable from his monstrous counterpart.[9] Indeed, it is almost as if what was mere spectacle in the case of the prodigy (and "infants" of this sort were routinely spectacles during this time)[10] is simply raised, in the example of the Winander boy, to a sublime pitch:

many a time
At evening, when the stars had just begun
To move along the edges of the hills,
Rising or setting, would he stand alone
Beneath the trees or by the glimmering lake,
And there, with fingers interwoven, both hands
Pressed closely palm to palm, and to his mouth
Uplifted, he as through an instrument
Blew mimic hootings to the silent owls
That they might answer him. And they would shout
Across the wat'ry vale, with quivering peals
And long halloos, and screams, and echoes loud,
Redoubled and redoubled—concourse wild
Of mirth and jocund din.
(390–404)

It scarcely requires saying that the example of the Winander boy is intended to contrast favorably with that of the "dwarf man," whose shrunkenness is meant to set the Winander boy's growth—his education by Nature—into sharper relief. At the same time, the two boys have much in common in that they both appear odd or even freakish. In the prodigy's case, freakishness is part and parcel of the satiric apparatus, whereas the Winander boy's freakishness is strangely unintended. The representation of the boy mimicking the birds, which is undoubtedly meant to show a more vital, less mediated, interaction with the world, modulates to a level of virtual grotesquerie before lapsing into the somewhat stilted description "of mirth and jocund din."

There may be no accounting, finally, for this labored and ambiguous description. Yet one possible reason—and still another ground for comparing the two boys—is that while the Winander boy is *meant* to be different from the infant prodigy, his "difference," in accordance with this adversarial stance, mandates an assertion or refiguration of the authority that knowledge or science, with its "engines" of mediation and power ("telescopes, and crucibles, and maps"), allegedly confers on the dwarf man. These engines may, in the case of the Winander boy, be nothing more than his hands and mouth and his human brain; yet the orchestration they perform, and the response they conspire to evoke, make the Winander boy even more successful (and more grotesque by virtue of his successes) in controlling the world he inhabits. Thus, when Wordsworth observes somewhat belatedly that the boy of Winander died prematurely "in childhood ere he was full ten years old" (415), the sense of loss struggles, in a strange way, against the propriety of the boy's passing. For like his counterpart, the Winander boy is similarly a "dwarf man," whose development, although plainly conditional upon his remaining fixed "where he was born" (417), is in the disposition of the Poet's argument tantamount to a kind of confinement.

By no means am I suggesting that Wordsworth had some sinister purpose in mind for the Winander boy, nor am I implying that his description of the boy here was meant to be anything other than laudatory. I am indicating simply that Wordsworth's attacks here on science and on education have, more obliquely *and concertedly* than in earlier works, the effect of exposing flaws and contradictions in what can be termed the poem's "humanistic" or "progressive" argument. Wordsworth's attack on the prodigy, for example, seems motivated largely by the child's achievements: by a mind whose particular growth is held in opposition to the "unreasoning progress of the world," in which a "wiser spirit is at work for us" (384–85). However, the subsequent use of the Winander boy as an exemplar of this latter progress impresses us not only with a sense of progress but with a sense of *unreason* ("long halloos, and screams, and echoes loud, / Redoubled and redoubled")—if only in that progress now, as the prodigy has already shown, is aligned with a program that the Poet alternately finds dehumanizing and confining.

Thus, the question must be asked: what of that "progress," notably the growth of the poet's mind, of which *The Prelude* is an account and of which the Winander boy is presumably a related instance? Is such progress still progress? Or is it, as the latter's premature death signifies, the antithesis of progress? The answer is by no means clear. However, it may be argued surely that such progress is ultimately a fiction insofar as it is based *as progress* on a denatured stance toward the world of which the infant prodigy may be an instance but in which the Winander boy need also excel. In other words, by making good on his humanistic "argument"—by casting in epical/biblical form what he later terms "the discipline / And consummation of the poet's mind" (13.270–71)—Wordsworth has no choice but to resist himself in *The Prelude:* both by recourse to a circular, biblical structure, whose progressive aim is to return paradoxically to the beginning ("the vale where he was born"), and, more centrally, by recourse to the individual, "enfranchised" (1.9) subject—either the poet "above all" (13.73) or the Winander boy in book 5—as the notably authoritarian hero of such a narrative. And what of the infant prodigy, who clearly bears the brunt of reflexivity in *The Prelude*—the awareness of the poem's decidedly nonprogressive posture? Well, the prodigy, by curious reversal, turns out not only to be less appropriative or less successful at appropriation than his naturalized counterpart. More important, the prodigy turns out to be comparatively deferential to the world, which thanks to the instruments of its mediation ("telescopes, and crucibles, and maps") is more often than not a visible, merely palpable world, whose peculiar autonomy is figured (along with the prodigy himself) in its describability—in its spectacular rather than specular nature.[11]

Such an interpretation of the infant prodigy requires, of course, that we do substantial violence to the theme and tone of *The Prelude*'s book on "books." Yet this violence has been initiated already by the poem itself, whose attacks on "science" or "knowledge" have the effect of projecting onto science precisely the features that are more properly—and deleteriously—*The Prelude*'s own. Thus, scientific mediation is not only charged here with offenses it did not necessarily commit; like the mechanical Diorama, which both threatened Constable yet managed somehow to render the painter a sovereign subject among "magpies," the attention here to scientific mediation serves the more reflexive function of allowing *The Prelude* to reflect back onto *itself* the very ideals, notably the "knowledge *not* purchased with loss of power" (5.449, emphasis added), that technology and science with their comparatively nonsubjective, nonappropriative and (I would further argue) nontotalizing orientation, tend curiously to resist. Far from abandoning the romantic prejudice against scientific knowledge and against the visible, observable world in which it necessarily issues, *The Prelude* continues this prejudice. But what it discloses in so doing is a conspiracy of knowledge and power sufficient to render science—not poetry—the more "genuine inmate of the household of man."

This intervention in Wordsworth must be distinguished from a poststructural critique that ultimately sees no intervention here at all, as well as from the more conventional or humanistic viewpoints that either applaud his romantic prejudice or, worse, seek to redefine science so as to render it more congenial to a romantic metaphysics. Whether science itself, with its particular emphasis on observation and objectivity, may perform this intervention on its own, or *independently* of literature, is beyond the scope of this study—and is, in any case, a matter of great debate among philosophers and epistemologists.[12] What concerns me is the way a romantic encounter *with science,* which amounts also to a resistance to science, manages willy-nilly to reinvent poetry and science in each other's image—compelling poetry to objectify its adversarial tendencies as human "expression" in contrast to science, which operates as a demystifying and, paradoxically, a more human agency.[13]

A reversal of this very sort occurs earlier in book 5 in the well-known Arab dream, where the relationship of science and poetry, alternating between opposition and equivalence, ultimately issues in what can only be deemed a critique of both poetry and the imagining subject. As readers of *The Prelude* will recall, the Poet's recollection here of a friend's dream involving an Arab and that Arab's quixotic efforts to save science and poetry from cataclysm is prefaced by the speaker's own fear for the fate of books "should earth by inward throes be wrenched throughout, / Or fire be sent from far to wither all / her pleasant habitations, and dry up / Old Ocean in his bed" (29–32).

In the dream of the Arab, which immediately follows these speculations, the speaker's fears are at once allayed and deconstructed by a single device: the figurative transposition of books of science and poetry into a stone and a shell respectively:

> the arab told him that the stone—
> To give it in the language of the dream—
> Was *Euclid's Elements*. 'And this', said he,
> 'This other', pointing to the shell, 'this book
> Is something of more worth.' 'And, at the word,
> The stranger', said my friend continuing,
> 'Stretched forth the shell towards me, with command
> That I should hold it to my ear. I did so
> And heard that instant in an unknown tongue,
> Which yet I understood, articulate sounds,
> A loud prophetic blast of harmony,
> An ode in passion uttered, which foretold
> Destruction to the children of the earth
> By deluge now at hand. . . .'
>
> (86–99)

There is much in this passage that warrants comment—not least the undecidable or indeterminate character of poetry, which modulates in the Arab's description from "this" to "this other" to "this book".[14]

But more to my purpose here is the fact that a stone and a shell are among the very few things that would survive the deluge. What would not survive would be the human culture, composed of figures such as the Arab, whose rather arbitrary "consecration" of books is underscored here in two ways: in the transformation of books into two objects whose value would, to the majority of the poem's readers, probably appear comparable and quite slight; and second, and more important, in the Arab's equally arbitrary claim that the shell "is something of more worth" than the stone. This valuation not only does violence to what, in the material transformation of books, is a virtual equivalence of science and poetry; it manages at the same time to deconstruct the whole notion of value by demonstrating that the shell (and by implication poetry) is "something of more worth" simply in its congeniality to subjective or specular sanctions.[15]

The "articulate sounds" uttered by the shell are, no less than the articulate utterances of the speaker in the initial lines of book 5, what the subject—in this instance the Poet's friend—fears and what he is compelled always to give expression to. This is equally true of the remainder of the dream, where the truth and the authority of the vision are conditional upon the persistence of the dream. Initially of course the fact that the Arab is ultimately chased by "the fleet waters of the drowning world" (136) would seem to confirm both the superior worth of the shell and the friend's almost equally superior ability to comprehend its message. But when the friend, upon envisioning the flood, immediately wakes in terror, the superiority of both poetry and the vatic dreamer is immediately contested by disclosure of their specular relationship. We are, according to this episode, moved more by what we imagine and by what is therefore untrue than we are impressed by what is true and therefore beyond the jurisdiction of the individual subject.

This narcissism and its negative implications for poetry are already hinted in the mock-heroic character of the Arab (deemed a semi-Quixote) as well as in the friend's rather revealing wish, upon listening to the shell, to cleave unto the Arab and share his errand with him (116–17)—thereby imitating the poem's speaker, who has already made *his* friend a double or surrogate of himself.[16] But, in the end, it devolves upon what is mostly absent in this episode, or barely disclosed—the merely measurable or "scientific" reality, whose concretion is appropriately figured in the stone and whose ultimate impenetrability is later figured in the various scientific instruments with which the prodigy may only take its measure—to cast the Poet or romantic subject into proper critical relief. This "reality," as most readers are aware, is generally absent in *The Prelude* or, when present, invariably subsumed under the category of Nature, whose function, here and elsewhere in Wordsworth, is often to minister to the subject either as a maternal guide or in the capacity of a largely passive, malleable poetic object. Nevertheless, in the very way that the infant prodigy casts the Winander boy (and by implication the Poet) into critical relief, so it is sometimes the case that the "stone" turns the tables on the "shell": that reality—the world viewed through nonsubjective or *scientific* means—breaks through the largely resistant surface of the poem, exposing both the arbitrariness of its representation and, to follow the parable of the Arab even further, the sheer fatuity of the Poet's will to power.

The notable instance of this reversal in book 5, as both Cynthia Chase and Paul de Man have already noted, is the episode of the Drowned Man of Esthwaite, whose "ghastly" discovery Wordsworth apparently witnessed as a boy. For de Man and Chase this episode is important chiefly as an allegory of the rhetoric of romanticism, whereby what is represented manages always to be vulnerable to the contingency of both figuration and language.[17] There is a great deal of merit to these arguments, especially Chase's extraordinarily relevant comparison of the lake—subsequently disrupted by the drowned man's body—to the specular (and mimetic) nature of the poem. Nevertheless, the episode also functions in a more specific way: namely, to reverse the customary relationship in *The Prelude* between subject and object and, in the particular example of the drowned man, the generally mystified relationship of man to nature.

The ostensible purpose of the episode is to dignify books, specifically fairy tales, whose own representations of terror were sufficiently familiar to the eight-year-old Wordsworth to gird him from the actual terror of the man "bolt upright . . . with his ghastly face" (471–72). Yet the poem's recollection of the episode (a recollection that typically suppresses the fact that the drowned man was by occupation a schoolteacher) tells a different tale altogether. In this tale, the "illusion of mastery" (as Susan Wolfson has appropriately termed it) is exposed not only in the way the experience, particularly on recollection, challenges the Poet's claims to have ever mastered it (as Wolfson shows)[18] but also in the way the drowned man himself allegorizes this very failure:

> Twilight was coming on, yet through the gloom
> I saw distinctly on the opposite shore
> A heap of garments, left as I supposed
> By one who there was bathing. Long I watched,
> But no one owned them; meanwhile the calm lake
> Grew dark. . . .
> . . . .
> . . . The succeeding day—
> Those unclaimed garments telling a plain tale—
> Went there a company, and in their boat
> Sounded with grappling-irons and long poles:

At length, the dead man, 'mid that beauteous scene
Of trees and hills and water, bolt upright
Rose with his ghastly face, a spectre shape—
Of terror even. And yet no vulgar fear,
Young as I was, a child not nine years old,
Possessed me, for my inner eye had seen
Such sights before among the shining streams
Of fairyland, the forests of romance—

(459–77)

The schoolteacher's failure to take sufficient measure of the lake—a failure *not* of science or knowledge (as evidenced, again, in Wordsworth's refusal to make the most of this coincidence)—effectively parallels and unmasks the speaker's assertion of having overcome the shock of recognition by agency of imagination. As Chase observes, the representation of the drowned man "bolt upright" imposes itself on the very text of the poem—the experience as recollected in tranquillity—in much the same way that both the young poet and "the dead man" are subjected to what in the 1799 version of this episode Wordsworth perspicaciously (after Shakespeare) termed the "accidents in flood or field" (1.280).[19] In the case of the drowned man, this imposition is substantially assisted by a teacher's failure to heed the lessons of his vocation in taking sufficient measure of the natural, physical world. The young poet's example is a little more complicated; for he is asserted not only to have borne the experience comfortably enough thanks to fairy tales, but along with the community, to have surmised it by constructing a comparatively "plain[er] tale" out of the swimmer's unclaimed garments.

Nevertheless, the fact that Wordsworth recurs to the memory in the manner he does—in the context that he does—attests less in the end to the power of imagination than to the power of "accident." It shows the ability of unrecuperated, undomesticated nature (or mere contingency)—the ability of spectacle—to offer up the subject, be it the beholder or the beheld, on the very altar of his or her illusions. It devolves, therefore, to *some other* way of seeing—to a way likely enabled by such instruments of mediation as employed by the infant prodigy (and apparently eschewed by the drowned man)—to foster an alternative mode of perception: a way of regarding the world now that, according to the *logic* of the poem and its claim for a sovereign subjectivity, must also be resisted.

III

Writing over a century later about the transformations in art currently at hand "in the age of mechanical reproduction," Walter Benjamin numbered as chief among them the dissolution or "brush[ing] aside" (as he put it) of "outmoded concepts, such as creativity and genius, eternal value and mystery—concepts whose uncontrolled (and at present almost uncontrollable) application would lead to a processing of data in the Fascist sense" (218).[20] To Benjamin this transformation was most evident in motion pictures, and it was a transformation, further, that hinged on something of a paradox: "precisely because of the thoroughgoing permeation of reality with mechanical equipment, [film offers] an aspect of reality which is free of all equipment" (234). On the face of it, this seems little more than a waggish conundrum intended to provoke or to rouse readers from complacency. However, if we return to Benjamin's initial assertion, the target of which would seem to be the mystified individual or sovereign subject—the "creator" or "genius" whose creations invariably inspire awe and adulation in the beholder—there is much to ponder in Benjamin's assertions regarding "reality" in film.

In the first, according to Benjamin, film meets or "enables the original to meet the beholder halfway" (220) by devices ranging from the mediation of the camera to the collective, nonauthoritarian nature of filmmaking (in which no single entity—neither actor, nor director, nor cameraman—holds complete sway), to the beholder's own proclivity to "distraction" (239), to which the "constant, sudden change" (238) of film is all too congenial. Second (and related to the first), the "reality" made available to the viewer (in the company of other viewers) through the filmic medium simultaneously challenges that viewer's privatizing tendencies—for example, the spectatorial "contemplation" that painting (unlike film) "invites" (238)—by restricting all affinity between the beholder and the creative genius.

To students currently wrestling with the politics of representation in film, particularly with the alleged claims of the medium on our constitution as bourgeois subjects, there is undoubtedly something sentimental, if not wrongheaded, in the "revolutionary demands" that film, in Benjamin's conception, would simultaneously exert on both art and its audience. Yet it is testimony to the power of Benjamin's observations—particularly as a corrective to the fashions of film studies in our time—that they have a virtual, if reluctant, progenitor in William Wordsworth.

That Wordsworth's largely negative representation of his response to the shows and spectacles of London in book 7 of *The Prelude* may be identified with the effect that film ideally creates according to Benjamin is not so outrageous an observation today as it might have seemed a generation ago. Despite the fact that many film historians disagree with Benjamin on the revolutionary accomplishments of film, they are in general agreement on what Michael Chanan, among others, terms the "prehistory" of film, the manifestations of which registered a "demand" that (as Benjamin himself observes of the new public art galleries in the nineteenth century) more developed and sophisticated modes of mechanical reproduction such as film would subsequently satisfy.[21]

The problem, then, has really to do with the precise nature of that demand. Chanan and other neo-Marxists tend to regard the demand within an ideological framework that traces the control and manipulation of the individual through the largely bourgeois illusion of individual autonomy that film and the film industry mutually foster. Nevertheless, we have—thanks to the reluctant testimony of Wordsworth in 1805, and to the material culture to which he was attesting—substantial evidence that Benjamin's comparatively sentimental Marxism is an equally valid, if possibly more sensitive, register of the subversive power and subversive potential of a mechanized, democratized *art:* a power to which, in the current fascination with ideological and state apparatus, we have not given nearly enough credit.

Benjamin speaks early on in "The Work of Art" of what he provocatively (and not a little ambiguously) calls the "aura" either of the work of art or of what is represented in the work of art. Using the analogy of "natural [objects]," Benjamin defines aura "as the unique phenomenon of a distance, however close it may be," and he gives an example: "If, while resting on a summer afternoon, you follow with your eyes a mountain range on the horizon or a branch which casts its shadow over you, you experience the aura of those mountains, of that branch" (222–23). In other words, "aura" must not be confused with the reality of the mountains or the reality of the branch; what aura represents is merely the experience of these phenomena from a singular, privileged, and obviously leisured vantage. For aura to exist, there must first be a unique, private, autonomous subject whose perception of the real ensures, and is reciprocally underwritten by, a sense of "the uniqueness of . . . reality" (223)—"uniqueness" being little more than a reflection of the subject's sense of self.

However with film (as with other precinematic institutions such as public art galleries and, as we seen, the Panorama and the Diorama) we discover, according to Benjamin, something altogether different. Here, "the contemporary decay" of "aura" (222), as Benjamin celebrates it, is revealed in two ways: in the reproduction and reproducibility of the image itself, which "differs [unmistakably] from the image seen by the unarmed eye"; and in the collective of nature of the viewing, which further shows "the adjustment of reality to the masses and of the masses to reality" by demonstrating "a sense of the universal equality of things" (223). Where "uniqueness and permanence" (223) invariably characterize the aura of a thing witnessed and administered by an individuated, privileged beholder, so "transitoriness" and seemingly endless "reproducibility" (223) properly describe the "real" divested of aura. Moreover, it is the "meanness" of this divestment, what Wordsworth had earlier deemed inimical to the "sublime notion of Poetry," that reflects the challenge that "reality" now—with assists obviously from various modes of production and reproduction such as the Panorama—poses to the distant, private, hitherto "unique" subject.

IV

Book 7 of *The Prelude* provides a virtual "case history" in support of Benjamin's thesis. And it does so through its reluctant, if notably spectacular, resistance to the very "aura" or sublimity to which, in its celebration of the individual poetic mind, the poem is otherwise committed. Moreover, just as Benjamin speculates, this resistance remains a function of the masses: "the comers and the goers face to face— / Face after face" (172–73), and the "sights and shows" (109)—the Panorama, the music halls, the "raree-shows" and, of course, Bartholomew Fair—that properly characterize "their" culture.

Wordsworth's aversion to London in *The Prelude* has not exactly escaped the attention of his readers, the majority of whom, it is safe to say, would prefer that it were otherwise. Peter Stallybrass and Allon White have recently argued, for example, that "Wordsworth's remote and observant solitude, his lack of intimate concern for the collectivity [as described in book 7]," reveals—"despite [the poet's] *own* kind of avowed democratic populism"—his fundamental aversion to the "bourgeois progressive and idealist strand of thinking about popular festivity to which Bakhtin"—and, I would add, Benjamin—belong.[22] There is no question that Wordsworth wishes, in retrospect, to maintain his distance and to assert his difference from all that he remembers experiencing while living in the city. We see this very clearly in his response to the Panorama. Yet the very existence of what is, in effect, Wordsworth's "London Journal" reveals how even this resistance is insufficient to suppress that "other" resistance that the masses and their culture—the art in the age of mechanical reproduction—both foster and, in so fostering, help to reproduce. To put it bluntly: what Wordsworth sees, or what he *remembers seeing* in London, he comes finally to reproduce—even if he does so reluctantly.

Initially this is not the case. Wordsworth begins "Residence in London" with a virtual analogue (actually several analogues) to the "aura" of natural objects as described by Benjamin. Reverting momentarily to the poetic present—to an interval marked by the freedom and enfranchisement to which the Poet was always destined (according to the poem) to become heir—the speaker remembers hearing "yester-even"

> A quire of redbreasts gathered somewhere near
> My threshold, minstrels from the distant woods
> And dells, sent in by Winter to bespeak
> For the old man a welcome, to announce
> With preparation artful and benign
> . . . .
> That their rough lord had left the surly north,
> And hath begun his journey. . . .
> . . . .
> And, thereafter, walking
> By later twilight on the hills I saw
> A glow-worm, from beneath a dusky shade
> Or canopy of yet unwithered fern
> Clear shining, like a hermit's taper seen
> Through a thick forest. . . .
> . . . .
> The voiceless worm on the unfrequented hills,
> Seemed sent on the same errand with the quire
> Of winter that had warbled at my door,
> And the whole year seemed tenderness and love.
> (7. 21–48)

This expatiation on the birds and on the glowworm, indulging the subject's impulse to refigure and appropriate the real, is a representation less of nature than of the speaker in complete and inviolable self-possession. The sustained (and not particularly interesting) allegory of winter, the simile of the hermit's candle and, last and most important, the representation of the year as one of tenderness and love, all derive their authenticity from a proximity to, and as a reflection of, the mind capriciously beholding them. However, when the Poet begins to recall his experience in London, and the effect of the sights and shows of that city at the time he initially experienced them, the effect is to loosen the hold of the "enfranchised" Wordsworth over the very space and time of which he appears in total command.

The "loosening" begins even before the Poet actually enters London, as he recalls his fantasies about the city prior to visiting it, all of which transport him, even as "imaginations" (136), into a world of veritable "distraction." Although composed of the usual landmarks—"St Paul's," "the tombs of Westminster," "Bedlam," "the Monument, and Armoury of the Tower"—this "fond[ly]" imagined world is sufficient to preclude the control and self-possession demonstrated in the previous descriptions of nature. But it is ultimately up to "the real scene" (139) with its "motley imagery" (150) to effect a change that only "science"—with its particular resistance to the subject—has managed, however indirectly, to accomplish in the poem thus far:

> the quick dance
> Of colours, lights and forms, the Babel din,
> The endless stream of men and moving things,
> . . . .
> The wealth, the bustle and the eagerness,
> The glittering chariots with their pampered steeds,
> Stalls, barrows, porters, midway in the street
> The scavenger that begs with hat in hand,
> The labouring hackney-coaches, the rash speed
> Of coaches travelling far, . . .
> . . . .
> Here, there, and everywhere, a weary throng,
> The comers and the goers face to face—
> Face after face—the string of dazzling wares,

Shop after shop, with symbols, blazoned names,
And all the tradesman's honours overhead.
. . . .
And sights and sounds that come at intervals,
. . . a raree-show is here
With children gathered round, another street
Presents a company of dancing dogs,
Or dromedary with an antic pair
Of monkies on his back, a minstrel-band
Of Savoyards, single and alone,
An English ballad-singer. Private courts,
Gloomy as coffins, and unsightly lanes
. . . .
May then entangle us awhile,
Conducted through those labyrinths unawares
To privileged regions and inviolate,
Where from their aery lodges studious lawyers
Look out on waters, walks, and gardens green.
(156–204)

I quote from *The Prelude* at length, not only to make absolutely clear the extent to which distraction has taken precedence over intention in this section but to illustrate the process by which the reproduction of the London spectacle leads inevitably (or so it appears) to an objectification and critique of a privatized, poetic vantage. Caught up in a spectacular whirl that, even upon recollection, holds sway over the shaping powers of imagination and symbolic control, the Poet is finally removed by "the masses" away from the very station or identity which not two hundred lines previously appeared so "inviolate."

We see this transformation most clearly in the sequence of images (and pejoratives) with which the description is brought temporarily to a halt, beginning with the "English ballad singer [single and alone]," and culminating in the scene *as seen* from the "privileged regions" of the inns of court. Linking these two descriptions, furthermore, is the somewhat pointed reference to "private courts / Gloomy as coffins." It is probably tendentious to claim that this judgment on the "private" finds a comparable, equally adverse counterpart in the objectification or displacement of poetic identity in the body of the "single [singer]." Nevertheless, a privatized vantage is clearly *not* what Wordsworth is experiencing at the moment or inclined to reproduce. The comparatively tepid description of the world viewed from the inns of court is more than simply a surmise offered in lieu of an actual experience; indeed, it remains, in its peculiar "absent-minded[ness]" (Benjamin, 241), evidence of the "shock effect," as Benjamin describes it (238), that the "sight of immediate reality" (233) has had on the hitherto contemplative subject.

To Benjamin this shock effect is most readily available in the experience of the cinema. And, not surprisingly, it devolves upon such precinematic institutions as the Panorama (244–80) and the music hall (281–310), in addition to such related "adjustment[s] of reality to the masses" as Bartholomew Fair or the Exeter Change menagerie,[23] to force repeated shocks upon the fabric of Wordsworth's text and on the constitution of the hero represented therein. The issue, however, is not necessarily the poet's prescience in both intuiting and reproducing (albeit reluctantly) an art better served by mechanical agency. The situation is, in fact, a little more complicated. Like the treatment of the prodigy in book 5, book 7 is largely about the *resistance* of spectacle (or of the tyranny of the eye, as Wordsworth later describes it) in the experience of spectacle. In other words, like the opposition of prodigies, which book 5 alternately promotes and deconstructs, the resistance waged by spectacle in book 7 is at base a resistance to spectacle that, only by circuit of repression, becomes a capitulation to the visible and to the dramatic changes in the subject that spectacle effects.

This particular dynamic achieves its most complete and conclusive demonstration in the well-known encounter with the blind beggar (609–23), whose overall effect on the speaker amply justifies the seemingly excessive designation of the man as "spectacle." At first glance, the sight of the "blind beggar, who, with upright face, / Stood propped against a wall, upon his chest / Wearing a written paper, to explain / The story of . . . who he was" (612–15), seems hardly deserving of its designation as "spectacle" (616), especially in comparison to other descriptions in book 7. If anything, the experience of seeing the beggar appears more closely aligned with Benjaminian aura, conveying to the Poet "the unique phenomenon of a distance" despite the beggar's rather close proximity. This is echoed, furthermore, in the Poet's reaction to "view[ing]" the man "amid the moving moving pageant" (610–11), whom he "look[s at], / As if admonished from another world" (622–23).

And yet, if the Poet remembers experiencing the aura of the beggar, his rather circumspect "as if" simultaneously indicates a decay of aura, or an ability to separate the object *from* its aura, which justifies the beggar's designation as spectacle. It is the anatomizing of aura by the beggar—his exposure of a suddenly unwarranted interposition of distance between subject and object—that renders him a spectacle and alerts the beholder to precisely which "worlds" the blind man (with and without aura) is alternately a reproduction of.

Hence, the blind beggar turns out to be less a spectacle in his own right than an object whose resistance to "aura" reveals just how spectacle, the spectacle of London, has been sufficient to wean the beholder from his privileged identity as a private subject. It is important, for example, that the beggar materialize accidentally rather than intentionally, that it is the Poet's "chance," rather than his wish, "abruptly to be smitten with the view / Of a blind beggar" (610–12). And it is even more important, if inevitable by now, that the immediate efforts to reverse this balance of power or "might"—to smite the view with symbolic language—all founder on the "world" viewed:

> My mind did at this spectacle turn round
> As with the might of waters, and it seemed
> To me that in this label was a type
> Or emblem of the utmost that we know
> Both of ourselves and of the universe.
> (616–20)

It may be objected, certainly, that the final transformation of the beggar into a representative man is simply another way of conferring aura on an otherwise proximate, neutral aspect of reality. Yet these objections are easily answered by recalling that aura, as Benjamin conceives it, pertains to an object's "unique existence" (and, by implication, to the uniqueness of its beholder, of whom the object is a reflection), whereas here uniqueness ultimately gives way to a "plurality of copies" (Benjamin, 221), of which beggar and beholder are equal versions.

Even so, to ascribe as dark a view as the Poet does to human knowledge will strike many readers as a pathetic fallacy. Yet the seeming tragedy and apparent arbitrariness of this pronouncement must be weighed once more against the triumph of knowledge (or of science again) *over subjectivity* in the "spectacle" of the beggar. It is not, in other words, that we are all, according to the speaker, blind supplicants casting about in a universe over which we have absolutely no control (though this is a way, certainly, to read the passage). Rather, it is Wordsworth's altogether more subtle point that the world viewed independent of, or in opposition to, subjective controls is all we really know on earth and all we need to know. Indeed, the "utmost that we know" is not "blindness" as symbolized by the beggar; it is what is *gained* by virtue of the beggar's *resistance* to symbol as he literally wriggles out from one designation after another—from "label," to "type," to "emblem." The "[o]ther world" from which the speaker is "admonished" is no longer some transcendental or metaphysical order apprehended by imagination. Rather, in a total recanting of the "passage" from the "earthly" to the "celestial," this world is the sublunary, visible, historical world whose "knowledge" is suddenly accessible thanks to the sights and shows of London.[24]

V

The episode of the beggar, and the larger episode to which his "spectacle" is attached, can be said, then, to recover a decidedly revolutionary, or, as Burke would call it, "subversive," aspect of spectacle that more recent studies of spectacle are inclined to minimize. It is more often argued that spectacle—despite its experience of free play—is "a *containment* . . . in which awareness of any realities other than the spectacular gives way to a pervading image of sense as something that simply happens, shows forth, but that can't be told."[25] Using cinema as the *locus classicus* of spectacular containment, Dana Polan interprets the "will-to-spectacle" in film to "asser[t] that a world of foreground is the only world that matters or is the only world that *is*" (135). Grounded, he contends, in a "philosophy of realist individuation," spectacle effectively sees to it that the "imagistic surface of the world" militates against "any depth of involvement with that world" (137).

This sense of spectacle as a vehicle conducive to the very detachment that spectacle (I would argue) actively resists undoubtedly owes much to the paradigms of film study, which has long lamented the hegemonic discourse to which the cinema, especially in its classic formulation, has proven permeable. But there are also a number of problems with this assertion, all of which cluster around the issue of history. One problem, to be sure, is the absence of a history of cinematic spectacle: namely, the spectacles and other institutions of seeing such as the Diorama, all of which anticipate the revolutionary, nonindividuating cinema as Benjamin conceives it.

A more immediate problem involves the history that spectacle makes readable, the "world" upon which spectacle necessarily opens. For this turns out to be the very world that spectacle, according to Polan, necessarily suppresses: a world whose otherness, accessibility, and "incomprehensibility" (to borrow Schlegel's term again) distinguish it from a world that is defamiliarized in the guise of being understood. The "world," certainly the world Polan wants to see represented and thereby understood, will undoubtedly render any art a version of containment. Nevertheless, what makes Wordsworth's spectacle—or the spectacle of the blind beggar—so special and so prescient is precisely its ability to foreground, and paradoxically to see through, blindness. While blindness is surely a characteristic of the sighted object, it is at the same time an admonishment that only the *visible* spectacle of the blind man can perform. The beggar, to be sure, stands distinct from the world. But he remains, like the detached speaker in his image, "amid" a world whose peculiar, suddenly visible, otherness is at once a function of and a challenge to the speaker's blinding self-consciousness: a consciousness that, commensurate with a blindness brought suddenly into visible relief, is less specular and more spectacular and self-reflexive.

The potential of spectacle not only to admit an historical "other" but, in the process, to relocate the beholder within a world previously inadmissible can be further illustrated by recalling what spectacle would have meant to Wordsworth. We have already seen the spectacle to which London, in retrospect, appears tantamount. However, this sense of London, where spectacle and the "world" are demonstrably equivalent, also owes something to spectacle per se—to spectacle in a somewhat narrower, theatrical sense—whose peculiar resonance, and responsiveness to the world, Wordsworth undoubtedly knew first hand. And he knew this (as several commentators have variously suggested) in light of his experience in France at the time of the Revolution, which, though mostly chronicled in subsequent books of *The Prelude,* not only predates but quite literally flanks the *represented* London of book 7, informing the "spectacle" therein.[26]

Wordsworth is by no means alone in understanding spectacle to be the conjunction of foreground and background or, with special reference to France again, as that "imagistic surface" on which the real world is always traceable. Wordsworth is anticipated in this conception by none other than Burke himself, whose excessively graphic account of the "atrocious spectacle" of October 6, 1789, in which Louis XVI and Marie Antoinette were chased from their bedchambers by a "band of cruel ruffians and assassins," forces Burke "directly into a meditation on the nature of spectacle itself" (Mitchell, *Iconology,* 145). In "such spectacles," writes Burke,

> we learn great lessons; because in events like these our passions instruct our reason; because when kings are hurl'd from their thrones by the Supreme Director of this great drama, and become the objects of insult to the base, and of pity to the good, we behold such disasters in the moral, as we should behold a miracle in the physical order of things. We are alarmed into reflexion; our minds . . . are purified by terror and pity; our weak unthinking pride is humbled, under the dispensations of a mysterious wisdom.—Some tears might be drawn from me, if such a spectacle were exhibited on the stage. I should be truly ashamed of finding in myself that superficial, theatric sense of painted distress, whilst I could exult over it in real life. With such a perverted mind, I could never venture to shew my face at a tragedy.[27]

Although Burke clearly means to underscore the similarity between theatrical tragedy and the "spectacle" which (as Mitchell observes) he has himself created, there exists, by Burke's own demonstration, a very crucial difference between spectacle and tragedy. The difference is in the way "spectacle"—thanks chiefly to its composition from the "physical order of things" or from the "real" world (specifically the events "of the 6th of October")—supersedes theatrical tragedy by working to eliminate the so-called "invisible wall" between drama and life. Burke, for his part, would retain this wall in order that we may continue to read and respond appropriately to the tragedy of "real life." But it is spectacle's function to militate against this restoration (and the catharsis that attends it) by "alarm[ing us] into reflection," by which art and life, spectacle and spectator, are effectively intermixed.

Reflection, in other words—the response into which we, the spectator, are alarmed or interpellated by spectacle—is coextensive with the reflection whereby "life" is simultaneously spectacularized and set free. Thus it is especially fitting that Burke, in describing the deliberations of the French Assembly several pages earlier, depicts a theater with no stage, where vision and response, text and world, are necessarily permeated by one another:

> The Assembly . . . acts before them the farce of deliberation with as little decency as liberty. They act like the comedians of a fair before a riotous audience; they act amidst the tumultuous cries of a mixed mob of ferocious men, and of women lost to shame, who, according to their insolent fancies, direct, control, applaud, explode them; and sometimes mix and take their seats amongst them; domineering over them with a strange mixture of servile petulance and proud presumptuous authority. As they have inverted order in all things, the gallery is in the place of the house. This Assembly, which overthrows kings and kingdoms, has not even the physiognomy and aspect of a grave legislative body. . . . They have a power given to them, like that of the evil principle, to subvert and destroy; but none to construct, except such machines as may be fitted for further subversion and further destruction (161).

Burke, to be sure, attempts to naturalize the "order [of] things" by summoning the "physiognomy . . . of a grave legislative body." However, it is hardly surprising that one function of the spectacle he describes would be to expose this mystification by allowing the "body"—the group of men and women—to distinguish itself from, and ultimately to displace, any other embodiment or form.

A similar (and similarly deconstructable) opposition obtains in the machinelike status of the mob. For in the same way that the spectacle of men and women quite literally interrupts and demystifies the legislative body, so the attempt to reconstruct or to refigure the mob as a body whose function is solely to produce machines emphasizes the "further subversion" through which spectacle by introjection of the world—by replacement of personification with persons—resists both naturalization and the imaginative, artistic authority that attends it. Burke suggests as much when he comments subsequently on the "perversion" that the "profane burlesque" visits upon a "sacred institute" (161). For although Burke clearly means to criticize the spectacle of the Assembly, what he witnesses (or allows spectacle to represent) amounts now to an *institution* of the profane. The distinction between the sacred and the profane that Burke draws would no doubt limit his horror (and his "alarm") to an authoritative claim. However, it is a claim that ultimately founders, and a horror—accordingly—that proliferates, in the way the spectacle merely institutes, or restages, the very machinery it is not.

Wordsworth, as we have seen, certainly shares Burke's aversion to spectacle. Yet, unlike Burke, Wordsworth is apparently willing to grant spectacle a function in *The Prelude* as "another" way of alarming him into reflection.[28] Theatricality and the Revolution are linked less, then, according to Wordsworth's conservatism and to the antitheatricality endemic to his private, mediative posture. Indeed they are linked because, as Burke suggests (and as Wordsworth himself could not but have recognized), spectacle had threatened at one time and in one place to characterize almost everything. Spectacle, in this way, involves more than a visual chaos or the conflation of the sacred and the profane; it encompasses the subject-position that obtains when horror can no longer be directed outward, when the spectacle of the beggar is by turns the spectacle of oneself: the knowledge of a spectator/actor "amid" the "moving pageant." This transformation is echoed in the very language of Wordsworth's description of the beggar, which necessarily recalls Burke's vertiginously alarming spectacle. But where this *vertige* immediately becomes a modern-day catharsis for Burke ("We are alarmed into reflection; our minds . . . are purified by terror and pity"), "mak[ing] revolution," as Mary Jacobus argues, "the paradigm of Tragedy" (368), it signals the admission of history to *The Prelude* and the permeability of an aesthetic, or humanistic field, to what the speaker (referring earlier to the Winander boy and subsequently to the "unmoving man" amid the moving scene) calls "knowledge."

I propose, then, that the experience of France at the time of the Revolution, which Wordsworth recollects in books 9 and 10 of *The Prelude,* is more accurately represented in the earlier description of London where the Poet's complicity with the Revolution, so to speak, is less a matter of displacement or of guilt than of being caught up in a "moving pageant" in which the word and the world, self and society, are continually indistinguishable. In a recent article that attempts, like Jacobus's, to historicize Wordsworth's aesthetics by attending to his aestheticization of history, Reeve Parker begins "by placing Wordsworth in the audience at the Théâtre de la République, Rue de Richelieu, on the evening of November 26, 1792, at the *représentation pre-*

mière of one of the more bizarre spectacles of revolutionary Paris theatre, an *Othello* contrived by the playwright Jean-François Ducis, the best-known eighteenth-century French adaptor of Shakespeare."[29] Parker admits to having "no warrant for putting [Wordsworth] in the audience" apart from the fact that the poet was in residence at the time. Yet he does so for the purpose of underscoring the bearing of the French *Othello*—which suppressed Iago's treachery and denigrated Desdemona's loyalty to her father—on Wordsworth's postrevolutionary play, *The Borderers.*

With respect to *The Borderers,* which bears the marks of the "tendentious, propagandistic spectacles" of Paris (despite repudiating their function), a great deal is gained by locating Wordsworth in the theater on November 26. But with reference to *The Prelude,* specifically the London section, which is postrevolutionary in fact (or compositionally) but not in substance or in disposition, it is no longer necessary to confine Wordsworth to a specific seat. All that is necessary really is that Wordsworth have been in Paris in 1792 inasmuch as being there at that moment was tantamount to being in the theater. Marvin Carlson puts the point succinctly in his authoritative study, *The Theatre of the French Revolution.*[30] "While the Revolution entered the theatre," he writes, "affecting audience, actors, and repertoires, theatrical manifestations now also entered the Revolution, and when the nation celebrated the anniversary of the fall of the Bastille with a grandiose Festival of Federation" (on the very day, it turns out, that Wordsworth arrived in France), "theatrical people were not surprisingly among the leading contributors to the occasion" (34). Like the London of *The Prelude,* then—a London mediated by the experiences in France that both preceded and followed Wordsworth's stay there—Paris had no place, not even for the displaced Burkean xenophobe, as we have seen, to stand apart: no place, that is, which was *not* the theater and no spectacle that was not Paris.

Nor is this simply a conceit, or a way to wax theoretical about events and about a time when the quotidian and the excessive were increasingly indistinguishable. Rather, the spectacularization of the quotidian, the normalization of the spectacle, and the destabilizing effect of this interchange upon an audience that was alternately the object of its own regard were quite literally facts of life in revolutionary Paris. Parker is undoubtedly correct in emphasizing the tendentious character of the Parisian theater during the Revolution which, in the years of the Terror particularly, was constrained to serve Jacobin interests with uncompromising severity. What it is not to his purpose to emphasize, however, with respect to either France or Wordsworth, is the radical as opposed to revolutionary aspect of spectacle in the years and months preceding the Terror: namely, the breakdown of hierarchy and, with it, the privatized spectatorial vantage that public spectacle in France effectively accomplished.

This breakdown was reflected first and foremost in the theater itself. In the years preceding and leading up to the Revolution, not only did the theater expand beyond the Comédie Française, the Comédie Italienne, and the Opéra to include twenty-three new (hitherto illegal) theaters with a combined seating capacity virtually equal to the entire population of Paris (Carlson, 111); the theater had managed, commensurate with the virtual (or at least potential) incorporation of the citizenry within it walls, to reproduce that influx in a variety of ways. Chief among these reproductions, of course, were plays, among them Beaumarchais's *The Marriage of Figaro* and later Chénier's *Charles IX,* that spoke directly to the political and social transformations currently at hand.

But the more crucial transformation involved what can only be described as a permeability of spectacle to audience and of audience to spectacle such as would horrify Burke. This permeability was figured noticeably in the galleries of the new theaters, where, as Simon Schama describes it, "drastically different social worlds were pressed together like sardines."[31] And it figured more pointedly in situations in which the spectacle was the audience—for example, the Palais-Royal,

> where promenading, . . . gazing, and inspecting were a major pastime, [with] conditions and classes . . . indiscriminately jumbled together. In the melee it was easy to mistake a flashily dressed courtesan . . . for a countess. . . . Young soldiers dressed to impress girls with their uniforms, on which insignia of rank were either unmarked and indeterminate. In their black robes noble magistrates from the Parlement were dressed in much the same fashion as humble barristers and clerks. And it is evident that contemporaries relished this social potpourri. Louis-Sébastien Mercier, who had railed against the boulevards for encouraging feeble-minded dissipation among "honest citizens," adored the Palais-Royal, where he witnessed "the confusion of estates, the mixture, the throng." And Mayeur de Saint-Paul, who wrote

> even more lyrically, insisted that "all orders of citizens are joined together, from the lady of rank to the dissolute, from the soldier of distinction to the humblest official in the Farms." (136)[32]

At this point, needless to say, we are very near the "blank confusion" (7.696) of Wordsworth's London, where the "swarm of . . . inhabitants" are "melted and reduced / To one identity" (699–704). The difference, of course, is that, where the melting pot is a source of delectation and excitement for the French citizen, a means by which, as Schama contends, the subject effectively submits to his or her construction as citizen, it poses a threat to a subject not yet inured to his place in the community of men and women. London for Wordsworth is a place where knowledge—a recognition of the subject's place in time and space—is necessarily purchased with loss of power and individuation.

The blind beggar is undoubtedly the key instance of this spectacular exchange, which is both a resistance to and, more importantly, a resistance *by* spectacle. But it is far from the only resistance. Not twenty lines earlier, the Poet remembers saying to himself that "the face of every one / That passes by me is a mystery" (597–98). As in the spectacle of the beggar, the apparent mystification of the object (with its allusion to still another theatrical category) leads by turns to the demystification of the subject, whose sudden knowledge of the world prohibits him at last from seeing his own face in everyone he meets. Accordingly, the "mystery" the speaker bestows on every face he sees serves not only to mystify these objects in a somewhat desperate assertion of individual authority; it marks the deference to a world that is mysterious only to the extent that it is fathomable, visible, as if for the first time.

> And all the ballast of familiar life—
> The present, and the past, hope, fear, all stays,
> All laws of acting, thinking, speaking man—
> Went *from me,* neither knowing me, nor known.
> (604–7, emphasis added)

Such resistance to an individual perspective, where knowledge previously figures the capacity to be known (and vice versa), is generally an exception to *The Prelude* and to its representation of the Poet's enfranchisement. Nor is it long before "Residence in London" gets subordinated, along with the Poet's revolutionary disappointment, to a more "familiar" narrative structure that brackets the sights and shows of London (and the history behind them) into an interval in which "paradise" is necessarily, but only temporarily, lost. Still, in the very way that the infant prodigy earlier exerts pressure on his humanistic counterpart, the Winander boy, so it is similarly the case that the Wordsworth once shorn of power marshals the "knowledge" purchased by agency of spectacle *against* the "Wordsworth" returned to full strength.

When in book 11, for example, the Poet speaks reverentially of the "spots of time" (257)—the privileged moments of imagination that continually remind him of his potential as an enfranchised individual—it should not surprise us that the spots, whose liberating effects may be observed in their opposition to "the most despotic of our senses" (173)—the "eye" (171)—are simultaneously moments in which "the mind / Is lord and master, and that outward sense / Is but the obedient servant of her will" (270–72).

I will not linger over the obvious contradiction in this claim, where despotism in one instance becomes liberation in the other. I want only to suggest that such contradictions as do exist in the final books of *The Prelude* (or for that manner in many of the poet's "high romantic" works) are less a result of blindness or unawareness (as observed by some including Hartman and de Man) than of a consciousness—what Benjamin later described as "unconscious optics" (237)—that recognizes all too well the truth of being made "subservient . . . to the great ends of liberty and power" (11.182–83).

CHAPTER FIVE

Lamb and Hazlitt: Romantic Antitheatricality and the Body of Genius

I

Despite the fact that the London theater grew substantially during the romantic period, with the enlargement of the two main patent houses (Covent Garden and Drury Lane) and the evolution of spectacle, pantomime, and melodrama (all of which were performed in a variety of newer venues), and despite the fact, too, that many of the Romantics, notably Coleridge, Byron, and Hazlitt, were actively involved in the theater at one time or another during the first decades of the new century, one of the central characteristics of British romanticism, in the estimation of a virtually every critic and historian, remains its antitheatrical bent. My formulation, then, already admits a certain resistance to this consensus—but the resistance that I propose to discuss comes from something more than a simple contradiction that tracks the permeability of an avant-garde movement to the very world to which it is necessarily opposed. The resistance endemic to romantic antitheatricality, like the resistance to and by spectacle in *The Prelude,* begins *according to* the conventional wisdom: it accepts and even draws strength from the fact that the Romantics were not only an antitheatrical coterie (despite their demonstrated interest in things theatrical) but were strangely justified in this particular—some might argue paradoxical—antipathy.

To speak of the Romantics' "justification" in any issue, much less in this one, represents a challenge to the conceptions of romanticism now current, many of which take a rather dim view of the privatizing—and, in the case of drama, clearly closeted—tendencies of a movement whose alleged radicalism or republicanism appears, in the minds of most romanticists today, attenuated by a prevailing inwardness. Nor does this sense of the Romantics' justification accord much better with the "old" historicism, which can scarcely overlook the puritan origins of the romantic aversion to the theater.[1] My conception, then, of a justified antipathy to the theater effectively stares both the new and the old historicism in the face—but not, it must be emphasized, by some mystified indifference to fact. It is precisely fact that forms the basis of such a view. For despite the ideals of privacy, privilege, and individual genius that routinely inform romantic encounters with the theater, the established theater in the early nineteenth century (as distinct from the open-air theaters of both France and urban London) was the scene more of crisis than of change.

This is not to suggest that the theater was not a popular forum in these years and the gathering place for an increasingly heterogeneous, always vocal, audience. It is simply to observe that unlike the contemporaneous institutions of the Panorama, and later the Diorama, which were products of a public they managed both to attract and to construct, the theater in the age of Kemble, Kean, and Siddons (among other actors) was, for all its seeming variousness, a fundamentally conservative and increasingly irrelevant institution.[2] Much of this conservatism can be seen in the repertoire, which was dominated by Shakespeare (including such bowdlerized plays as Colley Cibber's *Richard III* and Nahum Tate's *Lear*) and, in Shakespeare's absence, either by Jonson and Beaumont and Fletcher or by more recent but decidedly conventional playwrights such as Sheridan and his Restoration predecessors (Donohue, *Theatre,* 84–104).

Furthermore, the theatrical works that premiered during the romantic period, including Gothic dramas and melodramas, were characterized less by innovation than (the complaints of Coleridge and others notwithstanding) by an unflinching morality. In the case of melodrama, this morality exceeded virtually all bounds of mimetic plausibility as the meek and the good were bound by convention to inherit the earth, no matter how intractable and unpredictable that environment. And then, there was the physical arrangement of the theater itself. Partitioned into the pit, the gallery, and the essentially panoptic box whose inhabitants (following the restoration of both patent houses) were empowered to see without being seen, the theater, as Joseph Donohue details, worked largely to "contai[n] a socially stratified society." "Despite a certain mobility reflected in the seating choices made by some members of this audience," writes Donohue, "patrons had [in selecting one or another of these three possibilities] in effect identified themselves, at least for the evening, as being of a certain class of spectator" (*Theatre,* 150).

The very nature of this mobility, to be sure, chiefly the masquerade of forsaking one's accustomed or proper place, does not lack for subversive intent, any more than the "Old Price" riots that gallery and pit goers waged in 1809 to protest an increase in both ticket prices and the number of private boxes reflect a desire merely to return to an older, more established order.[3] As a public place, and as an institution dependent on the public, the theater—like the Panorama—was necessarily responsive to change, even if by change I mean a widening rather than a consolidation of social groups (Donohue, *Theatre* 150). Nevertheless, unlike the Panorama and the Diorama, both of which militated against that division—including the division implicit in the romantic subject-position of enfranchised individuality—the theater, with its conservative or concessionary bent, proved less a challenge to the Romantics than a foil. Indeed, even so obvious an accommodation as the right of the people, chiefly those in the pit, to air opinions vocally during a theatrical performance was less a response to public pressure—a radical or mass initiative—than a centuries-old sanction.

Faced with an institution that managed to preserve a stratified society and to contain that society by, among other means, containing subversion or revolt (the theaters' response to the old price revolts, for example, was to roll back prices, thereby placating the masses), the Romantics were on uniquely solid ground in opposing theatricality. The characteristic romantic turn from the theater—either through closet drama (deliberately unperformable plays such as Wordsworth's *The Borderers,* Byron's *Manfred,* and Shelley's *Prometheus Unbound*) or through the so-called theater of the mind, against which any actual performance of a play might be found wanting by a romantic critic—is scarcely beyond reproach, much less ideology.[4] My point is simply that nowhere is the privatizing impulse more *justified* in British romanticism: the "self" that holds itself in opposition to theater during the romantic period, whether by the creation of plays that defy theatrical production or through a necessary resistance to the production of just about any play (most especially those of Shakespeare), is a self in opposition to the very containment in which there is no place, no role, for the individual. Thus, where a revisionist approach to romantic inwardness would undoubtedly position this "opposing self" in one of the boxes whose very privacy figures the privileged isolation of the romantic subject, the romantic aversion to theater is, at least in part, an aversion to *that* structural mandate as well.

That romantic antitheatricality ultimately represents an aversion to the box and the pit alike, to an institution whose particular containment or manipulation of the people permits the romantic writer to cast off the role of "citizen"—or as man speaking to men—is doubtless its least attractive consequence. Yet it is an effect, strangely, that the Romantics are alternately capable of exposing and, in the example of Coleridge, as I will show, of even correcting. And, again, it devolves upon the theater: not the actual theater this time but a hypothetical or repressed theater—a theater of the "mind's eye," if you will—to adumbrate and finally to manage this contradiction.[5]

A theater of the mind's eye must be distinguished, then, from the "mental theater," as Byron termed it, that we customarily associate with romanticism.[6] The former, far from subsuming a visible, sensible order within a strictly visionary or personal framework, actually reconstitutes and imagines a visible order in ways that the theater of the time, encumbered by numerous conventions, simply could not. Such a theater works (much like London in *The Prelude*) to return the opposing self to the world, transforming genius into a visible or fleshly rather than omniscient entity. In so doing, it represents the final stroke—the belated and often repressed countermovement—of romantic antitheatricality as it is customarily understood and as the Romantics, for their part, routinely expressed it. Working less in accordance with a challenge posed by the actual theater, such a theater operates more in conjunction with a challenge posed by the antitheatrical prejudice of the day. In its peculiar preoccupation with a uniquely sensible (if still hypothetical) world, with a world subject to the unities and constraints of space, time, and culture, such a "theater" necessarily counts on the justifiable turn from theater as a necessary first step, whose theatricalization *in turn* is both possible and also necessary.

Like other aspects of the visible in British romanticism, including (as we have just seen) Wordsworth's spectacular resistance to spectacle, the romantic theater of the mind's eye figures a refinement of the very republicanism to which the Romantics, even in the aftermath of the French Revolution, were committed. The significance of the individual, chiefly the individual lives of the poets themselves, which was so much a feature of romantic writing and, for better or worse, of the "romantic ideology" during this period, remains in the vicissitudes of romantic antitheatricality—and in the visible world it alternately substitutes for the actual theater—a prelude rather than a dead end. In what is ultimately a reflexive turn, genius or the individual mind—the mystified source and site of representation according to romanticism—is systematically "brought down," in Lamb's apt description of this new theater, to the "standard of flesh and blood" (1:98).[7]

Thus when Lamb, apropos of the "level[ling of] all distinctions" on stage, speaks of the revulsion he experiences at the "actual sight" of the "courtship and wedded caresses" of Othello and Desdemona, or when Hazlitt, in his well-known review of Kemble's *Coriolanus,* is moved by the example of the central character into an indictment of imagination as an "anti-levelling" faculty that is both "monopolizing" and "aristocratical," or when Coleridge, in his 1812 lecture, literally glimpses Hamlet, whose "greatness of genius . . . [leads him] to a perfect knowledge of his own character," as "a man *living* in meditation" (my emphasis), each of these critics is referring less to an actual performance (though Hazlitt was no doubt provoked by Kemble's "representation") than to a *hypothetical* actualization: a performance wherein genius—whether it be Hamlet's "knowledge," or Coriolanus's "power," or Othello's "mind"—is variously subverted by the body in which it is housed and by the visible field to which that body is in turn restricted.

Such a transformation, as a rule, is not immediately welcomed by the Romantics—not even by Coleridge, whose visibly static Hamlet interrupts and inverts a larger argument for Shakespeare, who, in "appeal[ing] to the imagination & not to the senses," is otherwise "above the iron compulsion of space & time." Nevertheless, as the example of Coleridge will confirm—and as we have already seen in both Wordsworth and Constable—the romantic tendency to expose, indeed to conceive, a visible world (however actualized), in contrast to an inner world of imagination, must be understood apart from the pejoratives with which it was almost always visited. As the example of romantic antitheatricality shows, in fact, what is often available to the "bodily eye" during the romantic period must also be understood as that lack or gap that, in characteristically bad faith, the Romantics are inclined to demonize but that, in paradoxically good faith and by some inevitable turn of mind, they are disposed by turns to admit.

II

Of the three romantic commentators—Lamb, Hazlitt, and Coleridge—whose engagement with the theater in the early nineteenth century gives the fullest sense of the possibilities and permutations of the antitheatrical bias at this time, Charles Lamb is probably the most conventional and also, paradoxically, the most extreme. In a series of essays, notably "On the Tragedies of Shakespeare, Considered with Reference to Their Fitness for Stage Representation" (1811), "On the Artificial Comedy of the Last Century" (1822–23), and "Stage Illusion" (1825), Lamb set forth what many construe to be the quintessential, if somewhat simplified, romantic attitude to theater.[8] This view is that the actual performance of a play, especially one by Shakespeare, represents an assault upon the beholder's "mind"—whose "slow apprehension" of the "power of originating poetical images and conceptions" in the act of "reading"—is "thus crampt and pressed down to the measure of a strait-lacing actuality" (1:97–99).

It would be easy to construe Lamb's complaint as simply an attack on actual performances of Shakespeare. But the fact remains that Lamb's consideration of the problem turns less on a given performance of Shakespeare (including Kemble's Hamlet and Mrs. Siddons's Lady Macbeth, to which he alludes only cryptically and in passing) than on a very specific, very privileged, communion with the text, *only after which* the "body and bodily action" as "shewn to our bodily eye" are threatening and "revolting" (1:108). Although Lamb argues, and indeed means to argue, that "the plays of Shakespeare are less calculated for performance on a stage, than those of almost any dramatist whatever" (1:99), he ends up describing something else.[9] He describes a challenge posed to a particular subject-position, which he calls "reading," by something that he terms "performance" or "acting" but that, in the absence of a specific production, seems more a reduction of the world to flesh. Lamb's quarrel in his Shakespeare essay is less with the "artificial world" of the theater, as he protests it both here and elsewhere,[10] than with the real world: with the world of "bodies"—black and white, male and female—the mere sight of which is sufficient to wrench "the reader" from his solitary stance of "meditation" into a corporality, and a visibility, by which any disagreement or difference with community is immediately collapsed.

Lamb's squeamishness regarding the body and its functions is essentially about hierarchy, about the very "aristocratical" position of difference that Hazlitt would shortly declaim against in his review of *Coriolanus,* yet against which only the physical world—in Lamb's formulation, one body as perceived by another—continually proves a challenge.[11] Hazlitt's attack on power, chiefly the "monopolizing faculty" of the imagination, is not inconsistent with his generally tortuous effort to save the "spirit of the age" from a tendency to "ris[e] above the ordinary standards of sufferings and crimes"—a tendency that Hazlitt himself is disposed elsewhere (most notoriously in his defense of Napoleon) to support. Lamb, by contrast, admits no such complication. In fact, it is only by the sheer virulence of his position that a reaction of sorts takes place. This reaction comes most clearly in his discussions of *Othello* and, following it, *King Lear,* where his rhetoric becomes heated to the point of undecidability. For here at last, the particular relation of a visible field, to both romantic antitheatricality and the theatrical world it would repress, makes it difficult for Lamb to function as a critic, or to confine himself to showing the bad effects of an actual performance of Shakespeare.

Although Lamb's argument against performance begins with a quietistic description of the pleasures of reading versus "the instantaneous nature of the impressions which we take in at the eye and ear at a playhouse" (1:98), it soon modulates to a more sublime pitch, moving gradually from the reader in a closet to an intersubjective encounter with Hamlet in his closet. After making his much-quoted assertion that Shakespeare's plays "are less calculated for performance on a stage" than those of any other writer, Lamb offers some additional observations. He observes, presumably to justify his larger claim, that "their distinguished excellence is a reason that they should be so." Then, as if to qualify what he means by "excellence," Lamb observes that "there is so much in [the plays], which comes not under the province of acting, with which eye, and tone, and gesture, have nothing to do" (99). Shakespeare's plenitude, which is arguably a disposition of the works themselves, becomes on closer inspection a hermeneutic plenitude or fullness of understanding. It happens by rejection of one signifying practice—the interpretation of gesture by the eye—in deference to another, less sensible, practice on which "so much" in Shakespeare effectively depends. Thanks, that is, to a virtually invisible respondent, and through the sequestered agency "of the understanding in reading" (98), Shakespeare is suddenly fathomable.

Lamb is obviously not discounting Shakespeare's contribution to his own "distinguished excellence." But neither is he promoting

Shakespeare's excellence over, or apart from, the increasingly mystified distinction of its discovery. This is so much the case that the ensuing discussion of *Hamlet,* specifically those aspects of Hamlet's character that prove unsuitable for the stage, points less to the hero on the page than to the character of the reader, of whom Hamlet is almost a foreshadowing:

> But Hamlet himself—what does he suffer meanwhile by being dragged forth as a public schoolmaster, to give lectures to the crowd! Why, nine parts in ten of what Hamlet does, are transactions between himself and his moral sense, they are the effusions of his solitary musings, which he retires to holes and corners and the most sequestered parts of the palace to pour forth; or rather, they are silent meditations with which his bosom is bursting, reduced to *words* for the sake of the reader, who must else remain ignorant of what is passing there. (100)

It would seem that the publication of Hamlet's conscience in "words" is simply a concession to the reader, who, though no longer ignorant, is still an interloper in Hamlet's internal world. Yet it is also the case that *without* the reader—the beholder, as it were, removed from the "crowd"—Hamlet "himself" remains ignorant. Not only is Hamlet ignorant insofar as he appears so or is incapable, without words, of demonstrating what Coleridge would shortly term his "knowledge"; Hamlet remains ignorant as he is virtually destitute of knowledge, nine-tenths of which requires a "transaction *between* [Hamlet] himself and his moral sense."

The conception of a solitary Hamlet, sequestered in an unpresentable contemplation, is in many ways a romantic commonplace that not even Hazlitt, who was far more accepting of the theater, could resist. However, in the case of Lamb this stereotype works less to render Hamlet a representative "self" than to install a hypothetical reader as Hamlet's (and to some degree Shakespeare's) better self. Thus, as Lamb expatiates on the character of Hamlet, Hamlet begins more and more to resemble the reader, his vocal effusions becoming, in an important qualification, "solitary meditations" experienced in the privacy of his "palace." It is the reader—not Hamlet—who is the moral touchstone in *Hamlet,* the truly privileged figure whose plenitude of understanding renders him the "conscience" in effect, on whom Hamlet, no less than Shakespeare, relies. No longer imitating or recapitulating Hamlet in merely comprehending his words, the reader, in reading Shakespeare, is somehow privileged to read herself: to retire to a closet where Hamlet is already "sequestered."

The reader to whom Lamb is referring at this moment may well be a generic reader, an everyman who has the ability to read. Yet it is clear, especially from the ensuing discussions of *Othello* and *Lear,* that the reader in Lamb, like the lyric persona of much romantic poetry, is far more exemplary than representative. This exemplary quality is most apparent in the way Shakespeare's characters become "objects of meditation" (106) for Lamb, interpretations who are the reflections of the subject reading them. When, for example, Lamb elaborates on the "texture of Othello's mind, the inward construction marvellously laid open with all its strengths and weaknesses, its heroic confidences and its human misgivings, its agonies of hate springing from the depths of love" (102); or when, in reference to the "great criminal characters . . . Macbeth, Richard, even Iago," he speaks of the "inner mind in all its perverted greatness" (106); or when, in dramatically identifying himself with Lear ("while we read it . . . we are Lear"), he elaborates "a grandeur which baffles the malice of daughters" and "a mighty irregular power of reasoning, immethodized from the ordinary purposes of life, but exerting its powers . . . at will upon the corruptions and abuses of mankind" (107), he is speaking not so much about Shakespeare's characters (to which these observations might well apply) than he is speaking from a subject-position, the authority of which is simply reflected and recapitulated in the characters he reads. It is not, in short, that "we are Lear" in the act of reading; it is really the other way around. The act of reading is, in this writing *of* reading, an act of projection and, in the specific eloquence of its presentation here, a self-advertisement.

To argue, of course, that reading per se is an act of self-projection is to say nothing new or especially profound. Had Lamb's essay demonstrated only this fact, it would scarcely warrant our attention. But the point to stress about Lamb's antitheatricality is not just its self-projection but rather the particular self projected. This self is more than simply an invisible or omniscient self, above or otherwise apart from the "crowd"; it is a self that remains powerful as long as it can stay *out* of theater or be removed from what (in reference to *The Tempest* and its supernatural apparatus) Lamb calls "a quantity of the "*hateful incredible*" (109). "Hateful" in these moments, and a threat to the peculiar sovereignty of Lamb's "reader," is a *materialization* that "levels all distinctions" (104): a reversion of the word to flesh, of which the union in *Othello* of a white woman and "a *coal-black Moor*" is perhaps the central example:

> But upon the stage, when imagination is no longer the ruling faculty, but we are left to our poor unassisted senses, I appeal to every one that has seen Othello played, whether he did not find something extremely revolting in the courtship and wedded caresses of Othello and Desdemona; and whether the actual sight of the thing did not over-weigh that beautiful compromise which we make in reading; —and the reason it should do so is obvious, because there is just so much reality presented to our senses as to give a perception of disagreement, with not enough of belief in the internal motives,—all that which is unseen, —to overpower and reconcile the first and obvious prejudices. What we see upon a stage is body and bodily action; what we are conscious of in reading is almost exclusively the mind, and its movements: and this I think may sufficiently account for the very different sort of delight with which the same play so often affects us in the reading and the seeing. (108)

Although it is possible to attribute the extremity of Lamb's complaint to a "benighted racism" (Barish, 330)—of which Lamb was sufficiently sensible to smooth over in an appended footnote comparing Othello and Desdemona to the denuded and equally disturbing images of Adam and Eve in certain paintings—Lamb's revulsion points to more than mere "prejudice" activated by seeing. It points to a leveling, a "reduc[tion of] every thing" (100), of which racial equality, no less than the fleshly synonymity of all humans (Adam and Eve included), is merely a single, "incredible" instance.[12]

And yet, by qualifying *his* notion of the "incredible" as "hateful," Lamb inadvertently tips his hand. Hateful, again, and necessarily resisted by Lamb, is not the incredible as such—"that beautiful compromise which we make in the reading" or in suspension of disbelief. "Hateful," rather, is the *uncompromising* disposition of a "reality" so powerful and threatening that it becomes an object only of the most intense and abject loathing. And this should hardly surprise us. In the wake of "so much reality"—of the materialized "body" suddenly eviscerated of all inwardness and authority—the privileged projections of the "ruling" reading subject, which have added up to "so much in Shakespeare," are suddenly vulnerable and subordinate to "things" as they are.

Lamb, it goes without saying, is no more reconciled to or willing to concede reality's power over the subject than, say, Kristeva's abject subject is aware of something beyond "horror" in those moments when, "at the boundary of what is assimilable [and] thinkable," "'subject' and 'object' push each other away" (*Powers*, 18). Nevertheless, the plenitude of what Lamb discloses here and discloses (*pace* Kristeva) with a characteristically unmanageable candor—namely, a visible world both strangely uniform and strangely uncontainable—is sufficient to overwhelm the fullness of his closeted reading.

Thus, when at the height of the peroration on *Lear,* Lamb asks, "What has the voice or the eye to do with such [sublime] things?" (107), the answer is necessarily twofold. The preferred answer is, of course, "nothing": the eye has nothing to do with the sublime (or the "I") except to serve as a kind of irritant. Yet as a *distraction*—the "reality" on whose suppression "so much in [Shakespeare]" depends—the "eye" and its produce have apparently everything to do with Lear, since they actively resist "the sublime identification . . . with that of the *heavens themselves*" (107), in which "we" are not only "Lear" but "are Lear" so long as we *cannot* see. In other words, far from simply removing us from an identification with either Lear or even the "heavens themselves," the introjection of "so much reality" by the "eye" does something even more important, which Lamb acknowledges only by resistance. It manages, in the wake of a romantic reading, to force an identification with *Gloucester:* the unwitting, self-absorbed figure in *King Lear* whom Lamb, with predictable (dare I say identificatory?) blindness, doesn't even mention in his essay.

Thus, if Lamb succeeds in discrediting the theater as a proper site for Shakespeare, his particular method of discreditation cuts both ways. All that Lamb deems characteristic of the theater here and its appeal to the eye—the abolishment of difference through a materialized leveling of all distinction—turns out, simply as an object of dread, to be a function of antitheatricality itself. It belongs to a theater whose particular mentality is more an aid to distraction—to the inevitable *resistance* (or theatricalization) of a "ruling" subject-position—than a stay against equality. Lamb may very well assert his identity with Lear in this essay, but it is Gloucester whom his criticism inadvertently reprises.[13]

III

If Lamb's intended stance toward the theater is essentially humanistic and, despite its appeal to the "we" who "are Lear," fundamentally nonegalitarian, then William Hazlitt leans in the opposite direction, relying on the theater as an occasion to enter political speculations on modern individuality and its aristocratic bearing. Unlike Lamb, who adamantly defends and privileges a self in opposition to the theater, Hazlitt marshals the theater, or more properly the task of thinking about it, in the service of more recognizably republican ends.[14]

This is not to say that Hazlitt is somehow immune to the romantic cult of the individual, or that his position to the theater is unprejudiced. He is just as capable of impatience with the theater as Lamb, vowing in one memorable instance "never [to go] to another representation of a play of Shakespear's as long as [he] lived . . . *by choice*" (5:234).[15] And he virtually echoes Lamb in observing that "all that appeals to our profounder feelings, to reflection and imagination, all that affects us most deeply in our closets, and in fact constitutes the glory of Shakespear, is little else than an interruption and a drag on the business of the stage" (5:222).[16]

Yet where Lamb is remarkably direct in his particular loathing of the stage, and just as transparent in his vulnerability to the visible world it suggests, Hazlitt is less directly hostile, and less immediately sensitive, to the more subversive or self-reflexive theatricality that derives its strength from a hatred of the theater as such. As we have seen, Lamb distinguishes sharply between the "reading" and the "seeing" of a Shakespeare play. But Hazlitt, in characteristically dialectical fashion, actually combines these extremes, accommodating the stage to the closet by imparting a certain humanism or privacy to the actual theater. Thus, in the very way that Lamb's uncompromising or repressive stance proves strangely liberating, Hazlitt's more nuanced attempt at synthesis turns out to be more of a compromise in the end, and more confining. Unlike Lamb, who under pressure of the eye submits to the leveling he opposes, Hazlitt, by essentially compromising the eye, reconstitutes Lamb's hierarchy and—in what is almost a commonplace regarding Hazlitt—discovers himself in opposition to everything, including the very leveling or democracy of which he remains an impassioned advocate.

Without a doubt, Hazlitt's dialectic of humanism and theatricality is staged powerfully in the teeth of romantic antitheatricality in its more conservative manifestation. Even so, this dialectic works to shore up the very subject-position that Lamb—in his abject hatred of "so much reality"—manages, by turns, to undermine. For all his political circumspection regarding modernity and its tendency to both solipsism and disengagement, Hazlitt finds himself in a classically liberal dilemma: hewing, in his dialectic, to a position of absolute rectitude, which also figures the very singularity or monopolizing power he finds deplorable. This contradiction is at the core of Hazlitt's most bracing criticism—his attack on *Coriolanus*—in which the sum of his critical position is effectively demonized in what can finally be termed a theater of the mind's eye. But to understand the importance of this particular essay, specifically as a figuration of its author in opposition, we must first trace the path by which Hazlitt is led finally to a place where (like Lamb in the throes of revulsion) he is empowered to stare—blindly—at himself.

Central to Hazlitt's rapprochement with the theater is an ideal of genius, which achieves its most complete development in Shakespeare but is necessarily dependent on another kind of genius more accessible to the senses. I am referring to the genius in acting, specifically to the actor Edmund Kean, who serves as a virtual signpost in Hazlitt's criticism to that invisible place (and towering perspective) that is "Shakespear." While it is possible to regard Hazlitt's reviews, with their lengthy analyses of plot and motive, as the product of a mental or preconceived theater against which an actual production is simply measured, there is a more necessary relation, I think, between what Hazlitt calls "conception"—the meaning or intention of the play—and what he calls "articulation" or performance (5:181). Despite the hierarchy implicit in this taxonomy, it is the case not only that all roads lead to a "higher conception" (including the ones that fail to get us there) but that certain "articulations" emanate from this conception as well. The comprehension of conception depends less (or less exclusively), according to Hazlitt, on the understanding in reading than on a very different signifying process that verges on originality. And this, again, is the process of acting, specifically Edmund Kean's acting of Shakespeare, the particular genius in which refers inevitably to something beyond Kean.

This "higher" referent—an originality and comprehensiveness of vision—is everywhere a feature of Hazlitt's Shakespeare criticism, including his theater reviews, later collected in *A View of the English Stage* (1818), as well as the essays in *Characters of Shakespear's Plays*

(1817), many of which are revisions of the reviews as they appeared earlier in the *Examiner* and the *Morning Chronicle*. Thus, we routinely read that Shakespeare "embodie[s] his characters so very distinctly, that he stands in no need of the actor's assistance to make them more distinct" (5:222); or that the "exclamation of the ancient critic—Oh Menander and Nature, which of you copied from the other! would not be misapplied to Shakespear" (4:183); or that "the capacious soul of Shakespear had an intuitive and mighty sympathy with whatever could enter into the heart of man in all possible circumstances" (19:83). We also read that Shakespeare (unlike Chaucer) "saw both sides of a question, the different views taken of it according to the different interests of the parties concerned, and he was at once an actor and spectator in the scene" (4:225). Often godlike in Hazlitt's accounts, Shakespeare's originality is either equal to or capable of actually subsuming nature: "Shakespear does not suppose himself to be others, but at once *becomes* them. His imagination passes out of himself into them, and as it were, transmits to him their feelings and circumstances. . . . His plays can only be compared with Nature—they are unlike every thing else" (5:191). Thus, Shakespeare's "characters are real beings of flesh and blood. . . . Each object and circumstance seems to exist in his mind as it existed in Nature. . . . In the world of his imagination every thing has a life, a place and being of its own" (5:185).

The most complete observation regarding Shakespeare's singularity probably occurs in the review of Kean's performance of *Macbeth:*

> If *to invent according to nature,* be the true definition of genius, Shakespear had more of this quality than any other writer. He might be said to have been a joint-worker with Nature, and to have created an imaginary world of his own, which has all the appearance and truth of reality. His mind, while it exerted an absolute controul over the stronger workings of the passions, was exquisitely alive to the slightest impulses and most evanescent shades of character and feeling. The broad distinctions and governing principles of human nature are presented not in the abstract, but in their immediate and endless application to different persons and things. The local details, the particular accidents have the fidelity of history, without losing any thing of their general effect. (5:204)

Hazlitt, to be sure, did not invent "bardolatry"; his particular praise of Shakespeare looks back, like Lamb's, to over a century of hagiography.[17]

Yet what is altogether unique in Hazlitt's praise of Shakespeare, which counts very clearly on the poet's singularity, is the way it works alternately to disclose and to displace a humanistic or romantic argument. In Lamb, as we have seen, the "romantic" argument is transparent and immediate in the "we" who "are Lear": in the "genius" made manifest in "the understanding in reading." In Hazlitt, by contrast, where one is continually reminded of those minds that are *not* Shakespeare—for example, Wordsworth, whose "poetical egotism would prevent his writing a tragedy" (18:308) or even Iago, who is dubbed "an amateur of tragedy in real life" (5:215)—the argument is, with deference to Shakespeare's particular capacity, more dynamic and slippery. Shakespeare is less a model or representative self in Hazlitt—the authority whom, in Lamb, for example, the "reader" at once imitates and usurps. Instead, Shakespeare is an ideal that can only be approximated or referred to. His genius is more often than not typologically configured: it is an origin or plenitude routinely anticipated in, for example, Kean's acting but, despite its manifestation there, never realized or repeated.

Hazlitt very clearly means to have it both ways in this criticism, acceding to an imperial self or to a godhead, which he proceeds, for political reasons, to situate at a perpetual remove.[18] Thus, while the romantic ideal of mind-over/as-nature is a model still in Hazlitt, it is an ideal that must, for the sake of equality, be abandoned or never quite reproduced. There are moments, of course, where this configuration is sharply tried, where not only Hamlet, but the readers in his image, find themselves in a privileged realm that is ordinarily and ideally inaccessible. Where Shakespeare's other characters are, like actors in a way, the features or synecdoches of a larger totality called "Nature" or "Shakespear," Hamlet, in Hazlitt's rendering, seems a virtual stand-in for his creator. More than a mere product of genius like other Shakespeare characters, "the character of Hamlet *is itself* a pure effusion of genius" (5:185, my emphasis), which effectively attributes genius to two separate sources. The "magnanimity of genius," which is "shewn more [in this play] . . . than in any other," is a plenitude that literally spills over into the main character, whose "refinement of thought and feeling" (5:185) makes him "probably of all others the most difficult to personate on stage" (5:186). In this way, Shakespeare's "magnanimity" extends ultimately to the "romantic" reader, of whom a readable Hamlet is also an effusion: a "shadow" that (in Hazlitt's apt description of this appropriation) cannot be "embod[ied]" (5:186).[19]

The visible embodiment of genius invariably threatens a certain kind of romantic subjectivity, just as genius disembodied or made invisible—whether at the source or the site of creation—properly describes the essential (or, for my purposes, preliminary) subject-position of romanticism in general. And by and large, Hazlitt's altogether unique achievement as a theater critic was to have provisionally avoided either of these extremes: both the privatization that appropriates genius "in the reading" and the actualization that effectively levels it in the "seeing."[20] Moreover, Hazlitt accomplishes this not by rejection, or by a gesture that allows finally for a return of the visible. He accomplishes it through a quite subtle maneuver in which the body is effectively pressed into the service of genius so as to partake of it and thereby refer to it.

The fortuitous occasion of this rapprochement was the appearance in 1814 of Edmund Kean, whose emergence as the dominant figure on the English stage coincides with Hazlitt's emergence as a critic of the theater. Hence, while it is difficult to imagine Hazlitt's theater criticism without Kean, it is important, in light of this coincidence, to understand Hazlitt's criticism not only as a praise of Kean, but more importantly as a defense of acting. For in his particular celebration of Kean, Hazlitt establishes a *via media* between genius and the body—or between the invisible and the visible—by which the body on stage is credited even as it is given a subordinate role.

This is not to say that Hazlitt's criticism is necessarily about someone other than Kean, whom the actor merely represents. In many ways, Hazlitt's writing further confirms the "remarkabl[e] consisten[cy]" in the responses to Kean at this time, most of which were variations on Coleridge's striking (and apparently borrowed) comparison of Kean's acting to "reading Shakespeare by flashes of lightning" (Donohue, *Theatre,* 59). At the same time, the most telling aspect of Hazlitt's criticism regarding Kean remains its curious impatience with Kean, whose particular accomplishment, however unequaled, is almost always prelusive to something larger. Even in his famous first review of Kean's Shylock, which is taken up almost entirely with Kean's contribution to the production, Hazlitt's attention is constantly flitting elsewhere. Early on, Hazlitt digresses from the performance of Shylock to "other parts" by Shakespeare in which, he speculates, "[Kean] will . . . become a greater favourite." Following these speculations, he speaks of "a buoyancy and elasticity of spirit" in Kean's performance that is misapplied to the "morose, sullen, inward, inveterate, inflexible malignity of Shylock" (5:179). On the heels, then, of a generalized Shakespeare to whose many "parts" Hazlitt looks ahead, it is no coincidence that Kean's singular genius becomes thoroughly implicated in a movement from genius *to genius,* whose referent—given the inequality of actor to role—remains Shakespeare.

Shakespeare's primacy is even clearer in the second of the Kean roles that Hazlitt reviews, Richard III. In this review, which sets forth the distinction between "conception" and "articulation," Kean's articulation of the part is, for all its brilliance, subordinated to a "higher conception," which passes, in effect, from Kean, who intermittently grasps it, to Richard, who figures it, to Shakespeare, who originally and ultimately conceives it. "To be perfect," contends Hazlitt, the character of Richard "should have a little more solidity, depth, sustained, and impassioned feeling, with somewhat less brilliancy, with fewer glancing lights, pointed transitions, and pantomimic evolutions. The Richard of Shakespear," he continues, "is towering and lofty, as well as aspiring; equally impetuous and commanding; haughty, violent, and subtle; bold and treacherous; confident in his strength, as well as in his cunning; raised high by his birth, and higher by his genius and his crimes; a royal usurper, a princely hypocrite, a tyrant, and a murderer of the House of Plantagenet" (5:181). Although it is probably placing too much weight on a simple phrase to argue that "the Richard of Shakespear" indicates a link between character and playwright, it is to Hazlitt's purpose to make "Richard" a more lofty figure of genius than the man playing him. While the "Richard of Shakespear" may only mean Richard as Shakespeare invented him, "Richard" remains, in the upward, onward trajectory of Hazlitt's description, decidedly different from the Richard of Kean.

This discrimination is already evident in the characteristically romantic aversion to the visible personification of genius in "glancing lights, pointed transitions, and pantomimic evolutions." But the real distinction comes less in Kean's impedance to elevation than in a hierarchy that properly *begins* with his articulation, and continues in the conception articulated, before culminating in Shakespeare, or in language spoken by the main character and now quoted by Hazlitt (5:181):

> But I was born so high;
> Our airy buildeth in the cedar's top,
> And dallies with the wind, and scorns the sun.

These lines, which (as Hazlitt observes) were omitted in the version of the play performed by Kean, convey the "towering" stature to which, in his confinement to the stage, Kean can do no more than point. And just as characteristically, the stature to which Kean *does point* on stage accords perfectly with the idea of genius regarding man and nature that Hazlitt regularly uses to describe Shakespeare. While it is possible to exaggerate and even to misrepresent Hazlitt's recourse to citation at this juncture in the essay, it is impossible to deny the overwhelming sense that Shakespeare's mind is where everything, for Hazlitt, originates and ends.

Nowhere, however, are the typological configuration of Kean and Shakespeare more in evidence, and the implications of their relationship more explicit, than in the review of Richard II. In this review, written over a year later, the movement from Kean's genius to Shakespeare's genius is not only negotiated in the usual way; it is negotiated in a way that sharply underscores the fundamental asymmetry in which, in "stimulat[ing] the faculties of the actor more," Shakespeare "enables [actors] to shew themselves off" (5:222).

Thus, Hazlitt begins in an antitheatrical vein, alluding to the "abuse" of Shakespeare's genius "even by the best actors" (5:221) only to proceed, in a tentatively protheatrical way, to distinguish "Mrs. Siddons and Mr. Kean" as "the only exceptions . . . to this observation" (5:222). Just as "Shakespear" is distinguishable from or beyond the playwright "represented" in the theater, so there is also, in Hazlitt's view, a distinction to be made between the "best actors" and the "best actors." Now, this last clearly seems a contradiction. But it is typical of the larger contradiction of Hazlitt's scheme—which valorizes a humanistic ideal by narrowing the number of humans who display genius—that he makes this observation.

Nevertheless, in valorizing genius as he does, Hazlitt ultimately creates a situation in which the potential of the individual is so much an ideal, so much the ideal of democracy, in fact, that it can no longer be contained or easily restricted. Thus, Hazlitt can observe "that in acting Shakespeare there is a greater number of good things marred than in acting any other author" *after just noting* the "effects and refractions of [the genius of Shakespeare] in [the actor], who is essentially a "priest at the altar . . . inspired with the god" (5:223). The virtues, in fine, that are exclusively Shakespeare's are—for all their exclusivity—not always or prohibitively inaccessible to others.

With a Kean or a Siddons, however, the situation is somewhat different. In their cases, the word is no sooner made flesh than it reverts to the word or to "god" again. But when the instances of genius multiply as they will, when the declension of the word to flesh involves a resurrection of the flesh and the formation of a priestly class—when, under pressure of the humanistic ideal, aristocracy effectively becomes democracy (and vice versa)—a problem occurs.

And the problem, as Hazlitt's "altar" scene makes clear, is that hierarchy only finally becomes hierarchical—is only visibly and effectively an antileveling principle—when there is *democracy* or more than one authority. Under Hazlitt's humanistic dispensation, which renders Shakespeare a god, the reader or beholder everyman, and Edmund Kean a go-between, democracy is provisionally removed from its deep structure of "everyman a king." But this removal is scarcely tantamount to a disavowal of that structure. If anything, democracy is removed by the transposition of its structure to a place and person—Shakespeare—where the humanistic basis of democracy and the democratic ideal remain intact. Such a schema allows for a vision of uniformity, on the one hand, a nation or culture *under* Shakespeare in which all men and women are created equal, and for a vision of perfectibility on the other, which is the only condition—the only *promise* really—under which the first vision is in any sense bearable. It is important, of course, that these leveling and antileveling visions be simultaneous: that Edmund Kean be our representative and, at the same time, Shakespeare's representative. But it is just as crucial that they be independent: that the body of genius be here and then elsewhere—or that Kean revert to bodily form only *after* having been absorbed into a plenitude beyond the reach of our bodily eye.

IV

Hazlitt's dialectic, his rapprochement between the body and genius, is effectively a way to buy time: to forestall the inevitable deconstruction of democracy—with its fundamentally aristocratic notions of power and enfranchisement—in the hope of discovering better, more revolutionary, terms for freedom. In the meantime, Hazlitt's immediate response to the sudden meeting of his respective visions in the republic of "inspired" actors, is to go backwards: to reassert the ideal of inimitable, unpresentable genius by recalling the deleterious effects of acting in general. But since this inimitable ideal or referent is still the basis of democracy, whose principle, consequently, is both leveling and antileveling, a more drastic measure is required.

This measure, which is taken nearly two years later in the review of Kemble's *Coriolanus,* involves two crucial turns: a disavowal of Shakespeare as being of the other "side" (at least in this play) and a critique of genius or "imagination" as fundamentally "aristocratical." Where previously Hazlitt is able to remove genius sufficiently to preserve the contradictory ideals of perfectibility and equality, genius as performed in *Coriolanus* is not only demonized but essentially discredited as a species of modern selfishness. Where previously Kean could be pressed—prospectively and retrospectively—in the service of an invisible, omniscient Shakespeare, it is the effect of *Kemble's* performance now to show the truth of that omniscience. Thus, while Hazlitt speaks generally about the character of Coriolanus as if these reflections were independent of the performance he was reviewing (and, in fact, reviews only cursorily), one cannot help feel that his response to the play was in some way provoked by Kemble's articulation.

I say this not because Kemble was demonstrably a worse actor than Kean (though their styles were assuredly different).[21] I say it because—as the best actor as distinct from the "best actors"—Edmund Kean was the linchpin in Hazlitt's critical mythology: the body of genius who became invisible *as a body* or subsumed in something larger. Remarking, at another point, on the impossibility of acting Hamlet, Hazlitt compared the deficiencies of Kean's and Kemble's performances. "Mr Kemble," according to Hazlitt, "unavoidably fails in this character from a want of ease and variety":

> [He] plays it like a man in armour, with a determined inveteracy of purpose, in one undeviating straight line, which is as remote from the natural grace and refined susceptibility of the character, as the sharp angles and abrupt starts which Mr. Kean introduces into the part. Mr. Kean's Hamlet is as much too splenetic and rash as Mr. Kemble's is too deliberate and formal. His manner is too strong and pointed. He throws a severity, approaching to virulence, into the common observations and answers. There is nothing of this in Hamlet. (4:237)

Apart from the fact that Kemble endures a somewhat greater ratio of blame than does Kean—Kean simply adds to the character, whereas Kemble "unavoidably fails" in the role—most important in this comparison is the visible field into which Kemble, in particular, casts the hero. Where Kean's performance is kinetic, energetic, and difficult to fix or visualize, there is something demonstrably cartoonish and monolithic in the image of Hamlet "in armour."

And this, it seems to me, is what Hazlitt most means when he observes immediately before the adduction of Kemble's performance that "we do not like to *see* our author's plays acted, and least of all, Hamlet" (4:237, my emphasis). Like Lamb, what Hazlitt most dislikes in the performance of *Hamlet* is the relocation of genius to a visible or social field. The difference between the two critics is that where Lamb's "visible" immediately attacks the sovereign self and is thus a "level[ling of] all distinctio[n]," Hazlitt's "visible" is both a version of democracy—a "reduction" of "Shakespeare" to "Kemble"—and a version of aristocracy consistent with the "anti-levelling" character of the humanistic ideal. If Hazlitt manages to overlook the visible in a performance by Kean by looking ahead, as it were, to Shakespeare, the visible and the corporeal are nevertheless something that, following the fragility of Kean's typological and political function, Hazlitt will observe in a performance by someone else.

A week before his performance of Coriolanus, Kemble appeared in the role of King John, which furnished Hazlitt with a further occasion to compare him and Kean. The comparison is noteworthy for a number of reasons, not the least being the metaphor of "religion" that Hazlitt employs to describe the passing of authority from Kemble to his successor. Beginning with a rather excessive observation—"we wish we had never seen Mr. Kean"—Hazlitt goes on to explain that Kean "has destroyed the Kemble religion . . . in which we were brought up":

> Never again shall we behold Mr. Kemble with the same pleasure that we did, nor see Mr. Kean with the same pleasure that we have seen Mr. Kemble formerly. We used to admire Mr. Kemble's figure and manner, and had no idea that there was any want of art or nature. We feel the force and nature of Mr. Kean's acting, but then we feel the want of Mr. Kemble's person. (5:345)

Although Kean clearly had to be "seen" to be distinguished from Kemble in this way, the sight *of Kemble* is unquestionably the more immediate, more wrenching, experience. Kean, after all, is essentially invisible to Hazlitt; he is the new religion or god who is a synecdoche of an even larger totality. Thus, Kean's "art" is ineffable, powerful, or Shakespearean (insofar as Shakespeare and "nature" are virtually synonymous), whereas "the want" or liability "of [Kemble's]" physical "person" is unavoidable and curiously indelible: "an old and delightful prejudice is destroyed," writes Hazlitt, "and no new enthusiasm, no second idolatry comes to take its place" (5:345).

It is possible that the religion of Kean is also an idolatry. But the term—with its visible, corporeal freight—seems more a way to counter a false religion, which involves the declension of the word to flesh, in deference to a new religion that involves the ascension of man to creator. Both of these religions, to be sure, are ways of talking about the same thing, which is the secularized humanism or perfectibility that Hazlitt locates in Kean and, more ideally, in Shakespeare. However, in what is likely a last ditch effort to deny the synonymity of these faiths, to keep humanism immaculately clear of as much humanity as possible, Hazlitt consigns Kemble to a visible order, and Kean, whose ascension to godhead depends on his being "seen," to a metaphysical realm. In other words, the initial "wish" never to have "seen" Kean is less an exaggeration than a truism, since this wish pertains not only to Kemble, who has become unwatchable, but more urgently to Kean himself, whose visibility is finally at cross-purposes with his function.

And what of Kemble in this regard: what is *his* function? Well, it is Kemble's function to assert the claim of the ordinary so that genius and authority are either removed or, better still, made invisible. In commenting on a moment in the play when King John approaches Hubert, Hazlitt remarks that "Mr. Kemble's look . . . was exactly as if he had just caught the eye of some person of his acquaintance in the boxes, and was trying to suppress a rising smile at the metamorphosis he had undergone since dinner" (5:346). At this point, of course, we are but a hairsbreadth from Lamb, and from his revulsion "at so much reality." But where Lamb is concerned more with the greatness that is lost in the theater, Hazlitt attends more to what is actually *gained* by this introjection. And he is attentive, I would argue, because the quotidian, no matter how detrimental its "look," contains more than a kernel of the very leveling, of the very democracy, which is no longer necessarily linked to its opposite. Although Hazlitt's inclinations are elsewhere in this review—specifically with Kean and ultimately Shakespeare—his look at "Kemble's look" remains, in the contradictory nature of those humanistic inclinations, somewhat overdetermined.

There is, by contrast, precious little overdetermination in the ensuing review of *Coriolanus,* which must rank among Hazlitt's most searing and unambiguous works of criticism. The reason for this clarity is that while the essay ultimately reinscribes the very problem it seeks to redress—which is the problem, again, of a sovereign subject-position—it concedes from the first that genius and imagination are fundamentally "aristocratical" and that Shakespeare, "perhaps from some feeling of contempt for his own origin," was in favor of such a hierarchy (5:347). Moreover, in the very way that Shakespeare—once mystified—represents an ideal for Hazlitt, so Shakespeare demystified (or psychologized) seems almost a figure for the essayist himself. Like Hazlitt, the author of *Coriolanus* entertains "arguments for and against aristocracy, or democracy, on the privileges of the few and the claims of the many, on liberty and slavery, [and] power and the abuse of it" (5:347). But there is also a crucial difference. Where previously, as the description implies, one argued "for and against" democracy at once, there is—independent of the use to which Shakespeare was previously put—a new ideal, a new notion of democracy now, as distinct from the humanistic ideal.

And so Hazlitt moves immediately to reverse his earlier scheme —situating genius and democracy in mutually *exclusive* camps. "The imagination," Hazlitt writes,

> is an exaggerating and exclusive faculty: it takes from one thing to add to another: it accumulates circumstances together to give the greatest possible effect to a favourite object. The understanding is a dividing and measuring faculty: it judges of things, not according to their immediate impression on the mind, but according to their relations to one another. The one is a monopolizing faculty, which seeks the greatest quantity of present excitement by inequality and disproportion; the other is a distributive faculty, which seeks the greatest quantity of ultimate good by justice and proportion. The one is aristocratical, the other a republican faculty. The principle of poetry is a very anti-levelling principle. . . . It admits of no medium. It is every thing by excess. It rises above the ordinary standard of sufferings and crimes. It

> presents an imposing appearance. It shews its head turretted, crowned and crested. . . . It puts the individual for the species, the one above the infinite many, might before right. (5:347–48).

It can be argued, as David Bromwich has done, that Hazlitt did not come by this formulation overnight, that his aversion here to imagination and the concomitant promotion of what is called the understanding, have a history and a context at least as old as the *Essay on the Principles of Human Action* (1805).[22]

At the same time, the remarkable determinacy of the imagination here, and the concomitant indeterminacy of the understanding (or what Hazlitt would have elsewhere called the sympathetic imagination), recall and even recapitulate the earlier commentaries on Shakespeare. Even as Hazlitt is quite effective in bringing genius down to earth and in placing it firmly before our view as if for the first time, he is necessarily ineffective in describing the alternative to imagination. This is because that alternative, what Hazlitt calls "the understanding," is essentially no different from genius or from the monopolizing power of a decidedly un-sympathetic imagination. The understanding depends, if anything, on the very idea of genius—specifically the omniscient or infinite capacity to take in all "things"—that has hitherto been synonymous with Shakespeare. The only difference—and it is surely an ironic difference—is that where such loftiness is previously sustained in conjunction with Kean, and as the basis of democracy in effect, the loftiness of the understanding (and of the democratic ideal it apparently serves) is characterized entirely by an opposition to everyone, past *and* present.

The moral high ground, to which Hazlitt rushes in democracy's cause here, and from which he ultimately surveys "the history of mankind," is (even more than Shakespeare's previous elevation) remarkably inaccessible: a sublime alternative to an utterly degraded world. "The whole dramatic moral of *Coriolanus*," Hazlitt famously concludes,

> is, that those who have little shall have less, and that those who have much shall take all that others have left. The people are poor, therefore they ought to be starved. . . . They work hard, therefore they ought to be treated like beasts of burden. They are ignorant, therefore they ought not to be allowed to feel that they want food, or clothing, or rest, that they are enslaved, oppressed, and miserable. This is the logic of the imagination and the pas-

> sions; which seek to aggrandize what excites admiration, and to heap contempt on misery, to raise power into tyranny, and to make tyranny absolute; to thrust down that which is low still lower, and to make wretches desperate: to exalt magistrates into kings, kings into gods; to degrade subjects to the rank of slaves, and slaves to the condition of brutes. The history of mankind is a romance, a mask, a tragedy constructed upon the principles of *poetical justice;* it is a noble or royal hunt, in which what is sport to the few, is death to the many, and in which the spectators halloo and encourage the strong to set upon the weak. (5:349–50)

There is little doubt that Hazlitt means to take up the "claims" of the people here, reminding his readers of the "many" who are essentially forgotten in either "romance" or in the "history" art imitates. Still, if it is Hazlitt's purpose to recall how poetry (nominally Shakespeare's) always puts the "one above the infinite many," then this is done paradoxically by placing the "infinite one"—the critic with his Pisgah vision of all life and art—"above the many." It would be difficult, I think, to imagine a democratic appeal more "aristocratical" than this one, whose cartoon of the enfranchised, including those liberated according to humanistic or revolutionary initiatives, is exceeded only by the mass terms—"slaves," "brutes," "wretches"—attached to those whom Hazlitt would presumably retrieve from degradation.

That Hazlitt seems altogether unaware of this most recent contradiction, that his "pride" and "obstinacy" are such that, like Coriolanus, he effectively "turns arms against his country" (5:348), should not surprise us. Hazlitt's blindness, like Lamb's in his commentary on Lear, is a blindness plainly visible, a performance so completely palpable that there is scarcely any need to refer to the actual performance itself.

Of that performance, then, Hazlitt has almost nothing to say, except to observe that "Mr. Kemble in the part of Coriolanus was as great as ever" (5:350)—an observation whose barely stable irony nearly catches the ironist in his own judgment. Some months later, however, on the occasion of Kemble's retirement, Hazlitt offered a more considered account of this performance. "In Coriolanus," recalled Hazlitt,

> [Kemble] exhibited the ruling passion with the same unshaken firmness, he preserved the same haughty dignity of demeanour,

> the same energy of will, and unbending sternness of temper throughout. He was swayed by a single impulse. His tenaciousness of purpose was only irritated by opposition; he turned neither to the right nor the left; the vehemence with which he moved forward increasing every instant, till it hurried him on to the catastrophe (5:376).

Although it is too melodramatic—and too prescient at this point—to consider Hazlitt's critical position as similarly catastrophic, Kemble's performance seems nearly a portrait of the reviewer six months earlier: it figures a lofty, oppositional stance that—even when he contrived to remove it from sight or to see it only briefly in the body of Kean—Hazlitt always valued enough to protect. Just how much Hazlitt valued this position will become much clearer when, in response to Coleridge's *Biographia* and the theater criticism eventually appended thereto, he inveighs against apostasy as something not unlike a leveling of all distinctions. For at the heart of Hazlitt's theater criticism—and at the center of his *Coriolanus* essay—is a justifiable fear of democracy, whose power to raise "magistrates into kings," or writers like Shakespeare "into gods," is effectively the same power that "degrade[s] subjects," including sovereign subjects, "to the rank of slaves."

Nevertheless, if Hazlitt feared democracy, he also understood democracy, or something called "democracy," to be the best of all possible arrangements. Thus, he sought, by keeping genius at remove in Shakespeare, to accomplish two things. He sought to keep democracy at bay or otherwise distinct from equality, and he sought to preserve the democratic ideal, chiefly the ideal of enfranchisement, as a status to which all people might still aspire as equals. The key to this double strategy was the actor Edmund Kean, whose ability to be in time and space as well as out of them, simultaneously and independently, figures a human potential in which equality may well be another word for freedom.

At the same time, Kean's tendency to disembodiment in referring to Shakespeare exposed the reality of this potential freedom, specifically the autonomy or plenitude that was both democracy's deep structure and, as Hazlitt had already intuited, a fundamentally false guide to liberation. Democracy, in accordance with Kean's function, was less a leveling than an antileveling initiative: a principle according to which the number of magistrates, however great, would always be exceeded by the number of slaves.

So the question now becomes: why was it Kemble and not Kean who illustrated this last point? Whose performance in *Coriolanus,* with its notably aristocratic bearing, would prove a deconstruction of Kean's mediation? The answer rests with Kean himself, whose contradictory disposition, as I have just described it, bespeaks a nearly obdurate optimism that denies any contradiction. Thus, it is Kemble —the not-Kean—who occasions the suspension of denial here and permits a more skeptical Hazlitt to disclose what remains hidden or invisible in his treatment of Kean. As the body in which genius has been degraded and made visible, Kemble is conveniently the demon against whom Hazlitt *remains* a "democrat" and a Kean supporter.

But this, of course, is only one aspect of Kemble's function vis-à-vis Kean. The other involves the way Kemble's very "figure and manner," which contrast *unfavorably* with Kean's more symbolic figuration, are a register nonetheless of Hazlitt's continued optimism—denying, as they do, any denial in the "religion of Kean." Kemble may well be that "person" who embodies denial simply by performing *Coriolanus,* which Hazlitt (correctly or not) deems a reactionary play. But as Kemble/Coriolanus he has a more important role as that figure into whom Shakespeare's, or Kean's, or Hazlitt's authority is at once telescoped and displaced. Bearing the stigma of the antileveling forces whom he works simultaneously to exonerate, Kemble-as-Coriolanus is a materialization who, merely by reprising a position of authority and exteriority, is essential to what is undoubtedly Hazlitt's severest *and* most sympathetic piece of theater criticism.

CHAPTER SIX

Coleridge's Antitheatricality: The Quest for Community

I

To the extent that Hazlitt's "view" of the English theater submits finally to its own theatricalization, to a reflexive turn in which Coriolanus as performed by Kemble reprises the critic-in-opposition, it prepares for Coleridge's equally reflexive and dramatic response to the contemporary stage in his critique of the Gothic drama *Bertram*. Yet where Hazlitt's submission is chiefly an act of denial, a resistance that, like Lamb's hatred of "reality," ultimately recoils on itself, Coleridge's objectification of himself amounts also to an acceptance of his humanity—which is to say his materiality. The difference between Hazlitt and Coleridge becomes especially clear in Hazlitt's virulent attack on Coleridge's apostasy, as it appears both in the *Biographia* and in the theater criticism appended to it. In this charge, Hazlitt explicitly contrasts his subject-position, and the "democracy" in whose cause it allegedly functions, to the arguably greater democracy of Coleridge's position, which effectively admits no distinctions and certainly no position of exteriority. In the meantime, the particular similarity of these critics, which is a prelude to Hazlitt's ultimately prelusive status, is most evident in Coleridge's lectures on Shakespeare, which were contemporaneous with Hazlitt's and were likely delivered to many of the same people.[1]

In light of the fact that Hazlitt and Coleridge were in competition regarding Shakespeare, it is customary to emphasize the difference in their approaches. Where Coleridge is often seen to be more directly influenced (in fact, too influenced) by A. W. Schlegel, who imagined Shakespeare as a contemporary and developed a number of critical categories, notably organic form, in support of that view, Hazlitt's stance toward Shakespeare is often seen to be transhistorical and, at the same time, more immediately political.[2] Nevertheless, an important aspect of Hazlitt's theater criticism—the promotion of Shakespeare's genius—is equally a feature of Coleridge's Shakespeare criticism, which is by and large antitheatrical in treating the plays exclusively as literature. Thus, even as he sidesteps the theatrical typology, by which the body of an actor is made an intimation of Shakespeare, Coleridge nevertheless concurs with Hazlitt in the humanistic use to which he puts Shakespeare. And he is in agreement here because his humanism, unlike Lamb's wholesale promotion of genius, is also somewhat qualified: genius, in Coleridge's view, is less a status we must all ascend to, a representative state, than an exemplary or ideal state that may, like Hazlitt's ideal, be held in abeyance.

That Coleridge's praise of Shakespeare, including the identification of his "genius" as "Romantic" in the "appea[l] to the Imagination" (1:467), is more tentative and more complicated than Lamb's praise—or even Hazlitt's for that matter—is evident in a number of ways.[3] It is evident in Coleridge's refusal to allow even the "enlightened reade[r]" more than the barest access to "the poet's power" (1:351–52). And it is evident in the very terms of Coleridge's criticism, especially the pejorative notions with which both Shakespeare and romanticism are routinely compared and contrasted. These terms—all of which describe a world or "reality" bound by a sensory discipline of time and space—ultimately highlight an alternative, more distinctly romantic, vision independent of sensory reality. Nevertheless, by engaging this comparison, such a rhetoric imagines a counteraesthetic to romanticism as well—whose antithetical function is necessary to Coleridge but necessarily excessive.

Time and again, Coleridge will *compare* Shakespeare and the veritably "religious" work of his poetry (1:325) to something else. Shakespeare, therefore, stands distinct from "Science" whose "Object is the . . . acquirement or communication of Truth" (1:217); he operates beyond the "narrow sphere which [the] hand can touch or even [the] eye can reach" (1:325); he creates by meditation rather than "from the outward watchings of life" (1:306), and, most important perhaps, Shakespeare differs from the ancient dramatists in his "appeal to the imagination & not to the senses" and in otherwise being "above the iron compulsion of space & time" (1:350).

Not much is often made of Coleridge's antipathy regarding the unities, or of the fact that the values that continually ground his appreciation of Shakespeare are essentially contested by what, in reference to the Greeks again, Coleridge disparages as a "refined & elevated Sensuality" (1:439). Generally it is the practical criticism of Shakespeare, descendent from his (and Schlegel's) notion of organic unity, that garners the most attention.[4] Nevertheless, a closer look at organic unity—particularly the use to which Coleridge puts the Schlegelian concept—points to the most practical and problematic aspect of his Shakespeare criticism: the subjugation of a visible world to a metaphysical or "religious" one in which "Time & Space" are "obedient only to the Laws . . . the Imagination acts by" (1:467).

Despite its appeal to a natural model, or to a rhythm of existence that is concrete and palpable, organic unity is simply another name for a totality or principle of unity that imagination apprehends and only genius in effect controls. Thus, in an 1819 lecture on *Romeo and Juliet,* Coleridge typically postulates an alternative unity to the unity of action inherent in "Athenian Drama":

> Yet instead of Unity of Action I should great[ly] prefer the more appropriate tho' scholastic and uncouth words—Homogeneity, proportionateness and Totality of Interest.—The distinction or rather the essential difference betwixt the shaping skill of mechanical Talent, and the creative Life-power of inspired Genius. . . . Whence the Harmony that strikes us in the wildest natural landscapes? In the relative shapes of rocks, the harmony of colors in the Heath, Ferns, and Lichens, the Leaves of the Beech, and Oak, the stems and rich choc[ol]ate-brown Branches of the Birch, and other mountain Trees, varying from varying Autumn to returning Spring—compared with the visual effect from the greater number of artificial Plantations?—The former are effected by a single energy, modified ab intra [from within] in each component part—. Now . . . this is the particular excellence of Shakespearian Dramas generally. (2:362)

There is no question that the homogeneity that Coleridge values here is another description of organic unity, in which (as he observes in another lecture) "Poetry" becomes "in its essence a universal spirit . . . which in incorporating itself adopts & takes up the surrounding materials" (1:511). Still and all, the particular defense of "inspired Genius" over what Coleridge disparagingly terms "mechanical Talent," is necessary as much for what it defends—the shaping power of the mind—as for what, in accordance with the notion of organic unity again, "Genius" must appropriate and inform. As Coleridge's description makes abundantly clear, genius informs a "visual" world of potential distraction, the apparent "harmony" of which seems more a wish-fulfilling fantasy than a *fait accompli*.

This is not to say, of course, that this criticism is, at base, a defense of something other than genius, or an argument against "the great prerogative of genius . . . to swell itself into the dignity of a god" (1:308). It is to show only that the ostensible position of Coleridge's Shakespeare criticism is sharply tried by a discipline of space and time that, in spite of disparaging, Coleridge seemingly never loses an opportunity to acknowledge. Thus, in praising Shakespeare's "psychological genius to develope all the minutiae of the human heart," Coleridge observes how the poet "makes visible what we should otherwise not have seen: just as after looking at distant objects through a Telescope when we behold them afterwards with the naked eye . . . we see them with greater distinctness than we should otherwise have done" (1:306). And regarding human nature in *Othello*, Shakespeare apprehends such things not by mere observation, but "with the inward eye of meditation on his own nature" (1:310). Or, in a related observation that echoes Hazlitt, Shakespeare is alleged

> to paint truly a vast multiplicity of characters by simple meditation; he had only to imitate such parts of his character, or to exaggerate such as existed in possibility and they were at once nature & fragments of Shakespeare. It was like men who seeing the vast luminary of the world thro' various optics, declared it to be square, triangular or round, when in truth it was still the sun. So with the characters of our Poet whatever forms they assumed, they were still Shakespeare or the creatures of his meditation. (1:289)

The question, of course, remains: what is gained in this ability to "thro[w] objects of . . . interest at a distance from us" (1:325)? Does such propulsion, as Coleridge avows, "subserv[e] the interest of our virtues" in effectively "rescu[ing]" us from the "slavery" of our "senses" (1:325)? Or is it the other way around: is it the work of genius to enslave the senses out of fear of what a world, mediated simply by the "naked eye," or bound by "the iron compulsion of space & time," might look like?

The answer to this, at least from Coleridge's perspective, is probably "yes"—on both counts. So long as it remains "independent of Time & Space," "appeal[ing] to the Imagination rather than to the Senses" (1:467), genius is indeed godlike and its poetry a religion apparently worth defending. But when things are reversed (as they apparently always threaten to be), when "Imagination" or genius is "obedient only to the Laws" of time and space, something very different occurs. What occurs is a reconception of genius so startling and so inevitable that it well explains Coleridge's continued recourse to the asymmetry of matter and mind.

This refiguration is especially evident in Coleridge's discussions of *Hamlet* (1812–13), which variously recall Lamb's submission to a "reality" produced by the "bodily eye." Yet where visible reality returns to Lamb as something repressed, Coleridge is more willing—even driven in a way—to accommodate what Lamb is forced only in the end to acknowledge. This is clear, for example, in Coleridge's rhetoric of comparison, which resists the autonomous imagination even as it abets it. Not only do Coleridge's comparisons work to cast imagination into sharper relief; they privilege imagination by positioning it *against* an equally autonomous visual field. Accordingly, the most notable aspect of Coleridge's discussion of *Hamlet* is less its sympathy with Hamlet (such as both Lamb and Hazlitt show) than a tendency to visualize "the character of Hamlet" independent of either a particular performance or, as in the case of Lamb, a generalized one.

Coleridge's visual compulsion begins at the level of metaphor with his initial query: "What did Shakespeare mean when he drew the character of Hamlet" (1:386)? But it moves very quickly to the more essential issues regarding visual perception and individual genius in the ensuing answer that Shakespeare "meant to pourtray a person in whose view the [external] world and all its incidents [and objects] were comparatively dim, and of no interest in themselves, and which began to interest only when they were reflected in the mirror of his mind." In other words, Hamlet as Shakespeare invented him "beheld external objects in the same way that a man [of vivid imagination] who shuts his eyes, sees what has previously made an impression upon his organs [of vision]" (1:386).

Coleridge might well have added that, in this sense, Shakespeare probably conceived Hamlet as a version of himself insofar as Hamlet has apparently internalized the very "telescope" that was his creator's imagination: the instrument that perceives objects only at a distance or sees what is indistinct to the bodily eye. But Coleridge does not make this connection. And he resists making it, I would argue, not because it was inconceivable, but because it was all too conceivable: because the conception of Hamlet here is less Shakespeare's invention or self-portrait than a repetition of Coleridge's own, distinctly romantic, conception of Shakespeare. It is Hamlet now who "sees through the [very] souls of all who surround him" and who has "[as it were] a world within [himself]" (1:386).

But there is, in any case, a difference between Shakespeare and his character. While Shakespeare can be said to have asserted his independence over and against the constraints imposed by a merely visible order (in the logic of romanticism at least), such an assertion is no longer possible for a man with his eyes closed—whose blindness is suddenly visible to the naked critical eye. Thus, it is hardly a coincidence that Hamlet's genius is very much an issue in Coleridge's visualization, that Hamlet's "retire[ment] from all reality" is plainly the "result of having [the greatness of genius] we express by the terms a world within himself" (1:388). In this way Coleridge does not deny Hamlet's "greatness of genius," or that such genius involves a mental appropriation of the physical world. He merely regards genius—be it Hamlet's or Shakespeare's—from the outside in, allowing a discipline of the senses to assert its claim over a mind accustomed to transcending it. The effect of this inversion is not to stare blindly at genius (or at oneself) as both Lamb and Hazlitt effectively do; the effect, rather—in substituting the agency of sight for that of mind—is to do the very opposite: that is, to stare critically at blindness.

Coleridge, it must be added, does not refrain completely from entering Hamlet's mind, or from remarking sympathetically on the nature of his meditations. Nevertheless, these entries are also blocked or deflected in the visible image of Hamlet as "a man *living* in meditation" (1:390, emphasis added). Thus, no matter how much Coleridge presses this image in an intentionality that renders Hamlet a cautionary example—in which "no faculties of intellect however brilliant can be considered valuable, or otherwise than misfortunes, if they withdraw us from or render us repugnant to action" (1:390)—intentionality and will are things that the critical "eye can reach" as well as repulse. In spite of the efforts to reverse the asymmetry of sight and mind by recourse to what Shakespeare *intended* in *Hamlet,* the most striking aspect of Coleridge's demonstration remains the image of Hamlet drawn: the *sight* of genius with its eyes shut. No longer a matter of intrinsic superiority or of will, genius has become a matter of extrinsic difference. Genius counts as an arbitrary aloofness from both a physical and a social world, where uniqueness may be nothing more than a denial of materiality and community.

It must be emphasized, again, that these disclosures or theatricalizations are hardly the wrenching disclosures of either Lamb's revulsion at Othello's blackness or of Hazlitt's self-portrait in Kemble/Coriolanus. If anything, the tendency to theatricalize is sufficiently endemic to Coleridge that it is scarcely necessary for him to have seen a performance of *Hamlet,* or to have imagined seeing one, in order to see Hamlet.[5] Where it devolves upon the actual theater to do the work of demystification for other romantic critics—a work they accordingly resist—Coleridge appears willing to assume the demystificatory role even in conjunction with the "greater romantic" project of promoting Shakespeare's genius. Thus, Coleridge can (in reference to Hamlet, again) distinguish the "healthy processes of the mind," in which a "balance [is] maintained between the impressions of outward objects and the inward operations of the intellect," from "an overbalance in the contemplative faculty" that—even as it continues to "distinguis[h Man] from the animal"—also renders him "a creature of meditation" (1:543).

Coleridge goes on to grant Shakespeare a supervisory role in this process, crediting him (according to the transcript of the 1813 lecture as reported in the *Bristol Gazette*) with having "conceived a mind . . . with this overpowering activity of intellect" (1:543). Yet this concession to genius is scarcely sufficient to overcome the demystificatory drift of the criticism, which is headed in the opposite direction: to a place or site where, as a "creature of meditation," "Man" is essentially an "animal" whose distinction from other animals (and people) is increasingly arbitrary. The failure to distinguish sufficiently between the "activity of intellect" in Hamlet and the "activity of intellect" in conceiving such a character is no accident or ambiguity introduced into the transcription without provocation. In addition to making Shakespeare and Hamlet equals and therefore equally cautionary, Coleridge's (over)sight serves an even larger principle of equality. It points to a leveling of all distinction by agency of sight: to a society of visible objects and a world of visible, vital "creatures," following whom the "activity of intellect" (as Coleridge so aptly terms it) seems almost an oxymoron.

To readers familiar with Coleridge's other theater criticism—notably the series of letters on Maturin's play *Bertram,* which subsequently became chapter 23 of the *Biographia Literaria*—his inclination toward the material and the active in describing Shakespeare will seem odd, especially given the virulence of his attack on the modern theater as a "Jacobin" institution. But precisely because Coleridge's virulent antitheatricality (and antirepublicanism) is *itself* a theatrical apparatus—a means, as we shall see, for the critical persona to take on the role of Hamlet with his eyes shut—it is worth considering what is finally at stake in a world in which genius, or an authoritative critical position, is "reachable" by the "eye." And here, we are as much helped by Coleridge's Shakespeare criticism, with its insistent image of a visible world wherein all objects are equal, as by Hazlitt's well-known criticism of Coleridge's *Biographia* with its infamous charge of apostasy. For, in many ways, the apostasy systemic to a text like the *Biographia,* according to Hazlitt, is another term for the reversal inherent in Coleridge's treatment of Hamlet.

The difference, then, is that where apostasy clearly values the integrity of a given subject-position so that a new position amounts to a renunciation of a previous one, the kind of reversal endemic to both the *Biographia* and Coleridge's Shakespeare criticism is more properly an objectification—a leveling of difference—in which one object or position is no better than or different from another object or subject. As a result, the pages that Coleridge was forced to append to the *Biographia,* culminating in what is essentially the sum of his contemporary theater criticism (Badawi, 203), not only resemble the treatment of *Hamlet* in the way such criticism remains consistent with the text that precedes or surrounds it; these pages recapitulate the treatment of *Hamlet* in having virtually the same impact on genius, which is adduced in the *Biographia* from the examples of Wordsworth and Coleridge as well as Shakespeare. At the heart of the *Biographia* is less an apostasy, a massive swing from one orientation to another; at the heart, rather, is an inconsistency so utterly pervasive that the sanctity or privilege of any given position amounts to an insensitivity, even a kind of violence, to all other outward objects and subjects.[6]

The discussion that follows, then, which takes up the question of apostasy and, following it, the question of genius at times moves from the more immediate problems posed by visibility, or even by the materialized subject, to more general issues regarding both Coleridge and romanticism. This is because the issues that the visible continually verges on are, in the main, issues involving community in its various and not always consistent manifestations. A liberationist ideal, on the one hand, and the desired end of what either Lamb or Hazlitt would have called a leveling initiative, community is also, as Coleridge will show, another term for hegemony, whose ideals, most notably those of genius, are ones that a materialization of the self or leveling by sight can no longer simply militate against or contain. Far from securing a place beyond culture, then, the visible becomes, if anything, a point of entry for Coleridge, following which his antitheatrical posture—with its potential for contradiction—is variously pressed in both a reassessment and a revision of his romanticism so called.

Thus, it is in the *Biographia,* in the account of Coleridge's "literary life," rather than in any of his letters or other criticism, that the visible as such discovers its most expansive treatment. For what is at stake finally in the romantic visible, at least for Coleridge, is neither the exception to the rule, nor a new or better orientation waiting to be born. At stake, rather, is something that only the *Biographia,* with its unparalleled mixture of retrospection and prospection, can expose: namely, a possibility that counts paradoxically on impossibility—or, as Coleridge reiterates it in his defense of Burke, on a visible field bound to a discipline of space and time. No longer accessible from a position of exteriority, such a field is accessible or comprehensible solely from a position of *inclusion,* wherein the ability to see all things is necessarily dependent on one's being, like *all things,* visible and contained. Only by declension to the material, that is, or by otherwise joining Hamlet, regardless of whether their juncture represents hegemony or community or both, can Coleridge see through things simply by seeing them. For the peculiar transparency of the world now, which alternately admits and precludes possibility, renders the spectacle of oneself—which is also the act of belonging and of being beside oneself—less an end, or fall from authority, than a beginning or, as Gramsci would describe it, an "active unity."[7]

II

That the *Biographia* is caught up in a rhythm of subversion or renunciation is so much a commonplace these days that to deconstruct Coleridge or to enlist him in the wisdom of deconstruction can scarcely add to our understanding of his achievement here.[8] What does add to our understanding, strangely enough, is the Coleridge demonized by Hazlitt in his review of the *Biographia,* since the instability of *this* Coleridge (or his apostasy, as Hazlitt charged in the review) is somewhat more restrictive, and as a result more palpably disruptive.

Like his Coriolanus, Hazlitt's Coleridge is more than a figure demonized, a Coleridge who has betrayed an earlier, more politically correct, republicanism. Like Coriolanus, Coleridge is also the product or fantasy of a sensibility that regards *itself* as comparatively stable and therefore recoils on itself in ways more apposite to the ends of deconstruction than the position(s) Hazlitt criticizes. Such recoiling happens in two ways in this encounter. It happens in the way Coleridge shucks off Hazlitt's charge of apostasy in suggesting the synonymity or (to use his own coinage) the "desynonymity" of all positions of difference; and it happens in the way the very charge of apostasy, centering on Coleridge's irregularity and "effeminacy," becomes a self-defeating imputation, whose masculinist basis, with its intimations of difference and superiority, is effectively exposed by Coleridge and made to look ridiculous. To the extent, in other words, that Coleridge may be deemed subversive in the *Biographia,* it is not by wisdom of hindsight or by some transhistorical agency that turns canonical works to contraband and vice versa. Rather, he is contestational in terms that are as fundamental as they are fundamentally *opposed* to romanticism: according to certain notions of democracy and freedom on which romanticism can be said to rely but that can be better served (as we have seen) by repudiation.

Still, if Hazlitt collaborates with Coleridge in the latter's vindication (and in his own subversion, as it were), it is only because Coleridge manifestly needs a Hazlitt—the orthodox if contradictory romanticism Hazlitt exemplifies—as the last barrier or obstruction to seeing himself (and other selves, notably Burke, Southey, and even Wordsworth) as part of a larger community. Accordingly, my treatment of the *Biographia,* with particular attention to the consistency, even the centrality, of its appended sections on the theater, begins by *following* Hazlitt.

It is not, of course, that I agree with Hazlitt's charge, which in any case has more than its share of contemporary adherents. I begin with Hazlitt's famous review of Coleridge's "literary life" because its fault line is precisely where he and Coleridge ultimately agree: because the instability or "licentiousness" characteristic of anti-Jacobinism and apostasy, according to Hazlitt, is altogether consistent with Coleridge's logic of "desynonymization."[9] The very extravagance, which renders Coleridge a "dangerous leader" and a "treacherous follower," according to Hazlitt, is an extravagance in which these discriminations are abolished; it is an excess wherein no two subject-positions are the same any more than they are objectively different. It is an instability, whose only consistency is community and solidarity—in a "democracy" (for want of a better term) toward which Hazlitt inclines by his own assertion but whose "levelling" or negation of a sovereign position he also actively and perversely resists.

Apart from the usual imprecations, which picture Coleridge either in a Kantian haze or "going up in an air-balloon filled with fetid gas from the writings of Jacob Behmen and the mystics," what distinguishes Hazlitt from the roster of Coleridge detractors is his obsession with Coleridge's apostasy, chiefly the latter's political descent "in a parachute made of the soiled and fashionable leaves of the Morning Post" (16:118). This descent, moreover, involves not only the betrayal of Coleridge's earlier Jacobin principles but an irregularity or instability that Hazlitt is sufficiently stung by to label effeminate.

Citing Coleridge as representative of contemporary anti-Jacobinism, particularly as it is manifest in poetry increasingly disposed to "an ideal world of [the poet's] own" (16:137), Hazlitt observes how modern poets invariably "make strange work with matter of fact":

> They indulge only their own flattering dreams or superstitious prejudices, and make idols or bugbears of what they please, caring as little for 'history or particular facts,' as for general reasoning. . . . Their inordinate vanity runs them into all sorts of extravagances; and their habitual effeminacy gets them out of them at any price. Always pampering their own appetite for excitement, and wishing to astonish others, their whole aim is to produce a dramatic effect, one way or other—to shock or delight their observers; and they are as perfectly indifferent to the consequences of what they write, as if the world were merely a stage for them to play their fantastic tricks on.—As romantic in their servility as in their independence, and equally importunate candidates for fame or infamy, they require only to be distinguished, and are not scrupulous as to the means of distinction. Jacobins or Antijacobins—outrageous advocates for anarchy and licentious-

> ness, or flaming apostles of persecution—always violent and vulgar in their opinions, they oscillate, with a giddy and sickening motion, from one absurdity to another, and expiate the follies of their youth by the heartless vices of their advancing age. (137)

The imprecation of "habitual effeminacy" in the modern spirit implies a masculine alternative. And this last, needless to say, Hazlitt provides. Nevertheless, the most striking aspect of this alternative is its opposition to *everyone:* men and women, Jacobins as well as anti-Jacobins.

The movement, then, from the particular to the universal here, from Coleridge the apostate to the apostasy of the age as exemplified by Coleridge, is neither inadvertent nor, as the *Coriolanus* essay has already made plain, especially unusual in Hazlitt. It constitutes the characteristic rush in Hazlitt to the highest moral ground: to a sovereign subjectivity whereby Hazlitt is indeed (and rather redundantly, as Mary Shelley apparently understood the phenomenon) "the last man." Double-parked beside the very space and time he occupies, Hazlitt is the exception, the independent, whose unwavering stability and comprehension of both "history" and "fact" highlight and, in effect, prove the "giddy" dualism of everyone around him.

When Hazlitt speaks therefore of a romanticism characterized by either servility or independence, and of the apparent interchangeability of Jacobins and anti-Jacobins, he is scarcely acknowledging the sameness of these positions or that their sameness is the thing that provokes and is simultaneously sustained by an increasingly mystified sense of their difference. He is, in fact, arguing the very opposite: these positions have been degraded to a kind of sameness, and their "distinction" profaned by an irregularity of purpose, which only the critic—the last Romantic and last of the independents—is capable of resisting. The question of Jacobinism, to be sure, poses a slightly different problem because the term itself had by this time become an all-purpose pejorative (Bate, *Shakespearean Constitutions,* 159–62). Yet even so, what is remarkable in the exchange of Jacobinism and anti-Jacobinism, as Hazlitt imagines it, is not that they are the same any more than servility and independence are conceivably the same. The remarkable thing about them is that they have been *made* synonymous by a habitual effeminacy, which Hazlitt—the manly apostle of a more glorious revolution and a more sublime democracy—is alternately above and opposed to.

There is, however, an irony to Hazlitt's fantasy of the age. And it has to do with the way Coleridge, in his enlargement as representative man, becomes the reflex of the critic, who sustains a comparable magnification. Although Hazlitt stands sufficiently apart from his contemporaries to render a universal judgment upon them, he is effectively driven to this position by Coleridge, whose swelling into the "spirit of the age" suggests the enormity of a counterexample that Hazlitt can do no more (and no less ultimately) than rise above. This counter, to be sure, embraces many forms in the *Biographia,* not the least being Coleridge's oft-noted tendency to digress from the "details of [his own] life" (115) in a work presumably devoted to it. Yet for the purposes of my discussion, especially given its bearing on the imperial self and the contestation of this self by Coleridge, the challenge most worth scrutinizing is Coleridge's political inconsistency, which Hazlitt vigorously contests in reference to the *Biographia*'s defense of both Southey and Burke.

In one sense, Hazlitt could not have chosen a better point of attack in his review; both Southey's conversion from Jacobin to royalist and the amnesia apparently separating Burke's support of the American Revolution from his opposition to the French are transformations difficult to defend. Yet it is precisely the unconventionality of Coleridge's defense—his ability to see beyond the praise and blame of the day to a larger desynonymity of all positions on revolution and change—that spells problems for Hazlitt and renders him a victim of his own essentialism.

In interrogating the defense of Southey, who "has not only taken to write against democracy in his maturer age, but has abused and reviled those who adhere to his former opinions," Hazlitt derides Coleridge for avoiding this fact and for vindicating Southey according to his "private character":

> Some people say, that Mr. Southey has deserted the cause of liberty: Mr. Coleridge tells us, that he has not separated from his wife. They say, that he has changed his opinions: Mr. Coleridge says, that he keeps his appointments; and he has even invented a new word, *reliability,* to express his exemplariness in this particular. . . . It is further alleged, that he is arrogant and shallow in political discussion, and clamours for vengeance in a cowardly and intemperate tone: Mr. Coleridge assures us, that he eats, drinks, and sleeps moderately. It is said that he must either have been very hasty in taking up his first opinions, or very unjustifiable

> for abandoning them for their contraries; and Mr. Coleridge observes, that Mr. Southey exhibits, in his own person and family all the regularity and praiseworthy punctuality of an eight-day clock. (120–21)

It is difficult to imagine Hazlitt on more solid ground than he holds here, or to imagine a position more assailable than the one he so confidently cartoons.

Nevertheless, a look at Coleridge's actual defense of Southey suggests not only that Hazlitt has been lulled into a position of rectitudinous radicalism but, more important, that this position is interesting solely for its misplaced confidence in a stable, unwavering selfhood. Contrary to Hazlitt's description, Coleridge begins *not* by praising Southey's private character. He begins with the "genius" that Southey "possesses" but, he adds, "is not possessed by" (1:66).[10] This last, I think, represents an important qualification, especially if we construe possession "by" genius to mean possession by the *ideal* of genius, or by a structure that is otherwise divisive and differentiating. Because different Southey assuredly is not.

If anything, it is Southey's ordinariness, his exceptional ability to absorb and regurgitate almost everything, his hewing to a position marked by variousness or irregularity, that constitutes his achievement. "His prose," writes Coleridge,

> is always intelligible and always entertaining. In poetry he has attempted almost every species of composition known before, and he has added new ones; and if we except the highest lyric, . . . he has attempted every species successfully: from the political song of the day, . . . to the wild ballad; from epistolary ease and graceful narrative, to the austere and impetuous moral declamation; from the pastoral charms and wild streaming lights of the "Thalaba," . . . to the more sober beauties of the "Madoc;" and lastly from the Madoc to his "Roderic," in which . . . he has surpassed himself in language and metre, in the construction of the whole, and in the splendour of particular passages. (1:64)

If this list of accomplishments fails to damn Southey with faint praise, it scarcely does much more than that. Just when Southey is about to distinguish himself in this litany, something inevitably drags him down. This impedance may be nothing more than the accomplishment of mere intelligibility, with which Coleridge begins the list; or the failure to have excelled in "the highest lyric"; or even the way the comparative excellence of "Roderic" casts a retroactive pall on the achievements that precede it.

But whatever its form, the impedance serves two related purposes. It diminishes Southey, as Hazlitt so ably shows. And it also marshals the *diminished* Southey—the Southey of "matchless industry and perseverance," generously submissive "to tasks of transitory interest" (65)—in a critique of the very standards and structures by which certain "men" apparently "deserve a higher record" and with "whose characters it is the interest of their contemporaries, no less than that of posterity, to be made acquainted" (64). Such greatness, Coleridge argues through the comparatively pedestrian and distracted "genius" of Southey, is paradoxically a matter of conformity, of satisfying some preordained or perennial standard. Furthermore, greatness of this sort requires a stability, an integrity in one's public as well as private person, that is both unrealistic and largely impossible.

And it is in conjunction with the impossibility of greatness that we must consider Coleridge's apparently mindless defense of Southey's private "virtues," which are explicitly (and ironically) connected to his failure to be "possessed by" genius. These "virtues," which range from the "regular and methodical tenor of his daily labours," to the "dignified simplicity of his manners," to his "punctual[ity] in trifles" as "in the performance of highest duties," do not merely pale next to the more sublime virtues to which the tag "reliability" would be nothing less than an insult. They measure the only stability, the only regularity if you will, that Coleridge deems possible. All other positions that pretend to stability, that are unwavering in their particular commitment and are otherwise possessed by the ideal of genius, are as likely characterized by instability, or by apostasy, or by ordinariness, as that of the "genius," who acts "not in obedience to any law or outward motive, but by the necessity of a happy nature" (66).

A "happy nature," to be sure, is not the kind of private integrity that would impress a Hazlitt. But it is the only disposition about which Coleridge is in any way confident. All other orientations, as he conceives them, are subject to the same irregularity, the same resistance of possession, the same susceptibility to change, as are Southey's:

> As son, brother, husband, father, master, friend, he moves with firm yet light steps, alike unostentatious, and alike exemplary. As a writer, he has uniformly made his talents subservient to the

> best interests of humanity, of public virtue, and domestic piety; his cause has ever been the cause of pure religion and of liberty, of national independence and of national illumination. . . . [Future critics will] not fail to record, that as no man was ever a more constant friend, never had poet more friends and honorers among the good of all parties. (66–67)

Here, with the mention of "all parties," we encounter for the first time the issue of Southey's politics—and they are politics that are anything but stable. The pairings of religion and liberty, of independence and illumination, can undoubtedly be pressed in some synthetic arrangement, an arrangement virtually characteristic of "high romanticism." However, the allusion to "all parties" leaves little doubt that despite the synthesis that a secularized humanism contrives to enact, this union is but another name for apostasy, for a rhythm of reversal in which the combinatory initiative is simultaneously a renunciatory one.

Thus, Coleridge begins the political discussion in a startling way: with a list of Southey's various private or interpersonal roles. The effect of this list is neither sentimental vindication (as Hazlitt would have it) nor to cast blame in the wake of that visited upon Southey by "quacks in politics . . . and quacks in criticism" (67). The effect, in enumerating Southey's various roles, is to suggest rather that *no* subject-position of any weight—no position beyond simply getting on or being on time—is stable or necessarily immune to the charge of instability. All other roles, personal or private, are sufficiently blameable or, from another angle of vision, sufficiently desynonymous (in the way "son, brother, husband, father," etc., are desynonymous) that there is no reason to castigate one for changing one's position anymore than there is cause to assume that *any* position necessarily differs from any *other* position. All positions are alike in the way they are different *and* vice versa, all of which makes the charge of apostasy—and the equality it ostensibly serves—an *anti*leveling initiative.

A similar argument is made with reference to Burke, and it is an argument that Hazlitt is at equal pains to rebut. Construing Coleridge's argument to be the consistency of Burke's positions on the American and French revolutions, Hazlitt asserts that, in his antipathy to the French, Burke "abandoned not only all his practical conclusions, but all the principles on which they were founded":

> In the American war, he constantly spoke of the rights of the people as inherent, and inalienable: after the French Revolution,

> he began treating them with the chicanery of a sophist, and ended raving at them with the fury of a maniac. . . . The burthen of all his speeches on the American war was conciliation, concession, timely reform, as the only practicable or desirable alternative of rebellion: the object of all his writings on the French Revolution was, to deprecate and explode all concession and all reform, as encouraging rebellion. . . . In the one case, he took part with those who were actually rebels against his Sovereign; in the other, he denounced, as rebels and traitors, all those of his own countrymen who did not yield sympathetic allegiance to a foreign Sovereign, whom we had always been in the habit of treating as an arbitrary tyrant. (16:130–31)

As in the case of Southey, Hazlitt's argument against Burke—and against Coleridge's defense of him—does not lack polemical verve. What it does lack is simply the understanding that Burke is in large part a device: like Southey, he is marshaled as much for his own sake here, or for his particular example, as on behalf of a larger argument for desynonymity and community.

Not surprisingly, then, Burke is adduced in the *Biographia* on the heels of a discussion in which "unanimity" is alleged to exist not in spite of, but in conjunction with, various "fixed opinions":

> Let the scholar, who doubts this assertion [of unanimity], refer only to the speeches and writings of EDMUND BURKE at the commencement of the American war, and compare them with his speeches and writings at the commencement of the French revolution. He will find the *principles* exactly the same and the deductions the same; but the practical inferences almost opposite, in the one case, from those drawn in the other; yet in both equally legitimate and in both equally confirmed by the results. Whence gained he this superiority of foresight? Whence arose the striking *difference*, and in most instances even the discrepancy between the grounds assigned by *him*, and by those who voted *with* him, on the same questions? (1:191)

The answer to this question is not an easy one, particularly if we eschew or take a harder look at the one Coleridge immediately provides, which credits Burke with the capacity to "se[e] all things." For the real answer—the really interesting answer here—would appear to diminish Burke in deference to that very capacity of sight: in deference to a world sufficiently visible (and constrained by space and time) that the site of Burke's "fore*sight*" (the "whence") is necessarily the site of palpable, perceptible "*difference.*" In other words, it is not that Burke is omniscient or that he knows more; it is that the different positions Burke adopts—those for and against revolution—are sufficiently "the same" and, on the evidence of the "results," sufficiently interchangeable that the support of one is tantamount to support of the other.

This is not, to be sure, what Coleridge specifically argues here or is arguing as explicitly as he is something else. Clearly, Coleridge is also pursuing a patriotic theme in which "unanimity"—in particular the British reaction to the revolution in France—is both testimony to a fundamentally democratic England and to a fundamentally democratic Burke. Nevertheless, lurking in this essentialist position is a more compelling argument (and a more compelling democracy) that only Hazlitt's essentialism—his support of Burke "in the one case" and denigration of Burke "in the other"—finally highlights. And this is the fact that Burke, in apparently seeing all things, remains, like Southey in a way, all things visible. Not merely steadfast in his principles, Burke is also *unanimous* in his opinions, as the multiple positions he maintains are, regardless of their apparent differences, always the "same."[11] Thus instead of assigning Burke a position of exteriority, in which he allegedly comprehends "all things, actions, and events" (in the manner of a romantic Shakespeare), Coleridge actually levels him to a position of inclusion in which disagreement or "discrepancy" is less a point of exit than a point of desynonymity or belonging: a point of entry in which the "laws" Burke *sees*—laws that "circumscribe . . . possibility"—are the very laws he also lives by.[12]

III

Coleridge's conviction in the unanimity that exists among different positions and narratives, all of which leads to a sense of impossibility or stasis, does not on the face of it lend much hope or luster to his democratic vista. Yet it is consistent with Coleridge's leveling, and with his logic of desynonymization, that less is usually more: that possibility—so long as it is "circumscribed" or removed from a totalizing narrative of change and plenitude—is always/already upon us. What is necessary is that we somehow abandon or relinquish the subjective correlative of unbounded possibility: that we consent to our place among the "outward objects," who, under a similar compulsion of space and time, are ourselves. And this leads, in turn, to the return of the visible, or more precisely to the return of genius—be it Hamlet, Wordsworth, or ultimately Coleridge himself—to a visible or social or corporeal field.

Such consent or submission, needless to say, flies in the face of the phenomenological drift of romanticism, both as we have come to understand it and as it was variously promoted at the time—not least by Coleridge himself. Thus, we must never forget that even as it reverses the romantic subject-position in regarding the world and its creatures as barely distinguishable entities (or from the opposite end of the Shakespearean "telescope"), the romantic visible requires an idealized interiority, and the concomitant belief in the significance of *individual* lives, to function as it does. Only in conjunction with these humanistic initiatives, in fact—compromised either by a prevailing blindness or by undue reverence for individual achievement—does a leveling by sight, or in a theater of the mind's eye, carry any real weight or political valence.

The *Biographia* would seem to illustrate this very point, granting both genius and its humanistic freight a seminal, if still preliminary, role in their ultimate reintegration. Yet even with the appended sections to the *Biographia,* upon which the task of reintegration devolves, this turns out to be more than a structural mandate. The discussion of Wordsworth's genius, for example—in many ways the heart and soul of the *Biographia*—is curiously proleptic or preliminary to another conclusion. This is certainly detectable when, in speculating on Wordsworth's future achievement, specifically the ability to produce "the FIRST GENUINE PHILOSOPHIC POEM" (2:156), the text opens onto a kind of blankness that is as much a function of Coleridge's reluctance to "prophesy" such a poem as of a larger refusal, to which the anticipated failure (or the uncertainty of Wordsworth's achievement) is curiously congenial.

This reluctance also undergirds Coleridge's famous insistence on pointing up the difference between Wordsworth's pronouncements regarding his own poetry (recently republished in the 1815 edition of Wordsworth's poems) and the excellences of the works themselves. Often attributed to Coleridge's personal hurt or to his competition with Wordsworth (following the publication of his collected poems in *Sibylline Leaves*), this strategy has the effect, certainly, of reversing the Wordsworth-Coleridge hierarchy in making Coleridge the arbiter of genius, if only for the time being.[13] Nevertheless, it works also to separate Wordsworth from the authority or intentionality that, in the example of Shakespeare, as we have seen, is otherwise the hallmark of genius. When Coleridge observes, for example, that a "literal adherence to the theory of [Wordsworth's] preface *would* exclude . . . two-thirds at least of the marked beauties of his poetry" (2:106), or "that the *supposed* characteristics of Mr. Wordsworth's poetry . . . are as little the *real* characteristics of his poetry at large, as of his genius and the constitution of his mind" (2:119), he is doing more than peevishly educating "genius" in its own achievement; he is (as he did in the discussion of Southey) also identifying genius as a specific order or ideal to which Wordsworth inadvertently conforms.

Hazlitt, whose review of the *Biographia* sidesteps most of Coleridge's "discussion of the merits of his friend Mr. Wordsworth's poetry," is moved, not surprisingly, to contest Coleridge's position on Wordsworth's theory of poetry. Defending Wordsworth's well-known claim that he had "endeavoured to bring [his] language near to the real language of men," Hazlitt asserts that Wordsworth's achievement on this particular score is "so obvious, . . . so generally acknowledged, that nothing but a pitiful affectation of singularity could have raised a controversy on the subject" (134–35). Hazlitt is undoubtedly right in sensing something singular in Coleridge's dissent. Still, the sheer defensiveness of Hazlitt's position—even as it is clearly justified by Coleridge's example—ultimately proves Coleridge's point: the singularity of *Wordsworth's* achievement cannot be described in terms of the poet's representativeness. As Coleridge argues, rather, Wordsworth's theory (and, by implication, Hazlitt's defense of that theory) deploy commonality more as wish-fulfillment: as a distraction to the business of genius, rather than a necessary feature of it.

Thus while Coleridge and Hazlitt are, in their respective ways, opposed to singularity, it is Hazlitt who is sufficiently challenged by Wordsworth's intimations of immortality to stigmatize Coleridge with them. Where Coleridge is seemingly untroubled by Wordsworth's difference, Hazlitt's strategy requires that these attributes be dismissed or elided: that Wordsworth not be discussed on this occasion, and that the poet's singularity—a potential problem in an otherwise democratic poetry—be transposed to Coleridge. Nor is Coleridge, for his part, averse to this transposition. His views regarding Wordsworth in the *Biographia are* elitist and aristocratical: he neither challenges Wordsworth's singularity, nor the genius that sets Wordsworth apart from the very men with whom he claims linguistic proximity. The only problem here—and it is not immediately clear that it is a problem for

Coleridge—is that singularity as such is not singular. Rather, Wordsworth's genius remains something he is "possessed by": a role or "affectation" whereby he consents to the taste by which he is already "of interest."

The conjunction, then, of ascension and accession in the *Biographia,* of the figure of genius and the figure of the critic on whose sanction that singular distinction depends, ultimately cuts both ways. On the one hand, it allows Coleridge, as both I and others have shown, to exploit Wordsworth and to become the self, the origin, the very afflatus, that effectively animates Wordsworth.[14] On the other hand, this conjunction makes singularity a distinction marked paradoxically by conformity, by the poet's ability to satisfy the critic. Hence, even if Coleridge can be said to exploit Wordsworth in this exchange, or to replace him, he is the beneficiary of what amounts to his own dubious praise. This is because the putatively singular object of Coleridge's "copious discussion" is paradoxically (and demonstrably) a copy of singularity.

That Coleridge's critical bequest to Wordsworth turns out to be this much of a problem, with singularity becoming almost a kind of blame in the *Biographia,* is evident, again, in the reluctance to "prophesy" whether Wordsworth will in fact produce the first genuine philosophic poem. In addition to expressing legitimate doubt about Wordsworth's ability to produce such a work, this reluctance is directed at the anticipated work itself, which was Coleridge's idea to begin with. In other words, Coleridge is concerned less in the end with Wordsworth's ability to write the great poem than with the entire circuit in which Wordsworth's great poem would be one that only Coleridge might deem successful. For in this circuit singularity is both paradigm and paradox, both an achievement and an affectation: it measures the taste, once again, by which it is already important.

If Wordsworth's conformity ultimately constitutes a disappointment in the *Biographia,* a recognition of the standards and structures that govern and control not only critical judgment but its humanistic argument, then the reluctance to prophesy a culminating achievement for Wordsworth is in many ways a recantation of Coleridge's famous definition of Imagination, which precedes and effectively prefaces the discussion of Wordsworth in volume 2. The definition, appearing at the very end of the first volume, is of course familiar: "The primary IMAGINATION I hold to be the living Power and prime Agent of all human Perception, and as a repetition in the finite mind of the eternal act of creation in the infinite I AM" (1:304).

In this definition, then, "the prime Agent of all human Perception" turns out *not* to be "imagination," as Coleridge authoritatively claims. It turns out to be God Himself: the authority whose apparent universality, or repetition in the finite mind, is necessarily restricted rather than dispersed. After all, were this authority everywhere and unrestricted (as the definition implies), it would not matter as it now does—since it is the very *centrality* of this authority "in the infinite I AM" that makes the alleged dispersion of authority in imagination a considerable event for "*all* human[s]."

Accordingly, Coleridge's definition requires an example like Wordsworth rather than either Southey or Burke: an example whose status hinges on his being exemplary rather than "our" representative. In being brought closer to the very authority that his *human* example might militate against, Wordsworth shows how, in fact, it is the other way around: how the "I" conjugated by "AM" is less a declension of the infinite to the finite than an ascension to godhead that only certain individuals can achieve. The putatively radical dispersion of authority in imagination, in the prime agent of all human perception, amounts, then—whether in fact or in Wordsworth—to a proliferation of God.

Coleridge's solution to this contradiction was to distinguish immediately between the primary Imagination, the agent "of *all* human Perception," and the secondary Imagination, which comparatively fewer humans possess. Unlike primary Imagination, secondary Imagination requires the "conscious will," which in turn makes it "identical with the primary in the *kind* of its agency, and differ[ent] only in *degree,* and in the *mode* of its operation" (1:304). But this distinction between imagination-as-perception and imagination-as-creation (specifically poetic or artistic) was finally no solution—if only because those possessed of secondary imagination, of the ability "to idealize and to unify," were no longer like "all" other humans.[15]

A more dramatic solution to the contradiction of divine dispersion—or to the "degrees" of equality as Coleridge conceived them—was clearly in order, and it was a solution, not surprisingly, that would eventually turn on the problem of conformity. If conformity in the humanistic sense leads ultimately to God, to a proximity with the "infinite," for which "I" and "Wordsworth" are simply other names, then it is only by conformity, again, by a leveling of all distinction, that other possibilities will be served. Consequently, Coleridge moves in the appended sections of the *Biographia* to accomplish several things, almost all of which either hinge upon, or are closely related to, the return of genius to a visible or social or corporeal field. The return of genius to a terrestrial or theatrical state, where it necessarily lacks distinction—where Wordsworth, for example, lacks even a name when he is next referred to in the *Biographia*—marks the severance, most obviously, of genius and God. Accordingly, when we encounter Wordsworth in the appendix to the *Biographia* he is not only anonymous or a mere body; he is a seasick body conscious *solely* of his bodiliness and nothing else.

But not even this return can ultimately prevent the reestablishment of those ties that a materialization of genius apparently disrupts. For the metaphysical ties linking man to God in Coleridge's conception of genius, though clearly breached by the return of the visible, recall the culture—a hegemony bound equally to a discipline of space and time—of which the humanistic critic (no less than his object) remains a part.

The theatrical impulse in Coleridge, which is most evident finally in his theater criticism, proceeds in two, somewhat separate, directions, therefore. The first and most obvious direction involves a return of the visible, whereby genius, in the image of Hamlet, is distinguished by no feature other than its refusal to be part of the visible, social world to which it demonstrably belongs. The second direction is more tortuous and harder to demarcate. Here, Coleridge does more than simply join Hamlet as an authority demystified; he actually takes his place in a culture to which both he and Hamlet have belonged: in an order whose values and ideals he has not revised or opposed so much as perpetuated. What this ultimately means for community, or for the possibility that counts on a sense of solidarity and belonging, is unclear. All that *is* clear by the end of the *Biographia* is that by joining or returning to community (as the case may be), Coleridge, in anticipation of such twentieth-century thinkers as Antonio Gramsci, takes a necessary first step in reimagining what he has joined. Beyond the recognition that all positions are the same or desynonymous, there is the further recognition in the *Biographia* that desynonymity and synonymity are more properly synonyms: that a position of critical authority, more than capricious or even arbitrary, makes Coleridge (like either Wordsworth or Hamlet) one of a hegemony.

IV

The story of how Coleridge came to enlarge the *Biographia* does not, on the face of it, bode especially well for this interpretation of its appended parts—comprised of the three "Satyrane" letters and the "critique," following them, of Maturin's play *Bertram.* Informed by his publisher that the *Biographia* had to be expanded to fill two volumes of equal size and to avoid the "disproportion" that currently existed in a work unevenly divided between aesthetic philosophy and the practical criticism of Wordsworth's poetry, Coleridge was apparently at a loss as to what to do. Writing to the printer in Bristol, he frantically envisioned the solution as "writing *a hundred and fifty pages* additional—on *what, I* am left to discover" (4:661). He appears to have solved the problem by writing nothing new at all.[16] In the end, Coleridge simply expanded the *Biographia* by republishing a pastiche of letters from 1798, which he had already revised for *The Friend* in 1809, and by republishing his critique of *Bertram,* which he was in the process of sending to the *Courier* at the time he received word of the need to expand.

Of the two additions to the *Biographia,* the Satyrane section detailing Coleridge's and Wordsworth's 1798 trip to Germany was (as even Coleridge implied) the more germane to the "title" and subject of the *Biographia:* both to the commerce of German theory and English philosophy as well as its apparent issue in Wordsworth's poetry.[17] In contrast, the critique of *Bertram* seems relevant only insofar as it was important to Coleridge at the time he was actually completing the *Biographia* and smarting over the recent rejection of his own play *Zapolya* by Drury Lane. This, more or less, is the conventional wisdom regarding the additions to Coleridge's text. Nevertheless, the choice to republish these *particular* works, and to do so on the very heels of a fantasy regarding Wordsworth's inability to write the first great philosophic poem, was more powerfully motivated, in my view, or at least differently motivated, than commentators have allowed.[18] This motivation is most evident, again, in the theatrical turn of these additions, which entails not only a rather deliberate theatricalization of the critical persona but an objectification of the very community, of the very culture in fact, that the authoritative persona inhabits and continually serves.

We do not know exactly what provoked Coleridge in 1809 to publish and, in two cases, to combine and radically amend seven letters that he had written to his wife and to his friend Thomas Poole at the time he and the Wordsworths traveled to Germany in 1798. But the republication of the revised letters in the *Biographia* suggests that it was the purpose of the three "Satyrane" letters (as Coleridge dubbed them at the time of their inclusion in *The Friend*) to reflect retrospectively on that moment in Coleridge's career when, for want of a better term, he became a "Romantic" with all the privileges and problems attached thereto. Reminding us, more recently, that among the things accomplished on this trip was an avoidance of the draft in England or of what had been "the greatest *levée* of the Volunteers in the whole decade" (167), E. P. Thompson has argued that Coleridge's German tour necessarily taints romanticism as a postrevolutionary movement. In his apparent flight from sedition, according to Thompson, Coleridge was sufficiently removed from a radical or revolutionary matrix that his "romanticism" can actually be deemed a movement toward conservatism or toward what Thompson disparagingly calls "default."[19]

Like Hazlitt's, then, Thompson's assessment of romantic politics admits a hierarchy of values that finds political radicalism firmly at the top and political conservatism—the anti-Jacobinism that effectively drove Coleridge out of England and that Coleridge, in consenting to be driven, came inevitably to embrace—at the bottom. In the middle of this hierarchy is something called "disenchantment," by which Thompson distinguishes one account of romanticism—in which radicalism and privatization are congenial bedfellows—from *his* account, in which it is the privatizing tendency (nominally reflected in Coleridge's flight to Germany) that distinguishes romanticism from the revolution that spawned it. More recent assessments, chiefly by critics affiliated with the new historicism, have been even harsher in describing the romantic turn inward, eliminating all but the most reactionary links between a radicalism on the one hand, with its inevitable openness to people and to history, and a meditative humanism on the other.[20] Unlike Thompson or Hazlitt, who at least credit romanticism with a radical inheritance, some recent critics find apostasy too light a charge. For them, romanticism was always in "default"—even and especially in those moments when, flushed with a sense of their democratic rectitude, the Romantics expressed a faith in the significance of individual human beings.

In returning to that moment, then, when romanticism burgeoned in all its contradictoriness, Coleridge would show an almost identical sensitivity to what later critics have found wanting in the romantic program. The only difference really is that Coleridge was responsive *without* a moral alternative, a vocabulary sufficiently empowering that he could apparently blame others in lieu of himself. Thus, while blame remains a prevalent activity in the three Satyrane letters (as well as in the critique of *Bertram*), it does not succeed in shoring up a privileged, comparatively blameless counterposition. In fact, the blame cast by "Satyrane" (and later by "Wordsworth") in the three letters—blame of the slave trade, blame of the contemporary theater, blame of the German poet Klopstock—actually renders Satyrane, who is named thus because he is "the Idoloclast, or breaker of Idols" (*Friend,* 2:185), a builder of consensus: a figure whose perpetual transit from democrat to aristocrat (and vice versa) makes him, like Burke in a way, the embodiment of community.

But there is, in any case, a critical difference between community as imagined in the figure of Satyrane—and after "genius" in effect—and community as it was previously imagined according to Burke and Southey. Where Burke and Southey were enlisted, like the visible Hamlet, to contest the possibility of inviolable difference or exteriority, community in the wake of Wordsworth's singular achievement is also seen through a glass darkly: as a hegemony in which there are few options and in which even desynonymity is probably too supple, too dynamic, a description of consensus. Instead, it is the inevitable sameness of all positions *however singular,* a unanimity or consensus no longer dependent on difference, that arguably describes the human world for Coleridge.

Thus, even more than the criticism previously inclined toward community, the appendix to the *Biographia* requires an apparatus of the visible, whereby the idoloclast is, by turns, the man in the street and individual *performance,* or selfhood, is a parabola between fixed, opposed, and ultimately *similar* positions. In speaking of this apparatus, then, I am speaking once again of theatricality—a term used here neither loosely nor because the theater as such is increasingly the central topic of the added sections. "Theatricality" is the operative term because it is, in fact, the only one that properly describes the essential moments in the Satyrane letters, at least two of which—the encounter with the Dane in letter 1 and the dialogue about the contemporary theater in letter 2—are cast specifically in dramatic form.

The third essential moment, which can be described as a dramatic monologue by Wordsworth himself, gives an even fuller sense, perhaps, of what is at stake in Coleridge's recourse to theatricality. For Wordsworth's meeting with Klopstock, whose peevish and pedestrian character is both recorded and recapitulated in notes quoted by "Satyrane," marks the first time that Wordsworth speaks in propria persona in the *Biographia*, or independent of the evidence of imagination on which his genius—and in large part, the entire humanistic project—depends. With this objectification, then, all difference between Wordsworth the poet and Wordsworth the ordinary, nearly anonymous body is finally collapsed, as the temporal and spatial discipline to which Wordsworth is exposed—which fixes him according to one standard or another—precipitates a movement in which "Wordsworth" is essentially remarkable and indistinguishable all at once. Theatricality in the *Biographia* would appear to accord, then, with Michael Fried's use of the term (discussed in chapter 3). Not only does theatricality level a decidedly romantic authority to a merely material status; it allows this leveling or subjugation of authority to *figure* the peculiar conformity or synonymity that is also genius, or (if you prefer) genius to begin with.

Consequently, when we next encounter Wordsworth in the *Biographia* we encounter him scarcely at all, despite the fact that it was known that Wordsworth and his sister had accompanied Coleridge on the 1798 trip. Instead, the anonymity to which Wordsworth is deliberately consigned by "Satyrane"—he may or may not be the "gentleman" standing "near" Satyrane to whom the latter speaks briefly upon embarkation but is almost certainly one of the passengers who soon go below consumed by seasickness—points, in a strange way, to the anonymity, or better still the synonymity, of Wordsworth as a celebrated person. While the specter of a nearly anonymous Wordsworth responsible, among others, for the noxious "exportations from the cabin" (2:161) has an effect analogous to that of Hamlet "living in meditation," it goes one step further in canceling any difference between "genius" and the world to which genius now belongs. After all, where something is inevitably gained by Hamlet's replacement to a visible field—a sense of solidarity perhaps—Wordsworth's conformity, his return to a vomiting body, both echoes and recapitulates what was gained *and lost* in his previous accession to genius.

Later, in recounting Wordsworth's transcription of the meeting with Klopstock, Coleridge is rather more explicit regarding the identity of the monologuist whom "Satyrane" describes in characteristically eighteenth-century fashion as "my friend W——" (2:199). This gesture of conferring and withholding identity in a single stroke remains an even more precise articulation of the point at issue. Much like the consignment of Wordsworth to anonymity, to a body conscious only of its bodiliness, the point here is that there is literally no difference between Wordsworth and the not-Wordsworth, between the great man and the ordinary man. To be a body, an object in space and time, is to be part of the cultural field that produces genius or, if you prefer, produces "W——." It is to belong to a world that produces a man whose identity and singularity are a reading—an arbitrary, if directed interpretation of him such as we have just witnessed in the *Biographia—and* at the same time (as the present formulation plainly suggests) a reading against the grain.

All the same, it devolves upon the Satyrane persona himself, and to his dramatic encounters in particular, to confirm how Wordsworth's materialization "below"—the sight of him under erasure—circumscribes not only the three Satyrane letters but, with its particular bearing on genius, both the *Biographia* and the romantic project as a whole. Hence, it is worth remembering what Coleridge initially said of Satyrane when he introduced him in *The Friend* in 1809. After explaining the meaning of Satyrane's name, Coleridge expatiated on the personal characteristics of his "idoloclast":

> He had a greater and more heart-felt delight in in the superiority of other men to himself, than men in general derive from belief in their own. His readiness to imagine a superiority where it did not exist, was indeed, for many years his predominant foible. His pain from the perception of inferiority in others, whom he had heard spoken of with any respect, was unfeigned and involuntary; and perplexed him, as a something which he did not comprehend. In the child-like simplicity of his nature he talked to all men, as if they were, at least, his equals in knowledge and talents. . . . When he was at length compelled to see and acknowledge the true state of the morals and intellect of his contemporaries, his disappointment was severe, and his mind, always thoughtful, became pensive and almost gloomy: for to love and sympathize with mankind was a necessity of his nature. (*Friend,* 2:186–87)

Whether this counts as veiled autobiography or even self-hagiography is manifestly less important than the portrait of the "breaker of idols" as a defender of the status quo: as promoter of the very hierarchies and correspondences on which a democratic vista (everyman my superior) is disingenuously founded.

Thus, even so slight a contradiction as Satyrane's "comprehension" of a world allegedly peopled by his betters, points to what is most essential to him and later confirmed by his compulsion to concede the opposite. For Satyrane's disappointment in others, which he had deferred for a time in the guise of sympathy and fellow feeling, was always his position. As a result, Satyrane's principle "foible"—his imagining "a superiority where it did not exist"—is more than a little ironic. In addition to underscoring Satyrane's superiority relative to the world he imagines superior to himself, it suggests more importantly how this very sense of superiority—the only vocabulary that Satyrane has—is as misplaced at its source (in the subject prone to comprehension) as it is misplaced *by* its source or in the Satyrane prone to disappointment. Superiority, whether given or taken away, whether appropriated or dispersed, always emanates from the same structure: it issues from a subject-position that, for all its apparent concern and sympathy, is about as far from its professed radicalism, and consequently from itself, as is possible.

The point in emphasizing the "Idoloclast's" sense of superiority is not to underscore his hypocrisy but rather to show how the Satyrane so constituted—unlike either Burke or Southey—is marshaled in a critique of romanticism that is no less a disclosure of hegemony. Where previously the desynonymity of all positions implied a leveling of those positions—and a community, by extension, whose mitigation of autonomy allowed for its improvement as a community—things are here reversed. Now, in a virtual recapitulation of abiding dominance, the initiatives of equality and fellow-feeling are subsumed by an antileveling initiative. Superiority is as characteristic of the blameworthy—of the apparent enemies of freedom and solidarity—as of the blamer himself, who is no less the enemy of equality and solidarity. Oscillating rather between positions that are sufficiently proximate, dissent or idoloclasm comes parabolically (more, perhaps, than paradoxically) to consent and idolatry. As a result, Satyrane's radical or liberationist initiatives—beginning with his detestation of the Danish slave trader—end up recapitulating and participating in the very thing they oppose.

The highly theatrical encounter with the Dane provides an excellent instance of Satyrane's function as a blamer. In addition to belonging to the least revised of the original letters, the encounter belongs to a letter whose revisions as such make clear what Coleridge was after when he undertook to reuse his letters ten years after they were first composed. The first, and possibly most notable change in the letter of 3 October 1798 (from which the first Satyrane letter derives), remains the reduction of Wordsworth to anonymity. Where Wordsworth was mentioned by name in the original letter to Mrs. Coleridge and was described there as having "followed" his sister in retiring "to the Cabin" (1:421), he is nowhere to be found in this letter to the world except below deck, or among the various others whose "brotherhood" is marked entirely by seasickness. A second revision involves essentially two things: a more sanctimonious meditation on the "brotherhood" of boat travel (as opposed to coach travel), and following it, the transposition of the encounter with the Dane into dialogue or dramatic form.

Nevertheless, unlike Wordsworth's consignment below, or the rather self-serving notion of community and "communication" elaborated in the 1809 text, the dialogue with the Dane does not differ substantially from the transcription of the conversation as Coleridge first reported it in 1798. In both letters, the Dane is presented as a hypocrite whose reiterated belief in human equality is sharply countermanded by his experience in the slave trade:

> THE DANE: I was sent ofer to dhe Vest Indies—to our Island, and dhere I had no more to do vid books. No! no! I put my genius another way—and I haf made ten thousand pound a year. Is not dhat *ghenius,* my dear friend!—But vat is money! But vat is money! I dhink the poorest man alive my equal. Yes, my dear friend! my little fortune is pleasant to my generous heart, because I can do good—no man with so little a fortune ever did so much generosity—no person, no man person, no woman person ever denies it. But we are all Got's children. (164–65)

This speech as reproduced by Satyrane differs scarcely at all from the (ironic if still chauvinist) statements reproduced by Coleridge in his earlier letter. But there is one notable exception, the exclamation "Is not dhat *ghenius,* my dear friend," which Satyrane means to have founder on its own rhetoric.

And this, needless to say, is an important addition—if only in that Coleridge's role in the *Biographia,* particularly regarding Wordsworth, has been to repeat that very gesture. Thus, far from simply vindicating Satyrane, the emphasis on "*ghenius*" ultimately subjects Satyrane to an interrogation not unlike the one *his* transcription would wrest from the Dane's rhetoric. While the Dane is undoubtedly an object of ridicule according to Satyrane, he is in the transcription of Satyrane's transcription (in which there are now two chauvinists) more nearly Satyrane's double. This is already clear in the assertions regarding equality (all of which recall Coleridge's description of Satyrane in the introduction to *The Friend*). But the real issue is the way Satyrane is necessarily transformed by the dramatic form—indeed by his very recourse to dramatic form—into a figure who is both the Dane's antagonist and as such the defender of true genius and true equality.

V

Referring, then, to the contradiction inherent in the humanistic position, the movement from Coleridge *to* Satyrane in the *Biographia* is (for want of a better term) self-reflexive, since it both follows and ultimately exceeds the parent text in revealing the way equality is effectively construed along lines of superiority, and how genius, far from being singular, is more a matter of conformity. This contradiction, of course, is one of the many lessons of poststructuralism and of the revisionist approach to romanticism, in general. But it is more immediately, I would urge, a lesson of the *Biographia Literaria,* that Hazlitt, among others, clearly failed to heed.

In an 1821 essay, "On Consistency of Opinion," Hazlitt continued his attack on Coleridgean apostasy by distinguishing his own "sympath[y] *beforehand* with the different views and feelings . . . that prevents my retracting my judgment, and flinging myself into the contrary extreme *afterwards*" from a "sympath[y] with others" (17:23) based on a a desire to please. This latter "sympathy," according to Hazlitt, yields an "inconsisten[cy]" not "at different times, but at all times" (29) and is thus a "sympathy" in which Coleridge is, again, representative: "He is a sophist, a casuist, a rhetorician, what you please; and might have argued or declaimed to the end of his breath on one side of a question or another, but he never was a pragmatical fellow. He lived in a round of contradictions, and never came to a settled point" (29). Nor is it only Coleridge who is inconsistent. It is virtually everyone with the exception of Hazlitt, whose "consistency" is such that not even the "high and heroic" souls, who "think to scale the heights of truth and virtue at once" (27), can possibly compete with him in their steadfastness. Yet precisely because Hazlitt assumes his customary position of exteriority in this essay, a position so consistent that it is literally unrepresentable except as an inferable alternative to Coleridge, he necessarily works to prove Coleridge's point—or the point made through the Satyrane's example. As Hazlitt shows, in fact, the only "uniform consistency" remains the "spirit of contradiction" (28) or the "round of contradiction" in which Coleridge lives: the "inconsisten[cy] . . . at all times" (as he terms it), which is really another name for hegemony. Unlike the desynonymous or unanimous world glimpsed earlier through the examples of Southey and Burke—a world whose essential sameness both admits and even requires difference—the world, according to Satyrane (and in addition to Hazlitt), is precisely a world of contradiction: a world where difference is either canceled or sufficiently leveled that it no longer counts as difference.

Nevertheless, unlike Hazlitt, whose own sense of difference is figured not only in the attempt to reconcile singularity and equality in (for example) the treatment of Edmund Kean, but more reflexively in the attack on Coriolanus, the Satyrane persona advocates both equality and genius as if they were in no need of reconciliation. Thus, where Hazlitt sees himself only inadvertently or by accident, Satyrane sees himself not at all. Coleridge's recourse to dramatic form, both here and in the ensuing chapter, is more than a countermovement to a blinding humanism, therefore; it is a strategy that clearly distinguishes a writer increasingly cognizant of his place in space and time from a critic like Hazlitt, whose denial of community issues only in an unconscious objectification of that refusal. While the dramatic encounters in letters 1 and 2 necessarily separate Satyrane from the Dane and the defender of modern drama respectively, the very transposition to dramatic form demarcates a spatial, social environment that cannot, as Coleridge sees it, be transcended or transgressed. If anything, every effort at transgression or transcendence—every movement toward a position of exteriority or consistency—merely returns Satyrane (and later Wordsworth) to the very company from which he cannot in any case remove himself, literally or figuratively.

This point, I think, is made unequivocally in the dialogue with the Dane in which Satyrane becomes fixed and formulated as a better version of the Dane: as a man whose belief in the equality of "all Got's children" is rivaled only by his belief in "Got" or in the "ghenius" in "Got's" image. Nevertheless, it is the second letter with its lengthy dialogue on the contemporary theater that drives the point home—theatricalizing, in effect, the very antitheatricality that holds to a position of exteriority and difference.

The dialogue on the contemporary theater—though apposite to Coleridge's concerns when he was completing the *Biographia*—was, like virtually every other revision in these letters, an invention of 1809. Thus, to attribute the antitheatrical drift of the added sections of the *Biographia* to Coleridge's anxiety regarding the recently rejected play, *Zapolya,* overlooks the extent to which antitheatricality as such—with its humanistic or romantic legacy—is a central object of interrogation. Like other aspects of "high romanticism," notably the superiority underwriting both "ghenius" and equality, antitheatricality evinces an inconsistency *at all times* for which hegemony is still the better term.

But hegemony is not the only term for such continual inconsistency. Such inconsistency or contradiction remains—in its necessary confinement (in any given moment) to one orientation as against another—tantamount to the very agency or resistance that Paul Smith describes. The difference, then, is that where resistance to hegemony transpires, according to Smith, in the space between one interpellated position and another, or in a space continually created by the "round of contradiction" within a hegemonic order, the peculiar agency, which the visible both serves and signifies, requires what is in some ways a longer *view* of the situation. For here, the movement among, or oscillation between, subject-positions turns out be less a destabilizing activity than a figuration of sameness, which is deplorable in one sense and yet in another sense desirable. That is, the contradiction "at all times" figures what is in the end a counterhegemony as well, which (in addition to being a means of resistance, according to Gramsci) is in large degree the *goal* of resistance: the leveling according to which contradiction and consistency, and the various subject-positions from which these two terms derive their value, become virtually interchangeable and, by turns, meaningless.

There are, to be sure, many moments in the Satyrane letters where inconsistency is necessarily more hidebound and more conventionally hegemonic: for example, in the jingoism that routinely intrudes upon Satyrane's efforts to "bond" with his fellow human beings abroad. However, there are two instances in letter 2—each an addition of 1809—whose hegemonic inconsistency necessarily looks ahead to the theatrical performance that follows in imagining a counter-hegemony, the peculiar *consistency* of which is anything but restrictive or oppressive. Rather, the synonymity of this imagined order, which counts paradoxically on a leveling by sight or the reduction of the subject to material status, remains a goal that, even as it is always beyond us and interfered with (as in these instances), is literally within our ken.

The first of the two instances, Satyrane's expatiation on "the character of a *gentleman,*" concludes with the rather remarkable definition of "*gentlemanly* character aris[ing] out of the feeling of Equality acting, as a Habit, yet flexible to the varieties of Rank, and modified without being disturbed or superseded by them" (2:175–76). Without debating the accuracy of this description, which effectively locates the gentleman in a hierarchy from which he is ostensibly removed, we can conclude that the gentleman is not only a figure of contradiction, but of a contradiction that literally knows no limit, no end.

There is, to begin with, the notion of equality itself, which is introduced and undone in what amounts to a single breath. "Equality" is so clearly a performance, so inextricably an affectation, that it necessarily issues in (and helps mask) the very hierarchy it opposes. And, too, there is the concluding observation—bearing Satyrane's endorsement—that despite behavior that is evidently contradictory, the gentleman represents a resistance to hierarchy, and a defense of equality, in the way he avoids being superseded or modified by his betters.

To deploy the gentleman as an archetypal republican is problematic enough. However the image of equality as inequality—of being equal, in effect, to one's betters—suggests that there is more at stake in the deployment of Satyrane than either simple surrogacy or even self-irony; inherent in his praise is an acuity that, were it not contradictory "at all times," would likely count as deconstruction—since it is the gentleman, the everyman unsuperseded and unmodified, who remains the quintessential subject of the *Biographia:* the very genius whom Coleridge both endorses and yet militates against.

Several pages later, in reference to the French "emigrant" (and monarchist) who initially prompts the discourse on gentlemanliness, Satyrane has occasion to compare and contrast the revolutions in England and in France:

> My heart dilated with honest pride, as I recalled to mind the stern yet amiable characters of the English patriots, who sought refuge on the Continent at the Restoration! O let not our civil war under the first Charles be parallelled with the French revolution! In the former, the chalice overflowed from excess of principle; in the

> latter, from the fermentation of the dregs! The former, was a civil war between the virtues and virtuous prejudices of the two parties; the latter between the vices. (2:181)

The concluding jingoistic turn, which cancels an otherwise apposite parallel between the revolution *under Cromwell* and the French Revolution, is only the last in a series of contradictions beginning with an implicit parallel of patriotism and monarchism. Indeed, just as the French monarchist in exile leads Satyrane into speculation regarding the "English patriots," whose flight owed undoubtedly to their advocacy of regicide, so Satyrane is obliged by the logic of this parallel to dub the Puritan Revolution "our civil war under the first Charles." Such a euphemism does two related things: it marks the equivalency and the interchangeability of patriotism and monarchism; and more important, it makes the only good "revolution" a Glorious Revolution. While Satyrane is quite explicit in identifying the monarch associated with the English Revolution, his situation of that revolution "under Charles" reveals his nostalgia for what came after—specifically, the conversion of levelers into patriots that only the Restoration, the revolution "under Charles," would achieve. Thus, even as he means to distinguish the French and English revolutions according to the relative morality of the "parties" involved in each, Satyrane's position remains circumscribed by an ideal of "revolution" that is really counterrevolution; it is contained by an ideal in which patriotism, like equality, is figured by the monarchist in exile: by the "gentleman" who is sometimes but never finally his own sovereign.

In all of this, needless to say, there is plenty with which to indict Coleridge, and to compel agreement with Hazlitt. But such an indictment requires that we discount the interrogatory function of the Satyrane persona, and that we minimize the dramatic apparatus—both here and in the chapter that follows—with which Satyrane's introduction into the *Biographia* is explicitly connected. Thus, while the ensuing dialogue on the contemporary theater, which features Satyrane in the role of "Plaintiff," resembles similar pronouncements made by Coleridge in his own person, it nevertheless allows Coleridge a second chance with these pronouncements in putting that complaint, with its peculiar inconsistency, to different and more productive use. And the proof of this, again, is not only in the "Plaintiff's" virulent anti-Jacobinism, in which he reveals the "secret of dramatic popularity" to be "the confusion and subversion of the natural order of things"

(2:190); the proof is in the way the encounter itself reveals this alleged "order" to be a *naturalized* order that, in recapitulating the structures of social and metaphysical organization, resists both man and nature.

It is not necessary to engage in a complete reading of the dialogue on the theater, which ranges, in any case, from the contemporary appetite for narrative or story to the demand for sensation and spectacle, before settling on the more important issues of subject and character. Nor is it necessary really to observe the often accurate, and otherwise convincing, protests levied by the Plaintiff (Satyrane) against what was, after all, an institution in crisis. Instead, the point to emphasize is that Satyrane's perfectly sensible, even canonical view, lauding "the personages of Shakespeare, and the Greek Tragedians" (2:189) over the "good friends and next-door neighbours" (2:188) in contemporary drama, moves from an unassailable position to a position that *becomes* assailable simply in disclosing the aristocratical basis of judgments that are otherwise humanistic.

In discussing, then, the importance of the characters in contemporary theater, Satyrane wonders how the "Defendant" can possibly "connect with such men and such actions that dependence of thousands on the fate of one, which gives so lofty an interest to [Shakespeare's characters]," or "connect with them that sublimest of all feelings, the power of destiny and controlling might of heaven, which seems to elevate the characters which sink beneath its irresistible blow" (2:189). In all of this, to be sure, the Plaintiff is doing little more than reciting the standard prescriptions for tragedy dating back to Aristotle. However, what is unique to Satyrane's argument, or unique at least for the purpose to which his argument is being put, is the peculiar bias whereby human value—indeed "human nature" (2:189)—is essentially opposed to humans in general.

Thus, in contesting the Defendant's counterassertion that "we seek and find on the present stage our own wants and passions, our own vexations, losses, and embarrassments," Satyrane reminds his adversary that "it is your own poor pettifogging nature . . . which you desire to have represented before you . . . not human nature in its heighth and vigour," but rather a "libelling [of] your superiors" (2:189). It is clear, if only from the tone of this exchange (and from the contradictory position into which Satyrane has been forced), that a reversal has taken place. Moreover, this reversal owes less to any intrinsic excellence on the part of the Defendant (who continues to be weighted down by his cause) than to a transformation on the part of

Satyrane himself, for whom human nature is, by definition, an elevated and fundamentally denatured condition. While it may be tempting to credit Satyrane (whose invention the encounter is) with the ability to have sympathized with two positions at the same time, it is clear—if only from the futility of the defense—that the Plaintiff's hysteria is very much to *Coleridge's* purpose: that theatricality is recuperated only in the way it is a strategy that proves the breaker of idols wrong, or *demonstrably* an idolator, despite his being right about the theater.

That the theater is recuperated here as a legitimate counter to humanism (rather than for its own sake) becomes even more evident following the Defendant's rather silly taxonomy of the heroes and villains on the contemporary stage. Lauding the contemporary tendency to transform "moralists" into "traitors" and "men of spirit" into "men of honour" (2:190), the Defendant manages to goad Satyrane into an indictment of the "whole system of [modern] drama" as "moral and intellectual *Jacobinism* of the most dangerous kind . . . rewarding with all the sympathies that are the dues of virtue, those criminals whom law, reason, and religion, have excommunicated from our esteem" (190). If theatricality is necessarily vindicated in this exchange, it is not as an institution, much less a modern institution. It is vindicated simply by the way the last word in the exchange cannot be imbued with the authority that Satyrane apparently means it to carry. Authority, in fact, is all that is left: the very thing that prevents a humanistic discourse from being anything apart from a discourse wherein blame is essentially "excommunication."

The point—and the agency—of the dramatization, then, and it is central to the vindication of theatricality here, is that these two discourses are (and have been) fundamentally the same: humanism, following its canonical bent, is really a humanistic orthodoxy in which a thousand humans must be excommunicated for every one, for every genius, who is enshrined. Hence, the Plaintiff does more than demonstrate how hidebound things have become in a postrevolutionary era; he demonstrates the inconsistency of a revolutionary program as well: how romanticism—independent of its crudification on the contemporary stage—was "inconsistent at all times" if only by giving "superiority" complete rein in an ostensibly humane discourse. But this, of course, is only part of the story regarding inconsistency. The other part is about how inconsistency is simply another way of describing the ordinary: the "spirit of contradiction," as Hazlitt called it, which is so perennial that we no longer recognize it, particularly in the guise of singularity. Consequently, it is the spirit of ordinariness that pervades the last, and possibly the most critical of Satyrane's letters, the letter describing Satyrane's, and later Wordsworth's, interviews with the romantic poet Klopstock.

I have already mentioned the way letter 3 marks, among other things, the retrieval of Wordsworth from virtual anonymity—which is especially noteworthy insofar as Coleridge had initially obscured the identity of Klopstock's interlocutor in the version of the letter in *The Friend,* referring to him as "B——" rather than as "W——," as he is called in the *Biographia.* This is still a far cry from referring to Wordsworth as "Wordsworth," but it is a revision strangely proximate to the drift of Coleridge's criticism regarding Wordsworth in previous sections, where "Wordsworth" is a poet increasingly anonymous. Thus, it is altogether fitting that Wordsworth's retrieval from anonymity (according to the movement from "B——" to "W——") would be a return to anonymity as well: to an ordinariness that is as much figured by the still resistant nomenclature as it is proven in W——'s own words. For it is the ordinariness of the singular, its rather arbitrary claim to difference where none is visible, that is its most dramatic feature.

Thus, not only is Wordsworth put under erasure or returned to ordinariness in this final letter; Klopstock is as well: his movement from revolutionary ardor to "the most vehement Anti-Gallicism" (as Satyrane describes it [2:195, 198]) traces the parabolic and paradoxically ordinary arc of "idoloclasm" as it has been dramatized thus far. As a result, Satyrane's own description of their meeting, which precedes his transcription of W——'s notes of subsequent meetings with Klopstock, records a disappointment at once intellectual and physical—where the utter absence "of sublimity or enthusiasm in [Klopstock's] physiognomy" is recapitulated in his dreary and rather ill-informed "conversation" (2:195).

There is, it would appear, an irony to Satyrane's disappointment—and to Coleridge's actual disappointment as he related it to Poole in 1798 in the letter later transposed (*Letters,* 1:441). And it involves, quite clearly, a belief in genius so unqualified that there is virtual astonishment and even denial when the body of genius looks anything other than remarkable. If Klopstock did not look the part to Satyrane, then he was obviously not the part, as both Coleridge's and now Satyrane's account of him reveal. Yet where this recollection recoils on the hagiographer, who resists in every possible way the return of genius to bodily form, it is the purpose of the second recollection in letter 3—which is to say "W——'s" recollection—to foreground what Satyrane (and earlier Coleridge) were able, for their part, to deny. This, once again, is the very ordinariness, the synonymity, which is less a characteristic of Klopstock (despite W——'s efforts to the contrary) than of "W——" himself, whose notes reveal an observer who is anything but large-minded, or unique. If anything, "W——" is entirely the opposite and a reminder of how "Wordsworth," the character in the *Biographia* proper, is equally a conformist. His purpose, in conjunction with the nomenclature, is simply to dramatize how superiority or genius is a divestment akin to anonymity.

With this in mind, it is noteworthy that Coleridge's original letter to Poole, in which Wordsworth's meeting with Klopstock is recounted, contains no direct transcription of Wordsworth's impressions. Instead, Coleridge simply indicates what transpired between the two men, adding that, to him, it seemed very ordinary: "Wordsworth had a long [&] various Conversation on literature with Klopstock—but it [was] (& Wordsworth agrees with me) all very *commonplace*!" (1:444). It is this ordinariness, undoubtedly, that Satyrane means to emphasize in directly quoting "the mere transcription of notes, which my friend W—— made of his conversations with Klopstock, during the interviews that took place after my departure" (2:199). Yet even so, the existence of direct testimony from someone *other* than Satyrane, who is identified for the first time as "W——," is important in a different way. Not only does this testimony allow the *Biographia* to come to rest with the very figure on whom it effectively depends; it reflects what was likely at stake in 1809 but only became a matter of urgency in 1816, by which point Coleridge's retrospective view of romanticism, his literary life, had settled ultimately on the figure he could no longer refer to by name.

And so the rest to which the *Biographia* comes in this letter is anything but settled. Just as Coleridge had earlier closed on a blankness in Wordsworth's failure to write the first great philosophic poem, so the second (and penultimate) ending to the *Biographia* closes on a conversation whose own blankness owes entirely to the fact that it is an exchange between geniuses. It is an exchange in which the ordinariness of one party is rivaled only by the delectation in that ordinariness displayed by the other. Here is an example:

> Schiller's "Robbers" [Klopstock] found so extravagant that he could not read it. I spoke of the scene of the setting sun. He did not know it. He thought Don Carlos the best of his dramas; but said the plot was inextricable.—It was evident, he knew little of Schiller's works: indeed he said, he could not read them. Bürger he said was a true poet, and would live; that Schiller, on the contrary, must soon be forgotten; that he gave himself up to the imitation of Shakespeare, who was often so extravagant, but that Schiller was ten thousand times more so. (202)

A fuller transcript of these and similar notes of Wordsworth's meetings with Klopstock, with their particular attention to the latter's envy and, more important, his incapacity ("He could not read it. . . . He did not know it. . . . He knew little of . . ."), was recently retrieved from manuscripts and journals and published as "Conversations with Klopstock."[21] While the more complete extract (the majority of which Coleridge quotes) does not particularly enhance Wordsworth's reputation any more than do the majority of the poet's prose works and letters, it does not as an independent text bear the impact that it does as a potential conclusion to the *Biographia Literaria*. With the weight of the age bearing down on it now, an age whose philosophical humanism found its issue in William Wordsworth according to the *Biographia,* the exposure of the poet as a stickler for details, overly concerned with catching Klopstock's various inconsistencies or lapses in knowledge, is more than a piece of character assassination by either Satyrane or Coleridge. It is an anticlimax that carries just about everyone down with it, including the Satyrane figure, who is sufficiently removed from the Coleridge he represents that his endorsement of W——'s transcript, with its endorsement of the latter's authority, additionally figures Coleridge's disaffection with his (and Wordsworth's) enterprise.

Of the actual transcript itself, there is little to add except to reiterate that "W[ordsworth]" is *quoted* here—or reproduced in his particular historicity—and further, that his words are bracketed by the disclaimer that "these notes, &c. are not intended as specimens of Klopstock's intellectual power" and have "little other interest . . . than what is derived from the celebrity of the person who made them" (2:205). Undoubtedly, Satyrane is referring to Klopstock's "celebrity" as justification for the notes' inclusion. However, as Wordsworth's celebrity is already the focus of the *Biographia* as a whole, the ambiguity of this disclaimer, beginning with an intentionality that exonerates Satyrane in effectively inculpating Wordsworth, cannot be taken lightly. Not only does this slippage further objectify W—— in the image of his equally commonplace subject; it provides further testimony to the ordinariness of "celebrity" as such, which is of no interest apparently apart from our continued inability to behold it as ordinary. If these "remarks" are "of interest" on account of the "celebrity" of their subject, it is not because they are recuperated by either Klopstock or Wordsworth. It is because "interest" creates, even as it is created by, "celebrity," all of which allows Wordsworth (or Klopstock) to be rescued from ordinariness *by* conformity. Like Klopstock, in other words, Wordsworth is so much a part of culture now that he is really "W——," a celebrity necessarily anonymous.

VI

It is customary, in light of its contemporaneity, to regard the critique of *Bertram* in chapter 23 (with which the *Biographia* effectively concludes) as filler: as a text whose interest is for the most part topical rather than central to the author's "literary life." Nor is this custom necessarily discouraged by Coleridge, whose rather clumsy effort to justify the inclusion of the critique as proof that "I have been . . . falsely charged with . . . fickleness in my principles of *taste*" (2:208) founders on the demonstrable fact that this taste as such—a vehement antitheatricality—was both a late addition to the *Biographia* and a relatively recent addition to the Coleridge canon. This is not to say, of course, that Coleridge was always enamored of the theater, or even that the *Biographia* does not sometimes verge on the antitheatrical. In a letter to Wordsworth in early 1798, Coleridge complained of "one of Kotzebu's Tragedies" in ways that would seem to anticipate his later criticism (1:378–79). Nevertheless, in light of the disingenuous deployment of Satyrane's second letter as a specimen of that earlier thinking, critics are probably justified in treating the *Bertram* critique in terms of Coleridge's actual relationship to the theater, especially in the wake of his recently rejected play *Zapolya,* rather than to the age or sensibility with which the *Biographia* is otherwise a coming-to-terms.[22]

A recent attempt by Jerome McGann to do just the opposite—that is, to link the *Bertram* critique both to the *Biographia* and to Coleridge's aesthetic and political orientation in general—certainly flies in the face of conventional wisdom.[23] Yet it also comes closer, in my view, to the real issues inherent both in the critique itself and, more important, to its deployment on this occasion. And here, not surprisingly, the question of theatricality—of theatricality as a successive and necessary accompaniment to antitheatricality—is absolutely central.

According to McGann, the critique of Maturin's play may be likened to the treatment of Wordsworth in the *Biographia* in exposing the fundamental "conservatism" of Coleridge's critical position. Regardless of whether Coleridge was "right" in understanding Wordsworth's achievement as a poet, he was nevertheless wrong, or politically incorrect, in contesting the materialist, "nonsubjective" basis of Wordsworth's own theory. As McGann regards it, Wordsworth's emphasis on ordinariness—with its implicit attention to "human intercourse and social life" (243)—represents, at the very least, a will to transcend the romantic ideology that binds Coleridge (and ultimately Wordsworth, as Coleridge showed) to a unificatory or idealistic position. "In Wordsworth," contends McGann,

> Coleridge is constantly being brought up against resistant particulars, details that somehow evade—or rather, details that seem *determined* to evade—the necessary poetic harmony and reconciliation. Coleridge calls this Wordsworth's "*accidentality,*" and he says that it contravenes "the essence of poetry," which must be, he adds, "catholic and abstract." "Accidentality" works against Coleridge's idea that poetry is the most philosophical of discourses because it alone can reveal the general in the especial, the sameness in the differences. (244)

In conceiving Coleridge as an enemy of the ordinary, or as a critic encumbered by a world bound down to a discipline of space and time, McGann is not misrepresenting Coleridge any more than Coleridge misrepresented himself. To a great extent, as we have seen, Coleridge's criticism *is* a criticism wherein the ideal of genius is sharply tried by a visible, material world.

But this is not, as we have also seen, the full extent of Coleridge's obsession with the material. In his Shakespeare criticism, almost all of which is contemporary with the *Biographia,* there is a tendency not only to promote genius over sensory reality, but also to return genius to a visible order—to a virtual "sameness" if you will—where genius (in the example of Hamlet) becomes a matter of holding oneself aloof and, to appropriate Hamlet's own words, of protesting too much.

This is likewise a tendency in the *Biographia,* whose impulse to objectification is such that the complaint regarding matter-of-factness, on which McGann rightly centers, is as much a humanistic retrenchment as it is a materialization of that position (anticipating Satyrane and later "W——"), for which McGann probably takes a little too much credit.

The tendency, then, to deny Coleridge any circumspection regarding his romantic orientation is similarly an issue in McGann's reading of the Maturin critique, which counts on Coleridge to prove the critic's point without so much as wondering why this point is provable or self-evident. Following Byron's lead in actually focusing on this aspect of the *Biographia* (despite the fact that Byron's attention was, as even McGann notes, a function largely of his efforts to get Coleridge a hearing at Drury Lane and to his perception, afterwards, of Coleridge's ingratitude on that score), McGann credits chapter 23 as "one of the most *interesting* chapters in the book" because it is among other things "the least creditable" and "shows Coleridge's literary criticism operating at its most polemical moral level" (247). That Coleridge managed to produce a chapter that was simultaneously his "least creditable" and most moral is an achievement for which McGann is understandably grateful. For McGann's real interest is not with the *Biographia;* it is in showing how Byron's animus to this chapter, with its repeated charges of indecency and immorality, found its eventual issue in *Don Juan,* where opposition to "this sort of bourgeois moralism" proved an opposition as well to the "wrong revolutionary poetical system" (as Byron called it), of which the *Biographia* in general was a defense.

There is scarcely any point in debating either the idealist basis of Coleridge's aesthetics in the *Biographia,* or their problematic status, according to both McGann and Byron, in claiming a revolutionary function. What must be contested is simply the assumption that Coleridge was somehow ignorant of this fact: that the obdurate moralism of the *Bertram* critique represented a position to which he was led unwittingly by an unflinching and unitary vision. If anything, what inspiration Byron may have received from the *Biographia,* or the inspiration into which he was apparently provoked by Coleridge (according to McGann), he might have gathered just as easily by *following* Coleridge's example—since this example involves the transposition of tragedy, and of the Don Juan myth in particular, into a comic spectacle encompassing both myth and mythmaker.

That McGann would virtually ignore this Byronic aspect of Coleridge's chapter in favor of such minor points of contention as the attack on Gothic drama, against which both *Manfred* and *Don Juan* are deemed "antithetical move[s]," or the ridicule of Bertram's "powers as a swimmer," which Byron would ridicule in turn in *Don Juan* 2 (248–49), points not only to an essentialism in which Byron, unlike Coleridge, "covets surprises and the upsetting of balance, antithetical moves of every kind, and what he called, in a wonderful portmanteau word, 'opposition'" (254); it points to an essentialism that Coleridge understood sufficiently, I think, to broaden and sophisticate. While Coleridge is surely a straight-man in these pages, and a straight-man, more importantly, who writes under the signature of Samuel Taylor Coleridge (rather than "Satyrane"), he is capable in that dual role—in the role of both authentic commentator and everyman—of an "opposition" more oppositional than the one he *seemingly* resists. And this is initially signaled by his reflexive promotion of the Don Juan narrative.

Following an attack on contemporary German drama, which is "*English* in its origin, *English* in its materials, and *English* by re-adoption" (2:212), Coleridge recurs to an earlier play, indeed to a theatrical tradition stemming from "the old Spanish play *Atheista Fulminato*" and issuing in, among other works, Thomas Shadwell's *Libertine,* as a counter to the deleterious Englishness of Maturin's Gothic drama. Striking in Coleridge's adduction, however, turns out to be the peculiar indigenousness of the Don Juan plays: an "imaginative[ness]" or romanticism in which their central characters, far from "belong[ing] to the real world," are more properly "creatures of the brain" (2:213). In this indigenousness, then, the "brain," like Lamb's in the act of reading, is a seat whose provisional lack of an occupant figures an intersubjective relationship in which the beholder has the same privileged access to the purely imaginary character as does the creator. Thus, Don Juan or Don John is of "interest," not merely because he is an "abstraction" but because he is interesting in the only way possible: namely, as a projection or image of his beholder.

And because he is so interesting, Don Juan is necessarily a character into whom "the spectator or reader" is absorbed:

> There is no danger (thinks the spectator or reader) of *my* becoming such a monster of iniquity as *Don Juan! I* shall never be an atheist! . . . But to possess such a power of captivating and enchanting the affections of the other sex! . . . To be so loved for

> my *own self,* that even with a distinct knowledge of my character, she yet died to save me! this, sir, takes hold of two sides of our nature, the better and the worse. (216)

In tracing, then, the circuit of absorption, which is essentially "an outward confirmation of *that* something within us" ([216–17] as it is thematized in a woman's love), Coleridge is remarkably candid about the kinds of appropriation and self-legitimation that routinely inform what can only be deemed a closeted approach to the theater: an approach centering on some species of "intellectual power" or "superiority" (217) as it is reflected back upon the spectator/reader. The only difference is that Coleridge's closeted approach, far from distinguishing itself as uncommon, recapitulates the commonality (beginning indeed with the gendering of superiority) to which his contemporaries, and the contemporary theater by his reckoning, presume themselves opposed. Where other versions of romanticism—and of romantic antitheatricality—tend to mask their ordinariness by some valorization of the human or the individual, Coleridge moves effortlessly and without any sense of contradiction from promoting these plays as self-representations to privileging them as representations whose "sole purpose" is to "displa[y Don Juan's] hollowness, and . . . to put us on our guard by demonstrating [his] utter indifference to vice and virtue" (221).

Moral turns such as this one are the very thing that irks McGann and undoubtedly disturbed Byron when he first read the critique in the *Biographia.*[24] Nevertheless it is important to remember that Coleridge's moralism in these pages is ultimately coextensive with a position—a position of "separate self-subsistence" (2. 217)—to which his morality is both counterpoise and bulwark. If Don Juan's interest lies entirely in his autonomy, in the "superiority" or difference with which the "spectator or reader" cannot but identify, then this interest is nevertheless dependent upon and thereby continuous with the larger, and more static, order it opposes. We may be surprised, of course, or even disappointed, to discover that this "second Prometheus" (219) amounts finally to a cautionary example or parable. But from Coleridge's perspective, this is neither surprising nor disappointing. It amounts, if anything, to a necessary first (or perhaps second) step for him: the acceptance of his place in a community or culture that has so thoroughly fostered the ideal of superiority that it also cancels or at the very least subsumes all opposition in that guise.

Prior to this point, Coleridge's consent was registered (or verged upon) by other means, beginning with the treatment of Wordsworth and culminating in the figure of Satyrane, whose parabolic swings between equality and superiority, and between singularity and conformity, demarcated a contradiction "at all times" for which hegemony, again, remains the more proper designation. Yet where Wordsworth and Satyrane are, in their various ways, impediments to what is never quite a circuit of self-reflexivity, Coleridge's return in chapter 23 to his propria persona—retrieving him, significantly, from the anonymity under which he had previously published this critique in a series of letters to the *Courier*—completes a circuit of identification. This circuit involves both an assumption of critical authority and a return of that authority to the ordinariness or anonymity to which it originally and properly belongs. Coleridge moves in this chapter from being an authoritative reader of texts, who is typically absorbed by the superiority he admires in them, to a common reader who—through the apparatus of theatricality once more—takes his rightful place among the public, with whom he can no longer deny a kinship. The apparatus of theatricality—of theatricality as opposed to absorption—allows finally for a criticism (and a critical vista) that is essentially liberating; it allows for a materialization of the "critic," whose particular inclusion within a visible or social field effectively places the critic beside himself.

We see this very clearly in the concluding critique of *Bertram,* which follows on the heels of what, by comparison, seems an altogether labored (if revealing) adduction of the Don Juan plays. There, in characteristically authoritative fashion, Coleridge maintains a studied distance from those texts whose representation of authority he also mimes. But in the aftermath of this demonstration something very different occurs: in narrating and in ultimately lampooning Maturin's play, Coleridge literally becomes part of the text on which he is commenting, reconstituting *Bertram* with an eye toward his own situation. This is most evident in the *tone* of Coleridge's reading, which departs the high ground of humanistic authority for the common ground of wit, whose demonstrable self-irony makes Coleridge a part of the spectacle itself:

> We next learn from the best authority, his own confession, that the misanthropic hero, whose destiny was incompatible with drowning, is Count Bertram, who not only reveals his past for-

> tunes, but avows with open atrocity, his satanic hatred of Imogine's Lord, and his frantic thirst of revenge; and so the raving character raves, and the scolding character scolds—and what else? Does not the Prior *act*? Does he not send for a posse of constables or thief-takers to handcuff the villain, and take him either to Bedlam or Newgate? Nothing of the kind; the author preserves the unity of character, and the scolding Prior from first to last does nothing but scold, with the exception indeed of the last scene of the last act, in which with a most surprizing revolution he whines, weeps and kneels to the condemned blaspheming assassin out of pure affection to the high-hearted man. (227)

There is no question that Coleridge means to be critical of Bertram's play, but this criticism is delightful. Indeed, Coleridge has somehow marshaled a critical, essentially moralistic, stance so as to transform a sentimental tragedy into a comic spectacle whose reflexivity amounts to a partnership between Coleridge and the very text he renders undecidable. If the sublime, in other words, looks ridiculous in this account, it is not for the purpose of returning us to a better or more sober sublime. It is for the purpose of forgetting the sheer "interest" of the Don Juan plays, whose seriousness pales next to the spectacle of tragedy subverted.

Nor is it only tragedy, or the drama of absorption, that is subverted in Coleridge's critique. Also subverted is the conservative, authoritative discourse on which comedy is virtually dependent now. Although Coleridge is plainly endorsing the hero's incarceration over and against the strictures of narrative and character, his resistance to the play maintains an antithetical bent that, like Byron's in *Don Juan,* cuts several ways, contesting both a facile or "wrong" Jacobinism on the one hand and an equally wrong or reductive anti-Jacobinism on the other.

All of which suggests that Coleridge has arrived—whether intentionally or by accident—at yet another position of exteriority: at an adversarial stance that places him one step ahead of everyone, himself included. In a way, this is exactly what has happened. Literally beside himself, Coleridge has rejoined the world, from which there is no escape, or exteriority, apart from seeing oneself and where there is no comprehension apart from understanding both the acuity and stupidity of an imprecation such as "the shocking spirit of jacobinism." Hence, in the middle of rehearsing the very tragedy he has made into a comedy, Coleridge extends his participation even further by dramatizing his own response, which is already coextensive with the spectacle he is watching:

> I want words to describe the mingled horror and disgust, with which I witnessed the opening of the fourth act, considering it as a melancholy proof of the depravation of the public mind. The shocking spirit of jacobinism seemed no longer confined to politics. The familiarity with atrocious events and characters appeared to have poisoned the taste . . . and left the feelings callous to all the mild appeals, and craving alone for the grossest and most outrageous stimulants. The very fact then present to our senses, that a British audience could remain passive under such an insult to common decency, nay, receive with a thunder of applause, the human being supposed to have come reeking from the consummation of this complex foulness and baseness, these and the like reflections so pressed as with the weight of lead upon my heart, that actor, author, and tragedy would have been forgotten, had it not been for a plain elderly man sitting beside me, who with a very serious face, that at once expressed surprize and aversion, touched my elbow, and pointing to the actor, said to me in a half-whisper—"Do you see that little fellow there? he has just been committing adultery!" Somewhat relieved by the laugh which this droll address occasioned, I forced back my attention to the stage. (229)

It is difficult to say exactly what underlies Coleridge's "relief" or (*pace* Freud) his laughter here. Yet even in the present context, which deliberately distinguishes the critic's rather involved meditations from those of the "man . . . beside" him, relief is certainly bound up in what is obviously a reversal of that distinction: in a leveling that places Coleridge "beside" himself in exposing the literal sameness of his criticism and a morality of the most ordinary, most pedestrian, sort.

In one sense, then, relief here is relief at no longer being different, or *having* to be different, since with the movement from opposition to sameness, difference is a return to the very "public" or "public mind" that it *was* the function of criticism to enlighten. However, in another sense, the relief that Coleridge experiences he feels less by his own admission than on the strength of his text as I have described it. The relief that ultimately permits a theatricalization of the critic in the image of an elderly man is the relief of knowing all of the above: not just understanding what one's place is, but recognizing that one's place, in turn, is paradoxically the first and conceivably only step left to amelioration and change.

And this, of course, returns us to the problem of antitheatricality —specifically romantic antitheatricality—whose putatively radical or even humanistic legacy is both renounced as well as sophisticated in these pages. Unlike the reversals in either Lamb or Hazlitt, who variously glimpse the critic-in-opposition, Coleridge's more conscious theater of the mind's eye makes the materialization of that opposing self, his position as a body among bodies, the objective correlative of a stance that is no sooner *and no longer* adversarial. It is possible, then, that this reconstitution of community is no more than a mystification of a "conservatism" that came to force in the years preceding the *Biographia*. But it is just as possible, and a good deal more interesting, to consider the ways Coleridge's conservatism (in anticipation of such latter-day theorists as Gramsci) represents a profoundly radical circumspection.[25] Like Kierkegaard in fact—whose "reactionary" appeal to a discipline of space and time is primarily a critique of Hegel—or like Wordsworth, whose later "photographic" poems thematize (as we shall see) an escape from an authoritative subject-position, Coleridge's theatricality has a past and a future that can neither be denied nor wished away any more than the past or the future was forgotten.

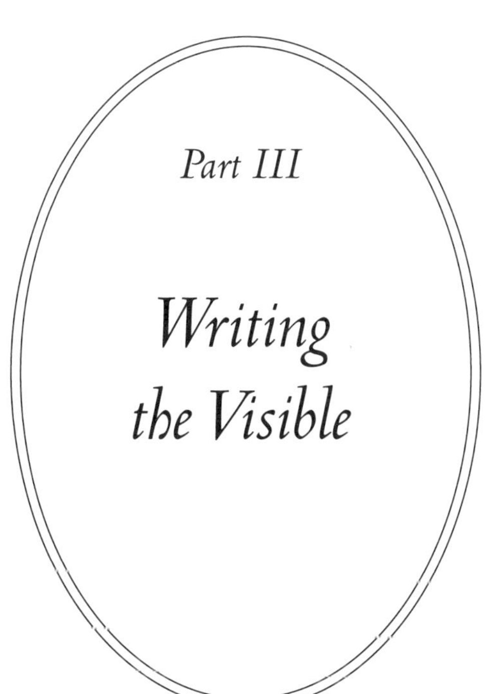

Part III

Writing the Visible

CHAPTER SEVEN

Wordsworth, Friedrich, and the Photographic Impulse

I

One attempt to eliminate the problems posed by visibility in romantic writing has been to discriminate good romantic poetry from bad poetry of the same period. In the case of Wordsworth this canonical practice begins in 1816, when Coleridge observes in the *Biographia Literaria* that "*accidentality* . . . contraven[es] the essence of [Wordsworth's] poetry," and that certain descriptive passages in *The Excursion* could be better rendered "by half a dozen strokes of [a draftsman's] pencil, or the painter with as many touches of his brush" (2:126–27). Coleridge's attempt to save Wordsworth from his infelicitous tendencies is notable less for its good intentions than for linking the contingent with the painterly. For in its particular aversion to the material (as McGann has argued), Coleridge's connection not only promotes "creation" over "painting" or sketching; it registers a fear—one closely related to antitheatricality, in fact—of an art (or version of creation) that, under the auspices of "fancy," dispenses with the intentionality in which art is ideally grounded (2:127–29).

Fancy, it is well known, assumes a subordinate status in Coleridge's taxonomy of faculties, where in contrast to both primary and secondary imagination "fancy" is a "mode of Memory emancipated from the order of time and space" (*Biographia,* 1:305). Nevertheless, the fact that fancy's is also a revolutionary (or emancipatory) function, exposing *and opposing* the hierarchical mystification of the individual in the function of imagination, becomes clear when "accidentality" and visibility collude in what amounts to a counteraesthetic. The importance of this aesthetic is initially minimized by Coleridge, chiefly through the argument that *"matter-of-factness"* is inimical to poetry (*Biographia,* 2:126). Yet, in the manner of his antitheatrical posture, no amount of protest by Coleridge is sufficient to protect poetry from the artificiality on which its defense rests. Indeed, Coleridge's defense of Wordsworth is really two defenses: a humanistic defense of man as creator and a more desperate defense against a world—a world plainly obedient to the "order of space and time"—in which "accidentality" and visibility rise up against the world of imagination.

Coleridge may well have been the first to praise Wordsworth for his "poetry" and not his "draftsmanship," but he is scarcely the last. From Matthew Arnold to A. C. Bradley to the present day, virtually all efforts to define and discriminate Wordsworth's achievement share Coleridge's fear of what the world, either viewed or accidentally admitted, might do to Wordsworth's poetry. This is clear, for example, in the peculiar commerce by which Arnold discriminates Wordsworth's "really first-rate work" from the "mass of inferior work" done "after [his] golden prime" of 1798–1808.[1] Unlike *The Excursion,* which Arnold dismisses as a "tissue of elevated but abstract verbiage, alien to the very nature of poetry," Wordsworth's "greatness" lies "in his dealing . . . powerfully" with "what is really life"—"in his powerful and beautiful application of ideas to life" (*Works,* 9:46–49). The very abstractions, in other words, alien to poetry are sufficiently instrumental and paradoxically native to poetry to allow it the distinction of being what Arnold hyperbolically calls "the reality" (48). The life to which ideas have been *applied* (rather than removed from, as in *The Excursion*) is ultimately truer, according to Arnold, more commensurate with the experience of the "real," than the "life" that stands independent of those ideas and of the "powerful and beautiful" controls of art.

This Wordsworthian commerce, by which ideas are applied to life, making "reality" conditional upon its idealization, is prevalent in twentieth-century criticism as well, where the Wordsworth canon contracts, not surprisingly, to the ten years Arnold designated "golden." In Cleanth Brooks' well-known reading of the "Intimations Ode," the poem is defended even though it is not always in control of the various paradoxes and ambiguities it exposes.[2] In failing to "accept the full consequences of some of his ironical passages" (Brooks, 125), Wordsworth, as Brooks reads him, dissociates his ideas from life so that life is not always conceived as paradoxical. Of course, it is the consciousness of paradox—the way an artifact shows an awareness of its ambiguities—that measures poetic success for Brooks. For this awareness simultaneously betrays a belief in clarity or wholeness—an "idea" of God—that, applied to life, yields "ambiguities, ironies, and paradoxes" (126).

That Brooks and other American New Critics were Christians and traditionalists, promoting poets who were themselves conservative Christians, is no great revelation. Nevertheless, both the larger canon they helped constitute, and the Wordsworth canon they managed to constrict, confirm judgments about poetical excellence with which Arnold would have been obliged to concur, since in the view of the New Criticism a poem is successful when neither life nor ideas conquer all. This view, not surprisingly, is reiterated by the great Arnoldian of our century, Lionel Trilling, whose own analysis of the "Intimations Ode" mounts a comparable defense—showing how the triumph of life, the diminution of the visionary gleam, is opposed by an equally triumphant idea: the "coming of the philosophic mind."[3] Arguing against Brooks that there is no paradox in Wordsworth's poem, Trilling manages like Brooks to have his paradox and its consumption too. The speaker's submission to the power of mutability may give him access to new powers or to a tragic sense, as Trilling asserts. However, this is still a contradiction whose resolution comes only in death, when, to the speaker at least, mutability will no longer be tragic. For Trilling, as for Brooks, it is life's ambiguity, the contradictions not resolved in life, that Wordsworth successfully represents and represents as a measure of success.

It is *this* "Wordsworthian complexity"—the way a certain application of ideas allows for the "bearing," as Leavis described it, "of [his] poetry upon life"[4]—that continually separates the readable in Wordsworth from the chaff. Thus, two issues must be borne in mind when discussing Wordsworth's reception: the infiltration of ideas on which canonical judgments are based, and the failure to sustain those "connexion[s]" (Leavis, 183) in consequence of which Wordsworth's poetry declined.

This dynamic is just as evident in the more recent, humanistic readings of both Geoffrey Hartman and Harold Bloom.[5] In these critics' view, Wordsworth's failure to fulfill an agnostic or humanistic agenda—a failure documented in his greatest works—is the very thing that makes him important. For this failure, which ultimately confirms what Shelley would later call the "triumph of life," is able in one gesture to promote the humanistic stance simply by making its failure, as it were, a failure at success.

Consumed by the antithetical imperatives of self and other, Wordsworth's poetry makes as powerful a case, in these critics' estimation, for the individual or imaginative autonomy it abandons as it does for the theism or nature worship it continually embraces. No matter how orthodox the "love of nature" seems in Wordsworth, such love is a secularized orthodoxy and always, in some sense, a "love of man." The agnostic impulse *behind* Wordsworth's greatest poetry manages amid compromise to find moorings nicely suited to the goal of poetic representation, which is the marriage, once again, of idea and reality. For it is in the vacillations of Wordsworth's poetry, in the applications that are only *applications,* that poetic success exists. The canonical Wordsworth does not, following Brooks, justify the ways of God to man with much greater success than he manages, according to Hartman, to contest those justifications. For both critics, as for Matthew Arnold, success in Wordsworth is strictly poetical—in the artifacts that bear on life by process of idealization.

The "bearing" that attends upon the application of ideas in Wordsworth becomes clearer when one looks outside the canon. In the case of Wordsworth this means looking at the period beginning around 1810, by which point, already at work on *The Excursion* (1814), Wordsworth was well into what in time would become known as his "anti-climax." This anticlimax is not only a phenomenon that romanticists, troubled by the poet's conservatism or his growing recourse to more traditional modes such as the sonnet, have lamented; it is a phenomenon that modern critics of every possible persuasion have long deplored. A crucial aspect of Wordsworth's decline involves, then, the failure of many of the later poems to meld "abstractions" with life in representing "what is really life." Such failures, it is commonly believed, were inevitable and inadvertent: Wordsworth simply changed and declined as a poet. It is my view, however, that Wordsworth knew all too well the place ideas had long occupied in his poems, that life to which ideas were unconnected—life unidealized—would be difficult, if not impossible, to read. Thus, many of Wordsworth's later poems prove a challenge to both reading and writing by dissociating or foregrounding the very ideas that, in application—or in "presentation" (as Lyotard terms it)—yield the eminently readable (or for Lyotard "unitary") reality that is the product of intentionality or nostalgia.[6] This dissociation allows Wordsworth to get beyond intentionality and to represent a life that is no longer paradoxical, arbitrary, or symbolic but one that, as Coleridge allowed, is merely contingent, visible, unwritten, and unreadable.

Wordsworth is not alone in this strategy. The commencement of his anticlimax coincides with the development of another medium inclined toward visibility and "accidentality"—namely, photography—which, like the poet's anticlimax, is both "another way of telling" (as John Berger calls it) *and* a "legitimate child of . . . Western . . . tradition."[7] Although there have been numerous attempts to recuperate photography as an application of ideas to life in the Arnoldian sense, it is the consensus among students of the medium such as Berger, Roland Barthes, Peter Galassi, and Rosalind Krauss, as well as aestheticians such as Roger Scruton, that photography's resistance to idealization is its greatest and most important feature.[8] That the photographed "moment" is necessarily divorced from "further moments," from various intentional, historical, or narrative structures (Berger, 88–92), is both photography's achievement and, these critics contend variously, the basis paradoxically for photography's unique place in tradition. The very demands that hastened photography's invention in the early nineteenth century are, I suggest, also those that Wordsworth placed on his writing so as to reverse an overly determined movement from the particular to the universal: from the visible or "viewed" (Krauss) to the authoritatively imagined. In this, Wordsworth and photography simultaneously challenge both "tradition" and posterity in exposing not only the conditions by which poetry and painting are deemed legitimate, but the illegitimacy, in turn, of what is normally considered "representation" (Scruton).

II

My story begins at the height of Wordsworth's career when in his autobiographical epic, *The Prelude* (1805), the poet complained about the "tyranny [of the eye]" (11.179).[9] This complaint, fostered by a humanistic belief in the renovating virtues of imagination, recurs throughout *The Prelude,* most memorably in book 6, where Mount Blanc appears as a "soulless image of the eye / Which usurps upon a living thought / That never more could be" (454–56). Later, in book 11, the same eye schooled by "mimic" (154) art—or by contemporary representational modes—is recalled to have been "master of [the poet's] heart, . . . the most despotic of our senses" (171–73). Still, as we saw in chapter 4, it is typical of Wordsworth's humanism at this juncture that the tyranny of which it complains supports yet another tyranny, which his complaint effectively masks. This other tyranny has less to do with the eye and its media—including Barker's Panorama in London—and more to do with the mind and its media: with the "words" used to "paint" (11.309–10) the poet's most privileged moments. In fact, less than a hundred lines after charging the eye with despotism, the poet observes that "mind," not the eye, is "lord and master" and that the "outward sense" is "the obedient servant of [the mind's] will" (270–72).

My purpose at this point is not to dispute the mind's mastery or the desirability of its regency as something vital to *The Prelude*. It is to suggest, as Wordsworth himself has suggested, that the mind and its media—in this case, poetic language—exert a tyranny in their own right. Thus, just as the tyranny of the eye proves a recurrent theme in *The Prelude,* so the tyranny of mind proves a growing phenomenon. *The Prelude*'s final books, in fact, particularly the last, find both Wordsworth and the character of "Wordsworth" laboring in the mind's service. This is evident in the determinedly heroic character of the poem's ending as well as in the appearance in the Poet's climactic ascent of Mt. Snowdon of a "mighty mind" (13.69) powerful enough to render "Wordsworth" an "under-presence" (72). The world encountered on Snowdon is impossible to figure visually, as the visible is usurped by *inland* sounds, by "streams / Innumerable, roaring with one voice" (58–59).

This interiorization, which locates the Poet here *and* elsewhere—rendering the mediations of the "I" more alien and more distant than those of the "eye"—runs counter to the conventional wisdom on Wordsworth. It is the tendency of most criticism not only to accept the unmediated originality of the poet's imaginings but also to applaud the predominance of imagination in what Wordsworth problematically terms the "picture of the mind."[10] Most criticism, in other words, either ignores or overlooks the fact that such picturing barely erases its own heritage, that the "passage," in de Man's words, "from a certain type of nature, earthly and material, to another nature which could be called mental and celestial" is, as Wordsworth reminds us, arbitrary and unstable. Far from masking this arbitrariness, the alleged tyranny of the eye in *The Prelude* would appear to unmask it. After all, not only does the eye's tyranny oppose, thereby exposing, an even greater tyranny of mind; it also opposes the mind's tyranny in revealing a tyranny over mind itself. In the end, then, the contest of eye and mind in *The Prelude* imagines both a liberation of the eye, and beyond this, a liberation of mind through the eye's emancipation.

One such liberating instance in Wordsworth's poetry occurs nearly a decade later in the final book of *The Excursion*—a work that Arnold, speaking as a canonical critic, deemed "alien to the very nature of poetry." Arnold was surely right to claim this of *The Excursion,* for central among *The Excursion*'s features is an authorial self who relinquishes the application of ideas to a number of other spokesmen. Nevertheless, for a brief moment in the poem's conclusion, the Poet suspends his role as silent witness to recollect an unforgettable "moment":

> Forth we went,
> And down the vale along the streamlet's edge
> Pursued our way, a broken company,
> Mute or conversing, single or in pairs.
> Thus having reached a bridge, that overarched
> The hasty rivulet where it lay becalmed
> In a deep pool, by happy chance we saw
> A twofold image; on a grassy bank
> A snow-white ram, and in the crystal flood
> Another and the same! Most beautiful,
> On the green turf, with his imperial front
> Shaggy and bold, and wreathed horns superb,
> The breathing creature stood; as beautiful,
> Beneath him, showed his shadowy counterpart.
> Each had his glowing mountains, each his sky,
> And each seemed centre of his own fair world:
> Antipodes unconscious of each other,
> Yet, in partition, with their several spheres,
> Blended in perfect stillness, to our sight!
> (9.433–51)

What differentiates this moment from other privileged sightings in Wordsworth, from the "spots of time" in *The Prelude,* for example, is its lack of privilege. The sight is witnessed by all and, by the speaker's claim, is entirely accidental: it is both accidentally glimpsed ("by happy chance we saw") and, as the water continues to be still, fortuitously sustained.

Moreover, in the context of *The Excursion,* the sight proves an alternative to the authoritative orientations that the Poet, in imitation of the reader, has long endured in the Wanderer, the Solitary, and the Pastor. It is interposed amid these others (*The Excursion* ends with the Wanderer's discourse and, following that, a prayer of thanks by the Pastor) as an alternative to the controlling voices of the poem. In its visual, accidental character, as well as in its readerly accessibility (rendered through its visibility), the scene not only challenges *The Excursion*'s spokesmen; it contests, or so it would seem, the authority contesting them—since with the intrusion of the "sight" the poem is also forced from its auditory format, in which the Poet remembers and reconstructs what he has previously witnessed.[11]

The ram scene was initially written ten years earlier, and because the version of it designated for *The Prelude* was subsequently dropped from the poem, a look at the earlier draft is most revealing. Here, amid recollections of his residence in France, Wordsworth remembers that

> Once coming to a bridge that overlook'd
> A mountain torrent, where it was becalm'd
> By a flat meadow, at a glance I saw
> A twofold image; on the grassy bank
> A snow-white ram, and in the peaceful flood
> Another and the same; most beautiful
> The breathing creature; nor less beautiful,
> Beneath him, was his shadowy counterpart;
> Each had his [glowing] mountains, each his sky,
> [And each seem'd centre of his own] fair world.
> A stray temptation seiz'd me to dissolve
> The vision,—but I could not, and the stone,
> Snatch'd up for that intent, dropp'd from my hand.[12]

The central difference in this passage, commensurate with the fact that it is only the speaker who observes the sight, is the urge to dissolve the vision. The urge, however, is not acted upon, and it is suppressed, I would argue, for at least two reasons. In one, the urge is suppressed because Wordsworth wants it suppressed, because the ram, as soon as sighted or "glanced" at, is made the object of the speaker's gaze and, by turns, a "vision." As the existence of the text verifies, the experience remains an act of mind akin to its representation in verse, making both the writing poet and the character of whom he writes "each" the "centre" of his "own" world.

Yet because this same text was finally elided, another possibility presents itself: the act of mind, which this sight *becomes,* may very well represent a situation in which the mind's cooptative powers are sufficiently coopted—that is, under a directive from some other authority—to make the observer-turned-visionary subject to his own observation. Only this, I think, would explain both the suppression of the written text and the suppression of the urge to disrupt the vision in the text subsequently suppressed. Not only do both texts—the written text *and* the text of experience—recapitulate an identical will to autonomy and power; they register, in their virtually identical suppressions of that will, what amounts to the same awareness: namely, that by exercising its prerogative the mind has somehow put itself in harness.

The "temptation" to dissolve the vision is worth pursuing, then, as much for what immediately provokes it—a sight more over- than underdetermined—as for the way this urge is later recast and then acted upon in *The Excursion.* I am referring specifically to the way the sight (which is itself an interruption) is interrupted in turn by the Pastor's wife, who exclaims:

> Ah! what a pity were it to disperse,
> Or to disturb, so fair a spectacle,
> And yet a breath can do it!
>
> (452–54)

Reflecting on both the sight and the Wanderer's discourse, she confesses to "sometimes feel[ing]"

> That combinations so serene and bright
> Cannot be lasting in a world like ours,
> Whose highest beauty, beautiful as it is,
> Like that reflected in yon quiet pool,
> Seems but a fleeting sunbeam's gift, whose peace
> The sufferance only of a breath of air!
>
> (467–73)

In making the wife both victim and requiter of his previous urge, Wordsworth articulates what he had surmised ten years earlier: certain sights, however accidental and visible, still bear the freight of intentionality. Here, the symmetry of the sight and the order it instills all point to an object less purely found than sought. This is true both of the sight's transcendental structure as picture (as the Pastor's wife intimates) and of its place in the poem in whose climactic book it characteristically appears. Thus despite articulating what in retrospect may well be an earlier surmise, the Pastor's wife differs substantially in function from the Poet, who earlier let the stone drop from his hand. For merely by *imagining* the sight's disruption (as the Poet surely did when he initially picked up the stone), the Pastor's wife does not actually disrupt the sight any more than she succumbs, strictly speaking, to the Poet's earlier temptation to dissolve the vision; it is more the case that she succumbs to one temptation to the extent of ultimately resisting another—which is the "spectacle" itself. The spectacle may be more contingent, surely, than other moments in Wordsworth. But, like other putatively contingent moments, it is far from simply visible.[13]

III

This situation, where a disruption or accident is necessary to recall a sight to an inherent or potential "accidentality," has a correlative in the work of another of Wordsworth's contemporaries, the German painter Caspar David Friedrich (1774–1840). I am referring specifically to those paintings by Friedrich in which there is a figure with its back to us, interposing itself between the beholder and a represented scene. Examples of such paintings include *Woman in Front of the Setting Sun* (ca. 1818, fig. 15), *Two Men Contemplating the Moon* (1819, fig. 16), and the often reproduced *The Wanderer above the Mists* (ca. 1818, fig. 17). The scenes before these *Rückenfiguren* (as they are commonly termed) are, as one art historian observes, discrete and momentary. However these same scenes contain supernatural elements as well and are effectively freighted with a transcendental narrative structure.[14] Such "freighting" is, of course, common in Friedrich as in most romantic painting, including Constable's. Undoubtedly less common is the employment of a mediating figure. More often it is a secondary or complementary figure—the *spectator ab extra*—who appears in Fried-

---

Figure 15 (opposite). Caspar David Friedrich, *Woman in Front of the Setting Sun,* ca. 1818. Museum Folkwang, Essen.

Figure 17. Caspar David Friedrich, *The Wanderer above the Mists,* ca. 1818. Kunsthalle, Hamburg.

Figure 16 (opposite). Caspar David Friedrich, *Two Men Contemplating the Moon,* 1819. Staatliche Kunstammlungen, Dresden.

rich, and who normally joins the viewer in witnessing the immanence of "another world"—usually figured by a boundless void onto which the painting opens (*Monk by the Sea* [1808–10, see pp. ii–iii], *Mountain Landscape with Rainbow* [ca. 1810, fig. 18]).

In contrast to the secondary figures, the *Rückenfiguren* with their backs to us—obstructing both our vision *and* Friedrich's—manage, like the Pastor's wife, to resist the vision before them. Thus, like the Pastor's wife, they not only interfere with the intentional structure of a particular sight or vista; they recall, by their very interference, the accidentality that has been canceled or appropriated by imagination. But accidentality is not the only thing such figures recall. Disruption is the paramount activity in these paintings because it is in large part an activity *anterior* to these paintings as well: because the vista currently obscured has already been disrupted or obscured by a human agent. Thus, the recapitulation of anteriority by a disruptive figure, or by what amounts now to *another* human agent, both recalls and resists an anterior authority. This is certainly the case in the most revealing of Friedrich's pictures in this vein: his well-known *Woman at the Window* (1822, fig. 19). Here, the woman not only stands before an arbitrary framing of the world from what is in fact the artist's atelier; she is before a world whose anterior *invisibility*—whose obscurity prior to her arrival at the window—may be said to figure the world elsewhere in Friedrich.[15] The visions before other observers in other Friedrich paintings (not to mention those paintings without observers) may be more capacious than the one barely visible through the already obstructive window, which is, again, the artist's window. But in no instance, suggests *this* painting, are they any less contained, or interrupted, by a human frame.

In a recent article that is specifically concerned with Friedrich's *Rückenfigur,* Joseph Leo Koerner insists that Friedrich's figures bear comparison with "halted travellers" in works by, of all poets, William Wordsworth. In such poems, Koerner observes, Wordsworth's speakers or poetical surrogates emphasize the privacy of a given scene by depicting "the artist in a landscape of memory."[16] Koerner is, of course, correct to underscore the shared emphasis on subjectivism in the works of Wordsworth and Friedrich. But his parallel requires elaboration. Unlike Wordsworth's traveler, who, in the earlier poems especially, is artist and traveler at once, Friedrich's *Rückenfigur* often "draws attention to itself," as Koerner writes, "arresting the movements of [the] eye about the canvas" (151). That is, instead of making distraction tantamount to vision (as happens in the initial ram scene), the *Rückenfigur* renders them opposed, effectively underscoring (as does the Pastor's wife) the arrangement or composition of the disrupted scene. While the halted traveler characteristic of the earlier Wordsworth willfully indulges both imagination and memory in the representation of a scene (one thinks, for example, of the ten thousand dancing daffodils in "I wandered lonely as a Cloud"), the *Rückenfigur* emphasizes the way imagination and memory have been indulged. And because "it is from his eye, not ours, that the painting seems to radiate" (Koerner, 152), the *Rückenfigur* bears what might be called the stigma of intention, since he or she also girds both the artist and the beholder from an imaginable experience. By foregrounding and displacing a "subjective standpoint" (Koerner, 152), Friedrich's figure, unlike, for example, Constable's dog, takes responsibility for a sight that has already obscured mere seeing.[17]

If the parallel between Wordsworth and Friedrich centers more on their resistance to rather than (as Koerner argues) their celebration of intentionality, it is a parallel that is especially helpful in understanding the *later* Wordsworth, whose works are normally dismissed as aesthetically conservative.[18] For this kind of resistance, which interferes with a union of the symbolic and the natural, necessarily looks beyond *The Excursion* to other poems by Wordsworth, among them the *Memorials of a Tour on the Continent, 1820* (1822). In these later poems and others contemporary with them the preoccupation with the visible is as inconsistent with Wordsworth's earlier and most overtly "romantic" writing as it is consistent with (then) contemporary developments in the visual arts that were similiarly implicated in a reconception of the romantic artist's role.

We have already seen how such innovations as the Panorama and the Diorama were as opposed to the visionary program of romantic writing as they differed in equally significant ways from the painting of the period, which was committed, more deceptively than writing perhaps, to an authoritative subject-position. But, as the example of Friedrich suggests, this was only part of the story regarding painting. Like romantic literature, in fact, which was alternately resistant and thereby vulnerable to the return of the visible, the pictorial conventions at this time prove an equally sensitive register of changes in the culture of seeing that painting both resisted and, at the same time, fostered.

Uncertain of its iconographic moorings, of the idealization to

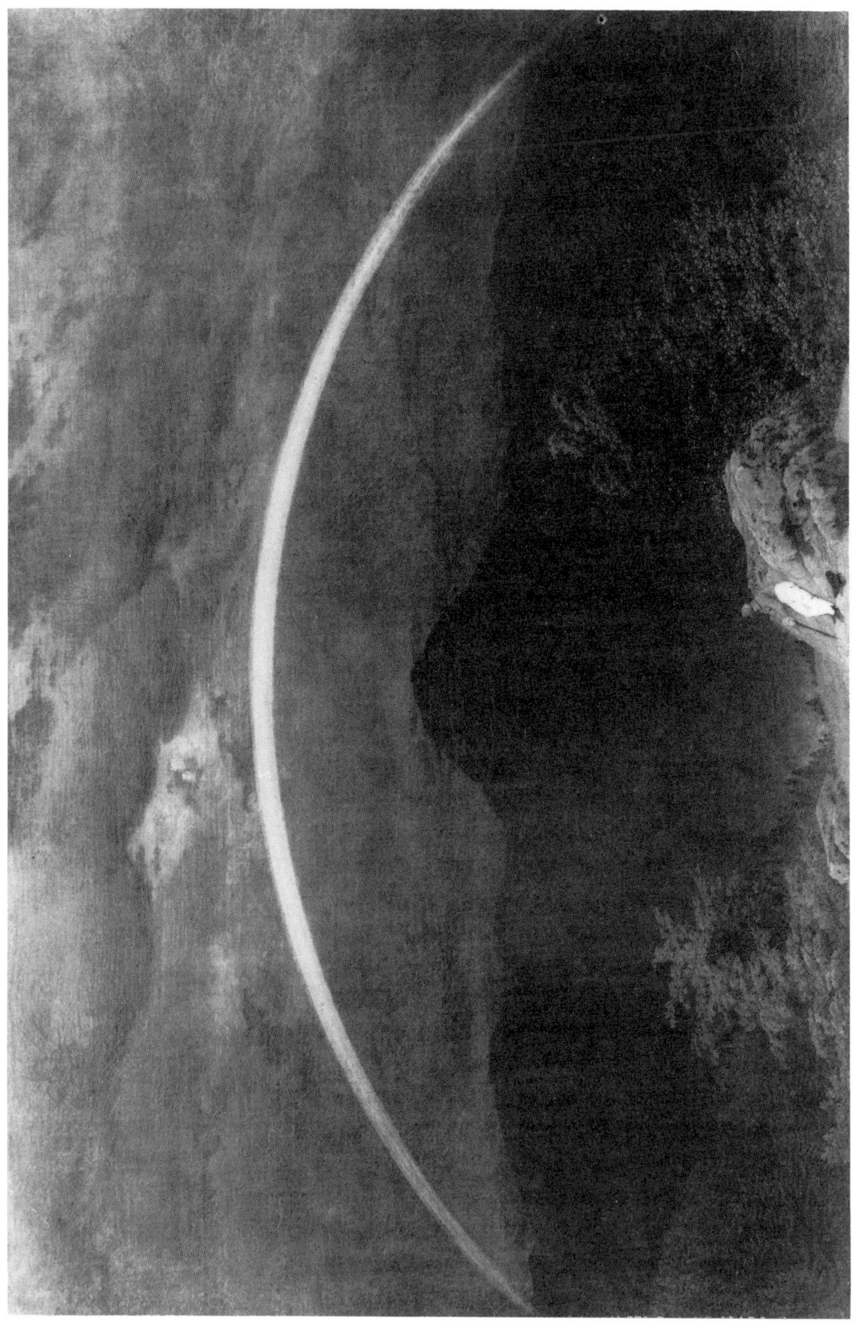

Figure 19. Caspar David Friedrich, *Woman at the Window,* 1822. Nationalgalerie, Berlin.

Figure 18 (opposite). Caspar David Friedrich, *Mountain Landscape with Rainbow,* ca. 1810. Museum Folkwang, Essen.

which the sensible world had been hitherto bound, the pictorial tradition at the turn of the century was also disposed to a way of seeing that was remarkably photographic—or noniconographic. Now, in numerous oil sketches and even full-sized canvases there was, as Peter Galassi has recently argued (and as Coleridge lamented perhaps disingenuously), evidence of a need on the part of many European artists to represent things in a more contingent or paratactic way. This need can be detected, as Galassi shows, in such British paintings as John Linnell's *At Twickenham* (1806, fig. 20) and John Sell Cotman's *Drop Gate* (1805, fig. 21), as well as in many of Constable's sketches, including *Study of Tree Trunks* (ca. 1821, fig. 22) and the remarkably photographic *Study of the Trunk of an Elm Tree* (ca. 1821, fig. 23). In all of these works, suffice it to say, there is clearly something that photography (or what later became that medium) would have made it easier to "present": "a new and fundamentally modern pictorial syntax of immediate, synoptic perceptions and discontinuous, unexpected forms" (Galassi, 25).

Two points are to be stressed, then, about protophotography or the motivation behind that (then) developing technology. The first and most obvious is that an impulse in painting precedes and anticipates the kind of picturing that photography would later facilitate and that the Panorama, as we have seen, had already begun to abet. The second point is that this need was—in light of its particular affiliation *with painting*—largely contestational. In other words, to the extent that there was a photographic impulse early in the nineteenth century, it was an impulse *opposed,* like Daguerre's "other" invention, to the intentional structures of romanticism. Obstructing the passage where, as Galassi writes, the "singular and contingent" give way to the "universal and stable" (25), it was the aim of this impulse to ensure that the "real" would not, as Walter Benjamin later wrote, "perish into *art.*"[19]

Precursors of postmodernism such as Benjamin as well as philosophers such as Stanley Cavell, to whom photography echoes the contemporaneous fall of philosophy into skepticism, subscribe wholeheartedly to the idea of a photographic impulse, or to a medium in which, as Cavell writes, the "mind had at once recognized . . . a manifestation of something that had already happened to itself."[20] But art historians are a different matter; not all of them accept the view that photography was an aesthetic impulse or that the impulse, such as it was, was in any sense photographic.[21] We need only summon Constable, whose preliminary studies can be said to reflect the photographic impulse but whose academy paintings assuredly do not, to appreciate their position. Nevertheless, even among those who do not subscribe to the idea of a photographic impulse, the efforts to account for it—or for some akin development—are especially noteworthy.

Kermit Champa has described the phenomenon as one of "actualization." In the process of actualization, according to Champa, a painter—in this case Friedrich—translates a symbolic image into the "form of an actual picture" (42). In actualizing such symbols, Friedrich uses the world—carefully rendered with fidelity to outward appearance—to justify that "other world," which viewers, long familiar with the particulars that have traditionally signified it (sunrises, sunsets, mountains, rainbows, full moons), re-view in what is essentially reverse sequence. The passage in Friedrich is not from the earthly to the celestial (to paraphrase de Man again); rather, it is to the earthly *by way* of the celestial, erasing in the process the distance that necessarily separates the physical and the metaphysical. Actualization, too, is what Morse Peckham (131–33) refers to when he speaks of Friedrich's photographic powers of observation and yet of the timeless, monumental character of images such as *Lone Tree* (ca. 1821, fig. 24). That is, despite arguing on behalf of narrativity in Friedrich, or against his breaking of the "monopoly" of "history . . . over time" (Berger, 109), both Champa and Peckham still credit Friedrich with having achieved what John Berger, in praise of photography, has called "another way of telling." The past, in these critics' view, is no more *passed* in Friedrich's paintings than the present—what the painter represents—is *visibly* a part of narrative.[22]

Fundamentally, such actualization is neither commensurate with photography nor necessarily reflective of the impulse to photography. If anything, Friedrich hovers at the point of impulse only to move backward to the symbolic (or to the allegorical). But the process, which contrives through actualization to telescope past, present and future into a single picture, must as actualization, or as "accidentality," stare intentionality in the face. All of which leads *in certain instances* to an aversion—a swerving from narrative—in the course of which a naturalized scene is essentially laid at the feet of a human imagination (as happens, for example, in *The Wanderer above the Mists*). Thus, even as he is determined *not* to "split [nature] from the human imagination" (Peckham, 134), Friedrich initiates a split for the purpose of then shoring up a union of mind and matter. "The artist," Friedrich famously

Figure 21. John Sell Cotman, *The Drop Gate,* 1805. Trustees of the British Museum, London.

Figure 20 (opposite). John Linnell, *At Twickenhem,* 1806. Tate Gallery, London.

Figure 23. John Constable, *Study of the Trunk of an Elm Tree,* ca. 1821. Trustees of the Victoria and Albert Museum, London.

Figure 22 (opposite). John Constable, *Study of Tree Trunks,* ca. 1821. Trustees of the Victoria and Albert Museum, London.

observed, "should paint not only what he sees before him, but also what he sees within him" (Börsch-Supan, 7). And this, surely, is contradiction enough that Friedrich is disposed not only to confess to this bad faith, which is nevertheless a demonstration of faith, but in so doing to "split" his *viewer* from the imagined natural scene. The disruptive figure, then, does more than disrupt Friedrich's natural scene in the same way that the painter confessedly marks or reinvents such a scene by the interposition of a human figure; the disruptive figure also interrupts the identificatory mechanism by which the viewer might be interpellated by such a scene and inclined, like the painter, to accept its naturalizing work.

To better understand the way this identificatory mechanism works in Friedrich, and how the interruption of it was consequent upon its deployment as a cooptative apparatus, a look at Richard Wollheim's recent treatment of the "internal" viewer in Friedrich proves most helpful.[23] Distinguishing the external spectator or actual viewer of a Friedrich painting from a subject-position or spectatorial vantage that is properly represented in and by a painting, Wollheim insists that a proper understanding of Friedrich must acknowledge the gap between the vision *in* the picture and a vision exterior to the picture *from which* the external or mere viewer is to be converted. Eschewing a "narrowly visual" sense of Friedrich's achievement, Wollheim argues instead that the representation of nature in Friedrich, particularly in paintings where there is no mediating figure, is undertaken to permit the beholder to "reconstruct the internal spectator's visual experience" (139), which differs from the actual perception of nature in its pietistic passage from the particular to the universal. In other words, while we are inclined as external viewers to regard nature with a bodily eye (or with what Wollheim, to distinguish it from a subjective or personal vision, erroneously terms "a mere disembodied eye" [130]), the particular relationship, even proximity, of the represented vision to normal vision, underscores a gap between Seeing and seeing that, thanks to the prevalence of a seemingly sensible or natural world in Friedrich, is potentially breachable.

Yet, even as Wollheim attends to the very important distinction between the internal and external viewer of a Friedrich image, he does

---

Figure 24 (opposite). Caspar David Friedrich, *Lone Tree,* ca. 1821. Nationalgalerie, Berlin.

not really consider the way this gap or difference is internalized by the artist, whose capacity of sight would necessarily precede the capacity to think, feel, and act (as Wollheim describes such "human" or "personal" characteristics [130]). Wollheim does not consider, in short, how the distinction between internal and external viewers, on which the rhetoric of Friedrich's art is founded, remains as relevant to the artist and to his way of seeing as it does to those ordinary viewers who are in apparent need of such art. The very distance that the painting invites the external viewer to cross, according to Wollheim, is a distance Friedrich must *repeatedly* cross or repeatedly imagine crossing in order to paint as he does. Indeed, this exemplar of "early-nineteenth-century Pietism," as Wollheim describes Friedrich, "who, disentangled from the exigencies of material life, gains a certain detachment from nature, which he then makes use of only so as to return to nature and make it the object of profound and devout contemplation" (Wollheim, 133), is with almost equal regularity entangled in the very material life his art opposes. This is provable not simply by images whose proximity to the actual or "objective" world virtually announces an impending return of the visible. It is evident on the strength of the visible itself, whose palpable containment in these same images both projects and resists a position into which a viewer *not always* Friedrich has been interpellated.

It scarcely requires saying that the gap between Friedrich and his pietistic subject is a gap or difference that the painter would prefer never existed. But it is a gap to which, as even Wollheim allows, Friedrich manages to give testimony. This is especially evident in those paintings in which a human agent—what I have called a disruptive figure—effectively usurps or appropriates that pietistic stance. Such a figure is, as Wollheim interprets him, a visual token of the internal viewer, and of the difference separating such a viewer from a comparatively unregenerate beholder (166–68). And in a way this is absolutely correct: the function of this figure is not only to register a detachment *from* "detachment," or from a distentanglement with the material that the actual viewer can rarely sustain; this figure functions also to interrupt that distentanglement, thereby countermanding the very absorption he or she apparently also signifies. Not only, then, does the *Rückenfigur* supplant the actual viewer, who is "recalled" (in Wollheim's apposite description) to his position *in front* of the canvas and to a loss of identification with the viewer in the painting. Such a figure simultaneously supplants the painter himself, who, in figuring the difference between seeing and Seeing by inclusion of the *Rückenfigur,* necessarily resigns the task of Seeing to another human whose vision is typically unrecoverable.

Furthermore, the painter relinquishes the burden of vision in such a way that any difference or detachment from the painted figure is directly proportional to the painted figure's inclusion in a field—at once visual and ideological—from which the painter and the beholder are mutually excluded. It does not matter, therefore, that such inclusion is also something Friedrich typically yearns for or that it represents a consciousness he would perennially rise to. What matters is that this ascent, that some disentanglement with the material, is continually necessary: the peculiar detachment from material life that such absorption requires, and that Friedrich's internal viewer apparently manifests, involves, by turns, an appropriation of the body and its capacity of sight that not even Friedrich—the painter who imagines imagination—can always submit to. It is more the case, rather, that virtually every work of Friedrich's trickles back (in Wollheim's phrase) to the materiality it would overcome: whether by process of actualization, where the passage from the earthly to the celestial is always subject to renegotiation, or according to an imagination that can never quite shake off, much less dominate, a world viewed.

I have referred already to Friedrich's nearly contradictory injunction that the artist paint what "he sees within him." What I did not observe, and what is particularly relevant to my discussion here, is that this injunction is further pressured by additional advice on what to do if there is nothing sightable within: "If, however, [the artist] sees nothing within him," continues Friedrich, "then he should also refrain from painting that which he sees before him. Otherwise his pictures will be like those folding screens behind which one expects to find only the sick or the dead" (Börsch-Supan, 7–8). The final declension to materiality, which follows typically upon the representation of a world that, by relinquishment of interior sanctions, is more properly photographic, is undoubtedly a romantic protest against the return of the visible. Yet the "triumph of life" projected in this maxim, beginning with the act of seeing and culminating in sickness unto death, is also a drift or an unacknowledged dispensation that Friedrich's ideal of painting abets as much as it resists. Indeed, the very admission of sight, or of a materiality paradoxically within, puts substantial pressure on Friedrich's position by making the marriage or so-called covenant of mind and nature an asymmetrical union that admits, however consciously, to an arbitrary and largely unsuccessful imposition of mind. It should not surprise us, of course, that a painter—*any* painter—would be compelled to take stock of a visible or material world. What distinguishes Friedrich's reckoning in this regard is that it more nearly follows the example of romantic *writing* in admitting a visible world in the acts of either demonizing or transforming it. Thus, even as he is committed to the primacy of the imagination, or to that visible world within, the link between theory and praxis in Friedrich is less a link of seamless commensurabilty, or wish fulfillment, than a connection sustained by inconsistency and by continuous wavering.

Nor is it only the painter's medium, again, with its ostensible fidelity to a visible or sublunary world, that is the source of this inconsistency. Friedrich's wavering owes far more, in the end, to a subject-position, or to romantic orientation, whose claim to enfranchisement and imaginative autonomy amounts (as he must have realized) to a compromised position. The characterization, then, of Friedrich as a "nineteenth-century Pietist" both penetrates and at the same time skirts the central issue regarding him. After all, it is the link *between* a pietistic tradition, according to which nature remains legible as the book of God, and a romantic or nineteenth-century idealism, extending the prerogative of authorship to that of readership and revelation, that Friedrich both registers and at the same time problematizes.

It is scarcely necessary, therefore, to dismiss the pietism *readable* in Friedich's paintings simply on account of those disruptions or acts of resistance that, as I have shown, frequently attend such narratives. These disruptions, which clearly count on a human center, work less to interrogate a pietistic tradition than to interrogate a more humanistic—even agnostic—orientation by authority of which the earlier tradition apparently survives. It is perfectly right, in fact, for Börsch-Supan, undoubtedly the most scrupulous of Friedrich's commentators, to observe of the *Woman in Front of the Setting Sun* (fig. 15) that the "woman's outstretched arms complement the arc of rays from the sun and thus unite the darkest and lightest areas of the picture—in other words, this world and the world hereafter,"—thereby "stress[ing] man's inherent affiliation to God" (108). For it is precisely "man's affiliation" with "God," figured also as a human center here, that permits and even sustains a reading that from a more romantic or humanistic viewpoint seems anachronistic at best.

In a recent study of Friedrich that follows his earlier article in examining the painter's responsiveness to certain paradigms of romantic subjectivity, Koerner is understandably impatient with readings such as Börsch-Supan's that insist on the "legibility" of elements of Christian devotion.[24] Arguing instead that the "peculiar interpenetration of nature and symbol, and of object and meaning" in Friedrich's paintings points more to "the universality of genius" rather than to the "validity of the religous faith" (124, 130), Koerner typically maintains that the symbolic or sublime landscape in Friedrich refers ultimately to the "cognitive act of a beholding subject," who is "himself another deity" (194). Committed as an artist to a "naturalization of the symbol" (142) by process of what Kermit Champa calls "actualization," such "naturalization," submits Koerner, "discovers the already symbolic character of nature" (142) as it "appeared" to the artist in a "moment" of his "life" (129–30).

In all of this, needless to say, there is not much to contest or to add, except to observe that the various sanctions to the individual subject that Friedrich undoubtedly absorbed from the philosophy and aesthetics of the day were sufficient only to move him—and the world within his ken—from an inherited narrative (such as Börsch-Supan discloses) to a less decidable if still symbolic narrative based on experience and invention. Despite the fact that Friedrich may have succeeded, following Kant and others, in retrieving the noumenal world from ways of apprehending that were fundamentally nonsymbolic and nonsubjective, he was anchored to a logic of redemption that was additionally one of imposition and authority. No matter how much his paintings echo and reflect certain (then) contemporary speculations about subjectivity and meaning, they remain—in demonstrably setting themselves against more traditional ways of seeing—always prelusive to yet "another way of telling," in which meaning might well be irrelevant or impossible.

That Friedrich would never reproduce such a world or such a narrative, despite approximating the visible in the various ways I have indicated, is hardly to impugn his achievement. It is simply to identify and even to privilege that achievement as verging on crisis: as a juncture when romanticism could, in remaining on the near side of tradition, finally define itself as provisional. And this, I would argue, makes Friedrich a very different Romantic from contemporaries of his such as the Schlegels for whom romanticism was also a *process,* albeit one that never came to rest. The provisional in Friedrich's romanticism is not the possibility onto which it forever opens; the provisional is the metaphysical or symbolic world on which Friedrich continually closes, whose particular imagination of the material is as much a desired end as it is also a dead end.

Hence, it is the peculiar pathos of the disruptive *Rückenfigur* in Friedrich not only to signify a goal or ideal from which the painter is capable of removing himself or his viewer: it is the pathos of the figure that the detachment it *variously* signifies—a detachment from the "exigencies" of "material life" as well as from the romantic disentanglement with the material—is possible insofar as the world before such a figure remains, as Friedrich previously enjoined, a world *seen*. Or to put it another way: the world available to such a subject leaves, by its constitution as something visible, something additional or excessive to the imagination, which the subject can neither control or exceed any more than the actual or external viewer can necessarily see the world beyond that internal figure. All one sees, whether one is in or outside the painting, is a self that is more precisely *oneself:* an imaginary, subjective relation to the world that is both literally *and scarcely* all there is to see.[25]

IV

The parallel between Wordsworth and Friedrich, which centers on the ram scene and the deployment in *The Excursion* of the Pastor's wife as a disruptive agent, tells us as much about Wordsworth as it does about Friedrich. For while it was the achievement of the "earlier" Wordsworth to have indulged imagination in a way that only the "middle" Wordsworth could apparently follow Friedrich in problematizing, it devolves upon the later Wordsworth—the Wordsworth after *The Excursion*—to admit a world that Friedrich no sooner broaches than he retreats from.

It is in the ram scene that these differences are initially apparent. Like any of the disruptive *Rückenfiguren,* or like the woman who interposes herself between the viewer and Friedrich's window, the Pastor's wife calls attention to the disruption or imposition, to which the world before her is virtually equivalent. This juncture of the visible and the intentional is, as we have seen, both an ideal and a limit in Friedrich. But in Wordsworth it is more properly a new beginning. That is, Wordsworth ultimately follows the photographic impulse in actually crossing Friedrich's threshold, eliminating (in the process) the need for a disruptive figure in the first place. Wordsworth's crossing, then, if both Wordsworth and Friedrich may serve as examples, demands the transformation of the vision that *precedes* this figure—its detachment specifically from the imagination and from its symbolic or metaphysical issue. Such a change invariably places greater emphasis on the purely random character of things sighted, rather than culled from symbolic tradition, and upon capturing "bits" and pieces of perceived reality.[26] The extent to which this actualization is intentional or reactive scarcely diminishes its contestational function. In contrast to realism, which followed in the nineteenth century, the photographic impulse—along with the related work of the Panorama and the Diorama—is exactly that: an impulse or hiatus, not a reconstitution.[27]

The hiatus becomes manifest in Wordsworth's poetry after *The Excursion* as well as in seemingly extraneous undertakings such as the notes Wordsworth dictated to Isabella Fenwick in 1843. In the latter, as Thomas McFarland observes, Wordsworth "again and again stresses the factuality of incidents that underlie his [earlier] poems, often with a curious sense of revealing something that makes the poem more important."[28] To McFarland, this "something" involves a paradox central to Wordsworth's greatness, whereby the urge to fantasy "was held in a fructifying tension" with "a drive to realism" that was also a resistance to imagination (5). But it may be, of course, that there is no paradox at all here: that the "matter-of-factness" stressed in the notes has less to do with a poem such as "Resolution and Independence" than with the "more important" efforts to write over that achievement by deflecting attention from imagination. An important means of deflection remains, then, the visual content of the poetry after *The Excursion,* most notably the tour poems of both Britain and Europe. But there are other means as well, among them brevity, which is generally achieved by recourse to the sonnet form.

Critics have long lamented Wordsworth's preoccupation with the sonnet, especially in his later phase.[29] Yet what is almost never stressed is the way the sonnet, especially in sequence, marks a repudiation of Wordsworth's earlier poetic forms—both the "personal epic" and "greater romantic lyric"—which are clearly expressions of personality.[30] Such repudiation of "greatness," then, involves more than the deployment of tradition as a counterpoise to individual talent (as arguably happens in Friedrich). In the absence of individual talent, of any real difficulty or "art," the sonnet characteristic of the later Wordsworth fails also to uphold tradition by refusing to revision the world.

Not only do poems like the *River Duddon Sonnets* (most of which were composed between 1819 and 1820) refer to something other than William Wordsworth (in comparison to either *The Prelude* or even *The Excursion*); the referent or represented itself poses a challenge to its recoverability. The dominant figurative mode in these poems is not metaphor—often regarded as a trope of power or authority—but simile, which (as Byron similarly emphasizes) uncovers the gap between poetic authority and what it strives generally to dominate. Mimetic in these poems, then, is the impossibility of mimesis (save for the visible), just as their remarkable determinacy—their continued deference to a world apart—is achieved through a renunciation whereby imagination and poetic language are undone in expiation for their "representations."[31]

Wordsworth's later poems contain—as do photographs in a way—their own critical history, a sense of what they are trying to do against what as poems they are somehow obliged to do. And this is plainly evident in many of the tour poems, notably the *Memorials of a Tour of the Continent,* where the visible actually replaces the disruptive figure—an intentionality materialized and foregrounded—as the agent of disruption. Unlike the ram scene in *The Excursion,* where the accidentality of the sight requires the supplementary intervention of the Pastor's wife, the world that passes before the eye in the *Memorials* succeeds in betraying what in another of his later tour poems Wordsworth calls "purpose"—usually the incorporation of a past into the present.[32] The betrayal, furthermore, is both immediate and cumulative. It is inherent in the individual poems and in the sequence as a whole, where, as in the contemporary *Ecclesiastical Sketches* ([1822] later the *Ecclesiastical Sonnets*), various phenomena make their transit before the eye both in inversion of the romantic stance to the world and in disruption of narrative.

I will conclude, then, by examining two of these *Memorials,* the sonnets "Bruges" (II) and "After Visiting the Field of Waterloo" (V), which is arguably mistitled. In both, the eye succeeds in frustrating a tyranny of mind.

> Bruges I saw attired with golden light
> (Streamed from the west) as with a robe of power:
> The splendour fled; and now the sunless hour
> That, slowly making way for peaceful night,
> Best suits with fallen grandeur, to my sight

Offers the beauty, the magnificence,
And sober graces, left for her defence
Against the injuries of time, the spite
Of fortune, and the desolating storms
Of future war. Advance not—spare to hide,
O gentle Power of darkness! these mild hues;
Obscure not yet these silent avenues
Of stateliest architecture, where the Forms
Of nun-like females, with soft motion, glide!

A winged Goddess—clothed in vesture wrought
Of rainbow colours; One whose port was bold,
Whose overburdened hand could scarcely hold
The glittering crowns and garlands which it brought—
Hovered in the air above the far-famed Spot.
She vanished; leaving prospect blank and cold
Of wind-swept corn that wide around us rolled
In dreary billows, wood, and meagre cot,
And monuments that soon must disappear;
Yet a dread local recompense we found;
While glory seemed betrayed, while patriot-zeal
Sank in our hearts, we felt as men *should* feel
With such vast hoards of hidden carnage near,
And horror breathing from the silent ground!

The Waterloo poem begins with the mind's regency conveyed appropriately in the image of a goddess who had "hovered . . . above the far-famed Spot." Yet with the introduction of this "spot"—the moment suddenly detached from idealization or narrative—the goddess vanishes, leaving a far sadder "prospect blank and cold / Of wind-swept corn, wood, and meagre cot." This "dread recompense," the speaker suggests, is a betrayal. However, it is equally clear that this betrayal owes its "dread" to what the "field" (the *panoramic* field of vision) necessarily opposes. To the extent, in other words, that the speaker ultimately "felt as [he] *should* feel / With vast hoards of hidden carnage near," he felt it, neither in memory of what remains hidden nor in recollection of the past per se. Rather, he feels as he should feel by forgetting the hidden and the past in deference to the present—the transit of which divides both the formerly patriotic poet and the equally freighted "spot" from their respective (and related) narratives, and in so dividing them transforms them.

The movement from transcendence, from the narrative or intentional structure of which the goddess is imagined to be a part, to immanence—specifically the breathing ground—has virtually nothing to do, then, with imagination. Although it looks like a pathetic fallacy, this breathing is, if anything, aligned with the peculiar "anonymity" (as Rosalind Krauss describes it) of many early photographs. In such photographs, "the phenomenological character of a view" frequently "opens onto a second feature" or "point of interest," thereby allowing for a "transfer of authorship from the subjectivity of the artist to the objective manifestations of nature."[33] This is the case, then, with the breathing ground. Less a flight of imagination, "this experience of the *singular*" (Krauss, 140) becomes in the dynamic of transference a *subject* now, whose "authority" quite literally supersedes the speaker's own. Moreover, in the poem that follows in sequence ("Between Namur and Liege"), the movement from "I" to the eye—from the beholder to the beheld—encounters significantly less resistance. Here, an idealized memory of war immediately defers to what in more than one sense now is "between" Namur and Liege: to the visible particularity of "monastic turrets" rising "from the smooth meadow-ground" (13–14).

In "Bruges" eye and mind wage a more dramatic contest with equally significant results. Here, the city "seen" in the light of setting sun struggles to resist the intentional structure that such transit of light invariably brings to mind. The same light that gradually transfigures motion and will ultimately suspend time initially *symbolizes* motion through what at first is an internalization of time. Internalized time—time as an idea—is abstracted here as mutability, which applied to life has the effect of making the present, specifically Bruges, a ruin of the past:

> and now the sunless hour,
> That, slowly making way for peaceful night,
> Best suits with fallen grandeur, to my sight
> Offers the beauty, the magnificence,
> And sober graces, left [Bruges] for defence
> Against the injuries of time, the spite
> Of fortune, and the desolating storms
> Of future war.
>
> (3–10)

By introducing the prophecy of "future war," Wordsworth reveals how those enslaved to history are condemned, if only in imagination, to repeat it. Yet, as if sensing this enslavement and the price it has exacted of the moment, the speaker reverses himself. "Advance not . . . Power of darkness," he exclaims—at which point the dreaded eventuality assumes a double meaning. In one sense, the power is that of change, of which nightfall is typically a measure. In another sense, the power is of the mind itself, whose usurpation of the visible (in summoning change) is further reflected in the way evening is made into a narrative figure.

The eye, for its part, has a quite different orientation, and in the sonnet's closing lines forsakes darkness—the darkness of both history and intentionality—for light and the details light illumines: for "mild hues," for "silent avenues," for "stat[ely] architecture," and most important perhaps, for "the Forms / Of nun-like females" who, "with soft motion, glide." It is crucial that these final figures are not nuns—whose existence and historical vocation are thoroughly integrated—but the "forms of nun-like females." In contrast to the initial image of a city appareled in light, they are figures who resist figuration. Figuration—like religion—requires more than the intervention of imagination; it derives from imagination's compact with tradition. In a present, then, in which they are forever visible and forever "transits o'er . . . optic glass" (as Wordsworth phrases it in another sonnet written at about this time, "Malham Cove"), the nuns are necessarily removed from a past that has usurped their sexuality and, with it, their form and movement.

There are numerous instances in the later Wordsworth where the photographic impulse intrudes to save the present from the past. But none is more revealing perhaps than the poem, "I Saw the Figure of a Lovely Maid," which begins the third and final section of the *Ecclesiastical Sonnets*. The ostensible purpose of the *Ecclesiastical Sonnets* was, of course, to trace the progress of the English Church from its origins to the present time. Yet because the task of representing this history would devolve to individual sonnets or to "sketches" (as they were initially called), the *Sonnets*' "history" quickly became a parahistory: a narrative where every station or sketch resists (at least in part) the ostensibly continuous, larger narrative that the individual poems also form. Nor is it at all a coincidence that the visible is often the means by which "accidentality" or "matter-of-factness" intervenes here, transforming a totality or history into a history that is more (and no less) than a sum of individual parts.

Such an intervention, with its particular resistance to narrative authority, is evident in the recollection of the figure of the maid. Recalling the lovely Maid "seated alone beneath a darksome tree" (2) Wordsworth juxtaposes the memory of her—the "bright corporeal presence—form and face" (9)—to her "dissolution" (14) *as a memory* or figure of the mind. In contrast to any number of Wordsworth's major poems, where objects are dissolved in order to be recreated, the actuality of the maid in the past ensures her presence in a way that the poet to whom she was *once* visible (and, in effect, photographable) cannot. In what amounts really to an abstraction of a photograph, the past—what was once visible to the speaker—persists despite the failure of both poetry and imagination to recover it.

Thus, it is also by failing as poems that Wordsworth's later poems, particularly his sonnets, protest what we are inclined generally to call good poetry. For by failing in the way they do, poems such as "Bruges" or "I Saw the Figure of a Lovely Maid" simultaneously reveal the failure of canonical texts to be much more than applications to life. Part of these sonnets' failure, to be sure, has to do with their failure at being sonnets, whose tradition—with its particular emphasis on figuration—they neither modify nor uphold. And yet, the failure of these poems probably has as much to do with their promotion of visible "figures" over figures, so to speak, as with their success in also summoning ideas that have little or nothing to do with the world viewed. Thus, it is not only the language of these poems that is frequently trite or lacks distinction. It is their sense or sentiment as well. The Waterloo poem, though it exposes a conflict of eye and mind, remains in purely poetical sense a hackneyed epiphany about the "horror" of war in the same way that "Bruges" never stops being a paean to that city in the eddy of time.

Nevertheless, the extent to which these sonnets may be deemed trite or unimaginative owes less to a diminution of Wordsworth's poetic powers (as customarily charged) than to a supervening intentionality that with the eye's mediation has finally replaced a romantic one. Such a replacement does more than reflect the betrayal to which language, especially the language of poetry, subjects the mind. It suggests, through the works themselves—which (like Friedrich's paintings) foreground so as to displace an irruption of the intentional—that this subjugation will persist so long as there is poetry. What Wordsworth first called the tyranny of the eye merely masked, he came to recognize, a tyranny at the center of the poetic enterprise. Thus, while he may have had the misfortune (as a former instructor of mine once aptly put it) to have lived to eighty, we might also ask how fortunate was the tyranny of his youth.

CHAPTER EIGHT

The Postmodernism of Childe Harold

I

In a journal entry made sometime in 1821, Byron's precocity, and the possible relation of his early "passions" to an ensuing "melancholy," gave way to a more elusive observation. "My earlier poems," he wrote, "are the thoughts of one at least ten years older than the age at which they were written,—I don't mean for their solidity—but their Experience—the first two Cantos of C[hilde] H[arold] were completed at twenty-two—and they were written as if by a man—older than I shall probably ever be."[1]

It is easy, certainly, to read these thoughts as the retrospection of a writer sufficiently removed from his earlier work (and from his earlier sexual self)[2] to be moved, in reconsidering them, to the kind of hyperbole whose referent is more realistically an anxiety about the present. Here, most readers would conclude, is simply another instance of the poet as his worst reader.

And yet, there is, in the precocity that exceeds the abilities of the "older man" so as to be more than a prolepsis, a deeply critical awareness that such early senescence might similarly exceed the ability of posterity to appreciate it. We see this most clearly in the distinction Byron makes between "solidity," by which he presumably means those aspects of the later poems that correspond to various aesthetic desiderata, and the "experience" of *Childe Harold,* which as any reader familiar with Byron will realize means something more than simply the events or experiences chronicled in the first two cantos.

Like "solidity," "experience" is largely an aesthetic matter—the experience *of Childe Harold*—which, as Byron and posterity have concurred, differs qualitatively from the experience of the later cantos and of the poems contemporary with them. The difference, then, is that where criticism has been uniform in preferring the second half of *Childe Harold's Pilgrimage* to the first, Byron effectively attributes this uniformity to the failure of criticism to have also recognized a challenge posed by the early cantos, which are more advanced, he implies, or differently conceived (recall, again, the equation of poetry and "thought"), than the work that followed.

This advancement, then—what, with special reference to Jean-François Lyotard, I call the "postmodernism" of *Childe Harold*—requires elaboration, for it bears directly on an issue of considerable importance not only with respect to Byron's poem, or to the contradictions inherent in the critical consensus regarding *Childe Harold* (where it is alternately valued as a romantic or modern document), but with respect as well to romanticism and literary history in general. I am aware, of course, that the prospect of *Byron's* postmodernism may seem—particularly to those already encumbered by the numerous possibilities and permutations of postmodernism—a needless elaboration. Nevertheless, I am provoked in my claim as much by the corroborating observations of Lyotard, for whom postmodernism "is not modernism at its end but in the nascent state,"[3] as I am by Byron's peculiar uncongeniality to the "deconstruction" of romanticism in our own time: a critical movement that, for want of a better term, is essentially postmodernist in orientation.

There are undoubtedly any number of deconstructive critics who have chosen not to "deconstruct" Byron simply because he is an easy mark—because the poet's apparent conservatism (unlike the more radical orientation of Wordsworth's "great period") says all that need be said about those other aspects of his writing that reflect a certain liberalism. Nevertheless, there are demonstrably more readers for whom Byron's uncongeniality to the fashions of literary history—most notably, the "romantic reassessment" of the 1960s—has remained a cover under which to read him as a protocontemporary. Whether it is Frank McConnell's notion of Byron's "anti-poetry," or Michael J. Cooke's assertion that "truth" in Byron is tantamount to "uncertainty," or Jerome McGann's emphasis on the paratactic, piecemeal way of comprehending the world in Byron, or even Anne Mellor's claim that Byron was forever engaged in a "constant process of creation and de-creation," Byron's admirers are in one sense perfectly eager to enlist Byron *against* the romantic or even modern "consciousness" in which, as Lyotard observes, there is "nostalgia of the whole" (81).[4]

This contemporaneity of Byron's is, in large part, a contemporary reaction to Byron's virtual exclusion from the more liberal, humanistic conceptions of the romantic achievement in the very influential studies in recent decades by critics such as M. H. Abrams and Harold Bloom. If Byron was not, as these critics have variously asserted, a "humanist" in some conventionally radical or agnostic sense, he was, his admirers have been forced to conclude, something else: an ironist, a "Catholic," a modernist and, insofar as the case for Byron has proved a reassessment (however unintended) of the "romantic reassessment," a postmodernist.[5] Thus, it is also impossible for Byron's admirers to separate the poet's "postmodernism," as they implicitly conceive it, from any of several orientations that, along with the "romanticism" these oppose, collectively subsume Byron within a counternarrative whose relative "maturity" also pries the poet from his "nascent" and potentially uncooptable position.

And, indeed, one does not have to look very hard among Byron's admirers to see in their "liberated Byron" a nostalgia for the wholeness that his "deliver[ance]," like the "humanistic" orientation it would correct, reflects (McConnell, 431). Whether it is the "uncertainty" that "truth" demands in Byron (Cooke, 139–40), or the "comprehension [that] is achieved only in successive, and relatively ignorant, perceptions" in a poem like *Childe Harold* (McGann, *Fiery Dust,* 39), or in the "greater creative power" to which as ironist Byron finally gains access (Mellor, 5), the readings of Byron in our time are reluctant finally to "wage a war" (as Lyotard describes it) "on totality" (82). It is more often the case that some totalizing vision is posited by criticism almost in compensation for the radical disposition of Byron's art.

Byron's postmodernism, in contrast, recognizes "totality" for what it is: an arbitrary orientation native to neither art nor life and, at the same time, a probable disposition (with particular regard to the subject) of both. Thus, where criticism is inclined to effect a truce between the poet and some totalizing vision, Byron, as I conceive him, tends to suffer totality as if it were a colonial garrison. In *Childe Harold's Pilgrimage* this sufferance is managed by a tension between Harold, who in the early cantos "sees," "watches," or "views" what he encounters as a passive onlooker, and the poem's narrator, who colonizes and writes over the world viewed according to a providential narrative of paradise lost. In contrast to the "postmodern" Harold to whom the world is visible, fragmented, and inchoate, the poem's narrator, with his peculiar nostalgia for the whole, reveals the similarity or modernity in those orientations that literary historians have capriciously distinguished as "romanticism" and "modernism." The putatively modernist narrative that privileges the past in *Childe Harold's Pilgrimage,* brooding (à la Pound and Eliot) on the decline of the West, is no different from, or no more conservative than, the revolutionary or "romantic" narrative that maintains hope in the future. The "selfish Sorrow [that] ponders on the past" (2.901), that feels, in the narrator's words, that "we are not what we have been," is no less selfish in its exercise of individual authority than the millenarian view that "deem[s]" that "we are not what we should be" (3.1033–34).[6] Both views put art, in this case poetic language, at the service of what Lyotard calls the "presentable" rather than performing the postmodern task of putting the present or, in Harold's case, the merely visible at the service of art.[7]

II

Lyotard figures centrally in my consideration of Byron. And he does so by agreement with Byron on the paradoxically advanced and reflexive character of what, in *Childe Harold* 1–2, is also a nascent, and as yet unformed, sensibility. No matter how much the narrator of the early cantos anticipates those orientations that are recognizably "modern," the presence of a notably reticent, inarticulate Harold concurrently enables Byron to foreground these "anticipations" as strangely belated.[8] Of special relevance to Byron's postmodernism, then, are Lyotard's notions of the "presentable" and the "unpresentable"—especially given Harold's ability to "subordinate thought to the gaze" (Lyotard, 79).

Drawing on the Kantian sublime, whose premodern disposition renders it a blueprint for "the postmodern condition," Lyotard distinguishes those "Ideas" (e.g., "totality," "simplicity," the "infinitely powerful") as ideas "of which no presentation is possible." "Impart[ing] no knowledge about reality" or "experience," such ideas, he argues, "can be said to be unpresentable" (78). "Modern aesthetics," however, is disinclined to accept the unpresentablity of these concepts. While modernism is scarcely naive in its presentation of certain ideas, it nevertheless "allow[s] the unpresentable to be put forward . . . as the missing parts," thereby "offer[ing] to the reader or viewer matter for solace and pleasure" (81).

Postmodernism, in contrast, aligns with Kant in calling for a "combination of pleasure and pain" in the experience of art, thereby resisting any "nostalgia" for what is missing. Indeed, it is the function of postmodernism "to put forward the unpresentable in presentation itself," making it impossible "to share collectively the nostalgia for the unattainable" (81). Postmodernism's task, then, is to search "for new presentations, not in order to enjoy them but in order to impart a stronger sense of the unpresentable" (81). No longer "supply[ing] reality" with some totalizing narrative or idea, it is "our business," submits Lyotard, "to invent allusions" to those ideas, effectively acknowledging them as concepts "which cannot be presented" (81).

If we follow Lyotard in assuming that certain totalizing ideas have neither a basis in nor a bearing on "reality," this means that the merely visible—those presentations that are necessarily not objects of enjoyment or nostalgia—also involves some aspect of un*representablity* (which Lyotard must mean in any case inasmuch as the term "unpresentable" doesn't exist in French in this sense). For visibility, in one way, actually reverses the tendency to represent ideas (in what Lyotard regards as presentation) by removing "reality" from the ideas to which the otherwise *seen* may previously or even simultaneously be imagined to conform. Thus, while it is presumably one function of postmodernism to foreground the totalizing tendencies of art, it is arguably a concomitant function to admit certain unrecuperable images. Lyotard suggests as much when he remarks that the gaze is frequently that means by which "thought" is turned away from the "unpresentable" in art. But where the gaze, in this apparently modern manipulation, is implicated in a project of "derealization," by which reality becomes accessory to concept, it is my contention that visibility—what is made available by agency of what Norman Bryson calls the "glance"—actually exposes the "incommensurability of reality to concept" (or the inapplicability of ideas to life), which both Kant (Lyotard, 79) and Byron posit against a more romantic, more "modern" tendency to totalize.[9]

Two things, consequently, must be borne in mind in reading *Childe Harold's Pilgrimage:* the tendency in cantos 1 and 2 to make the purely seen—what Harold sees—unrepresentable (as opposed to representing either a "dire universe" or Harold's "own enigmatic nature"

[B. Hirsch, 349]), and the tendency of what is otherwise represented to deploy "concepts" that are alternately "romantic" and "modern" in their hope and skepticism respectively. The distinction between Harold and the poem's narrator, to whom the task of representation initially falls, has often been observed and is customarily attributed to an uncertainty of voice or identity that gradually rights itself in the more univocal cantos of 1816 and 1818.[10] Nevertheless, what is striking about this tension is that it is as much a matter of silence as of utterance: language, rather than referring to the world, more often appears a means to appropriate it.

From the very advent of Harold's pilgrimage—which characteristically marks his departure from an appropriated world ("His house, his home, his heritage, his lands, / The laughing dames in whom he did delight, / . . . And long had fed his youthful appetite" [1.91–95])—there is a notable distinction between Harold who "views" the world passively (or impassively as the case may be) and the appropriative, aggressive narrator. In contrast to Harold's, the narrator's vision, as critics have frequently noted, is motivated by judgment—and in comparison to what Harold beholds—by an intentional structure.[11]

In the majority of instances, this motivation involves a "modern" or (to use Schiller's term) "sentimental" narrative of past and present, which insists that the actuality of Spain, Portugal, and Greece be contrasted to the greatness either of their pasts or of their idealized destinies. In other instances, the motivation is more gratuitously intentional (albeit characteristic of travel literature), involving jingoistic comparisons of the unregenerate nature of the Mediterranean sensibility and the more disciplined "north." These two narratives, moreover, are invariably intermixed, so that the effect is less a recuperation of the latter by the seriousness of the former than a deconstruction of their apparent difference or opposition.

The deconstructive dynamic can be observed with particular relevance in the narrator's ruminations on the ruins of Athens and the Elgin marbles. Unable to regard the temple of Saturn with the intractability of either Harold or "the Moslem," in whom the ruins evoke no apparent nostalgia, the narrator broods on the various plunderers, including Time, who have interposed themselves between what is "here" and its former totality (2.73–90). The "last" and "worst" of these spoilers turns out to have been Lord Elgin, whose appropriation of certain Greek artifacts for the British Museum points to a contradiction between "free Britannia" and the autonomy "she" is evidently willing to deny Greece (2.109–17). Yet even with this critique of England, the narrator cannot resist expressing thanks that Elgin was not English but Scottish. That is, just as the narrator is necessarily blind to what is before him, so he cannot criticize "freedom" without also mystifying it as a millennial ideal to which Greece was "once" privy and to which England, with all of its hypocrisies, is committed still.

Harold perceives things differently. The "little distance" from which he stands and "view[s]" the world (2.641–42) exposes not only the "incommensurability of reality to concept" but, with the narrator's overbearing counterexample, the commensurability of *one concept to another.* This is shown, for example, in the narrator's gyrations upon encountering Mount Parnassus, where ideas and concepts proliferate for the failure, as it were, to follow Harold's example. In contrast to his initial "survey" of Parnassus, whose visible actuality overwhelms the dreams and myths that had been associated with it, the narrator moves immediately to reinvest the mountain with significance. This resistance to the visible involves more than the mountain's mythological function as the seat of inspiration or even a nostalgia for its more noble past; it involves, more crucially, the speaker's own narrative of poetic vocation.

The issue, then, in making concepts presentable, or in representing the real, turns out not to be the concept brought, or even the reality reconstituted. At issue is the individual subject, whose primacy and sovereignty account for the forgetting, as Byron describes it (1.63), to which the nostalgia is paradoxically tantamount: the forgetting of things visible, such as the mountain, and the forgetting of things imagined or "presented" (e.g., the destiny of Spain), whose succession (and occlusion) attest, in different order, to the speaker's centrality. In contrast to the "little distance" at which Harold stands from the real, the narrator's distance is both greater and, in confirmation of that fact, much smaller: the world the narrator views is no more or less than himself.

III

Harold, for his part, is determined to remember. Yet his acts of memory, which are really perceptions, merely confirm the extent to which "the real," as Louis Althusser has noted, is—in contrast to Harold's reality—an "imaginary representation of the world" whose "constitutive" category is "the subject."[12] What is represented in most conceptions of the real, or in "ideology" as Althusser terms it, is "not the system of the real relations which govern the existence of individuals, but the imaginary relation of those individuals to the real relations in which they live" (165). Hence, just as the subject "is constitutive of all ideology," so all ideology has the reciprocal "function . . . of 'constituting' concrete individuals as subjects" (171–73).

I raise the issue of ideology (or "reality," if you prefer) not simply because Byron's narrator is an exemplary subject in the Althusserian sense. I raise it because the virtually seamless commensurability of subject and object, which is the proper "function" of "all ideology," is disrupted and foregrounded by the comparatively nonsubjective Harold. The key instances of this exposure involve those moments—such as the bullfight scene in canto 1 (756–91) or the Albanian revelry in canto 2 (631–48)—where a visible reality contests another, more idealized reality. Nevertheless, one instance in particular—the passage by Leucadia—reveals both the differences in the two perspectives and what is at stake in their differences.

The episode begins characteristically by revealing the distinction between the visible world and the "imaginary representation of [that] world":

> Childe Harold sail'd, and pass'd the barren spot,
> Where sad Penelope o'erlook'd the wave;
> And onward view'd the mount, not yet forgot,
> The lover's refuge, and the Lesbian's grave.
> Dark Sappho! could not verse immortal save
> That breast imbued with such immortal fire?
> Could she not live who life eternal gave?
> If life eternal may await the lyre,
> That only Heaven to which Earth's children may aspire.
>
> (2.343–51)

The closing ruminations on immortality reaffirm what is already apparent in the preceding lines: namely, the speaker's inability to regard the world in any but a self-concerned way. Unlike Harold, who views the mount and, in so regarding it, diverges from Penelope's more subjective example, the narrator necessarily follows Penelope in "overlooking" the world by imposition of *his* narrative, which in this case is one of poetic fame.

On the face of it, it would appear that the task of remembering devolves to the speaker here, who supplements Harold's inscrutable perceptions with the memories of Penelope and Sappho. However, in the same way that remembering Penelope involves *imitating* Penelope, so the appendage of "not yet forgot" to Harold's observations provides a transition between forgetting, or the imaginary representation that *is* memory, and the resistance to forgetting that the act of "viewing" (here as in the Diorama) provisionally wages. The "yet" looks in two directions at once: backward, to those perceptions that for the moment resist history, "pass[ing]" the image of Penelope overlooking the waves, and forward to those perceptions that make forgetting—the subject's imposition—a far greater likelihood.

There is enough in this one stanza to commend it to our attention. But it is in the ensuing two stanzas that the narrator's more subjective meaning is gradually subsumed within the more resistant or (to use Kristeva's term) "effective meaning"[13] of the episode:

> 'Twas on a Grecian autumn's gentle eve
> Childe Harold hail'd Leucadia's cape afar;
> A spot he long'd to see, nor cared to leave:
> Oft did he mark the scenes of vanish'd war,
> Actium, Lepanto, fatal Trafalgar;
> Mark them unmov'd, for he would not delight
> (Born beneath some remote inglorious star)
> In themes of bloody fray, or gallant fight,
> But loath'd the bravo's trade, and laugh'd at martial wight.
>
> But when he saw the evening star above
> Leucadia's far-projecting rock of woe,
> And hail'd the last resort of fruitless love,
> He felt, or deem'd he felt, no common glow:
> And as the stately vessel glided slow
> Beneath the shadow of that ancient mount,
> He watch'd the billows' melancholy flow,
> And, sunk albeit in thought as he was wont,
> More placid seem'd his eye, and smooth his pallid front.
>
> (2.352–69)

The initial allusion to itinerary, the narrative of longing of which Harold is both author and protagonist, is sharply qualified by the object of his longing—the sighted spot—whose immediacy and contingency erase all pretext for encountering the cape. Unlike the narrator, who is disposed to "mark" the world according to his design, Harold marks or observes the world independent of narrative. The "scenes of vanish'd war" are, in his view, precisely *those:* scenes, like Leucadia's "spot," where visibility and concretion take precedence over history.

The narrator perceives things otherwise, and just as he manages to retrieve various battles from invisibility (or Venus from her visible materialization as the "evening star"), so he is compelled, under similar authority, to mark Harold in an equally subjective way. The first of these markings involves Harold's supposed narrative of longing, which the pilgrim gives no evidence of sharing. Indeed, Harold merely observes what the narrator—in the sway of narrative—is disposed to represent. Then, too, there is the surmise regarding Harold's pacifism, which, however plausible, remains (particularly with the astrological allusion) still another effort to replace the visible—characteristically, the figure of Harold looking—with a "vanish'd" Harold.

Nevertheless, it is the ensuing protest against the uncommon nature of Harold's experience—"He felt, or deem'd he felt, no common glow"—that is most crucial in exposing both the differences between Harold and his counterpart, as well as what is at stake in them. Central, of course, is the surmise regarding Harold's surmise, which reveals the extent to which the speaker's world continually wears the speaker's face. In canto 1, for example, after twelve stanzas of uninhibited vituperation over matters ranging from the Convention of Cintra to the poverty of rural Portugal, the narrator remarks: "So deem'd the Childe" (315). At that point, the attribution was plainly erroneous and a means to introduce the very tensions that make the initial cantos of the poem more advanced (as Byron later suggested) than the later cantos. However now, with the implicit disagreement over the uncommonness of Harold's experience, the surmise takes on even greater significance. For it is by a *surmised* surmise that Harold's affinity with the speaker is at once demonstrated and his uniqueness—that is, the uniqueness of Harold's experience as against the speaker's—discredited.

There is a necessary relationship, in other words, between the *means* of contesting Harold's uniqueness and the need to contest that uniqueness. And here, Althusser's well-known observations on the lineaments of subjectivity, notably "the rituals of ideological recognition" (172) or of "hailing" (174), prove instructive. According to Althusser, it is the function of these various rituals to "guarantee for us that we are indeed concrete, individual, distinguishable and (naturally) irreplaceable objects" (172–73). The handshake is only one example of this ritual; there are other manifestations as well, including "the most commonplace everyday police (or other) hailing: 'Hey you there!'":

> [T]he hailed individual will turn round. By this mere one-hundred-and-eighty-degree physical conversion, he becomes a *subject.* Why? Because he has recognized that the hail was "really" addressed to him, and that it was *really him* who was hailed" (and not someone else). Experience shows that the practical telecommunication of hailings is such that they hardly ever miss their man: . . . the one hailed always recognizes that it is really him who is being hailed. (174)

In contrast to this "theoretical scene," the various instances of hailing in the passage by Leucadia's rock involve acts of "misrecognition," whose "function" is necessarily the "inverse" of ideology (172) and opposed to the subject thereby constituted. Unlike Althusser, whose concerns are with the subject hailed—whose recognition, in turn, both ensures and illustrates the subject's "interpellation" (174) by culture—Byron's more open scenario centers simultaneously on a subject doing the hailing. Harold's "hail[ing]" of the rock, which is repeated, is important for two reasons, then: first, because it is directed at a nonreciprocating *object,* and second, because this object is simultaneously the site of a subject's—Sappho's—dissolution. Harold's failure, in other words, to do the work of interpellation, or his success, if you prefer, in managing to "miss [his] man," is effectively echoed in Sappho's consent to nonbeing, which represents what is achieved now by her inability to *be hailed.*

Moreover, to disclose this breakdown in ideology (as "real art" apparently can, according to Althusser)[14]—specifically, that Sappho's inability to "turn round" imitates Harold's inability to hail her—we have the counterexample of the poem's narrator, whose "imaginary representation" of Sappho finds a correlative in his imaginary representation, or hailing, of Harold. The problem for the speaker, however, is that this ritual of recognition dissolves into misrecognition, exposing the narcissistic completeness on which ideology still relies. For failure, that is, to turn around, or to be interpellated, Harold forces the speaker to reinvent him in the speaker's own, necessarily "unique" image. But it is the ironic consequence of the narrator's invention—and proof of the way ideology departs the poem following Sappho—that "individuality," the "uncommon[ness]" of Harold's feeling, is additionally that means by which the narrator disparages Harold's individuality. For it is the rather self-serving, even clichéd, presumption of uncommonness, and *not* his uncommonness in fact, that marks Harold as a subject and as someone recognizable.

It becomes the achievement, therefore, of the first two cantos of *Childe Harold,* and testimony to their peculiar advancement, that Harold, like the very world he views, is visible as a reflex of his refusal to be recognized. In addition to compelling the narrator to fill the breach left by his absence, Harold's inscrutability makes it equally impossible to accept or to embrace the narrator's compensatory vision. Harold's unrecognizability has a double function, therefore. Not only does his failure to "turn round" relegate him to the margins of the poem; it manages—in a way that is almost antithetical to Friedrich's *Rückenfigur*—to prevent the reader from being similarly recognized or (in imitation of Harold "hailing" the site of Sappho's sacrifice) from recognizing himself *in anyone but Harold.* Such mutual dislocation is more than a matter of bringing theory to bear upon the poem, as I have done. It is also a matter, to quote Byron, of the "experience" of *Childe Harold,* which, as almost everyone agrees, improves in the later cantos. The difference is that while this improvement or repositioning of the reader is customarily understood at the expense of the earlier cantos and their narrator, it is the more theoretical function of the early cantos to oppose the very ritual of recognition or ideological identification that eventually provides "matter for solace and pleasure" (Lyotard, 81).

Such resistance to identification—to the ground not only for solace but for sadness as well—is especially evident at the very close of canto 2 as the narrator expresses grief over the death of a friend. Although poignant after a fashion, the poignancy of the narrator's expression is attenuated by its exclusivity:

> Thou too art gone, thou lov'd and lovely one!
> Whom youth and youth's affection bound to me;
> Who did for me what none beside have done,
> Nor shrank from one albeit unworthy thee.
> What is my being? thou hast ceas'd to be!
> Nor staid to welcome here thy wanderer home,

> Who mourns o'er hours which we no more shall see—
> Would they had never been, or were to come!
> Would he had ne'er return'd to find fresh cause to roam!
> (2.891–99)

Although one can certainly read and comprehend what the speaker is saying here, the ability to share or to recognize his grief is impeded by a syntax that, like the speaker's "being," is prisoner to an incessant doubling or circularity. The repetition of "youth," as well as the multiple conjugations of "do" and "be," perform at a linguistic level the very ritual of recognition by which the narrator stands in "imaginary relation . . . to . . . real relations." In the same way, in fact, that the narrator's being dissolves with the dissolution of a friend who "[has] ceas'd to be," he is reciprocally bolstered by one who (much like the figure of Harold "deeming") is invented by him: his friend, in short, is one whose loveliness is a condition of being loved.

Nor does this recognition move in one direction only. The narrator, who hails his beloved friend, demands as a matter of course that he be hailed or recognized in turn. However, it is testimony to the imaginary nature of their relationship, and of the imaginary identity their relationship underwrites, that the speaker must also suffer its fictiveness. Lamenting the hours they never more shall see, the speaker not only expresses regret that these hours had ever existed; he paradoxically, or so it seems, expresses the wish that there might be more hours to come. On the one hand, these two expressions simply register despair or nostalgia for experiences that will never more be realized. Yet their very conflation necessarily documents the way an imagined past—the "hours which we no more shall see"—holds sway over reality both now and in the future.

The speaker, at all events, is too immersed in being a subject and in being nostalgic to do much about this problem. But the poem, with its concomitant affinity for Harold or Sappho, enlists nostalgia in another function. This more critical or reflexive function is evident in the ensuing apostrophe—"Oh! ever loving, lovely, and belov'd!" (2.900)—which refers *interchangeably* to the speaker and his friend. Here, the ritual of recognition, where the speaker hails his beloved, shows by double referentiality how "ideology" in turn "hails or interpellates concrete individuals as concrete subjects" (Althusser, 173). The speaker, who also constitutes or invents reality is simultaneously (and literally) constituted by the reality he imagines—making the speaker both his own creation (in the image of his beloved) and a creation of something else.

A more direct disclosure in this vein follows immediately:

> How selfish Sorrow ponders on the past,
> And clings to thoughts now better far remov'd!
> (2.901–02)

Just as the narrator exchanges roles with his beloved in the previous apostrophe, so his exclamation with its notably interrogative pressure oscillates between a recognition and a criticism of that recognition. On the one hand, the speaker appears to realize his self-absorption and, still worse, the specifically fictive or imaginary nature of that nostalgia. Nevertheless, his self-injunction to remove his "thoughts" does not preclude their relocation or imposition elsewhere. If anything, as the poem shows, the narrator is calling for the replacement of one "reality" with a reality that is equally imaginary and arbitrary. This is clear in the various *interpolations* that divide the world and the speaker. It is not enough for the speaker to behold the world in sorrow. He must behold the world in sorrow that "ponders . . . [a]nd clings to *thoughts* . . . better far remov'd" (my emphasis). It is "thoughts," over anything to which "thoughts" might themselves cling, that are primary here—as well they should be. For while produced by the subject, thoughts in their peculiar autonomy are also constitutive of the subject. The prospect, then, of thoughts far removed involves two, exclusive possibilities: the removal of thought to another reality, in which the narrator is at once creator and created, and the removal of thought, following Harold's example, sufficient to redeem—in a more radical or postmodern way—both the physical and social world.

IV

Of the two possibilities broached by the early cantos, only one is realized in canto 3—and it is the possibility more congenial to the romanticism that, as Schiller describes it in *Naive and Sentimental Poetry,* is virtually synonymous with modernity as we frequently conceive it: a stance whose particular "striving after unity" or "approximation to an infinite greatness" simultaneously bears a "sadness at lost joys," or "at the golden age now disappeared from the world" (111–26). In *Childe Harold* this "sentimental" alternative is achieved in accordance with the narrator's transformation into a more integrated, more definable, and more autonomous "self." Indeed, even the famous early passage by which the speaker claims to have created himself, "gaining as [he] give[s] / The life [he] image[s]" (48–49), is less an etiology of self in the manner, say, of canto 2 than an "ontology of self" (Snyder) that implicitly distinguishes what the self creates from what also constitutes or constructs the self. A theory of self has been replaced suddenly by a theorizing self:

> What am I? Nothing; but not so art thou,
> Soul of my thought! with whom I traverse earth,
> Invisible but gazing, as I glow
> Mix'd with thy spirit, blended with thy birth,
> And feeling still with thee in my crush'd feeling's dearth.
> (3.50–54)

The claim to invisibility reveals nicely the extent to which the tensions of cantos 1 and 2 have been subsumed and virtually synthesized in canto 3. Although the speaker admits to a certain insubstantiality, his invisibility turns out to be "nothing" short of omniscience and a measure, consequently, of the invisibility to which he has reciprocally removed the "earth." Unlike the palpable, if unrecuperable, figure of Harold gazing at Leucadia's rock in canto 2, the narrator gazing in canto 3 restores a very critical distinction between one kind of vision and another. This distinction, which is a distinction really between the gaze and the glance (or between Seeing, in effect, and seeing) is necessary now. For unlike Harold, whose vision is thoroughly implicated in his materiality as a human (and characteristically visible) body—the narrator typically relinquishes being *something* only to redeem this self-proclaimed nothingness at a higher rate. The means of this redemption turns out, not surprisingly, to be "thought," the capacity for (or melding with) which not only retrieves the narrator from oblivion but has the simultaneous effect of making oblivion or nothingness a condition of everything that is *not* the speaker or not thought.

Thus it is scarcely a surprise that with the sudden prominence of the gaze over the glance, it would be Harold, whose access to the visible (and whose visibility in turn) had previously separated the gaze from the constraints of authority, who is suddenly and henceforth *invisible*. For in the very way that he had earlier resisted thought, or had exposed the imposition of narrative upon life, Harold is, in the present mandate, unthinkable. The customary explanations for Harold's disappearance, then—for example, that Byron no longer needs him or that Harold and the speaker are properly one—are not invalid so much as they are irrelevant. What matters now is that with Harold's invisibility (after which he is no longer sightable, much less recognizable) the possibilities and subversions to which his visibility and the visible in general have provided access are absent in kind.

Admittedly, this is a somewhat circuitous way around the problem. After all, no matter how much the "experience" of *Childe Harold* 3 owes to Harold's *disappearance,* it owes palpably more to the speaker's *presence,* which, in the absence of a counterexample, furnishes the reader with a direct access to poetic authority. The pleasure that canto 3 has long afforded readers—and the critical approbation for which it has been responsible—is here to be derived, owing largely to the omniscience, the capacity to totalize, to which the reader, as much as the speaker, is suddenly exposed. This power is much more than simply the satiric or ironic prerogative of "join[ing]" the speaker in "look[ing] down on other men's follies or sins" (as Wayne Booth might describe it).[15] Indeed, as the notably unsatiric description of the Duchess of Richmond's ball prior to the battle of Waterloo (181–225) shows, this power involves access to the very nostalgia, or participation in the very rituals of recognition, from which the reader has been previously excluded.

The particular attention to Frederick William, "Brunswick's fated chieftain," as the first of the revelers to hear the cannon's "roar," provides a case in point. Couched "within a windowed niche of that high hall" (199), the duke is observed not only to have heard the sound, but also to have "caught its tone with Death's prophetic ear" (202). One version of history, a sound heard dimly above the din of present revelry, is displaced by a sense of the past in which the momentary and contingent give way—under the narrator's imaginary retrospection (which is simultaneously Frederick's imaginary prospect)—to what is monumental, public, and readable.

Along with Brunswick, then, whose perceptions are necessarily secondary to the history they anticipate, the figures who are effectively "hailed" in canto 3 are no longer those out of Byron's past—for example the "beloved" friend Edelston, whose importance is essentially deconstructed at the end of canto 2. Rather, they are *public* figures—notably Napoleon and Rousseau—who focus the expectations and disappointments of a generation. The sudden recourse to a public narrative of desire and revolution cannot be minimized any more than its power, and the power it necessarily confers on the reader, can be discounted. This narrative, in fact, follows the disappearance of Harold in propelling the reader toward a more modern, more interpellated position, in which the gaze and mind are not only captivated by the likes of Napoleon or Rousseau but are captivated sufficiently for the reader to turn around. The genuineness of voice and consistency of vision with which canto 3 is customarily credited owes as much in the end to an interpellated speaker as to those whom he interpellates in hailing—all of whom are immediately readable and recognizable as versions of ourselves.

In this way, too, the constitution of the subject that had been opposed in the early cantos is validated in canto 3 in the only way it can be—namely, by identification of "poet" and reader. While it may be going too far to insist that the narrator and reader are one and the same here, they are at least as recognizable to one another in canto 3 as were the reader and Harold in cantos 1 and 2. The difference, of course, is that where affiliation with Harold was earlier a matter of resistance and disaffiliation—of substituting a real, barely fathomable, relation in place of an imaginary one—the identification with the speaker in canto 3 is predicated on an imaginary, if unavoidable, relation on the part of both Byron *and* his reader to Napoleon and to Rousseau. Such an identification, of course, both demands and invites participation in the "modern" narratives that by implication in the French Revolution and its Napoleonic aftermath are more urgent and also more relevant than the generalized (and, as I will shortly argue, feminized) millenarianism of the early cantos. For if paradise continues to appear lost, it is no longer lost by agency of providence or God. Paradise is lost in canto 3 by agency of *men* who are empowered thereby to desire it and whose sadness "at lost joys" is rivaled only by the expectation of joys forthcoming that the reader cannot but share.

The surprisingly sympathetic portrait of Napoleon as an "antithetica[l] mix[ture]," as both "conqueror and captive of the earth" (3.316–33), renders him—in the relative absence of nationalistic sentiment—a representative man. Such men—and notions—are common in Byron, most memorably in his character Manfred, whose composition of "dust" and "deity" is typically viewed as an index of the resigned, if still radical, humanism of the author. But where Manfred's plight is dramatized and sufficiently exemplary to be both heroic and cautionary, the example of Napoleon is remarkably sympathetic. Napoleon's failure is not in the presumption so problematically objectified in Manfred (and earlier criticized in canto 1); it is in the meanness that frustrates the greatness he is legitimately heir to.

The example of Rousseau provides similar access to an ideology that earlier would have seemed an imposition. Directing us to the French Alps, where Rousseau "sought . . . a refuge from the worldly shocks" (929–30), the narrator asserts that

> All things are here of *him*; from the black pines,
> Which are his shade on high, and the loud roar
> Of torrents, where he listeneth, to the vines
> Which slope his green path downward to the shore,
> Where the bowed waters meet him, and adore,
> Kissing his feet with murmurs; and the wood,
> The covert of old trees, with trunks all hoar,
> But light leaves, young as joy, stands where it stood,
> Offering to him, and his, a populous solitude.
>
> (941–49)

The "him" initially alluded to is "Love" or some pantheistic spirit, who is introduced in the previous stanza as "pervading light and life" (935). Thus, the retention of the pronoun in reference (presumably) to Rousseau not only has the effect of underscoring their equation; it is an equation that the reader must consider and, in that way, prove. Unlike canto 1, in which such homocentrism was contested by a visible reality removed from human thought, there is no way for the reader to escape the humanization or imagination of landscape. (Indeed, "Love" already hovers between a personification or representation of the deity on the one hand and a human emotion or subjective stance on the other.) To resist the pervasive agency of God or "Love," as the declension to "him" encourages, can only issue in the removal of man to God's place. The very identity forged through the narrator's pronominal style is thereby extended in the act of reading, which follows the Rousseaustic (or Napoleonic) agenda not only in rejecting God but in interpellating man in "H/his" image.

The totalizing tendencies of canto 3, which variously construct the reader as an imagining, desiring subject, are not restricted either to Napoleon and Rousseau or even to the absence of Harold. They incorporate, as did the duchess of Richmond's ball, potentially subversive or contingent instances as well. In the example of the duke of Brunswick, the sound of something is no sooner registered than it becomes history writing of a most conventional sort. This is equally true of the "broken mirror," to which the narrator now alludes in canto 3. No sooner is this mirror broached (and shattered) than it becomes a symbol of the human heart:

> Even as a broken mirror, which the glass
> In every fragment multiplies; and makes
> A thousand images of one that was,
> The same, and still the more, the more it breaks;
> And thus the heart will do which not forsakes,
> Living in shattered guise, and still, and cold,
> And bloodless, with its sleepless sorrow aches,
> Yet withers on till all without is old,
> Showing no visible sign, for such things are untold.
> (3.289–97)

It is probably a coincidence that the "visible," the human countenance, is made to appear trivial in contrast to the heart's narrative. But it is surely no accident that the palpably fragmentary image of the broken mirror reflects the primacy of the unitary narrative. Just as the heart lives on in shattered guise, representing the subject's indefatigability, so the shattered mirror—with its *visible* resistance to representation—bears a "thousand images of *one* that was." The mirror does not shatter in a postmodern, much less in a physical, way. Rather, the mirror multiplies and sustains both the represented and, by implication, the nostalgia underlying its representation. Canto 3, whose power and appeal owe largely to the interpellation of the narrator and the reader as subjects in kind, represents more than a reversal of cantos 1 and 2; canto 3 is, in fact, a sublation of the earlier cantos that, in a curious way, justifies their existence in the first place.

V

That Byron simply forgot the purport of *Childe Harold's Pilgrimage* by the time he got to canto 3 is a lot less plausible than the customary assumption that the relatively "nascent" orientation of the initial cantos is simply that and nothing more. Nor is the charge of forgetting made any easier by the fact that Byron is hardly faking it or being ironic: whoever is speaking in canto 3 is speaking as he speaks because he obviously wants to. But, as it happens, there is in canto 4 enough of what might be called a postmodern retrospection to redeem the initial cantos as precocious in the way I have suggested. Further, because redemption of the early cantos necessarily halts the more conventional progress of canto 3, consenting in effect to the shattering of the "one that was," it bears—in conjunction with its post- or protomodern retrospection—a more human, even psychological, retrospection.

Byron, for his part, suggests as much when he observes a propos of the remarkable maturity of the early cantos that they were written "*as if* by a man—older than I shall probably ever be" (emphasis added). But it is his poem finally—and canto 4 in particular—that justifies this assertion in all its implications. In the end, *Childe Harold's Pilgrimage* does more than contest the appropriative, symbolizing, and authoritative tendencies of a patriarchal or "man[ly]" disposition; the poem's maturity is marked equally by a recognition that a "revolution" (to use Julia Kristeva's term)[16] against the manly order must also exceed our abilities—certainly Byron's ability—to realize or represent it. The postmodernism of *Childe Harold,* then, is exactly as both Lyotard *and* Kristeva might conceive it: it is an orientation that can only adumbrate what it might be like to be on the "other" side of both modernism and culture.

This return to the proleptic instability of the early cantos is gradual, not immediate. Confronting the palpable fragmentariness of both the visible world and the subject who would unify it, the narrator adverts to a narrative of ruin or synecdoche:

> But my soul wanders; I demand it back
> To meditate amongst decay, and stand
> A ruin amidst ruins; there to track
> Fall'n states and buried greatness, o'er a land
> Which *was* the mightiest in its old command,
> And *is* the loveliest, and must ever be
> The master-mould of Nature's heavenly hand,
> Wherein were cast the heroic and the free,
> The beautiful, the brave—the lords of earth and sea.
>
> (4.217–25)

If there is a contradiction between the artificial, lifeless image of something cast, and Nature who is credited with having performed that molding, it is not that Byron is mixing metaphors; it is that his narrator is quite literally meditating "amongst decay." No matter how much the narrator contrives to reconstruct the past, imagining the wholeness of which the ruins are a trace, he is continually frustrated by Rome's visible and pervasive actuality, which resists his totalizing meditations. Where previously the broken mirror is reconstructed by the "one that was," the narrator is surrounded by fragments whose "isness" contests the "wasness" or wholeness to which he would restore them. The very tension earlier dramatized at the sighted site of Sappho's sacrifice is now internalized. No longer quite the authority of canto 3, the speaker, following the peculiarly antecedent character of postmodernism, is at the crossways of the comparatively infantile "childe," who beholds what is before him, and an individuated, "modern" subject, whose nostalgia for the whole is virtually a rite of exhumation.

But it devolves ultimately to a different kind of exhumation or memory, beginning with the speaker's recovery of Caecilia Metella in stanza 101, to align with Harold in an "older," more advanced opposition. In addition to contesting the nostalgic, synecdochical imperative, this exhumation elaborates its resistance by returning the subject to a presubjective and "feminine" condition (in Kristeva's sense of the term).

Staring at the palatial edifice of Caecilia's tomb, the speaker is moved, almost as a reflex action, to separate the facticity of Caecilia's life and body—for example, her hair—from the symbol commemorating her, which is an index merely of her husband's "pride." In contrast to this patriarchal memorial, the peculiarly visceral Caecilia whom the speaker visualizes—and with whom he consequently confesses an identity—involves what amounts now to his *feminization,* his passage from the "symbolic" to the more maternal, less subjective "semiotic" (Kristeva, *Revolution,* 20–106):

> I know not why—but standing thus by thee
> It seems as if I had thine inmate known,
> Thou tomb! and other days come back on me
> With recollected music, though the tone
> Is changed and solemn, like the cloudy groan
> Of dying thunder on the distant wind;
> Yet could I seat me by this ivied stone
> Till I had bodied forth the heated mind
> Forms from the floating wreck which Ruin leaves behind.
>
> (4. 928–36)

The conflation of the speaker's personal, barely memorable past with his sense of having "known" the woman otherwise entombed is neither accidental nor excessive. Just as he and Caecelia are variously trapped within the symbolic order—Caecelia in her husband's tomb, and the speaker within a mind disposed to consider her tomb a proper memorial—so the memory of a woman's body is sufficient to retrieve *both* of them from their respective prisons. In Caecelia's case this recovery is a matter of being granted a facticity or "[em]bodi[ment]" apart from the mythology or structure by which she has been written over.

The speaker's recovery is more complex. The recollected music, which Caecelia's body evokes, marks a return to a virtually prehistoric or "borderline stat[e]" (*Powers,* 1–31) that, as Kristeva theorizes, remembers the initial "relationship . . . to the mother":[17] a state that, in retrospect, "wavers between the *fading away* of all meaning" (most immediately, that of the symbolic tomb) "and the *ecstasy* of an ego that, having lost its Other and its objects, reaches, at the precise moment of this suicide, the height of harmony with the promised land" (*Powers,* 18). In the case of Byron's speaker, "the promised land" is registered in the "volition" to embody the very forms, preeminently Caecelia, that Rome has left behind. By this, Caecelia is not merely a substitute or *symbol* for the mother—the undifferentiated condition that the speaker's memory of a woman's body evokes; she is, commensurate with his retreat from all notions of surrogacy or otherness, as proximate to the maternal body as memory will permit.

There is, of course, a countermovement to this recovery as well, which is represented as much by the tomb itself—by whose wall the speaker is similarly bounded—as by the speaker's "could," the conditionality of which interposes a gap between those "other days" and the here and now. Yet even with this interposition, which is additionally figured in the continued recourse to highly symbolic language, the speaker's efforts to maintain a characteristically modern mode of memory or nostalgia are subsumed by the "recollected music," whose meaning is purposefully deferred.[18]

Unlike cantos 1 and 2, in which there is clearly a contest between one memory and another, there is, in the sudden deference to "form" as against image or symbol, an increased resistance in canto 4 to a system of signification that would follow the differentiating structure of subjectivism in instituting a more immediate gap between a thing and what it means. The meaning of Caecilia's form *is her form,* which accords nicely with Kristeva's "semiotic" in positing an anterior (and revolutionary) language whose lexicon is the body—the form of mother-child—rather than the order that Kristeva (after Lacan) calls the "symbolic." The "symbolic," with its notable insistence on the relationship or gap between signifier and signified, belongs to the "'subject-object' continuum" (*Revolution,* 52): it is at once "constitutive of language" yet "indebted to, induced, and imposed by the social realm" (*Revolution,* 48). The "symbolic," unlike the "semiotic," belongs to the realm of the Father (or Other) and is thereby implicated in hierarchic structures of both meaning and, as we have previously noted, identity.

Thus, it is the paradoxical destiny of the visible in *Childe Harold's Pilgrimage* that it becomes, by resistance to the "social realm," increasingly *invisible* or internalized. That is, just as Harold's *seen* had earlier opposed the narrator's authoritarian efforts at meaning or symbolism, so *Childe Harold's Pilgrimage*—which is *in* language—defers to the visible in the only way possible: by withholding the inherently "feminine" mandate under which Harold's resistance has been undertaken. The language that the poem's narrator speaks is increasingly fraught with a retrospection that is both postmodern in its characteristic aversion to an overarching narrative *and* genuine—or maternal/semiotic—in its concomitant aversion to meaning.

At once premodern and postmodern, such retrospection finds expression in the famous tableau of the dying gladiator, whom the narrator recalls at the site of the Coliseum (1252–69). In this reverie of a gladiator's thinking in the moments preceding his death, the gladiator's last thoughts are neither of himself nor a narrative of himself, but of a domestic scene that, in the urgency of his condition, recovers a connection more immediately severed by the "manly" (1253) realm in whose service he is pressed:

> He heard it [i.e., the shout which hailed the winner], but he
> heeded not—his eyes
> Were with his heart—and that was far away;
> He reck'd not of the life he lost nor prize,
> But where his rude hut by the Danube lay—
> *There* were his young barbarians all at play,
> *There* was their Dacian mother—he, their sire,
> Butcher'd to make a Roman holiday—
> All this rush'd with his blood—Shall he expire
> And unavenged?—Arise! ye Goths, and glut your ire!
> (1261–69)

The dissolution of the present in an internalized or retrospective "visible" ("his eyes / Were with his heart"), reveals with uncanny accuracy the maternal dispensation under which Harold and the speaker respectively function. The difference, then, is that while Harold is completely in the sway of this visible and is therefore absent and invisible, the speaker is necessarily present and additionally committed—as the final lines reveal—to an authoritative position properly characteristic of both poetry and the symbolic order.

And yet, for all its affinity with the symbolic, this commitment also highlights the "*there*ness" or remoteness of a less immediate, less manly orientation which the gladiator, under the pain of dissolution (and impending dismemberment), suddenly remembers. The double "there" emphasizing the gladiator's displacement ("*There* were his young barbarians . . . / *There* was their Dacian mother") is, with the additional resistance to language in "barbarian," a repetition of "their" ("their Dacian mother,—he, their sire"). The function of the auditory, noninscribed repetition recalls the locus of the feminine by appropriately nonreferential means. In contrast to what is "here," in the "social realm"—be it the poem or the gladiatorial contest—authority is "there" dispersed. There are, as it were, no subjects "there," no *single* entity—the mother, the children, or the gladiator, who has momentarily forgotten whether he has won or lost—maintaining ownership of or authority over another.[19]

A similar pattern is evident in the story of the Caritas Romana that follows at stanza 148. But unlike the gladiator tableau, which succeeds in glimpsing the "here" from the vantage point of "there,"[20] the Caritas Romana reverses this perspective by imagining the maternal "there" from a more conventional, more androcentric orientation.

Emasculation is, again, a possibility in this episode, but this time the speaker desperately resists it. In recollecting the legendary daughter who kept her imprisoned father alive by nursing him with milk from her breast, the narrator represents the scene of feminization—the "relationship to the mother"—in terms whose very conventionality proves problematic. In particular, the idealized manner in which the daughter is described initially, in which she is made an example of fertile, maternal womanhood, so precedes the account of her ministry that her repayment of "the debt of blood" (1344) is made to appear "abject" in its transgression of the norm. Such instances, according to Kristeva, invariably challenge the law of the father, revealing how, by institution of taboo, paternal law is kept distinct from maternal authority. But in the narrator's rendering of the Caritas Romana, the abject is, in a way, *too* abject, recoiling both from the challenge it potentially poses and, more important, from the origins of that transgression—the site of mothering—which is remembered through a glass darkly.[21]

There are numerous other instances in *Childe Harold's Pilgrimage* that, either by recourse to a remembered visible or by anatomy of the more symbolic inclination to forget, adumbrate a feminized or postmodern "unrepresentable." And while this retrospection devolves chiefly upon the poem's speaker, its proper referent is (as it has always been) Harold. Only by making Harold the remembered, if invisible, referent of canto 4, can Byron adhere to the feminine or postmodern trajectory. For if Harold's unrepresentability accords with the poem's overall resistance to the "social realm" (and its hierarchizing mode of signification), it is because Harold, unlike the *gazing* narrator of the Caritas Romana, is indistinguishable from the referent of his perceptions, which is his mother.

Harold, we learn quite early in the poem, "had a mother—not forgot, / Though parting from that mother he did shun" (1.82–83). These lines are, of course, customarily interpreted in reference to Harold's (Byron's?) anxiety about his mother, to whom he is unwilling even to say good-bye. Nevertheless, there is a more ironic reading, which is best glossed by the speaker's unanticipated recovery of Harold much later in canto 4. Brooding on Rome's heroic past and its various chroniclers, notably Cicero, the speaker stops himself:

> But I forget.—My pilgrim's shrine is won,
> And he and I must part,—so let it be,—
> His task and mine alike are nearly done;
> Yet once more let us look upon the sea;
> The midland ocean breaks on him and me,
> And from the Alban Mount we now behold
> Our friend of youth, that ocean . . .
>
> (4.1567–73)

The sudden union with Harold, which is a matter of remembering—and which makes "forget[ting]" the equivalent of nostalgic, sentimental writing—is reaffirmed by the remembered visible that "he and I" mutually "look upon." The speaker's assertion that he and Harold "must part" does not refer to their separation from one another. On the contrary, it suggests a mutual parting from the present, specifically the poem, which, as the speaker's subsequent axiom—"what is writ, is writ" (4.1661)—confirms, is virtually prewritten or subsumed by the social realm. Far from resisting the maternal order, the "parting" from his mother that Harold earlier "shuns" merely indicates the primacy of their union—a resistance to *their partition*—which Harold's subsequent acts of seeing and remembering (as against writing or narration) perpetuate and confirm.

Thus, just as Harold's relationship to his mother enables him to shun the symbolic order, so the narrator's relationship to Harold—and to the remembered visible to which Harold simultaneously has access—ultimately bears a maternal cast. But there is, again, an important difference between the two. While Harold shuns partition from his mother so as to *join* her as an unrepresentable/maternal referent, the speaker's union with Harold is strictly a matter of retrospection and always antecedent to the *writing* (in all its implications) to which he is "here" committed. Hence, the remembered visible—the ocean—moves, in the speaker's rendering, from the maternal referent he "look[s] upon" (along with Harold) to a phenomenon that by writing (and being written) is more properly a maternal symbol:

> And I have loved thee, Ocean! and my joy
> Of youthful sports was on thy breast to be
> Borne, like thy bubbles, onward; from a boy
> I wantoned with thy breakers—they to me
> Were a delight; and if the freshening sea
> Made them a terror—'twas a pleasing fear,
> For I was as it were a child of thee,
> And trusted to thy billows far and near,
> And laid my hand upon thy mane—as I do here.
>
> My task is done—my song hath ceased—my theme
> Has died into an echo; it is fit
> The spell should break of this protracted dream.
> The torch shall be extinguish'd which hath lit
> My midnight lamp—and what is writ, is writ,—
> Would it were worthier! but I am not now
> That which I have been—and my visions flit
> Less palpably before me—and the glow
> Which in my spirit dwelt, is fluttering, faint, and low.
> (4.1648–1665)

The "borderline" state, which the speaker enters in the final lines, follows the pattern of the Caritas Romana in both recalling and recoiling from an anterior condition that, in the present (comparatively exteriorized) vantage, is more suicide than ecstasy. The maternal "promised land," which might otherwise describe the dissolution of identity, is, for all its unforgettable allure, associated in the end with death and with the loss of power. Thus, the admission "I am not now / That which I have been" shows not only a failure to lose oneself, but, more important, a refusal to lose oneself. And it is refusal, more than failure, that is registered in the figurative apparatus, where the speaker's will to power or allegiance to the "social realm" is literally represented in the symbolic transfiguration of the "Ocean." The appropriation, by which the ocean is personified and made a symbol for the mother (and vice versa), is repeated in the refiguration of the ocean as horse, whose taming provides a bridge to the present. The very hand that the subject remembers having "laid upon [the Ocean's] mane" is the same hand, in effect, that "here" writes.

The notably postscriptive connection, then, between one who tames and one who writes—between a transfigured "there" and a transfiguring "here"—reveals with both poignancy and prescience the postmodern retrospection of *Childe Harold's Pilgrimage*. Although the speaker ultimately resists the inclination to be reborne on the mother's breast, his memory of having "loved" the "Ocean" succeeds nevertheless in anatomizing that resistance. The employment of "as it were" to qualify "child of thee" is more than a self-conscious effort to make clear the symbolic nature of this memory; it is a fairly compelled demonstration of the way language, or writing, has interfered with the ability to remember what it is truly like to be a child.

The very act, then, of calling a symbol a symbol does more than evince a certain control or self-possession; it uncovers a distance that simultaneously exists between the symbolizing writer and a prehistoric, prelinguistic subject who, like the gladiator, is displaced from the differentiated subject he has become. To be "as it were" a child is to be neither a "child" per se nor (with inescapable relevance) to be *Childe* Harold, whose proclivity to silence and the remembered visible merely highlights the "echo[ing song]" to which all writing is, in contrast, tantamount. If the speaker, like Harold, has "a mother not forgot," then both her memory and the speaker's union with Harold are sufficient only to remember how much the "modern" poet must *continue* to age in order to become as "old" a "man" as he was once.

POSTSCRIPT

The Feminization of Don Juan

If the most mature aspects of *Childe Harold's Pilgrimage* represent a resistance to writing (as distinguished, of course, from *écriture* in the Derridean sense) and to the totalizing visions writing ordinarily serves, then *Don Juan* would seem to confirm Byron's claim that his earlier poems were more advanced than anything he had produced subsequently. Unlike *Childe Harold* 1–2, *Don Juan* does more than "comprehend" the world in a unique, encyclopedic fashion; it reveals a notable faith in writing as the only cure either for writing or for the problems writing variously represents. Critics have frequently remarked on the radical disposition of Byron's magnum opus: the destabilizing character of *ottava rima* (where the couplet undoes all that precedes it), the antinarrative aspects inherent in the poem's compulsively digressive nature, and last and most important, the poem's effective endlessness—by which any ending or closure must appear arbitrary and inadequate.[1] Yet for all of *Don Juan*'s various subversions, it is also the case that these are circumscribed by writing—so much writing, as it turns out, that the poem's radical elements are all but ancillary to their mode of production.

By the time Byron was disposed to observe that the first two cantos of *Childe Harold* were "written as if by a man—older than I shall probably ever be," he was very much at work on *Don Juan*. No matter how advanced, in other words, or postmodern, the initial cantos of

Childe Harold remained, it was the author of *Don Juan* who recognized this about them. All of which would suggest that the same intelligence underlying Byron's appreciation of his earlier writing is prevalent in his last and greatest work. But there is, at the same time, a critical difference between these two works. Where the "promised land" is earlier presented or inferable in the "childehood" to which Harold is exclusively privy, *Don Juan* follows canto 4 in recognizing the irretrievability of such an end. Conversely, the effective endlessness of *Don Juan* reflects an optimism about writing—and its peculiar agency—that has all but vanished by the end of *Childe Harold*.

Thus, in 1821 Byron not only proposes that the earlier sections of *Childe Harold* were written by one "older than I shall probably ever be"; he allows, in apparent qualification of this senescence, that *Childe Harold* was in fact "written." More than simply resisting the maturity that Byron is skeptical of "ever" achieving, writing manages in this formula to enact that maturity by making it readable if somewhat incomprehensible. Writing, inevitably, has many functions—many of them in service of the "social realm." However, as we saw in canto 4, it is not the least of writing's functions to mark the difference between "here" and "there." To be "as it were" a "child" of the ocean not only imagines a connection with the world as mother; it makes the symbolizing imagination the inadequate—if only—bridge to those "other days."

All of this, of course, may seem peripheral to the peculiar difficulty and enormity of *Don Juan*. However, it can be argued, too, that the writing in *Don Juan,* like that in canto 4, is similarly motivated by a future, ungendered identity whose very impossibility, or unrepresentability, is figured in terms that, appropriately enough, are impossible to comprehend fully. The very failure of Juan to be the rakish "Don Juan" one expects owes less, then, to Byron's intentions as a satirist than to the failure of culture to take effect. In Kristeva's starkly clinical vocabulary, such failures are effected only by the most wrenching, instinctual efforts to undo the self (*Powers*). But it is characteristic of Byron's unrelenting sense of "historical catastrophe" (as Jerome Christensen calls it)[2] that his representation of this failure has virtually no clinical validity and simply lacks comprehensibility. Presented is an otherwise normal figure, Juan, who is sufficiently arrested in development—or not a self—to be unable to distinguish any woman from his mother. Women, for Juan, are not symbolic substitutes or replacements; rather they project, in their interchangeability, a presubjective or prehistoric inability to separate signifier and signified.

Such recalcitrance, were it comprehensible, would undoubtedly have other manifestations apart from Juan's remarkable pliancy. But it is consistent with the double function of Byronic writing as both pursuant and resistant to the social realm that there are virtually no other manifestations. On the contrary, the referent of *Don Juan,* at once maternal and (in large measure) unimaginable, is continually opposed by the represented, the meaning of which is always plainer and more accessible. It is far easier, indeed, to interpret Juan's relationships with Julia and Haidée in the first four cantos either as inversions of the Don Juan myth or (more philosophically) as paradigmatic of the behavior necessary in a chaotic, fluctuating world (Mellor, 42–76) than it is to read them as signposts to the unrepresentable, the very repetition of which discloses a world of relation that remembers no distinction between self and other. And this difficulty is scarcely mitigated by the poem itself, which more often than not proves an invitation to interpretation in some conventional, autocratic sense. Whether it is the sardonic observations about Wordsworth in conjunction with Juan's reveries on nature (canto 1), or the putatively earnest observations regarding his idyllic interactions with Haidée (cantos 2–4), there is, thanks to the compulsively double function of Byronic writing, something that both bars and confirms a prehistoric referent.

The observation about Wordsworth, whose "unintelligib[ility]" (1.713–28)[3] appears little more than a waggish accusation, has quite serious implications—especially since Juan's "communion" with nature, repeating the attachments to his mother and subsequently to Julia, is essentially a prelinguistic, presubjective, and in the present vantage, incomprehensible interaction necessarily characterized by "unutterable" thoughts. So, too, the interaction with Haidée, which is *represented* as a delightful interlude, reveals a contrast between Juan, to whom Haidée is still another mother, and Haidée herself, whose appropriation by the symbolic or paternal order is underscored by the fact that she is very much her father's daughter. Just as Juan resists Haidée's spoken language in deference to her "look," so Haidée's more conventional selfhood, attendant upon the "bar" between subject and object (and between signifier and signified [Kristeva, *Revolution,* 63]), is shown both in her possessiveness of Juan as object and, more vividly (and theoretically), in her famous dream in which that same "object" becomes a symbol for her father.

Still, for all its anticipation of postmodern theory, the most theoretical aspects of *Don Juan* simultaneously involve its resistance to theory, which entails, not surprisingly, a reliance upon writing or a recourse to poetic authority sufficient to render writing more a *justification* of agency than a means of intervention. Thus, in a manner altogether reminiscent of *Childe Harold,* the allusive and, in large part, unrepresentable disposition of the "childe" Juan in the first four cantos gives way in canto 5 to a critique of the subject that leaves virtually nothing to the imagination. The very interrogation of the subject and of gender construction that had proceeded by appropriately nonreferential means, and had thereby done the work that writing otherwise inhibits, is subsumed, by turns, within a satiric or representational apparatus that necessarily limits the poem's agency. It is not that there is nothing at stake in the episode detailing Juan's transfer to a harem, where he becomes "Juanna" in order to avoid detection by the other odalisques (among whom he is secreted) and finally, the sexual toy of Sultana Gulbeyaz, whose rank and marriage have conferred on *her* the prerogatives of masculine authority.[4] It is that the interrogation of sexual difference in cantos 5–6 is contained in virtually the same way that cross-dressing here—both Juan's and, in effect, the sultana's—merely recapitulates an order to which it is impossible, suddenly, to enact an alternative. Yielding to a position of exteriority or authority rather than to anteriority (as Kristeva would have it), "feminism" in these cantos comes to little more than being on the right side of the argument.[5]

Nor is it only on the question of gender that *Don Juan* is compelled henceforth to assert its rectitude and thereby to forget. In fact, the narrator's claim to authority is increasingly underwritten by and inclined to exploit, rather than to ameliorate, the very matters on which it focuses. This is certainly true of the episode in the harem, which differs from the treatment of gender in canto 1. Unlike canto 1, where Juan's incomprehensibility is part and parcel of the critical apparatus, he is made ancillary to criticism in cantos 5 and 6 in the way he is absorbed by (and into) the representation. In canto 1 the deformations of Julia, Inez, and Alphonse all derive resonance from Juan's inscrutability—from a resistance to formation by which Juan is not, among other things, the Don Juan we expect to encounter. In canto 5, by contrast, the deformation of Gulbeyaz, indeed of the entire social apparatus in which she is at once father and daughter, patriarch and wife, are localized and naturalized through Juan's—and our—absorption by them: for example, Juan's delectation and frustration at his proximity to the other concubines, and his vulnerability to the sultana's power. No longer opposed to the world of the poem, Juan is suddenly part of that world and, by dint of his interpellation, part of us.

Even more problematic, then, are the sections of the poem (cantos 7–8) detailing the siege of Ismail, where the horror of war is exactly that: a remarkably absorbing phenomenon on which it is impossible not to focus one's attention or one's indignation. Just as Byron's authoritative feminism allows for a vicarious, authoritative access to the world of the harem, pressing the reading body into a state of disembodiment or omniscience, so the seige of Ismail necessarily involves a similar manipulation of the act of beholding. Where distraction and attention were previously synonymous, particularly in *Childe Harold,* it is now the other way around; thanks suddenly to the various absorptive strategies and incentives, distraction is suppressed and the beholder wrenched from a position of anteriority and potential detachment into one of engaged, rectitudinous authority. Unlike the spectacle of Leucadia's rock in *Childe Harold* 2—where what is visible to Harold was alternately readable to the reader—attention requires an object sufficiently absorptive now, and a target sufficiently easy, that one is "hailed," as it were, in the very act of condemning it.

The facility of the latter sections of *Don Juan,* culminating in the so-called English cantos (10–16), has scarcely escaped the attention or, for that matter, the inattention of the poem's commentators, the majority of whom—it is safe to say—prefer to concentrate on the earlier sections. And yet, the peculiar necessity of *Don Juan,* from which these satiric sections issue, need not be counted merely as a liability. If anything, these sections give powerful testimony to their origins, to the apparently compelled writing responsible for them—for the poem Byron *had to write* no matter what he wrote—by which writing is recalled to its peculiar and potential feminization. This recollection, furthermore, is no paradox, nor a mystification of what is either less complicated or, at the very least, answerable to a less subversive motivation. In fact, the mechanism by which *Don Juan* is recalled to its "revolutionary" function—namely, the foregrounding of writing as authoritative action—is one with which both we, as readers of *Childe Harold's Pilgrimage,* and Byron are equally familiar.

The difference now is in the way this mechanism is activated: a difference as attributable, in a way, to Byron's belated appreciation of the earlier poem as it is immediately manifest in certain developments and permutations for which the earlier poem can be no more (and no less) than a grounding. Unlike *Childe Harold* 1–2, in which the speaker's authority is contested by the counterexample of Harold—the figure who watches at a distance—it devolves upon *the reader* of Don Juan to become that "childe." It is up to the reader, in other words, to see through the poem at hand: to make the readable visible (and what is visible readable) in lieu of simply being absorbed and interpellated by the text.

Don Juan, therefore, does not lack for incentives to reading against the grain. We need only look to the anti-Semitic fantasy regarding the conspiracy of Jewish bankers at the beginning of canto 12, in which "Jew Rothschild" (40) is observed to "hold the balance of the world" (33), for a *sign* that authority, however gratifying, is simultaneously a burdensome, unnatural charge. Yet, in the very way such signification effectively requires anti-Semitism, a discourse that by turns—and by turns only—opens onto something beyond what it necessarily represents, *Don Juan* can be said to cooperate with its ironization by doing, in effect, what it is supposed to do.[6] Only by writing "what is writ" in a conventionally satiric vein does Byron empower the reader to see what he or she is reading and, again, to see *through* the poem.

Thus, Juan's sudden encounter of a painting by Teniers in canto 13 leads inevitably to speculations by the speaker on an act of reading that, as an act of seeing, *resists* absorption and the subjectivity constructed thereby:

> Here sweetly spread a landscape of Lorraine;
> There Rembrandt made his darkness equal light,
> Or gloomy Caravaggio's gloomier stain
> Bronzed o'er some lean and stoic Anchorite:—
> But, lo! a Teniers woos, and not in vain,
> Your eyes to revel in a livelier sight:
> His bell-mouthed goblet makes me feel quite Danish
> Or Dutch with thirst—What ho! a flask of Rhenish.
>
> Oh, reader! if that thou canst read,—and know,
> 'Tis not enough to spell, or even to read,
> To constitute a reader—there must go
> Virtues of which both you and I have need.—

> Firstly, begin with the beginning—(though
> That clause is hard); and secondly, proceed:
> Thirdly, commence not with the end—or, sinning
> In this sort, end at least with the beginning.
>
> (569–84)

The question, of course, must be asked: What is it about the Teniers that is sufficient to reverse the trajectory from object to beholder, from one's absorption by a Rembrandt or by a Claude to a paradigm of reading that is more properly *about* reading—about the intentional, teleological structures according to which we read ourselves and our desires and not, in effect, what is before us? The answer to this involves a fair amount of conjecture, almost none of which is abetted by Teniers's actual paintings, including his tavern scenes, which are less arresting and disorienting than Byron indicates. Nevertheless, if we assume that what is at stake in this thematic tableau is less the painting's invitation to the world it represents than that "flask of Rhenish" that ultimately shatters the picture plane—radically altering the relationship of the subject to an otherwise seductive object—we can understand better what Byron means in his equally cryptic advice to the reader in the succeeding stanza.

Unlike a Rembrandt or a Caravaggio, which manages either by technique or by introjection of some narrative, to command our interest as spectators, the Teniers, according to this account, operates more on the order of still life or trompe l'oeil or a Panorama with its many details. Rather than interpellating the viewer as a social or deferential self, as a subject "hailed" by the painting, the Teniers in Byron's rendering "induces a feeling of vertigo or shock" that "breaks the bond of life," as Norman Bryson describes it, "between the subject who looks and the world that is seen." Like certain still lifes (according to Bryson), or the Panorama with its reconstruction of the public, the Teniers initiates a break between a social world of conviviality and "collective and . . . cultural solidarity," on the one hand, and an object world, on the other. It does this by bringing into view what "perception," according to Bryson, "normally screens out": a "visual field" or a visible *returned,* which, like the flask at once here and yet not here, "appears radically unfamiliar . . . and estranged" ("The Text of Still Life," 230–39).

And so it is with reading, or readable (according to Byron), in resistance both to our inclination as readers and to the speaker's as a poetic authority. The flask of rhine wine penetrates the pictorial plane only to elude the grasp of, and thereby to frustrate, the appropriative, beholding subject. So, too, it is the function, or potential, of writing to disrupt the hermeneutic circle. Reading in this latter sense is less an act of cooperating with some authorial intention or teleology, of "commencing with the end." Rather, reading is an activity suddenly mindful of and *made mindful by* the visible, verbal object before it.[7] Less a bond between authorities, whose goal is interpretation or understanding—the establishment of a "beginning" or intended meaning at the "end" of a text—reading as Byron would "constitute" it is more a matter of dislocation. It is a way to turn our interpellation as readers into a scrutiny of our absorption: a way to be double-parked not only alongside what we are empowered as readers to attend to and behold as if for the first time but beside what, as lesser readers and as subjects otherwise constructed, we are necessarily and simultaneously a part of.

With this in mind, we can better appreciate the function of a character such as Aurora Raby, who turns out to be the most remarkable figure in the concluding cantos and thus the figure with whom Byron and *Don Juan* effectively leave us. Moreover, like the flask of Rhenish, which interrupts the absorptive tour of the picture gallery in canto 13, Aurora's prominence in cantos 15 and 16 owes little to the fact that she is the object of Juan's desire and thereby part of the narrative involving Juan's marriage plans. Indeed, like the flask, which shatters both the representational plane and the subject-position contained by it, Aurora (along with the reconstituted reader, whom she arguably figures) stands apart from these cantos and the milieu they both represent and satirize. By lending weight, then, to Aurora's example rather than to her meaning, by emphasizing both her visibility and the visible world continually within her ken, Byron does two related things: he marks the feminization or the ungendered identity that previously has characterized Juan's heroism (and before him Harold's); and he reconfirms the orientation toward which the poem has verged thus far and, for all demonstrable purposes, will infinitely verge.

Nevertheless, it is characteristic of Byron's writing in which absorption and theatricality struggle for primacy and in which intervention is enabled, curiously, by a refusal to intervene, that Aurora can—indeed must—be read in two ways: as "a Catholic" and as "a Catholic too":

She was a Catholic too, sincere, austere,
As far as her own gentle heart allow'd,
And deem'd that fallen worship far more dear
Perhaps because 'twas fallen: her sires were proud
Of deeds and days when they had fill'd the ear
Of nations, and had never bent or bow'd
To novel power; and as she was the last,
She held their old faith and old feelings fast.
(15.361–68)

On the one hand, of course, Aurora's Catholicism and idealized spirituality make her an ideal match for the "represented" (and Spanish) Juan, who is ensconced at present in the company of Lady Adeline and her retinue of decadent, high-church Englishmen. Yet, as the space between "Catholic" and "too" (which is created, in effect, by the addition of the latter) suggests, Aurora's Catholicism, far from consuming her, is also beside the point. A measure of the consent by which she mitigates and reverses this obdurate legacy, Aurora's Catholicism, like Coleridge's antitheatricality, represents a way out for her precisely as a way in: a way to "bend" so as not to "bow."

This resistance to absorption or to strictly deferential behavior is borne out, furthermore, in the description of Aurora that follows, a description that corresponds to the overall trajectory of Byron's writing in verging off the page to a visible, incomprehensible order:

She gazed upon a world she scarcely knew
As seeking not to know it; silent, lone,
As grows a flower, thus quietly she grew,
And kept her heart serene within its zone.
There was awe in the homage which she drew;
Her spirit seem'd as seated on a throne
Apart from the surrounding world, and strong
In its own strength—most strange in one so young!
(369–76)

Aurora's remarkable self-enclosure, which exceeds not only her comprehension but the narrator's as well, is appropriately introduced by recourse to the visible.[8] For the unknowable world that is the object of both an interior as well as an exterior gaze has the reciprocal effect of defamiliarizing and removing to a more fictive or artificial plane the "surrounding" social world on which Aurora also looks.

It must be emphasized that, like Harold's gaze in cantos 1 and 2 of *Childe Harold's Pilgrimage,* Aurora's is not a "gaze" in the sense that Bryson or Laura Mulvey might describe it—the visual activity of an absorptive, otherwise dominant subject-position. In fact, Aurora's gaze can be deemed a gaze only insofar as the world on which it fixates *predates* the "historical catastrophe" of autonomy and subjectivity with which the gaze, specifically the "male gaze," is customarily associated. Aurora's world, in other words, has a history, indeed a prehistory, sufficient to transform her "glance" into a more durable, if incomprehensible, act of memory.

And this is further indicated in the *mise-en-abîme* of Aurora's "look," as Byron subsequently describes it. "Observing" Aurora while gazing from the vantage of his "nook," Juan "saw this much," according to the narrator, "which he was glad to see" (896):

> The love of higher things and better days;
>   The unbounded hope, and heavenly ignorance
> Of what is called the world, and the world's ways;
>   The moments when we gather from a glance
> More joy than from all future pride or praise,
>   Which kindle manhood, but can ne'er entrance
> The heart in an existence of its own,
> Of which another's bosom is the zone.
>
> (16:905–12)

From one perspective—the representational or writerly perspective—Aurora is a spiritual, meditative young woman who captivates Juan by her very aloofness and by her devotion to something greater and more valuable than the society in whose midst both she and he are cast. Yet from another perspective—that of the glance or the emphatic visibility that verges away from a "world" written and made readable—the sight of Aurora's seeing, which is simultaneously of a "world" viewed through her visible example (is there not an echo of "aura" in Aurora?), leads to another place and another possibility.

This place, which is still the repository of hope for Byron, is no longer a goal of narrative—the "better days" of some eschatology or teleology. It is an "unbounded," incomprehensible orientation, where narrative dissolves along with the regress *of* the visible (the reader looking at Juan looking at Aurora looking) away from a symbolic or metaphysical order. Such regress, which is at base a resistance to meaning, is arguably responsible for the ironization to which the notion of "heavenly ignorance / Of what is called the world" is immediately subjected. Referring on the one hand to a spiritual aloofness from society, such an image manages—under agency of the "glance" —to cancel that divine comedy by adumbrating a world whose contingency and unboundedness remove any and all connection between a comprehending heaven and the world, of which "heaven" is henceforth ignorant. It foregrounds a world that, so long as it is written or "called the world," will remain comprehensible in the same way that the subject, the self speaking, must re-present God in his peculiar, if unstable, omniscience.

But ultimately it devolves to the "glance," of which this stanza is clearly a representation—and to a "world" whose visibility is marked less by clarity than by incomprehensibility—to intervene in a way that only writing, or an art, in this case, reciprocally responsive to the visible, can. Despite its allegiance to a symbolic or metaphysical order, writing is aligned here with something else: with the memory of contingency (and vice versa) and with the theoretically ungendered, undifferentiated state it recalls. No longer encouraging the heart to an individuated or adversarial position, writing actually retrieves the heart (the same heart undoubtedly that sought to perpetuate the manly "one" in the shattered mirror of *Childe Harold* 3) from an existence of its own by returning it, in reading, to another's bosom. Thus, the stanza does more than invite the reader to remember by encouraging an identification with Aurora (or for that matter with Juan); it invites a reading now to the point of distraction. Compelling the reader to a state of being that is different again from comprehending, this stanza simultaneously sees to it that the means of understanding, in which to comprehend is to be interpellated, are momentarily suspended.

The return of the visible in *Don Juan* is not always a function of writing so elusive and allusive. However, like Aurora, who both repels and requires representation, Byron's visible writing continually oscillates between the social realm, where Aurora is clearly an object of adulation, and another world, whose distance and unrepresentability are reciprocally marked by language.

This is evident, for example, in the recourse to simile, notably the sequence of similes in canto 15 ("She gazed upon a world she scarcely knew / As seeking not to know it . . . As grows a flower, thus quietly she grew"; "Her spirit seem'd as seated on a throne" [369–74]). Unlike metaphor, which accedes to the social realm in refashioning and appropriating objects of the "world," simile tends in a more subliminal way perhaps to expose the arbitrary gap that is a proper condition of language and upon which our reconstitution as readers necessarily depends. Hence, the rather elaborate efforts to describe and narrate Aurora continually frustrate their aim by calling attention to themselves rather than the object of an increasingly uncomprehending (or too easily comprehending) subject. And it is *this frustration*—this resistance of writing to legibility and control—that allows "what is writ" a visibility, an incomprehensibility, and finally an escape from writtenness, which poetic language, like the environment that literally surrounds Aurora, resists and enables.

Notes

Introduction
The Visible Subject and the Agency of the Text

1. An argument for a less determined and more "excessive" cinema has recently been advanced by Timothy Corrigan in *A Cinema without Walls: Movies and Culture after Vietnam* (New Brunswick, N.J.: Rutgers University Press, 1991).

2. William H. Galperin, "Kubrick's *Lolita:* Humbert into Quilty," *Bennington Review* 15 (1983): 65–69.

3. Sigmund Freud, "The Uncanny," in *Studies in Parapsychology,* ed. Philip Rieff (New York: Collier Books, 1963), 51.

4. See, for example, Harold Bloom, "Visionary Cinema of Romantic Poetry," in *The Ringers in the Tower: Studies in the Romantic Tradition* (Chicago: University of Chicago Press, 1971), 37–52. Bloom is typical of most romanticists in privileging the romantic appropriation of the real by imaginative or prophetic means.

5. This is the theme of the majority of essays in Paul de Man's *Rhetoric of Romanticism* (New York: Columbia University Press, 1984). See also Cynthia Chase, *Decomposing Figures: Rhetorical Readings in the Romantic Tradition* (Baltimore: Johns Hopkins University Press, 1986). More recently, Chase has extended this position in ways that clearly jibe with my investigation. She argues (with Wordsworth as an example) that the very materiality of the linguistic sign also figures a history, or something exterior to the poetical text, of which the text itself, as "an intentional action of appropriation," is necessarily ignorant ("Monument and Inscritption: Wordsworth's 'Rude Embryo' and the Remaining of History," in *Romantic Revolutions: Criticism and Theory,* ed. Kenneth R. Johnston, Gilbert Chaitin, Karen Hanson, and Herbert Marks [Bloomington: Indiana University Press, 1990], 50–77.)

6. Carol Jacobs, *Uncontainable Romanticism: Shelley, Brontë, Kleist* (Baltimore: Johns Hopkins University Press, 1989), ix.

7. See especially Philipe Lacoue-Labarthe and Jean-Luc Nancy, *The Literary Absolute,* trans. Philip Barnard and Cheryl Lester (Albany: State University Press of New York, 1988), which attempts to found a deconstructive "theory of literature" in German romanticism, chiefly the writings of the Schlegels. So, too, J. Hillis Miller's *Linguistic Moment: From Wordsworth to Stevens* (Princeton: Princeton University Press, 1985), which uses romantic writing as a locus classicus for the kinds of aporia recurrent in a variety of works.

8. Tilottama Rajan, *Dark Interpreter: The Discourse of Romanticism* (Ithaca: Cornell University Press, 1980).

9. Galperin, "'Bad for the Glass': Representation and Filmic Deconstruction in *Chinatown* and *Chan Is Missing,*" *MLN* 102 (1987): 1151–70.

10. Garrett Stewart, "'The Long Goodbye' from 'Chinatown,'" *Film Quarterly* 28 (1974–75): 28.

11. Among the cinematic conventions, then, from which *Chinatown* stands removed is that of "realism." As Colin McCabe details, realism helps foster a dominant subject-position by homogenizing or transcending various contradictory discourses in a text. ("Realism and the Cinema: Notes on Some Brechtian Theses," in *Tracking the Signifier* [Minneapolis: University of Minnesota Press, 1985), 33–57.

12. The single or dominant subject-position inculcated by the cinematic text has become a real issue among feminist critics, several of whom claim that a divided subjectivity obtains when a female viewer is interpellated (usually only partially) to a male position. Laura Mulvey, in a now classic essay ("Visual Pleasure and Narrative Cinema," *Screen* 16 [1973]: 6–18), describes the appropriative fixation on the woman's body in film through the mechanisms of voyeurism and fetishism. Following Mulvey other critics, notably Mary Ann Doane (*The Desire to Desire* [Bloomington: Indiana University Press, 1987]) and Theresa de Lauretis ("Desire in Narrative," in *Alice Doesn't: Feminism, Semiotics, Cinema* [Bloomington: Indiana University Press, 1984], 103–57) have explored the divided subjectivity that occurs when a woman is exposed to the prerogative of the male gaze. More recently, Edward Snow has followed these initiatives in contesting—in ways with which I clearly concur—the alleged fixity of the male viewing position ("Theorizing the Male Gaze: Some Problems," *Representations* 25 [1989]: 30–41). Snow argues that recent feminist analyses of the "viewing situation," particularly their sense of "its hegemony and controlling power," would "grant to [the male gaze] exactly the reality it lacks," since feminist critique posits "a way of seeing" that "beyond ironizing and deconstructing desire . . . transfigure[s] and reabsorb[s] it" (40).

13. Paul Smith, *Discerning the Subject* (Minneapolis: University of Minnesota Press, 1988).

14. Jerome J. McGann, *The Romantic Ideology: A Critical Investigation* (Chicago: University of Chicago, 1983), 1.

15. For a critique of the new historicism and its failure to grant texts their

"incomprehensibility," see my essay, "The New Historicism: Comprehending the Incomprehensible," *Centennial Review* 35 (1991): 51–77.

16. See, for example, Miriam Hansen's discussion of Edwin Porter's 1907 *Teddy Bears,* "Adventures of Goldilocks: Spectatorship, Consumerism and Public Life," *Camera Obscura* 22 (1991): 51–71.

Chapter 1
The Return of the Visible

1. For a discussion of the "antipictorialist" position of the "canonical Romantic poets," particularly as it contrasts with Blake's absorption of the visible into language (and vice versa), see W. J. T. Mitchell, "Visible Language: Blake's Wond'rous Art of Writing," in *Romanticism and Contemporary Criticism,* ed. Morris Eaves and Michael Fischer (Ithaca: Cornell University Press, 1986), 46–95.

2. Jean Hagstrum, *The Sister Arts: The Tradition of Literary Pictorialism and English Poetry from Dryden to Gray* (Chicago: University of Chicago Press, 1958), 134.

3. "A Defence of Poetry," in *Shelley's Poetry and Prose,* ed. Donald H. Reiman and Sharon B. Powers (New York: W. W. Norton, 1977), 483.

4. In discussing Coleridge's views of language and poetry, Paul Hamilton regards the attack on the eye's despotism chiefly as a reaction against the "model of knowledge" in the philosophy of Hume and other British empiricists, which was "predominantly visual" in character—as opposed to Coleridge's model in which "language as a whole . . . exhibits the true shape of our knowledge" (*Coleridge's Poetics* [Oxford: Basil Blackwell, 1983], 27–35). While this probably goes without saying, it is important, I think, to map the postempiricist or idealist model of knowledge on a larger grid, by which the visible—as well as the attempts to demonize it—may be given a more political or cultural cast.

5. Rudolf Arnheim, *Art and Visual Perception: A Psychology of the Creative Eye,* 2d ed. (Berkeley: University of California Press, 1974), 303.

6. The standard modern study of the "radical shift to the artist in the alignment of aesthetic thinking"—from which treatments of romanticism have not substantially departed—remains M. H. Abrams's *The Mirror and the Lamp: Romantic Theory and the Critical Tradition* (New York: Oxford University Press, 1953).

7. For the revolutionary/counterrevolutionary disposition of romanticism as a privatizing movement (with particular attention to Wordsworth and Coleridge), see E. P. Thompson, "Disenchantment or Default? A Lay Sermon," in *Power and Consciousness,* ed. Conor Cruise O'Brien and William Dean Vanech (New York: New York University Press, 1969), 149–81. Paul de Man also shows, with reference to Wordsworth, how romantic nature imagery, for all its apparent and putatively radical organicism, is motivated in the end by a metaphysical and ultimately traditional impulse to move from

the earthly to the celestial ("Intentional Structure of the Romantic Image," in *Romanticism and Consciousness,* ed. Harold Bloom [New York: W. W. Norton, 1970], 65–77).

8. For Blake's radical emendation of the eighteenth-century notion of *ut pictura poesis,* see especially W. J. T. Mitchell, *Blake's Composite Art: A Study of the Illuminated Poetry* (Princeton: Princeton University Press, 1978). A broader theoretical investigation of both the possibilities for and the possibility of theorizing a composite art is offered in Mitchell's *Iconology: Image, Text, Ideology* (Chicago: University of Chicago Press, 1986). More recently, Murray Roston has asserted, in a largely synchronous study of verbal and visual texts of the period, that Blake's "painting and poetry conjur[ed] up in place of a glimpse of the celestial a projection of his own imaginative processes," giving "perhaps the first clear expression . . . to the primacy of the human imagination" (*Changing Perspectives in Literature and the Visual Arts, 1650–1820* [Princeton: Princeton University Press, 1990], 286–87).

9. See, for example, Vincent Arthur De Luca, *Words of Eternity: Blake and the Poetics of the Sublime* (Princeton: Princeton University Press, 1991). Remarking on what he calls Blake's "iconic style," De Luca observes that in such a style "we apprehend the verse not as a stream of passing signs, but as a single consolidated sign, a magnified word to celebrate the Word, as its order is in itself an encapsualted portion of the Divine Vision" (86–87). "What is original in Blake's use of the pattern [in the vortex passage of *Milton,* book 1] is the extent to which the very language and style describing the visionary center imitate its effective attributes. It ritualizes reading by demanding that it reenact the sacred experience presented in its space of words" (84).

10. Marilyn Butler is somewhat typical in the way she regards romantic conservatism as a falling off from the otherwise radical imperatives of the age (*Romantics, Rebels, and Reactionaries* ([New York: Oxford University Press, 1982]).

11. The return of the visible in British romanticism may thus be distinguished from the impulse merely to describe (and not, as it were, to narrate) that Svetlana Alpers details in her splendid analysis of seventeenth-century Dutch painting (*The Art of Describing: Dutch Art in the Seventeenth Century* [Chicago: University of Chicago Press, 1983]). Although, as Alpers shows, seventeenth-century Dutch art can be said to have resisted the narrative tendencies of Italian painting, it was far from a resisting movement per se, having been provoked rather by a host of positivistic influences ranging from the glass lens, to the Baconian imperative to observation, to the mapping impulse that necessarily accompanied Dutch commercial and colonial interests. Unlike the romantic visible, which opposes, however consciously, the oppositional, appropriative tendencies of a subjective stance to the world, the Dutch art of describing was surprisingly unconcerned and unaffected by artistic precedent. The commitment on the part of Dutch artists to an observable world was underwritten instead by an unwavering certainty—itself the result of theory, technology, commerce, and other forces—that the world to be represented

was already *there and present* and thus something to which the artist could only hope or be expected to bear testimony.

Nor is the romantic visible to be equated with what is visible to (and in) Foucault, where, as John Rajchman shows, the seeable pertains largely to the way "things [are] *given* to be seen" and is necessarily about limitation and control ("Foucault's Art of Seeing," *October* 44 [1988]: 89–117). Indeed, the return of the visible in romanticism is more akin to an "absence," as Foucault described it, which is the "art of seeing outside ourselves": the "open[ing of] one's time to what has not yet been seen," and the "transform[ation] or displace[ment of] one's instituted assigned idenitity at a time and place" (117).

12. It is because of his lack of agency (for want of a better formulation) that I have excluded a "visual" poet such as John Clare from this study. For although Clare is certainly unique among his romantic contemporaries in his almost exclusive preoccupation with visible particularity, the fact that this particularity is, as John Barrell has shown, firmly rooted in a "sense of place" puts substantial limits on its contestational function. (*The Idea of Landscape and the Sense of Place* [Cambridge: Cambridge University Press, 1972], 98–215.) Far from a visible returned, in other words, Clare's visible is something that really never leaves him—so much so, in fact, that by "failing to pass beyond" the particular to some metaphysical "knowledge," Clare *succeeds* at what is arguably a counterromanticism, replete with its own authority and intentionality. Although "knowledge," as Barrell argues, is "incapable of being abstracted" from description in Clare's poetry, "it is in its incapacity for being abstracted that . . . knowledge"—and, I would further venture the poet's authority—"consists" (131). Thus, no matter how much Clare's "aesthetic of disorder" with its "manifold of simultaneous impressions" (160–64) approximates what I would regard as the visible *in* romanticism, Clare's writing is completely consumed by a sense of identity, which, untouched or uncontaminated by any other subject-position, is more hegemonic in orientation than it is anything else. See also Juliet Sychrava, *Schiller to Derrida: Idealism in Aesthetics* (Cambridge: Cambridge University Press, 1989), who follows Barrell in marshaling Clare against a subjectivist or post-Kantian aesthetics that, as she argues, leaves no place in the critical imagination for a purely descriptive or symbolically "dense" writing. For Sychrava, as for Barrell, the visible in Clare is something excessive or accessory to romanticism rather than (as I would argue) a consequence of romantic subjectivity.

13. E. H. Gombrich's famous theory of illusionist representation as a predominantly conceptual art, or as a tug-of-war between schema and actuality, receives its fullest treatment in *Art and Illusion: A Study in the Psychology of Pictorial Representation* (Princeton: Princeton University Press, 1960). See also "Standards of Truth: The Arrested Image and the Moving Eye," in *The Language of Images,* ed. W. J. T. Mitchell (Chicago: University of Chicago Press, 1980): 181–217.

14. Norman Bryson, *Vision and Painting: The Logic of the Gaze* (New Haven: Yale University Press), 13–35.

15. See especially Julia Kristeva, *Revolution in Poetic Language,* trans. Margaret Waller (New York: Columbia University Press, 1984).

16. This intervention is shown to remarkable, if unappreciated, advantage in Coleridge's well-known poem "Dejection: An Ode," where the speaker's complaint about seeing—without also feeling—"how beautiful" the evening sky appears is countermanded by the palpably benificent effects of his sight, which is tantamount here to unmotivated, un-self-conscious distraction.

17. Many of my demonstrations, then, can also be seen as attempts to answer the question regarding the interaction of text and image that Mitchell puts forth in *Iconology:* namely, "To what extent is the battle of text and image a consciously articulated theme in literature, the visual arts, and the various 'composite arts' (film, drama, cartoons, narrative cycles, book illustrations) that combine symbolic modes?" As Mitchell observes, this question "takes us . . . away from 'what people say' about images toward the things they do with images in practice" (154). My investigation, then, may also be distinguished from Murray Roston's recent attempt to synchronize poetry and painting of the romantic period. Although "the relationship of poetry to the visual arts" was, as Roston concedes, "no longer a major principle of aesthetic theory," he nevertheless shows how "the dislodgement of mimesis . . . , coupled with the primacy now accorded to the subjective function of imagination, intensified the cherishing of individualism which was to become a hallmark" of romantic painting and poetry alike (*Changing Perspectives,* 341).

18. The romantic visible, as I conceive it, represents a stronger, more legitimate opposition to romanticism than the "aesthetic of particularity" endemic to Victorianism and Pre-Raphaelitism, which, as Carol T. Christ (among others) mantains, is at the center of the orientation that effectively succeeded romanticism in England (*The Finer Optic* [New Haven: Yale University Press, 1975]). In this way, the visible may be more properly aligned with the "detailism" that, as Naomi Schor theorizes, is repressed and stigmatized in Sir Joshua Reynolds's injunction against particularity, or in what Reynolds regards as the mere representation of nature. As Schor observes, Reynolds genders the representation of nature in its particularity as female and maternal, in contrast to the representation of the sublime, which for him is more masculine and imaginative. Like the Romantics in a way, and like the painter Constable, who was partly influenced by Reynolds, this aversion to detail points to "what is perhaps most threatening about [it]: its tendency to subvert an internal hierarchic ordering of the work of art which clearly subordinates the periphery to the center, the accessory to the principal, the foreground to the background" (*Reading in Detail: Aesthetics and the Feminine* [New York: Methuen, 1987], 20). For Reynolds's third and eighth discourses in which his arguments against detailism appear, see Sir Joshua Reynolds, *Discourses on Art,* ed. Robert R. Wark (New Haven: Yale University Press, 1975), 41–53, 145–65. In a related manifestation of the visible that relates both to detailism and, as such, to what is resisted and otherwise repressed in British romanticism, both Jean Baudrillard and, after him, Norman Bryson argue that the still life (and for Baudril-

lard the trompe-l'oeil) creates an illusionism in which "an object world . . . has dispensed with human attention and in a sense makes human attention and the human subject obsolete" (Bryson, "Chardin and the Text of Still Life," *Critical Inquiry* 15 [1989]: 235). However, in the same way that romantic painting necessarily eschews the merely visible, so it is incumbent upon the still life painter, as Bryson shows, to militate against this "defamiliarisation" by introjection of certain narratives through which the painting can then address the viewer "as part of a social and economic order" (245). For Baudrillard, on the other hand, it is the central achievement of the trompe-l'oeil that it "forgets all the grand themes and distorts them by means of the minor figuration of some object or other." For "only isolated objects, abandoned, ghostly in their exinscription of all action and all narrative, could retrace the haunting memory of a lost reality, something like a life anterior to the subject and its coming to consciousness" ("The Trompe-l'Oeil," in *Calligram: Essays in New Art History from France,* ed. Norman Bryson [Cambridge: Cambridge University Press, 1988], 53–62). This lost reality or alternative orientation adumbrated by the tromp l'oeil strongly resembles the operation of the visible as a repressed returned, particularly in the writings of Byron and Coleridge.

19. Bernard Edelman, *The Ownership of the Image: Elements for a Marxist Theory of the Law,* trans. Elizabeth Kingdom (London: Routledge & Kegan Paul, 1979).

20. For an excellent discussion of Burke and Lessing and their efforts to distinguish the function of poetry and painting, see Mitchell, *Iconology,* 95–149. The primary texts in this issue are of course Lessing's 1766 *Laocoon: An Essay upon the Limits of Poetry and Painting,* trans. Ellen Frothingham (New York: Farrar, Straus & Giroux, 1969), and Burke's 1757 *A Philosophical Enquiry into the Origin of Our Ideas of the Sublime and the Beautiful,* ed. James T. Boulton (South Bend, Ind.: University of Notre Dame Press, 1968).

21. See, for example, Stanley Cavell, *The World Viewed: Reflections on the Ontology of Film,* 2d. ed. (Cambridge: Harvard University Press, 1979), and Frank McConnell, *The Spoken Seen: Film and the Romantic Imagination* (Baltimore: Johns Hopkins University Press, 1975). A representative and indeed seminal critique of film in terms of its complicity with the (male) subject is Laura Mulvey's "Visual Pleasure and Narrative Cinema" (Introduction, n.12).

Chapter 2
The Panorama and the Diorama: Aids to Distraction

1. For a full treatment of the evolution and development of panorama painting in England, see Ralph Hyde, *Gilded Scenes and Shining Prospects: Panoramic Views of British Towns, 1575–1900* (New Haven: Yale Center for British Art, 1985).

2. The most detailed discussion of Barker's Panorama and its various nineteenth-century offshoots, including the Diorama, is Richard Altick's *Shows of London* (Cambridge: Belknap Press of Harvard University Press, 1978), 128–220. Hubert Pragnell offers an equally detailed and informed discussion of

Barker's Panorama of London and of the conditions surrounding the production and exhibitions of Panoramas generally in *The London Panoramas of Robert Barker and Thomas Girtin Circa 1800* (London: London Topographical Society, 1968). Both of Ralph Hyde's two important catalogues, *Panoramania!* (London: Barbican Art Gallery, 1988) and *Gilded Scenes and Shining Prospects*, deal extensively with Barker's London Panorama and, in the former (which contains an important introductory essay by Scott B. Wilcox), with the Panorama in London. Peter Galassi recurs to Barker's London Panorama in *Before Photography: Painting and the Invention of Photography* (New York: Museum of Modern Art, 1981)—which surveys the varieties of proto-photographic painting (chiefly oil sketches) during the late eighteenth and early nineteenth centuries.

3. Very much like the *flâneur* in Poe's "The Man of the Crowd" as subsequently described by Walter Benjamin in his famous essay on Baudelaire ("On Some Motifs in Baudelaire," in *Illuminations,* ed. Hannah Arendt, trans. Harry Zohn [New York: Schocken, 1969], 170–74), the "observer" who "succumbs to the fascination of [the street scene of a large city], which finally lures him outside in the whirl of the crowd," the Panorama viewer was also displaced—by the sight of images—from what he or she was. The *Examiner,* for example, observed of Burford's 1828 Panorama of Paris: "You not only see Paris before you, but a good specimen of its lively, helter-skelter, joyous, gallant, good-natured, intelligent, out-of-door living but not over-cleanly population. The Artist has presented to the eye a variety of groups, which . . . even more than the style of architecture, give you the idea *of standing* in the midst of a foreign people" (30 November 1828: 775, emphasis added). And *Blackwood's Magazine* not only argued in 1824 for the advantage of a trip to the Panorama over the inconveniences of actual travel but went so far as to assert that the viewer of the Panorama was "really" at a place made visible:

> *Berkeley* was a metaphysician; and therefore his word goes for nothing but waste of brains, time, and printing-ink; but if we have not the waters of the Lake of Geneva, and the bricks and mortar of the little Greek town, tangible by our hands, we have them *tangible by the eye*—the fullest impression that could be purchased, by our being parched, passported, pummelled, plundered, starved, and stenched, for 1200 miles east and by south, could not be fuller than the work of Messrs Parker's [sic] and Burford's brushes. (87:472–73, emphasis added)

4. A number of recent historical studies have examined the way seemingly consensual behavior, or the exercise of democratic prerogatives in the eighteenth and nineteenth centuries on the part of individuals, was, at best, a liberal illusion and the basis, if anything, of a more coercive, more hierarchizing "politics of deference." William Reddy has shown that the very institution of money—"as a medium of exchange between legal equals"—merely masked the "asymmetrical exchange" by which the poor "in their dealings with the rich" were invariably forced into a posture of "humility, deference and obe-

dience": "However freely both parties entered into the transaction, the owner had only inconvenience at stake; the tenant feared destitution" (*Money and Liberty in Modern Europe* [Cambridge: Cambridge University Press, 1987], 66). And, in his study of voting behavior in nineteenth-century England, David C. Moore shows how bloc voting, particularly in the instances where factory workers voted for the same candidate as did the owner, or where voters voted with their landlords, helped to "perpetuate" the "structure of the society" as well as "the conditions in which the selection and formulation of political issues were principally conditioned by the exigencies of cohesion of the particular varieties of group they formed and the exigencies of status of the leaders of these groups" (*The Politics of Deference* [New York: Barnes & Noble, 1976], 11–12). Thus, it is not surprising that the Panorama, for all its uniformitarian tendencies, would be equally vulnerable to an illusory liberalism, or to the illusion of a "free" England. The difference, then, is that the Panorama was also capable of *foregrounding* and thereby resisting this deferential imperative, whereas other liberal institutions, including many aspects of high romanticism, simply assimilated the conventional order of society.

5. Ruskin regarded the Panorama as an "educational institution of the highest and purest value" that "ought to have been supported by the government as one of the most beneficial school instruments in London." ("Praeterita," in *The Works of John Ruskin,* ed. E. T. Cook and Alexander Wedderburn, [London: George Allen, 1908], 24:117, quoted in Hyde, *Panoramania!,* 28).

6. For a discussion of the way a uniformitarian view of the shared feelings of mankind enabled Wordsworth to speak chiefly of himself (and thereby to oppose uniformitarianism), see Abrams, *The Mirror and the Lamp* (chap. 1, n.6), 100–14.

7. Jürgen Habermas, *The Structural Transformation of the Public Sphere: An Inquiry into a Category of Bourgeois Society,* trans. Thomas Burger (Cambridge: MIT Press, 1989), 128. That the public was in a state of flux—and that this flux involved among other changes a threat to the private autonomy of many individuals—may be inferred from the appeals to the public at large on behalf of individuals in economic distress, which frequently appeared, not coincidentally, alongside notices for the Panorama and other entertainments. Despite their obvious pathos, these notices, like the Panoramas, were the sites of a complicated fascination, both resisting and documenting change. The transformations to which they attest, though terrifying to some readers, were undoubtedly desirable to other readers (or may have seemed necessary to them), given the narrative prerogatives to which the destitute (or soon-to-be-destitute) were still publicly (and paradoxically) entitled. What these individual narratives pointed to, then, was not simply the plight of private individuals (which Habermas might deem a public concern); they pointed to a leveling or homogenization, which typically involved the expansion of the public to include those previously not a part of it: a transformation sufficient to make the public

sphere the site of a lost autonomy, which was the reflex in turn of a different kind of freedom.

8. This contrast was further emphasized in a later notice for the same exhibition (1 November 1800), in which "the same as reality," with its intimations of representational integrity, was changed to "as large as reality." The tension is equally evident in the subsequent views of Constantinople and of Nelson's attack on Copenhagen (1801–2), the notices for which not only alerted viewers to the accuracy and integrity of the depictions but reminded them as well of the "other" reality represented. The view of Constantinople was proclaimed a "most correct, satisfactory, *ocular* description of that ancient and magnificent City" (*Times,* 29 October 1801, emphasis added), and prospective viewers of the attack on Copenhagen, which for a time ran concurrently with the view of Constantinople, were advised not to miss these views "as they are both instructive and entertaining" (*Times,* 15 March 1802).

9. For a full discussion of the changes surrounding the exhibition of paintings and images in the late eighteenth and early nineteenth centuries, both the astonishing expansion of private, public, and semipublic art exhibitions and galleries and the larger and grander canvases by artists such as Benjamin Haydon and John Martin, which could physically accommodate an ever-growing audience, see Altick, *Shows of London,* 99–116, 404–19.

10. Although this particular advertisement ran only two or three times, and appears not to have attracted much attention—especially among those who might have wished to own a Panorama for their amusement—"someone," as Scott Wilcox observes, "did choose to speculate and, indeed, must have speculated successfully, for the Leicester Square paintings were exhibited in other cities at home and abroad until they were literally worn out" ("The Early History of the Panorama," in *Das Panorama in Altötting* [Munich: Bayerisches Landesamt für Denkmalpflege, 1990], 13). In other words, the ownership of the Panorama was subsumed yet again by the public need for such an image rather than by an appropriation of that image independent of the public.

11. Alan Liu, *Wordsworth: The Sense of History* (Stanford: Stanford University Press, 1989), 213.

12. It is interesting, too, that notices for the Panorama frequently appeared alongside notices for passage to places such as Sydney. This suggests, in turn, that the audience for the Panorama was the same body (often enough) as the one in transit.

13. For a full account of the development of both Hornor's Panorama of London and of the Colosseum in Regent's Park, where the Panorama eventually appeared, see Altick, *Shows of London,* 141–62.

14. See, for example, the review of the Panorama in the *Athenaeum* (5 February 1828: 89–90), which devotes nearly all of its attention to a history of the site of the recent engagement, whose difference from the earlier engagements proves the basis for evaluating the representation at hand.

15. Quotations are from the unpublished "Diary of a Painter of Burford's Panorama" (1833), which is in the library of the Victoria and Albert Museum, London.

16. The most detailed modern discussion of the Diorama is Altick's in *Shows of London,* 163–72. See also David Robinson, "Daguerre's Pleasure Dome," *Times* (5 February 1977).

17. For the differences between the high Gothic, with its totalizing cathedrals, and the late Gothic, with its more fragmentary churches, see Erwin Panofsky's *Gothic Architecture and Scholasticism* (Cleveland: Meridian, 1957).

18. For a discussion of this synecdochical aspect of romanticism, see especially Thomas McFarland, *Romanticism and the Forms of Ruin* (Princeton: Princeton University Press, 1981).

19. *John Constable's Correspondence,* ed. R. B. Beckett (Ipswich: Suffolk Records Society, 1968), 6:134.

20. For how a conceptual "schema, which can be molded and modified" by the artist, is necessary for the artist's imitation of reality, see Gombrich, *Art and Illusion* (chap. 1,n.13).

Chapter 3
Constable's Deception

1. *John Constable's Discourses,* ed. R. B. Beckett (Ipswich: Suffolk Records Society, 1970), 9–10.

2. See Gombrich, *Art and Illusion,* (chap. 1, n.13), esp. 174–78, 315–22.

3. In his well-known letter to Dunthorne, which expatiates on the ideal of "natural painture" (*Correspondence,* [chap. 2, n.19], 2 [1964]: 31–32), Constable reiterates and presumably endorses Reynolds's injunction that the way to a "pure and unaffected representation of scenes" or of "*Truth*" is strictly painterly and "can only be obtained by long contemplation and incessant labour in the executive part."

4. Michael Rosenthal, *Constable: The Painter and His Landscape* (New Haven: Yale University Press, 1983), 49.

5. According to Ronald Paulson, for example, Constable's "suppress[ion of] the human-centered [or literary] assumptions of the Claudian landscape" was pursued with such fervor that it allowed merely for the "return [of the human] in . . . the person of the painter" and "in his wish to paint 'one brief moment caught from fleeting time' " (*Literary Landscape: Turner and Constable* [New Haven: Yale University Press, 1982], 116). Constable's "aim to regard nature as independent whole-object" was necessarily "compromised," he asserts, "or complicated . . . by his ostensible desire to recapture a past . . . and his complementary desire to come to terms with the primal scenes that took place there" (153). In painting the Stour Valley almost exclusively, Constable painted a place that was "highly cathected" (129) and invariably informed by the specter of "parental figures" either "denying [Constable] the woman he loves [or] repudiating his work as an artist" (153).

Ann Bermingham's view of Constable (*Landscape and Ideology: The English Rustic Tradition, 1740–1860* [Berkeley: University of California Press, 1986], 9–54) is almost identical to Paulson's but is further historicized by the various sanctions that Constable inherited from the landscape painting that preceded and undoubtedly influenced him. As Bermingham shows, the tendency both of English landscape painting (Devis, Zoffany, Gainsborough) and of landscape gardening (Repton and Brown) to naturalize or variously to mask the impress of the human on the natural—chiefly the enclosure of the English countryside—made fidelity to nature a fidelity to what nature or naturalism could simultaneously hide and mystify. In the case of Constable, this fidelity was to the painter's self, by whose agency a determinedly objective rendering of a familiar landscape was automatically infused "with personal associative meaning" (126).

John Barrell argues that Constable's expressive tendencies as a painter were inclined less toward himself and his personal life and rather more toward the depiction of "a social vision—the image of a productive and well-organised landscape, as it relates to the idea of a well-organised society" (*The Dark Side of Landscape: The Rural Poor in English Painting 1730–1840* [Cambridge: Cambridge University Press, 1980], 133)—which is nevertheless complicated by a virtual *absence* of society in Constable's paintings. To represent the rural poor as they really were

> would have been a considerable embarrassment to Constable. . . . And so it was necessary for him to reduce his figures until they merge insignificantly with the landscape, to distance them, and even when they are in the foreground to paint them as indistinctly as possible, to evade the question of their actuality. The labourers do not step between us and the landscape—they keep their place, and it is a very small place, a long way away. (134)

Moreover, just as the poor are rendered indistinct to accord better with Constable's social and political ideals, so the distance that the painter had to interpose in order to represent those ideals registers his reciprocal remoteness from the "harmonious society" of his dreams (156). Thus, Constable's paintings do not only elide "what really happened . . . in the agrarian history of England." They also represent the myths and other fictions that did happen so as to compensate for the realities separating Constable, along with those whom he could not truly represent, from "an enviable . . . and almost relaxed relationship with the natural world" (164).

6. Karl Kroeber, *Romantic Landscape Vision: Constable and Wordsworth* (Madison: University of Wisconsin Press, 1975), 18–19.

7. James A. W. Heffernan, *The Re-Creation of Landscape: Wordsworth, Coleridge, Constable, and Turner* (Hanover, N.H.: University Press of New England, 1984), 74–75, 117.

8. For additional discussion of the evolution of *The Hay-Wain,* with particular attention to the "little dog" who in the final version clearly dominates

the painting's foreground, see Alastair Smart and Attfield Brooks, *Constable and His Country* (London: Elek, 1976), 80–91.

9. In yet another preliminary study of *The Hay-Wain,* a very small oil sketch (ca. 1820), currently at the Yale Center for British Art, the parity of man and dog, is underscored in the virtual absence of the dog, who is scarcely visible, as well as in the highly impressionistic nature of the sketch, whose details are sufficiently blurred to render them the object of what is alternately (and simultaneously) a man's-eye and a "dog's-eye" view. For a discussion of the possibility of extending an "internalist account" to animals, as Constable may well be doing in this sketch (alternately admitting and containing the visible), see the exchange between Arthur C. Danto and Martin Donogho in *Visual Theory: Painting and Interpretation,* ed. Norman Bryson, Michael Ann Holly, Keith Moxey (New York: HarperCollins, 1991), 201–20.

10. An actual visit to the painting's site, which belongs now to the British National Trust, reveals that there is no physical vantage point from which Constable could have seen the scene he painted. The elevation was characteristically, and suitably, his creation.

11. Citations to Michael Fried are, unless otherwise noted, to *Absorption and Theatricality: Painting and Beholder in the Age of Diderot* (Berkeley: University of California Press, 1980).

12. See, again, Barrell, *The Dark Side of Landscape,* 131–64.

13. For discussion of a "dog's-eye-view," see Martin Donogho, "Minding the Animals—or, Can Pigeons be Hopeful?," in Bryson et al., *Visual Theory,* 216–20.

14. Michael Fried, "Art and Objecthood," *Artforum* 5, no. 10 (1967): 15. More recently, of course, Fried has sought—chiefly in his discussion of the American painter Thomas Eakins—to identify a mode of representation that, like Constable's painting, allows for a "dividedness of point of view" in which "the effort to project oneself imaginatively into the represented scene is openly in conflict with the desire, also stimulated by the painting, to keep one's distance" (*Realism, Writing, Disfiguration: On Thomas Eakins and Stephen Crane* [Chicago: University of Chicago Press, 1987], 73–74). Nevertheless, where Constable's painting succeeds in subverting its absorptive dimension by disclosing what is effectively at stake in the viewer's annihilation/omniscience, Fried's more recent project (and his particular fascination with Eakins) is plainly dialectical and represents an attempt finally to subsume the rival claims of absorption and theatricality within a more unified, more authoritative, "tension." Thus, Fried's analysis of Eakins' *Gross Clinic* characteristically deploys the viewer's own materiality as a condition of both alienation and absorption: "[W]hat confronts us as viewers in *The Gross Clinic* . . . is an image at once painful to look at (so piercingly does it threaten our visual defenses) and all but impossible, hence painful, *to look away from* (so keen is our craving for precisely that confirmation of our own bodily reality). . . . [I]t is above all the conflictedness of our situation that grips and excrutiates and in the end virtually stupifies us before the picture" (65).

Chapter 4
The Mind in the "Land of Technology": Resistance to Spectacle in Wordsworth's *Prelude*

1. See, for example, Hans Eichner's essay, "The Rise of Modern Science and the Genesis of Romanticism," *PMLA* 97 (1982): 8–30, which details the "implications of the mechanical philosophy that made it unacceptable to the Romantics and that prompted them to branch out in new paths" (24). For an excellent summary of the issues confronting the discussion of literature and science today, particularly involving the "tightening [of] connections implicit in 'and' [in 'literature and science']," see George Levine, "One Culture: Science and Literature," in *One Culture: Essays in Science and Literature,* ed. George Levine (Madison: University of Wisconsin Press, 1987), 3–32. I am indebted to Levine both for his summary and for his ample and helpful references to other sources. A rapprochement between Wordsworth and science has recently been attempted by Fred Wilson in a heavily thematic reading of both *The Prelude* and "Tintern Abbey" ("Wordsworth and the Culture of Science," *Centennial Review* 33 [1989]: 322–92). According to Wilson, Wordsworth's reliance on "spontaneously experienced sentiments" and on the "faculty of imagination" as a ground for the "moral life of man" places him "squarely in that tradition of British philosophy that leads from Newton," which "did not attack science in the name of a higher, neo-platonic reason, as did Coleridge and the later idealists," but attacked instead "the associationist-utilitarian tradition." The appeal of this latter attack "was to experience, the very foundation of the Newtonian method." Because, according to Newton, "our ordinary moral feelings, and our feelings of the presence of God, are . . . unanalyzable," it "was *analysis* that was the enemy, and it was rejected on the grounds of *experience,*" the very grounds on which our moral and religious sense was defended (377–78). Wilson's argument may well count as a corrective to the conventional (and, as he suggests, Coleridgean) separation of romanticism and science, but to work as a corrective it demands not only that we thematize Wordsworth's poetry as moral philosophy but that we simultaneously transform Newton into the kind of Christian/moral humanist that both Wordsworthian subjectivity (with its intimations of agnosticism) and Wordsworth's own accommodations to science or to sensory experience, which are antihumanistic, resist.

2. Chief among these reassessments is Michel Serres's *Hermes: Literature, Science, Philosophy,* ed. Josué V. Harari and David F. Bell (Baltimore: Johns Hopkins University Press, 1982). See also Levine, "One Culture," 6–17.

3. Jacques Derrida, Roland Barthes, and Julia Kristeva are poststructuralists who, in various ways, see literature, writing, or "poetic language" as a resistance to or revolution against the cultural hegemony or linguistic imperialism that a more purely structural or semiotic approach to literary texts effectively countenances. Barthes describes this difficult dynamic most succinctly when he observes how the writer frequently confronts "the society of

his time" only to be "refer[red] back . . . by a sort of tragic reversal, to the sources, that is to say, the instruments of creation" (*Writing Degree Zero,* trans. Annette Lavers and Colin Smith [Boston: Beacon Press, 1970], 16).

4. Among the most important modern critiques of scientific method, particularly the ideal of induction as a method of observation independent of subjective bias or intentionality, are Karl Popper's *Logic of Scientific Discovery* (New York: Basic Books, 1961) and *Objective Knowledge* (Oxford: Clarendon Press, 1972), which maintain that no observation of, or encounter with, the outside world can transpire independent of a governing hypothesis. A similar, if potentially more disturbing, view is espoused by Paul de Man in reference to romantic nature imagery, whose claim to an organic freshness or belief in the "intrinsic ontological primacy of the natural object" is written over by an intentionality that necessarily returns nature—that is to say, nature represented—to the province of language and tradition ("Intentional Structure of the Romantic Image," chap. 1, n.7).

5. William Wordsworth and Samuel Taylor Coleridge, *Lyrical Ballads,* ed. R. L. Brett and A. R. Jones (London: Methuen, 1963), 104–6.

6. References to the 1802 Preface are to the text in *Literary Criticism of William Wordsworth,* ed. Paul M. Zall (Lincoln: University of Nebraska Press, 1966), 38–62.

7. References to *The Prelude,* unless otherwise cited, are to the 1805 version of the poem in William Wordsworth, *The Prelude: 1799, 1805, 1850,* ed. Jonathan Wordsworth, M. H. Abrams, and Stephen Gill (New York: W. W. Norton, 1979).

8. I adopt the standard practice of referring to the narrator of Wordsworth's autobiographical poem as the "Poet" simply because Wordsworth, though clearly writing about his actual life in *The Prelude,* has deliberately pressed that life into a representational structure sufficient, in turn, to render him a character. This is undoubtedly true of all autobiography, but it is especially acute in an epical/heroic poem.

9. For a reading of *The Prelude* as a progressive narrative, see M. H. Abrams, *Natural Supernaturalism: Tradition and Revolution in Romantic Literature* (New York: W. W. Norton, 1971), 73–140, 278–92.

10. See, for example, the notice publicizing the appearance in Hanover-Square Room of "that wonderful infant Master Parker" in the *Times* (19 April 1799).

11. For a discussion of how such mediating devices as the glass lens and cartography are leagued with the impulse in seventeenth-century Dutch art to describe the world in a way that necessarily resists the narrative impulses of pictorial convention, see Alpers, *The Art of Describing* (chap. 1, n.11). It is also worth speculating on the extent to which the very spectacle of a "prodigy" historically cut both ways, as in the case of "Master Parker" (*Times,* 19 April 1799). Although it was the purpose of the advertisement for this "wonderful infant" to garner interest in the four-year-old making his "first appearance" at Hanover-Square Room, the spectacle of the prodigy "speak[ing] some of

the choicest pieces of our stage with that energy and vehemence, joined with all the feeling, grace, and action of our first Performers" and "execut[ing] on the Piano Forte some of the most difficult Sonatas of Haydn, and other celebrated Authors, with that expression and precision which distinguishes a Professor," was by its very constitution ironic: that is, both a valorization and a parody of individual genius.

12. See, for example, Richard Rorty's overview of and argument against epistemology and foundational philosophies of science in *Philosophy and the Mirror of Nature* (Princeton: Princeton University Press, 1979). For a summary of the foundationalist versus antifoundationalist conception of science and its bearing on the relationship of science to literature, see Levine, "One Culture," 15–18.

13. I disagree with both D. M. Knight ("The Physical Sciences and the Romantic Movement," *History of Science* 9 [1970]: 54–75) and Edward Proffitt ("Science and Romanticism," *Georgia Review* 34 [1980]: 55–80), who by recourse either to romantic organicism (Knight) or to the romantic emphasis on observation (Proffitt) seek to dispel the traditionally oppositional relationship of romanticism and science. And I take issue as well with M. H. Abrams, who stresses the "metascience" with which the Romantics, and Coleridge in particular, displaced the Newtonian structure of reality ("Coleridge's 'A Light in Sound': Science, Metascience, and Poetic Imagination," in *The Correspondent Breeze: Essays on English Romanticism* [New York: W. W. Norton, 1984], 158–91). According to Abrams, the mechanistic science of Newtonian atomism reduces "the 'conceivable' . . . within the bounds of the '*picturable*,'" leaving effectively no room for an imaginable, metaphysical order. I agree that the "picturable" stands in opposition to both the imagination and the natural philosophy with which imagination is leagued, but only by agency of both art and imagination in what I term the "spectacular." Indeed, Abrams's assumption, here and elsewhere (e.g., *The Mirror and the Lamp* (chap. 1, n.6), 156–77, 298–335), that the mechanistic view of nature espoused by Newton, Boyle and others represents a uniform, thoroughly despotic view of things is a classic instance of the way the reification of an ideology—in this case the romantic ideology—does violence to both its context and its representation. Newton's recourse to a "*deus ex machina*" to explain "the genesis of law, order, and beauty in the world-machine" (*Mirror,* 164) would appear to link him to the pre-revolutionary world from which romanticism sought a break. Yet Newton's claim (cited by Abrams) that "this most beautiful system of the sun, planets, and comets . . . could only proceed from the counsel and dominion of an intelligent and powerful Being" (164) already indicates the subversive pressure that a mechanistic or merely picturable conception of nature ultimately brings to an organicist or natural-philosophic effort to resist the mechanistic by extrapolation of the metaphysical from the merely physical. Indeed, such pressure was arguably responsible for Coleridge's ultimate resort, as Timothy Corrigan shrewdly details, to the notion of "law" as a way of describing scientific (and, for that matter, poetic) principles. ("The *Biogra-*

phia Literaria and the Language of Science," in *Coleridge, Language, and Criticism* [Athens: University of Georgia Press, 1982], 123–56.) For the inherent arbitrariness of law effectively provides a middle ground between such relatively determinate mechanistic theories of the physical world as espoused by Newton and his followers and the comparatively indeterminate or merely speculative metaphysics of *Naturphilosophie* that Coleridge obviously found more congenial.

14. For a purely deconstructive reading of book 5, which emphasizes the way the various "forms of displacement" here, notably the substitution of the stone and the shell for science and poetry respectively, "pu[t] in question the possibility of literal naming and suggest that all names are metaphors, moved aside from any direct correspondence to the thing named by their reference to other names which precede and follow them in an endless chain" (139–40), see J. Hillis Miller, "The Stone and the Shell: The Problem of Poetic Form in Wordsworth's Dream of the Arab," in *Mouvements Premiers* (Paris: José Corti, 1972), 125–47.

15. For a related argument see Theresa M. Kelley, "Spirit and Geometric Form: The Stone and the Shell in Wordsworth's Arab Dream," *SEL* 22 (1982): 563–82. Kelley argues that the dream resists the rigid opposition of science and poetry by allowing the shell, with its peculiar symmetry, to "represent both geometric truth and poetry" (572), but she nevertheless concludes that Wordsworth's stance toward science is still antagonistic, whereas his stance toward poetry is relatively unchanged—even given its association with science. As I see it, the complementarity of science and poetry in book 5 has the simultaneous effect of rehabilitating science and, in light of Wordsworth's antipathy to science as stated in the Preface, of diminishing in significant measure the sovereign claims of poetry.

16. It is interesting to note, in this context, that in the 1850 text of *The Prelude,* Wordsworth reverses the apparatus of the "friend," whose confession now of "kindred hauntings" prompts the Poet to recollect the dream assigned previously to his companion, thereby "cleaving unto" him.

17. See Paul de Man, "Autobiography as De-facement," *MLN* 94 (1979): 919–30, and, as an expatiation on de Man's observation that "figures of depravation, maimed men, drowned corpses, blind beggars, children about to die, that appear throughout *The Prelude* are figures of Wordsworth's own poetic self" (924), Cynthia Chase, "The Accidents of Disfiguration: Limits to Literal and Rhetorical Reading in Book V of *The Prelude,*" *Studies in Romanticism* 18 (1979): 547–65, which focuses chiefly on the example of the drowned man as a paradigmatic instance of such defacement. I agree with de Man and Chase on the self-reflexive character of these figures, particularly in book 5, but I differ from Chase and de Man in regarding Wordsworth as a conscious, if still reluctant participant in the self-critical function of the figures. For a fuller account of these differences see my essay, "Authority and Deconstruction in Book V of *The Prelude, SEL* 26 (1986): 613–31.

18. Susan J. Wolfson, "The Illusion of Mastery: Wordsworth's Revisions

of 'The Drowned Man of Esthwaite,' 1799, 1805, 1850," *PMLA* 99 (1984): 917–935. In surveying the various versions of this key episode Wolfson shows how "revision" in this instance "is endlessly open, not simply because any field of vision is open to numerous, potentially infinite interpretations and organizations, but because each view discovers new motions, changes, and interchanges" (932).

19. "We can," writes Chase, "interpret the episode as a disruption of the specular structure of figuration: the effaced figure, or the dead letter, fractures the surface of the space that places sign and meaning. What emerges and breaks the liquid mirror of mimetic or metaphoric reflection is a disfigured face—itself a broken surface. Thus there emerges in the text something that disrupts our conception of literal language in contradistinction to figure" ("Accidents," 555–56).

20. References to Benjamin's "The Work of Art in the Age of Mechanical Reproduction" are to the text of that essay in Hannah Arendt (ed.), *Illuminations* (chap. 2, n.3), 217–51. For a relevant discussion of Benjamin's essay that concentrates similarly on the challenge posed by photography and film to "traditional art's authority," see Joel Snyder, "Benjamin on Reproducability and Aura: A Reading of 'The Work of Art in the Age of Its Technical Reproducibility,'" in *Benjamin: Philosophy, Aesthetics, History,* ed. Gary Smith (Chicago: University of Chicago Press, 1989), 158–74.

21. For the "prehistory" of cinema, see Michael Chanan, *The Dream That Kicks: The Prehistory and Early Years of Cinema in Britain* (London: Routledge & Kegan Paul, 1980). Other studies treating the origin of film include: Martin Quigley, Jr., *Magic Shadows: The Story of the Origin of Motion Pictures* (Washington, D.C.: Georgetown University Press, 1948), and C. W. Ceram, *The Archaeology of the Cinema* (New York: Harcourt, Brace & World, 1965). Altick's *Shows of London* (chap. 2, n.2) is an excellent and authoritative guide to virtually all precinematic institutions including art galleries, the Eidophusikon, the Panorama, the Diorama, the music hall, and various other "scenes optical, mechanical, spectral." See also Terry Castle, "Phantasmagoria: Spectral Technology and the Metaphorics of Modern Reverie," *Critical Inquiry* 15 (1988): 26–61, which examines in a more critical way the exteriorization of interiority, and the defamiliarization of the simultaneously familiar, in the phantasmagorias and assorted ghost shows in the nineteenth century.

22. Peter Stallybrass and Allon White, *The Politics and Poetics of Transgression* (Ithaca: Cornell University Press, 1986), 120–21.

23. Richard Altick locates Wordsworth in book 7 at the Exeter Change menagerie (*Shows of London,* 184).

24. For a relevant, but ultimately different view of the beggar's function, see Neil Hertz, "The Notion of Blockage in the Literature of the Sublime," in *Psychoanalysis and the Question of the Text,* ed. Geoffrey H. Hartman (Baltimore: Johns Hopkins University Press, 1978), 62–85. According to Hertz, the beggar becomes a means, amid the "baffling proliferation . . . of sights and sounds, objects and people," for the self to confirm "its own integrity, which

is only legible in a specular structure, a structure in which the self can perform that 'supererogatory identification with the blocking agent'" (78–79).

25. Dana Polan, "'Above All Else to Make You See': Cinema and the Ideology of Spectacle," *Boundary 2* 11 (1982–83): 129–44.

26. For a differently inflected discussion of the theatrical aspects of the description of London in *The Prelude,* which resembles Burke's description of the Revolution of France "in marking risky moments," in "uncover[ing] the Promethean excesses that both authors must conceal if their respective fictions of History and Nature are to be maintained," see Mary Jacobus, "'That Great Stage Where Senators Perform': *Macbeth* and the Politics of Romantic Theatre," *Studies in Romanticism* 22 (1983): 371–73.

27. Edmund Burke, *Reflections on the Revolution in France,* ed. Conor Cruise O'Brien (Harmondsworth, U.K.: Penguin, 1982), 164, 175.

28. The ultimate motive for placing spectacle in what amounts to a contestatory role with the individual mind can only, of course, be speculated upon. To Mary Jacobus, for example, theatricality is an issue in the London of book 7 chiefly in the way it exposes and cements a partnership of conservatism and humanism. London resembles Burke's France in that it too is "an open-air theatre in which Promethean art usurps on nature with the 'blank confusion' of indecipherability" (371). Hence, in Wordsworth's subsequent account of the Revolution in book 10, the allusion to *Macbeth* ("I wrought upon myself, / Until I seemed to hear a voice that cried / To the whole City, 'Sleep no more'" [75–77]) represents, according to Jacobus, Wordsworth's sympathy with the Revolution and—at the same time—a disowning of complicity in the regicide that was foreseeable at the time of his visit. In other words, the theatricality by which the world is set apart and simultaneously made proximate in *The Prelude* owes to Wordsworth's experience in France, insofar as the guilt to which that experience would lead in retrospect leads, in turn, to the "Restoration of an anti-theatrical imagination" (365), which follows in the poem. While I agree that an antitheatrical imagination is effectively restored in *The Prelude,* I take a more sanguine view of the theatricality that provokes and resists restoration. I discuss this theatricality, which is more properly an anti-antitheatricality, in the ensuing two chapters.

29. Reeve Parker, "Reading Wordsworth's Power: Narrative and Usurpation in *The Borderers,*" *ELH* 54 (1987): 300.

30. Marvin Carlson, *The Theatre of the French Revolution* (Ithaca: Cornell University Press, 1966).

31. Simon Schama, *Citizens: A Chronicle of the French Revolution* (New York: Alfred A. Knopf, 1989), 136.

32. The reconstitution of audience was also evident, with inescapable relevance to my argument, in instances of "charismatic science": for example, in the balloons or *globes airsotatiques,* whose public display "helped reorder the nature of public spectacle in France," generating "an audience that was hard to contain within the old regime's sense of decorum." The Montgolfier balloon of 1783 was launched at Versailles, and according to Schama,

no serious attempt was made to restrain numbers or to order them in the neat, ordained spaces generally required by old regime regulations. Nor was it possible, beyond giving special places to the immediate royal family, to preserve the hierarchies of court seniority in the huge pell-mell throng. Instead of being an object of privileged vision—the specialty of Versailles—the balloon was necessarily the visual property of everyone in the crowd. On the ground it was still, to some extent, an aristocratic spectacle; in the air it became democratic. (Schama, *Citizens,* 124–25)

Chapter 5
Lamb and Hazlitt: Romantic Antitheatricality and the Body of Genius

1. See, for example, Jonas Barish, *The Antitheatrical Prejudice* (Berkeley: University of California Press, 1981), 295–349. See also Altick, *Shows of London,* (chap. 2, n.2) 182–85. More recently, Janet Ruth Heller asserts that both the romantic "bias against spectacle" and the romantic "aversion to the senses in the arts"—particularly regarding theater—have a long tradition, beginning indeed with Plato (whom Barish also discusses), which the Romantics and their philosophical predecessors, chiefly Kant and Burke, can be said to have inherited. These notions, then, were not specifically Romantic, nor did they, according to Heller, develop simply as a reaction against "the limitations of early nineteenth-century theaters" (*Coleridge, Lamb, Hazlitt, and the Reader of Drama* [Columbia: University of Missouri Press, 1990], 7–42).

2. The decline of the theater at this time, most manifest in the decline in revenue and in the increasingly desperate efforts on the part of proprietors to gain a larger audience, was sufficient to compel Parliament to take up the problem in 1832. The result of that investigation, the *Report from the Select Committee on Dramatic Literature: With the Minutes of Evidence* (House of Commons, 2 August 1832), covered virtually every aspect of the theater ranging from repertoire, to licensing, to management in an attempt both to diagnose and to reverse the obvious decline of legitimate theater. For a discussion of this report with the benefit of hindsight, see Joseph Donohue, *Theatre in the Age of Kean* (Totowa, N.J: Rowman & Littlefield, 1975), who recurs to the document throughout his study.

3. See Donohue, *Theatre in the Age of Kean,* 52–56. See also Jonathan Bate, *Shakespearean Constitutions: Politics, Theater, Criticism 1730–1830* (Oxford: Clarendon Press, 1989), 42–45, who describes the theater owners' capitulation as "a triumph for the people." A more nuanced assessment of the politics of these riots, and their bearing on the development of melodrama, is offered by Elaine Hadley in "The Old Price Wars: Melodramatizing the Public Sphere in Early-Nineteenth-Century England," *PMLA* 107 (1992): 524–37.

4. For a discussion of the romantic emphasis on an "ideal performance" against which any actual performance would appear deficient see Joseph

W. Donohue, Jr., *Dramatic Character in the English Romantic Age* (Princeton: Princeton University Press, 1970), 280–312. For the elitism of romantic aesthetics with special reference to theater, chiefly the "retreat" (as exemplified by Lamb) "from youthful radicalism into a world of the self," see Bate, *Shakespearean Constitutions,* 132–35.

5. A similar concept has been recently introduced by Evlyn Gould in *Virtual Theater: From Diderot to Mallarmé* (Baltimore: Johns Hopkins University Press, 1989), which explores a theater that is effectively (and paradoxically) an "externalization of internal and energetic optical phenomena in the physical space of textual representation" (1). Yet where Gould's interest is primarily psychoanalytic and otherwise concerned with the "metapsychology of the actual spectator" (2), my deployment of this exteriorized interiority is more political and refers more to what is ultimately an appropriation of spectatorship rather than an investigation of it.

6. For an investigation of this aspect of romantic drama that echoes and refines earlier views in emphasizing the romantic theater's preoccupation with both individual consciousness and the "social element" of consciousness, see Alan Richardson, *A Mental Theater: Poetic Drama and Consciousness in the Romantic Age* (University Park: Pennsylvania State University Press, 1988).

7. References to Lamb are to *The Works of Charles and Mary Lamb,* ed. E. V. Lucas (London: Methuen, 1903), 4 vols., and *The Letters of Charles and Mary Lamb,* ed. E. V. Lucas (London: Dent & Methuen, 1903), 3 vols. It is interesting, of course, that the ultimate goal of romantic antitheatricality is precisely what a poet like Wordsworth claims he is doing in a collection such as *Lyrical Ballads:* namely, keeping his reader "in the company of flesh and blood" (*The Prose Works of William Wordsworth,* ed. W. J. B. Owen and Jane Worthington Smyser [Oxford: Clarendon Press, 1974], 1:130). However, as the trajectory of romantic antitheatricality shows, Wordsworth's goal is better accomplished by effectively abandoning—or at least resisting—an overtly and ultimately mystified communitarianism in which neither the author nor his reader is necessarily kept in the company of others, whose distinguishing (if shared) feature is their materiality.

8. See Bate, *Shakespearean Constitutions,* 47–48, 129–34. See also Donohue, *Dramatic Character in the Romantic Age,* 281–88. See also Heller, who compares Lamb's defense of reading to the reader-response criticism of our time (115–27), whose romantic elements—chiefly the identification of reading as a "creative process"—she overemphasizes and, to some degree, decontextualizes.

9. In his essay, "Artificial Comedy of the Last Century," Lamb makes a similar argument regarding the works of Wycherley and Congreve, whose "perusal" yields a pleasure in their purely "speculative" nature. Unlike modern plays, they have "no reference whatever to the world that is." "It is impossible," therefore, that these plays "should now be acted" (2:142–44) .

10. See, again, the essay, "Artificial Comedy," which complains of the "incongruities which Sheridan was forced upon by the attempt to join the

artificial with the sentimental comedy, either of which must destroy the other" (2. 145), as well as the essay, "Stage Illusion," in which Lamb observes how the "likeness" of something, as substituted in the theater for the "thing itself," is tantamount to misrepresentation (2. 163–65).

11. See, again, Bate, *Shakespearean Constitutions*, which compares Lamb's essentially private constitution of the theater with the decidedly public and political uses to which Hazlitt puts his Shakespeare criticism (129–35).

12. Bate stresses the antirevolutionary resonances in Lamb's use of "levelling" (*Shakespearean Constitutions*, 133). See also Jonathan Arac, "The Media of Sublimity: Johnson and Lamb on *King Lear*," *Studies in Romanticism* 26 (1987): 209–220, who argues that Lamb's treatment of *Lear* in the Shakespeare essay, with its appeal to the "sublime" and to the "elevation" caused by "genius," is ultimately a more conservative (though ostensibly more "democratic") treatment than Samuel Johnson's conservative, but more utopian, criticism of this same play.

13. Lamb's rather remarkable antipathy to a visible, material world is evident on other occasions as well, some of them quite proximate to the performance of Shakespeare as he describes it. In commenting, for example, on Boydell's Shakespeare Gallery, which featured scenes from the plays painted by popular artists of the day, Lamb complained generally of the "injury" done both him and Shakespeare by such representations and (in a language reminiscent of his response to *Othello*) of being "tied down to an authentic face of Juliet" (*Letters*, 3:393–94, cited in Bate, *Shakespearean Constitutions* 47–48). That a visible world, even a painted (and idealized) one, is effectively a world in decline for Lamb—or a world lacking the necessary distinctions—is further evident in a relatively late essay, "Barrenness of the Imaginative Faculty in the Productions of Modern Art" (1833 [2:226–34]), as well as in his notably detached response to the crowded street in "The Londoner" (1:39–40). Recalling how he would "rus[h] out into" the Strand in an effort to escape the "distaste" and "weariness" he felt at home, Lamb nevertheless brings an anterior, or closeted, orientation to bear upon the world viewed. In claiming "unutterable sympathies" with what he calls a "multitudinous moving picture," Lamb initiates a demonstrably *unsympathetic* idealization of the masses (both here and in a subsequent transformation in which this same crowd is described as "shifting pantomime") that refers us to the shaping powers of an imagination fundamentally opposed to the masses. Thus, unlike Walter Benjamin's *flâneur,* as described in the essay on Baudelaire (chap. 2, n.3), Lamb refuses to be swallowed up and leveled by the scene before him.

The well-documented failure of Boydell's Gallery gives rise to certain speculations. Although it is customarily asserted that the gallery failed on account of the wars with France, which deprived Boydell of an important market for his pictures (which were reproduced and sold) at the same time that it placed economic pressure on the market at home, it is clear, too, that the gallery was precariously positioned between a number of aesthetic *desiderata* and able, consequently, to satisfy no one. On the one hand, there were viewers like Lamb, who were put off by the declension of the word to image in, for example, the painting of Juliet. Yet, in light of other developments in the culture of the image at this time, or in what we might consider a mass culture, there were undoubtedly viewers for whom the declension was simply not strong enough: viewers who may have been troubled by the way the visible as such was too anchored in an ideal order. These viewers were undoubtedly less vocal than either Lamb or (as Jonathan Bate details) the cartoonist James Gillray, who mercilessly lampooned the gallery in his illustrations. But it makes sense that the failure of Boydell's venture would owe as much to a comparatively radical disappointment, in which the visible was just not visible enough, as to a "romantic" or conservative disappointment in which one idealization effectively falls short of doing its appointed work. That the gallery disappointed just about everyone, in other words, bears further scrutiny. For a discussion of Boydell's gallery, see Bate, *Shakespearean Constitutions,* 45–58. See also Altick, *Shows of London,* 106–8.

14. Although both my focus and my conclusions are substantially different, my discussion of Hazlitt's criticism is indebted throughout to Bate's extended treatment of Hazlitt, especially to the critic's politics and to his celebration of Kean, in *Shakespearean Constitutions,* 129–84. I have also benefited from the treatment of Hazlitt in Donohue, *Dramatic Character in the English Romantic Age,* 323–43.

15. References to Hazlitt throughout are to *The Complete Works of William Hazlitt,* ed. P. P. Howe (London: Dent, 1930–34), 21 vols.

16. That Hazlitt, like many of his contemporaries, found the "business of the stage" trivial is evident in any number of places, including, for example, his essay "On Actors and Acting" (4:153–56), which credits actors with "supplying" the "public" with "ideas and subjects of conversation"—much as baseball or the weather might.

17. For a discussion of the eighteenth-century background to the romantic approach to Shakespeare and to Shakespeare's genius in particular, see Jonathan Bate, *Shakespeare and the English Romantic Imagination* (Oxford: Clarendon Press, 1986), 1–21.

18. See, again, Bate's discussion of the politics of Hazlitt's Shakespeare criticism, particularly the preoccupation with power, in *Shakespearean Constitutions,* 144–84.

19. Nor is it surprising that in the revision of this very discussion in *Characters of Shakespear's Plays,* Hazlitt emphasizes even more a bond that effectively unites character, creator, and reader: "Hamlet is a name; his speeches and sayings but the idle coinage of the poet's brain. What then, are they not real? They are as real as our own thoughts. Their reality is in the reader's mind. It is *we* who are Hamlet" (4:232).

20. Janet Ruth Heller argues, to the contrary, that Hazlitt's treatment of Shakespeare's plays focuses ultimately "on readers and emphasizes the process

of sympathetic identification with a character by means of the imagination" (*Coleridge, Lamb, Hazlitt,* 106). Yet in this she is not discussing Hazlitt, the *theater* critic, but criticism that is at one remove from the theater (at least) and that (as she effectively shows) is more conventionally romantic if also less unique.

21. For a discussion of the different styles of Kemble and Kean, see Donohue, *Theatre in the Age of Kean,* 57–83.

22. See David Bromwich, *Hazlitt: The Mind of a Critic* (New York: Oxford University Press, 1983), 314–26. See also Bate's more historically inflected discussion of this review in *Shakespearean Constitutions,* 163–72.

Chapter 6
Coleridge's Antitheatricality: The Quest for Community

1. Not only were Hazlitt and Coleridge lecturing on Shakespeare at the same time (along with John Thelwall), but as Jonathan Bate reminds us (from the reminiscences of Henry Crabb Robinson), Hazlitt probably attended at least one of Coleridge's lectures in 1818 (*Shakespearean Constitutions* [chap. 5, n.3], 176–78); this is altogether consistent with his generally competitive attitude regarding Coleridge.

2. See Bate, *Shakespearean Constitutions,* 144–84, and *Shakespeare and the English Romantic Imagination* (chap. 5, n.17), 22–42. See also Donohue, *Dramatic Character in the English Romantic Age* (chap. 5, n.4), 189–215, 243–343.

3. References to Coleridge's Shakespeare criticism are to the various transcriptions of his lectures in *Lectures 1808–19 on Literature* (*Collected Coleridge,* vol. 5), ed. R. A. Foakes (Princeton: Princeton University Press, 1987), 2 vols.

4. See, for example, M. M. Badawi, *Coleridge: Critic of Shakespeare* (Cambridge: Cambridge University Press, 1973), 85–91. Certainly, Coleridge's condemnation of the "sensuality" of the Ancients owes something to the influence of the German critics, among them Schiller and Schlegel, whose aesthetics—including Schiller's "sentimental" and Schlegel's "incomprehensible"—were set up in opposition to the archly classical aesthetics of Winckelmann, who credited the Ancients with having actually embodied an ideal: both as a people and in their art. For the notion of the sentimental see Friedrich von Schiller, *"Naive and Sentimental Poetry" and "On the Sublime": Two Essays,* trans. Julius A. Elias (New York: Ungar, 1967), 83–90. For the "incomprehensible," see *Friedrich Schlegel's "Lucinde" and the Fragments,* trans. Peter Firchow (Minneapolis: Univeresity of Minnesota Press, 1971), 257–71.

5. But Coleridge, of course, did attend the theater, and although his hostility to actual performances of Shakespeare is well documented, it is clear, too, as Janet Ruth Heller notes, that his interest in the theater and in stage illusion departed in significant ways from antitheatricality so-called (*Coleridge, Lamb, Hazlitt* [chap. 5, n.1], 75–78). See also J. R. de J. Jackson, "Coleridge on Dramatic Illusion and Spectacle in the Performance of Shakespeare's Plays," *Modern Philology* 62 (1964): 13–21, who uses Coleridge's distinction between

"imitation" and "copy" to distinguish (like Heller) Coleridge's "antipathy to the stage . . . of the early nineteenth century" (13) from an ideal of dramatic representation that accords with a romantic aesthetic and is not "antitheatrical in any general sense" (20).

6. My position may be distinguished from two relatively recent approaches to Coleridge's apostasy: Thomas McFarland, "Coleridge and the Charge of Political Apostasy," in *Coleridge's "Biographia Literaria": Text and Meaning,* ed. Frederick Burwick (Columbus: Ohio State University Press, 1989), 191–232; and Jerome Christensen, "'Like a Guilty Thing Surprised': Coleridge, Deconstruction, and the Apostasy of Criticism," in *Coleridge's "Biographia Literaria,"* 171–90. McFarland, for his part, draws upon an encyclopedic knowledge of Coleridge in order to exonerate him of the charge, arguing that being "on all sides of a question at once" (194) was a necessary stage in a totalizing effort on the part of Coleridge to harmoniously reconcile all positions. Christensen, on the other hand, embraces "apostasy" as essential to a critical procedure that is deconstructive rather than totalizing: "The *Biographia* is a continuous falling away from itself that is a reading of itself, falling to know its constitution, falling to know the course of its descent—a narcissism providentially flawed by the apostasis that motivates a theoretically endless tracking" (180). Thus, where both of these critics treat apostasy as a stigma—even if, in the case of Christensen, they choose to embrace the stigma—my reading of the *Biographia* attempts to follow Coleridge in essentially destigmatizing the charge of apostasy as no more than the charge of *ordinariness:* the communal (or even hegemonic) activity, in effect, by which we continually become one another.

7. Antonio Gramsci, *Selections from Cultural Writings,* ed. David Forgacs and Geoffrey Nowell-Smith, trans. William Boelhower (Cambridge: Harvard University Press, 1991), 206.

8. For the "deconstructive" Coleridge, whose writings, particularly the *Biographia,* anticipate the wisdom of contemporary theory, see (among others) Christensen, "'Like a Guilty Thing Surprised,'" and *Coleridge's Blessed Machine of Language* (Ithaca: Cornell University Press, 1981); Thomas Vogler, "Coleridge's Book of Moonlight," in *Coleridge's "Biographia Literaria,"* 20–46; Kathleen M. Wheeler, "Coleridge and Modern Critical Theory," in *Coleridge's Theory of Imagination Today,* ed. Christine Gallant (New York: AMS Press, 1989), 83–102; and Timothy Corrigan, *Coleridge, Language, and Criticism.* For the new historical critique of Coleridge's conservatism, see Jerome J. McGann, *Romantic Ideology* (Introduction, n.14), 40–49, and "The *Biographia Literaria* and the Contentions of English Romanticism," in *Coleridge's "Biographia Literaria,"* 233–54.

9. For the bearing of Coleridge's notion of "desynonymization" on his conception of identity, in this case the identities of Wordsworth and Coleridge, see my essay "'Desynonymizing' the Self in Wordsworth and Coleridge," *Studies in Romanticism* 26 (1987): 513–26.

10. References to the *Biographia* are to the text in *Biographia Literaria* (*Col-*

lected Coleridge, vol. 7), ed. James Engell and W. Jackson Bate (Princeton: Princeton University Press, 1983), 2 vols.

11. Coleridge's logic of "unanimity" or the interchangeability of positions is something Hazlitt routinely overlooks or resists, rebutting (on another occasion) Coleridge's argument that Caliban in *The Tempest* is "a prototype of modern Jacobinism." Without entering into the motive behind this observation of Coleridge's—which is meant, in some sense, to recoil on the blamer—Hazlitt counters that Caliban "is strictly the legitimate sovereign of the isle, and Prospero and the rest are usurpers, who have ousted him from his hereditary jurisdiction" (19:207). In other words, by dubbing Caliban a Jacobin, Coleridge sets in motion a rhythm of exchange that is interrupted only by Hazlitt's essentialism, which demands, in turn, that usurpers and sovereigns be identified and then held distinct.

12. In this sense, then, there is an irony in the assertion here that Burke "was a *scientific* statesman . . . and therefore a *seer*" (1:191), if only in that the material limits that science both contends with and imposes (discussed in chapter 4) are the same limits that Burke neither transcends nor comprehends except by *seeing* them and thus by being in a position to be seen.

13. See, again, my essay "'Desynonymizing' the Self in Wordsworth and Coleridge."

14. See "'Desynonymizing' the Self." See also Raimonda Modiano, "Coleridge and Milton: The Case against Wordsworth in the *Biographia Literaria,*" in *Coleridge's "Biographia Literaria,"* 150–70, and "Coleridge and Wordsworth: The Ethics of Gift Exchange and Literary Ownership," in *Coleridge's Theory of Imagination Today,* 243–56; and Christensen, *Coleridge's Blessed Machine,* 148.

15. Contending that "Coleridge's threefold theory of imagination actually bears less on poetry"—and by implication Wordsworth's genius—"than it does on those things that always mattered most to him" (226), chiefly the metaphysical system that would unite freedom of the will and the existence of God, Thomas McFarland regards the secondary imagination in particular as a more representative or less exclusive power than do I ("The Origin and Significance of Coleridge's Theory of Secondary Imagination," in *New Perspectives on Coleridge and Wordsworth,* ed. Geoffrey H. Hartman [New York: Columbia University Press, 1972], 195–246). Nevertheless as Coleridge's metaphysical system is bound up entirely in a figuration of genius, effectively uniting individual and divine authority, the secondary imagination is as much a linchpin in this system (as McFarland argues) as a disclosure of the mythology (one alternately divine and humanistic) on which the system depends. If it is a solution in one sense, then, the secondary imagination is also a continuation of the problem that the metaphysical project, like the project of poetic genius, can scarcely resolve.

16. References to Coleridge's correspondence are to the *Collected Letters of Samuel Taylor Coleridge,* ed. E. L. Griggs (Oxford: Clarendon Press, 1956–

71), 6 vols. References to *The Friend* are to the text in *The Friend* (*Collected Coleridge,* vol. 4), ed. Barbara E. Rooke (Princeton: Princeton University Press, 1969), 2 vols.

17. Coleridge introduces the Satyrane letters as a portrait of himself in the "first dawn of my literary life" and as such "most pertinent to the title of this work" (2:159).

18. Two recent studies that attempt variously to historicize Coleridge's "critique of the stage" in terms of his own dramatic work, the politics of that work, and his relationship to Drury Lane are: John David Moore, "Coleridge and the 'Modern Jacobinical Drama': *Osorio, Remorse,* and the Development of Coleridge's Critique of the Stage, 1797–1816," *Bulletin for Research in the Humanities* 85 (1982): 443–64; and Alethea Hayter, "Coleridge, Maturin's *Bertram* and Drury Lane," in *New Approaches to Coleridge,* ed. Donald Sultana (London: Vision Press, 1981), 17–37. Hazlitt, who (as Hayter observes) "attacked the 'Critique on Bertram' violently and repeatedly" (34), echoed his other statements on the *Biographia* in using the critique as additional proof of Coleridge's apostasy, particularly his turn from the "*so-called* Jacobin principles he formerly possessed" (19:207). That Coleridge made this observation easy simply by including the critique in the context of his "literary life" does not seem to have occurred to Hazlitt, who was intent as usual upon catching Coleridge in contradictions.

19. E. P. Thompson, "Disenchantment or Default?" (chap. 1, n.7), 149–81.

20. See, for example, McGann, *Romantic Ideology;* Marjorie Levinson, *Wordsworth's Great Period Poems* (London: Cambridge University Press, 1986); and Liu, *Wordsworth* (chap. 2, n.11).

21. *Prose Works of William Wordsworth* (chap. 5, n.7), 1:87–98.

22. See, again, Moore "Coleridge and the 'Modern Jacobinical Drama,'" and Hayter, "Coleridge, Maturin's *Bertram* and Drury Lane."

23. McGann, "The *Biographia Literaria* and the Contentions of English Romanticism." See also Julie Carlson, "An Active Imagination: Coleridge and the Politics of Dramatic Reform," *MP* 86 (1985): 22–33. Contending, as I do, that there is a link between Coleridge's earlier idealism and his rampant antitheatricality in both the *Bertram* critique and the Shakespeare criticism, Carlson nevertheless regards their association in conjunction with what she takes to be a "desire" on Coleridge's part "to reconcile drama's ideal and sensory qualities" so as to "enhanc[e] his audience's imaginative faculties and maintai[n] the security of England" (28–29). Thus, instead of allowing Coleridge the ability to theatricalize his contradictory position as a Romantic, Carlson observes Coleridge in the midst of a contradiction—from which only the late twentieth-century critic apparently stands apart.

24. For Byron's response to Coleridge's critique, see the letter to Murray, 12 October 1817, in *Byron's Letters and Journals,* ed. Leslie Marchand (Cambridge: Harvard University Press, 1973–81), 5:267–68.

25. The parallel with Gramsci requires elaboration, if only because the solidarity based on leveling by sight in Coleridge would appear to approximate more precisely the "hegemony" that, in uniting intellectuals (like Hamlet or Coleridge) with the "people-nation," may be distinguished from a merely dominant order as a collective predisposed toward social change and amelioration. Yet precisely because a world bound merely to the discipline of the senses is more idealized and, in effect, more "utopian" (in Gramsci's conception) than the hegemony on which Coleridge settles in the *Biographia*—and in which he takes his rightful place as a critic—the parallel with Gramsci is better served (along with culture) by the latter formulation, which is clearly more a means than an end. This is not to say, then, that Coleridgean hegemony is identical to Gramscian hegemony, or as progressive. It is only to recall that Gramsci's own sense of hegemony is equally distinguishable from either a dominant or a utopian order in its rather pragmatic and nuanced sense of the ways social change and improvement can happen. Thus, even as Coleridge appears to take his place in an order that is otherwise immovable or characterized by a pervasive contradictoriness, such a juncture nevertheless admits a possibilty or "active unity" that a more humanistic or aristocratical stance—with its inevitable gap between some subjects and others—would inevitably close down. Indeed, like Balzac's realism, which Gramsci deems politically and socially reactionary, Coleridgean hegemony anticipates the productive potential of Balzac's "conception of the world" (as Gramsci praises it) in its perception that "man is the complex of the social conditions in which he has developed, and that in order to 'change' man one has to change this complex of conditions" (*Selections from Cultural Writings,* 259). In any event, Coleridge's identification with the audience, which is accompanied not surprisingly by detachment from his erstwhile stance as an authoritative intellectual, clearly anticipates Gramsci's injunction (directed primarily at the situation in Italy in the early twentieth century) for intellectuals and writers to forge an alliance with the people. I would further venture that this alliance in Coleridge—though clearly less Jacobinical than Gramsci would prefer (though by no means strictly anti-Jacobinical)—also informs Coleridge's conception in *On the Constitution of Church and State* (1829) of the clerisy or national clergy entrusted with cultivating and enlarging knowledge of various kinds. Although frequently lambasted by revisionist critics as evidence of a conservatism that was always prevalent in Coleridge, the idea of a clerisy bespeaks—in conjunction with other aspects of Coleridge, as I have endeavored to show—something far less or, to borrow from Gramsci again, far more hegemonic. For further discussion of Gramsci's surprising conception of hegemony, see especially Chantal Mouffe, "Hegemony and Ideology in Gramsci," in *Gramsci and Marxist Theory,* ed. Chantal Mouffe (London: Routledge & Kegan Paul, 1979), 168–204. For a different but related sense of Coleridge, whose opposition to culture is ultimately grounded in a "shared human identity," see Stephen E. Cole, "Coleridge and the Social Production of Agency," *Studies in Romanticisim* 30 (1991): 85–111.

Chapter 7
Wordsworth, Friedrich, and the Photographic Impulse

1. R. H. Super, ed., "Wordsworth," *The Complete Prose Works of Matthew Arnold* (Ann Arbor: University of Michigan Press, 1973), 9:42.

2. Cleanth Brooks, "Wordsworth and the Paradox of the Imagination," in *The Well Wrought Urn: Studies in the Structure of Poetry* (New York; Harcourt, Brace and World, 1947), 124–50.

3. Lionel Trilling, "The Immortality Ode," in *The Liberal Imagination* (New York: Scribners, 1976), 129–59.

4. F. R. Leavis, "Wordsworth," in *Revaluation* (London: Chatto & Windus, 1936), 170.

5. See, for example, Geoffrey H. Hartman, *Wordsworth's Poetry 1787–1814* (New Haven: Yale University Press, 1964), and Harold Bloom, *The Visionary Company,* 2d ed. rev. (Ithaca: Cornell University Press, 1971), 124–98.

6. For discussion of the way representation necessitates the imposition of "Ideas of which no presentation is possible" and that "impart no knowledge about reality," see Jean-François Lyotard, "Answering the Question: What is Postmodernism?" in *The Postmodern Condition: A Report on Knowledge,* trans. Geoff Bennington and Brian Massumi (Minneapolis: University of Minnesota Press, 1984), 71–82.

7. John Berger and Jean Mohr, *Another Way of Telling* (New York: Pantheon, 1982). Peter Galassi, *Before Photography* (chap. 2, n.2). For a corroborative, if more personal, conception of the aims and effects of photography, see Roland Barthes, *Camera Lucida,* trans. Richard Howard (New York: Hill & Wang, 1981).

8. Although Rosalind Krauss contests Galassi's assertion that photography belongs to a pictorial tradition that can be deemed "analytic," she nevertheless corroborates Galassi's argument on the fundamentally paratactic or nonauthoritative aspects of both photography and, more important, the photographic impulse. Concentrating on the way early photographs are essentially "views" rather than compositions, images whose actual "subjects" take precedence over the "subjects" beholding them, Krauss goes on to show that photography explicitly contests tradition in the way it continually dissociates the artist from any claim to "authorship." ("Photography's Discursive Spaces," in *The Originality of the Avant-Garde and Other Modernist Myths* [Cambridge: MIT Press, 1986], 131–50.) See also Roger Scruton, "Photography and Representation," *Critical Inquiry* 7 (1981): 577–603. According to Scruton, photography may be distinguished from painting, and thus from "representation," in the way it is "an entirely accidental matter" otherwise opposed to intentionality and to revealing any thought about what is represented.

9. References to *The Prelude* are to the 1805 version of the poem in *The Prelude: 1799, 1805, 1850.* All other citations to Wordsworth's poems, unless otherwise indicated, are to E. de Selincourt and Helen Darbishire, eds., *The Poetical Works of William Wordsworth,* 5 vols. (Oxford: Clarendon Press, 1952–59).

10. For the promotion of mind or imagination over the eye in Wordsworth and in the other Romantics, see Harold Bloom, "Visionary Cinema of Romantic Poetry," (Introduction, n.4), 37–52. For a similar view treating Wordsworth exclusively, see L. J. Swingle, "Wordsworth's 'Picture of the Mind,'" in *Images of Romanticism: Verbal and Visual Affinities,* ed. Karl Kroeber and William Walling (New Haven: Yale University Press, 1978), 81–90. Contemporary discussion of this issue begins with Frederick A. Pottle, "The Eye and the Object in the Poetry of Wordsworth," in *Romanticism and Consciousness,* 273–87.

11. For additional treatment of these issues, see my essay, "'Imperfect While Unshared': The Role of the Implied Reader in Wordsworth's *Excursion,*" *Criticism* 22 (1980): 193–213.

12. This fragment from MS. Y of *The Prelude* (1804) is cited in the notes to *"The Prelude" or Growth of a Poet's Mind,* ed. E. de Selincourt, rev. Helen Darbishire (Oxford: Clarendon Press, 1959), 581.

13. This argument regarding the ram scene is adapted from my earlier discussion of *The Excursion* in *Revision and Authority in Wordsworth: The Interpretation of a Career* (Philadelphia: University of Pennsylvania Press, 1989), 53–56.

14. William Vaughan, *Romantic Art* (New York: Oxford University Press, 1978), 142. See also Vaughan's essay in *Caspar David Friedrich, 1774–1840: Romantic Landscape Painting in Dresden* (London: Tate Gallery, 1972), 8–44. For the transcendental or natural-supernaturalistic structure of Friedrich's painting, see Robert Rosenblum, *Modern Painting and the Northern Romantic Tradition: Friedrich to Rothko* (New York: Harper & Row, 1975), 10–40. For additional treatment of Friedrich, see Kermit Champa, *German Painting of the Nineteenth Century* (New Haven: Yale University Art Gallery, 1970), 40–44, and Morse Peckham, *Beyond the Tragic Vision* (New York: George Braziller, 1962), 129–36. A relatively recent study that links Friedrich's art to German idealism and to its preoccupation with the subject—rather than to the metaphysical co tent of what the subject or, in this case, the painter imagines—is Joseph Leo Koerner's *Caspar David Friedrich and the Subject of Landscape* (New Haven: Yale University Press, 1990). The standard, and relatively orthodox or pietistic, interpretation of the meaning of Friedrich's paintings is Helmut Börsch-Supan, *Caspar David Friedrich,* trans. Sarah Twohig (New York: George Braziller, 1974). It is probably worth emphasizing, too, that my use of "narrative" here and elsewhere in this study essentially combines a phenomenological position, in which narrative or some symbolic movement from the particular to the universal is more or less imposed by the subject, with a postmodern or deconstructive sense that such a narrative is ultimately a totalizing one. A different view of Wordsworth's relationship to narrative, which nevertheless draws (like my sense of the visible) on Freud's "uncanny," has recently been offered by Jay Clayton in *Romantic Vision and the Novel* (Cambridge: Cambridge University Press, 1987), 103–21. According to Clayton, Wordsworth's antipathy to narrative as well as his attempt to shape narrative to his own poetic purpose

is shot through with a sense of repetition, leading ultimately (*pace* Freud) to a sense of an ending, which is also a sense of death. Thus, narrative, in Clayton's view, stands opposed to the very visionary structures that manage, in Wordsworth's poetry, to halt narrative momentum by effectively keeping the material or accidental or uncanny world at bay. Where I see narrative as fundamentally opposed to the visible (and, by turns, to the postmodern condition), Clayton aligns narrative with an apparatus very similar to the visible, whose return, no doubt, he would deem a narrative movement.

15. With this in mind, it is certainly worth noting that Friedrich had in 1805 produced two sepia drawings from his studio in Dresden that leave little doubt regarding the metaphorical equivalency of the window frame and the human artistic frame. Not only, in other words, are the framed and segmented worlds fraught with allegorical meaning (in the estimation at least of Börsch-Supan [25–27]); in one of them, which contains a partial reflection of the artist's eyes in a mirror adjacent to the window, there is, as Koerner observes (131), a clear equivalency between self-portrait and the "self" necessarily portrayed in what the artist gazes upon, frames, and ultimately of course represents. For a more conventional or humanistic solution to the problem of the human figure in Friedrich, see also Murray Roston (*Changing Perspectives,* [chap. 1, n.8], 377–82): "The eponymic figure, . . . with his back towards us," makes "it well-nigh impossible to resist the pull towards viewer identification and a vicarious sharing of his mood of rapt cogitation. . . . It is less the scene eliciting the mood that takes prominence, a scene often only dimly visible beyond the figure, than the emotional experience of the Sprecher himself, the Romantic persona projected into the canvas, soliciting our respect for the sensitivity and profundity of contemplation which the natural scene has inspired in *him.*"

16. Joseph Leo Koerner, "Borrowed Sight: The Halted Traveller in Caspar David Friedrich and William Wordsworth," *Word and Image* 1 (1985): 149–63.

17. Friedrich, as I have adduced him, may also be distinguished, then, from Neil Hertz's treatment of a somewhat similar configuration in Courbet (and elsewhere), where the position of the surrogate viewer is significant precisely in the way it is not significant—in the way "its *occupant* may be attentuated to the point of invisibility" and thus in "the *in*consistency of the subject occupying that position" (221–22). In this way, as Hertz shows, the position of subject or reader becomes as "attentuated" or "split" as the "doubled 'object'" on which it looks, precipitating a moment of unreadability or leading to what Hertz, in his particular modification of the sublime, terms "the end of the line" ("The End of the Line," in *The End of the Line: Essays on Psychoanalysis and the Sublime* [New York: Columbia University Press, 1985], 216–39.) It is precisely *against* this "sublime" or otherwise extreme idealization that Friedrich's various figures assert themselves, girding the viewer from a way of seeing that, however inevitable, is at the same time overdetermined.

18. I have already initiated a counterargument to the charge of aesthetic conservatism in *Revision and Authority in Wordsworth,* esp. 197–249.

19. Walter Benjamin, "Short History of Photography," *Artforum* (February 1977): 47. Although Daguerre figures in the history of photography as something of a scoundrel—inasmuch as his daguerrotype was based largely on the "heliograph" of Joseph Niépce, who (along with Fox Talbot in England) may be counted as the true inventor of photography—his legitmate invention, the Diorama, can be said to have responded to a similar impulse and to have achieved an end not unlike photography's. For a discussion of Daguerre's various machinations, see Helmut and Alison Gernsheim, *L. J. M. Daguerre* (London: Secker & Warburg, 1956).

20. Stanley Cavell, "What Photography Calls Thinking," *Raritan* 4 (Spring 1985): 2.

21. See, again, Krauss, "Photography's Discursive Spaces," who sees photography as out of the mainstream of nineteenth-century art. For a still different view, see Svetlana Alpers (*The Art of Describing* [chap. 1, n.11], 243–44), who concurs with Galassi that photography is indeed part of pictorial tradition but locates that tradition (thereby minimizing photography's uniqueness) in the departure from the "Albertian picture" already evident in "the [seventeenth-century] Dutch art of describing."

22. This view is reiterated by Charles Rosen and Henri Zerner, who, though challenging the conception of Friedrich as symbolist, nevertheless contend that for Friedrich (as for other romantic painters) "no phenomenon in Nature [was] too insignificant for art": while the "concentration is visual, . . . the meaning is general and inexhaustible." (*Romanticism and Realism: The Mythology of Nineteenth-Century Art* [New York: Viking, 1984], 51–70.)

23. Richard Wollheim, "The Spectator in the Picture," in *Painting as an Art* (Princeton: Princeton University Press, 1987), 101–85.

24. Joseph Leo Koerner, *Friedrich and the Subject of Landscape,* 124.

25. It is interesting to note that from 1818 on, or beginning about the time that figures (disruptive and otherwise) first appeared in his paintings, Friedrich's "paintings," as Börsch-Supan writes, "became more like direct, faithful impressions of nature" despite being "based on the same underlying thought that had determined his earlier works. The difference," continues Börsch-Supan, "is that [Friedrich] no longer talks in riddles which are recognizable as such" but instead "uses an ambiguous language which leaves the observer free to choose whether he wants to pursue the depths of the artist's thoughts or whether he wants to content himself with a superficial impression" (45). Although Börsch-Supan is clearly referring here to Friedrich's statements about his art, these statements are nevertheless applicable (as Börsch-Supan shows) to the art itself, whose particular movement from allegory to symbol, or from a recognizable riddle to a more ambiguous, less immediately decipherable immanence, installs Friedrich (and the viewer by extension) as an interpreter of landscape. As a result, we may read the inclusion of various human figures in the landscape as attesting—with varying degrees of reflexivity, to be sure—to the particular, more humanized authority of the new and ultimately dominant style. Thus, allowing even for degrees of reflexivity, such testimony is fun-

damentally a confession (more than it is necessarily an endorsement) of romanticism, if only in that it recalls and literally figures the intentional structures that—regardless of meaning—orginate in a human center and not in a world that is theoretically viewable.

26. *Before Photography,* 21. This "syntax of photography," as Galassi defines it, is in many ways a syntax of realism as well, albeit a syntax more contestational and less intended. According to Linda Nochlin, the emphasis in realism is always on "concreteness," on "the here and now of the event" (*Realism* [Harmondsworth: Penguin, 1971], 78). This emphasis, coupled with the need to present the "bare truth . . . stripped of all transcendental meanings and metaphysical implications" (60), often yields an "arbitrary segment[ing] of what might indeed be an inexhaustible reality" (81). This is particularly the case with *pleinairisme* and its urban correlatives, which variously seek to capture "the immediate present" (144) through a "fragmentary glimpse," through the "cutting off [of a] a scene arbitrarily" (162–63) in a "pictorial structure, which emphasizes the random and fortuitous and denies any literary meaning to the occasion of the work of art" (167).

27. Such a conception of photography may be contrasted to that of Rosen and Zerner in their analysis of Galassi's study (*Romanticism and Realism,* 99–110). Although they unite "realism" and "romanticism" through a shared emphasis on "the necessary presence of a distinctive perceiving subject," Rosen and Zerner are unwilling at the same time to grant photography the marginal and arguably disruptive status that (as they concede) Romantics and Realists alike were disposed to give it. Rosen and Zerner argue instead that far from contesting intentionality or authority, "the objective photographic vision depended paradoxically on means that stressed the subjective elements of perception" (109–10).

28. Thomas McFarland, "Creative Fantasy and Matter-of-Fact Reality in Wordsworth's Poetry," *JEGP* 75 (1976): 1.

29. See, for example, Stuart Curran, *Poetic Form and British Romanticism* (New York: Oxford University Press, 1986), 29–55.

30. Wordsworth did, of course, write approximately sixty sonnets between 1802 and 1807, or during his so-called great period, many of which were put in sequence or grouped under various headings in *Poems, in Two Volumes* (1807). Yet in the very way that such earlier sonnets as "Westminster Bridge" represent an attempt to modify and thereby extend the sonnet tradition, so the recourse to a sonnet *sequence* follows the later sonnets in simply recurring to tradition, which involves the rejection, in turn, of any claim to individuality.

31. I offer a related and sometimes intersecting argument in *Revision and Authority in Wordsworth,* 217–249.

32. I am referring to the 1818 sonnet "Malham Cove," which I interpret in a way that is quite relevant to the present argument in *Revision and Authority in Wordsworth,* 11–13.

33. Krauss, "Photography's Discursive Spaces," 140.

Chapter 8
The Postmodernism of *Childe Harold*

1. *Byron's Letters and Journals,* 9:40.

2. Louis Crompton, *Byron and Greek Love: Homophobia in Nineteenth-Century England* (Berkeley: University of California Press, 1985), 67.

3. Jeane-François Lyotard, "Answering the Question: What Is Postmodernism?" (chap. 7, n.6), 79.

4. For the contemporary or protodeconstructive Byron, see Frank J. McConnell, "Byron as Antipoet," *ELH* 37 (1970): 415–32; Michael G. Cooke, *The Blind Man Traces the Circle* (Princeton: Princeton University Press, 1969); Anne K. Mellor, *English Romantic Irony* (Cambridge: Harvard University Press, 1980), 31–76; and Jerome J. McGann, *Fiery Dust: Byron's Poetic Development* (Chicago: University of Chicago Press, 1968) and *"Don Juan" in Context* (Chicago: University of Chicago Press, 1976).

5. For a critique of the "romantic reassessment" that uses Byron as a counterexample, see Jerome J. McGann, "Romanticism and the Embarrassments of Critical Tradition," *MP* 70 (1973): 243–57.

6. References throughout are to the text of *Childe Harold's Pilgrimage, A Romaunt* in *Lord Byron: The Complete Poetical Works,* vol. 2, ed. Jerome J. McGann (Oxford: Clarendon Press, 1980).

7. Among the numerous readings of *Childe Harold's Pilgrimage* that examine the modern or romantic aspects of the poem, the most comprehensive is Robert F. Gleckner's *Byron and the Ruins of Paradise* (Baltimore: Johns Hopkins University Press, 1967), 39–90, 225–89. Although Gleckner allows that the poem is romantic in its concern overall with poetic consciousness and character, this consciousness is nevertheless modern or "Eliotic," embracing a universal vision of loss whose "unromantic" despair yields a "firmly romantic optimism" in the efficacy of art in human affairs" (83–84).

8. Bernard A. Hirsch, "The Erosion of the Narrator's World View in *Childe Harold's Pilgrimage,* I-II" (*MLQ* 42 [1981]: 347–68), anticipates my reading (albeit with a "modernist" inflection) in further distinguishing the orthodoxy and coherence of the narrator's perspective in the initial cantos from Harold, who "cannot see any such coherence" (349). Similarly, Frederick W. Shilstone (*Byron and the Myth of Tradition* [Lincoln: University of Nebraska Press, 1988], 15–45) stresses the narrator's recourse to a Spenserian, allegorical or conservative perspective, which strives to dominate but is ultimately contested by Harold's resistance of a "mythic consciousness."

9. The notion of an incommensurable reality is also explored by Lyotard in *Discours, figure* [Paris: Editions Klincksieck, 1984), 73–134, when he speaks of negation in language ("Le Non et la position de l'objet"). Of relevance here is Lyotard's third negation, the "opacity of the designated" ("l'épaisseur du désigné," 82–84), which, as Jerry Aline Flieger describes it, "emphasiz[es] the opacity of reality and the inexhaustible diversity that can never be adequately represented in language." According to Flieger, Lyotard's third nega-

tion "suggests the inaccessibility of 'reality,' . . . its resistance to comprehension in a single visual or verbal move, its refusal to be seen simultaneously from all angles. . . . This negation indicates that language is a symptom of impotence, a separation of the subject from his or her objects of desire, but paradoxically, it also implies a certain grasp of reality by the subject whereby the irretrievable object may be comprehended (in the field of vision/understanding) thanks to the irreducible separation between subject and object" (*The Purloined Punchline: Freud's Comic Theory and the Postmodern Text* [Baltimore: Johns Hopkins University Press, 1991], 153). Although the notion of comprehension jibes uncomfortably with the question of the visible, and with the peculiar "inaccessibility" of reality as Lyotrard describes it, it must be stressed that understanding, at least in the sense of the third negation, indicates the barest grasp of the object (probably by agency of the glance rather than the gaze) and not its derealization through a more appropriative subject-position.

10. See, for example, Peter J. Manning, *Byron and His Fictions* (Detroit: Wayne State University Press, 1978), 28–30; and Robert Lance Snyder, "Byron's Ontology of the Creating Self in *Childe Harold* 3," *Bucknell Review: Romanticism, Modernism, Postmodernism,* ed. Harry R. Garvin (Lewisburg, Pa.: Bucknell University Press, 1980), 19–39. Both McGann (*Fiery Dust*) and Gleckner also stress the stabilization of character in the later cantos. For a canonical view of the importance and stability of canto 3, see John A. Hodgson ("The Structures of *Childe Harold* III," *Studies in Romanticism* 18 [1979]: 363–82), who views canto 3 as representing "an all-important turning point in Byron's poetical career": specifically, the transmutation of the romantic or "Promethean" fire of Rousseau and Napoleon into a satiric mode, "whose weapons will be skepticism, wit, and irony" (381–82).

11. See, again, Gleckner, B. Hirsch and Shilstone.

12. Louis Althusser, "Ideology and Ideological State Apparatuses (Notes Toward an Investigation)," in *Lenin and Philosophy and Other Essays,* trans. Ben Brewster (New York: Monthly Review Press, 1971), 162–77.

13. Julia Kristeva, *The Powers of Horror: An Essay on Abjection,* trans. Leon S. Roudiez (New York: Columbia University Press, 1982), 202.

14. Althusser's well-known statement—"I do not rank real art among the ideologies" (*Lenin and Philosophy,* 221)—has recently come under attack by McGann and others, who question the extent to which art "escapes a subjection to ideology and preserves itself as a weapon for exposing the existence, the precise character, and the domain of particular ideologies (and, sometimes, of ideology in general)" (*Romantic Ideology* [Introduction, n.14], 155). While I agree with McGann that such a vision of artistic agency is overly sentimental and inclines toward an essentialist position, the peculiar agency in which romantic art is pressed by return of the visible clearly succeeds in foregrounding and undoing the very apparatus of repression that McGann calls the "Romantic ideology." Or, to put it another way, art does not *always* manage to do the things that Althusser insists that it can do.

15. Wayne C. Booth, *A Rhetoric of Irony* (Chicago: University of Chicago Press, 1974), 42–44.

16. Julia Kristeva, *Revolution in Poetic Language* (chap. 1, n.15).

17. See also, for particular relevance to my argument, Kristeva's brief essay, "Postmodernism?" in *Bucknell Review: Romanticism, Modernism, Postmodernism,* 136–41.

18. With this in mind, it is not surprising that the mode of discourse that best approximates "abjection" and best accommodates postmodernism, according to Kristeva, is "music"—"abject music in which we can survive without stopping up our eyes and ears. This is the modern, and I mean nontranscendent, variation of the truth" ("Postmodernism?" 141).

19. The antisocial dimension of the gladiator's reverie is further highlighted by the references to himself as "sire" and to his wife as "mother." While "mother" signifies a social and familial role, "sire" is a term of animal husbandry, which is sustained in the use of "butchery" to describe the gladiatorial contest. Paradoxically, then, the denaturing effect of society provokes the gladiator to naturalize and to resist the social, particularly its recourse to the authority of "fathers." I am grateful to Susan Wolfson for bringing this aspect of the reverie to my attention.

20. A similar exchange transpires later on in canto 4, when the speaker encounters the statue of Apollo Belvedere (1441–49). Although the narrator initially attempts to reposition the statue, or the moment it captures, in a larger narrative or continuum, he ultimately finds himself (as he did in the previous stanza regarding the statue of the Laocoon) captured by the moment: by a "glance," as he describes it, whose agency (and transport) is no longer represented by the statue solely but by its beholder—the speaker—as well. I am grateful to James A. W. Heffernan for calling my attention to the sculptural dimension of the gladiator tableau and its relationship to the more specific encounters with sculpture later in canto 4.

21. The resistance of the caritas Romana to its potential resistance is also indicated in its recourse to the masculine or idealized "gaze." "What do I gaze on?" the narrator queries—to which he answers "Nothing"—at which point the father and daughter materialize not as bodies but rather as "phantoms of the brain" (1325–27). So long, in other words, as seeing is tantamount to gazing, as opposed, say, to "glancing," the "seen," far from signifying a remembered visible, remains a remembered *invisible,* reflecting the appropriative or symbolizing tendencies of the subject. Gazing effectively ensures that the seen will be "nothing."

Postscript
The Feminization of *Don Juan*

1. See, for example, McGann, *"Don Juan" in Context* (chap. 8, n.4), and Mellor, *English Romantic Irony* (chap. 8, n.4), 42–76.

2. Jerome Christensen, "Byron's Career: The Speculative Stage," *ELH* 52 (1985): 60.

3. References to *Don Juan* are to the text of the poem in *Byron,* ed. Jerome J. McGann. The Oxford Authors. Oxford, 1986.

4. For a feminist reading of the Gulbeyaz episode and its bearing on *Don Juan* as a whole, which, although it interrogates "does not," according to the reading, "escape the roles fashioned and maintained by [Byron's] culture," see Susan J. Wolfson, "'Their She Condition': Cross-Dressing and the Politics of Gender in *Don Juan,*" *ELH* 54 (1987): 585–617.

5. This kind of authoritative (indeed male) feminism brings to mind the feminism of Sydney Pollack's 1982 film *Tootsie,* which has, not surprisingly, come under a fair amount of criticism. Marguerite Waller, for example, has observed the film's rather paradigmatic "failure to allow its feminist intentions to alter its male-centered mode of signification" ("Academic Tootsie: The Denial of Difference and the Difference It Makes," *Diacritics* 17 [1987]: 2–4). See also Elaine Showalter, "Critical Cross-Dressing: Male Feminists and the Woman of the Year," *Raritan* 3 (1983): 135–39.

6. For a fuller discussion of the way anti-Semitism operates as a vehicle for irony, indeed irony of a peculiarly subversive kind, in *Don Juan,* see my essay "Byron, Austen and the 'Revolution' of Irony," *Criticism* 32 (1990): 51–80.

7. A parallel argument for the fundamentally disruptive, destabilizing work of literary language—in this case as a materialized register of *sound*—has been advanced recently by Garrett Stewart in *Reading Voices: Literature and the Phonotext* (Berkeley: University of California Press, 1990).

8. Mark Storey has recently noted the way Aurora Raby effectively culminates Byron's preoccupation with the gaze (*Byron and the Eye of Appetite* [New York: St. Martins, 1986]); however, for Storey, Aurora's achievement is in the repose to which she effectively consigns her "passions" and the objects on which they otherwise seize.

Index

Principal discussions are indicated by page numbers in boldface type.

Index

Index

Index

The Return of the Visible in British Romanticism

Designed by Ann Walston

Composed by G&S Typesetters, Inc.,
in Bembo with Arrighi display

Printed by the Maple Press Company
on 60-lb. Glatfelter Eggshell Offset